Eighteenth Century
Collections Online
Print Editions

Gale ECCO Print Editions

Relive history with *Eighteenth Century Collections Online*, now available in print for the independent historian and collector. This series includes the most significant English-language and foreign-language works printed in Great Britain during the eighteenth century, and is organized in seven different subject areas including literature and language; medicine, science, and technology; and religion and philosophy. The collection also includes thousands of important works from the Americas.

The eighteenth century has been called "The Age of Enlightenment." It was a period of rapid advance in print culture and publishing, in world exploration, and in the rapid growth of science and technology – all of which had a profound impact on the political and cultural landscape. At the end of the century the American Revolution, French Revolution and Industrial Revolution, perhaps three of the most significant events in modern history, set in motion developments that eventually dominated world political, economic, and social life.

In a groundbreaking effort, Gale initiated a revolution of its own: digitization of epic proportions to preserve these invaluable works in the largest online archive of its kind. Contributions from major world libraries constitute over 175,000 original printed works. Scanned images of the actual pages, rather than transcriptions, recreate the works *as they first appeared.*

Now for the first time, these high-quality digital scans of original works are available via print-on-demand, making them readily accessible to libraries, students, independent scholars, and readers of all ages.

For our initial release we have created seven robust collections to form one the world's most comprehensive catalogs of 18th century works.

Initial Gale ECCO Print Editions collections include:

    History and Geography
    Rich in titles on English life and social history, this collection spans the world as it was known to eighteenth-century historians and explorers. Titles include a wealth of travel accounts and diaries, histories of nations from throughout the world, and maps and charts of a world that was still being discovered. Students of the War of American Independence will find fascinating accounts from the British side of conflict.

Social Science
Delve into what it was like to live during the eighteenth century by reading the first-hand accounts of everyday people, including city dwellers and farmers, businessmen and bankers, artisans and merchants, artists and their patrons, politicians and their constituents. Original texts make the American, French, and Industrial revolutions vividly contemporary.

Medicine, Science and Technology
Medical theory and practice of the 1700s developed rapidly, as is evidenced by the extensive collection, which includes descriptions of diseases, their conditions, and treatments. Books on science and technology, agriculture, military technology, natural philosophy, even cookbooks, are all contained here.

Literature and Language
Western literary study flows out of eighteenth-century works by Alexander Pope, Daniel Defoe, Henry Fielding, Frances Burney, Denis Diderot, Johann Gottfried Herder, Johann Wolfgang von Goethe, and others. Experience the birth of the modern novel, or compare the development of language using dictionaries and grammar discourses.

Religion and Philosophy
The Age of Enlightenment profoundly enriched religious and philosophical understanding and continues to influence present-day thinking. Works collected here include masterpieces by David Hume, Immanuel Kant, and Jean-Jacques Rousseau, as well as religious sermons and moral debates on the issues of the day, such as the slave trade. The Age of Reason saw conflict between Protestantism and Catholicism transformed into one between faith and logic -- a debate that continues in the twenty-first century.

Law and Reference
This collection reveals the history of English common law and Empire law in a vastly changing world of British expansion. Dominating the legal field is the *Commentaries of the Law of England* by Sir William Blackstone, which first appeared in 1765. Reference works such as almanacs and catalogues continue to educate us by revealing the day-to-day workings of society.

Fine Arts
The eighteenth-century fascination with Greek and Roman antiquity followed the systematic excavation of the ruins at Pompeii and Herculaneum in southern Italy; and after 1750 a neoclassical style dominated all artistic fields. The titles here trace developments in mostly English-language works on painting, sculpture, architecture, music, theater, and other disciplines. Instructional works on musical instruments, catalogs of art objects, comic operas, and more are also included.

Reflections upon ancient and modern learning. To which is now added a defense thereof, in answer to the objections of Sir W. Temple, and others. With observations upon the Tale of a tub.

William Wotton

bibliolife
old books, new life.

The BiblioLife Network

This project was made possible in part by the BiblioLife Network (BLN), a project aimed at addressing some of the huge challenges facing book preservationists around the world. The BLN includes libraries, library networks, archives, subject matter experts, online communities and library service providers. We believe every book ever published should be available as a high-quality print reproduction; printed on-demand anywhere in the world. This insures the ongoing accessibility of the content and helps generate sustainable revenue for the libraries and organizations that work to preserve these important materials.

The following book is in the "public domain" and represents an authentic reproduction of the text as printed by the original publisher. While we have attempted to accurately maintain the integrity of the original work, there are sometimes problems with the original work or the micro-film from which the books were digitized. This can result in minor errors in reproduction. Possible imperfections include missing and blurred pages, poor pictures, markings and other reproduction issues beyond our control. Because this work is culturally important, we have made it available as part of our commitment to protecting, preserving, and promoting the world's literature.

GUIDE TO FOLD-OUTS MAPS and OVERSIZED IMAGES

The book you are reading was digitized from microfilm captured over the past thirty to forty years. Years after the creation of the original microfilm, the book was converted to digital files and made available in an online database.

In an online database, page images do not need to conform to the size restrictions found in a printed book. When converting these images back into a printed bound book, the page sizes are standardized in ways that maintain the detail of the original. For large images, such as fold-out maps, the original page image is split into two or more pages

Guidelines used to determine how to split the page image follows:

- Some images are split vertically; large images require vertical and horizontal splits.
- For horizontal splits, the content is split left to right.
- For vertical splits, the content is split from top to bottom.
- For both vertical and horizontal splits, the image is processed from top left to bottom right.

REFLECTIONS
UPON
Ancient and Modern
LEARNING.

To which is now added
A DEFENSE Thereof,

In Answer to the Objections of Sir *W. Temple*, and Others. With Observations upon the *Tale of a Tub*.

By *WILLIAM WOTTON*, B.D.

ALSO A
DISSERTATION
Upon the Epistles of *Themistocles*, *Socrates*, *Euripides*, &c. and the *Fables* of *Aesop*.

By *R. BENTLEY*, D.D.

Third Edition Corrected.

LONDON:
Printed for *Tim. Goodwin*, at the *Queen's Head*, against St. *Dunstan's* Church in *Fleetstreet*. MDCCV.

TO THE
Right Honourable
DANIEL
Earl of NOTTINGHAM,

Baron FINCH of DAVENTRY.

May it please Your Lordship,

Since I am, upon many Accounts, obliged to lay the Studies and Labours of my Life at Your Lordship's Feet, it will not, I hope, be thought Presumption in me to make this following Address, which, on my Part, is an Act of Duty. I could not omit so fair an Opportunity of declaring how sensible I am of the Honour of being under Your Lordship's Patronage. The Pleasure of telling the World that one is raised by Men who are truly Great and Good, works too power-

fully

The Epistle

fully to be smothered in the Breast of him that feels it; especially since a Man is rarely censured for shewing it, but is rather commended for gratifying such an Inclination, when he thankfully publishes to whom he is indebted for all the Comforts and Felicities of his Life.

But Your Lordship has another Right to these Papers, which is equal to that of their being mine: The Matter it self directs me to Your Lordship as the Proper Patron of the Cause, as well as of its Advocate. Those that enquire whether there is such a Spirit now in the World as animated the greatest Examples of Antiquity, must seek for living Instances, as well as abstracted Arguments; and those they must take care to produce to the best Advantage, if they expect to convince the World that they have found what they sought for.

This therefore being the Subject of this following Enquiry, it seemed necessary to urge the strongest Arguments first, and to prepossess the World in favour of my Cause, varies little, if any thing, any farther than as Customs alter it, from one Age to another. Since therefore this Necessity always lasts, and that all the Observations requisite to compleat this noble Science, as it takes in the Art of Governing Kingdoms, Families, and Men's private Persons, cannot be made by one or two Generations; there is a plain Reason why some Nations, which wanted Opportunities of diffused Conversation, were more barbarous than the rest; and also, why others, which for many Ages met with no Foreign Enemies that could over-turn their Constitutions, should be capable of improving this part of Knowledge as far as *unassisted Reason* was able to carry it.

For, after all, how weak the Knowledge of the ancient Heathens was, even here, will appear by comparing the Writings of the old Philosophers, with those Moral Rules which *Solomon* left us in the *Old Testament*, and which our Blessed Saviour and his Apostles, laid down in the *New*. Rules so well suited to the Reason of Man, so well adapted to civilize the World, and to introduce that true Happiness which the old Philosophers so vainly strove to find; that the more they are considered, the more they will be valued; and accordingly they have extorted even from those who did not believe the Christian Religion, just Applauses,

Sir *William Temple* rightly concludes, that Common Sense is of the Growth of every Country; and that all People who unite into Societies, and form Governments, will in time make prudent Laws of all kinds; since it is not Strength of Imagination, nor Subtilty of Reasoning, but Constancy in making Observations upon the several Ways of Working of Humane Nature, that first stored the World with Moral Truths, and put Mankind upon forming such Rules of Practice as best suited with these Observations. There is no Wonder therefore, that in a long Series of Ages, which preceded *Socrates* and *Plato*, these Matters were carried to a great Perfection; for as the Necessity of any Thing is greater, so it will be more and more generally studied: And as the Subject of our Enquiries is nearer to us, or easier to be comprehended in it self; so it will be more thoroughly examined, and what is to be known, will be more perfectly understood. Both these concur here; Necessity of Conversing with each other, put Men upon making numerous Observations upon the Tempers of Mankind: And their own Nature being the Thing enquired after, all Men could make their Experiments at home; which in Consort with those made with and by other People, enabled them to make certain Conclusions of Eternal Truth, since Mankind
varies

report the Actions of their Governors. Great Skill in all the Arts and Secrets of Persuasion appear every where in *Demosthenes* and *Cicero*'s Orations, in *Quintilian*'s Institutions, and the Orations in *Thucydides*, *Sallust* and *Livy*. The Duties of Mankind in Civil Life, are excellently set forth in *Tully's Offices*. Not one Passion of the Soul of Man has been untouch'd, and that with Life too, by some or other of the Ancient Poets. It would require a Volume to state these Things in their full Light; and it has been frequently done by those who have given Characters and Censures of Ancient Authors. So that one may justly conclude, that there is no one Part of Moral Knowledge, strictly so called, which was not known by the Ancients, so well as by the Moderns.

But it would be a wrong Inference to conclude from thence, that the Ancients were greater Genius's than the Men of the present Age. For, by Sir *William Temple*'s Confession (*b*), the *Chineses* and *Peruvians* were governed by excellent Laws: And *Confucius* and *Mango Capac* may well be reckoned amongst the Law-givers and Philosophers of those which are commonly called Learned Nations; though neither of them, especially the Latter, can justly be suspected of learning what they knew by Communication from their Neighbours. From whence Sir

(*b*) *Essay* 3. upon Heroic Vertue, sect. 2, 3.

After-Ages had no need to invent Rules, which already were laid down to their Hands; but that their Business was chiefly to re-examine them, and to see which were proper for their Circumstances, considering what Alterations Time sensibly introduces into the Customs of every Age; and then to make a wise Choice of what they borrowed, that so their Judgment might not be question'd by those who should have the Curiosity to compare the Wisdom of several Ages together.

If we descend into Particulars, these Observations will, I believe, be found to be exactly true: The minutest Differences between Vertue and Vice of all sorts, are judiciously stated by *Aristotle*, in his *Ethics* to *Nicomachus*; and the Workings of our Passions are very critically described in his Books *of Rhetoric*. *Xenophon*'s *Cyrus* shews that he had a right Notion of those Things which will make a Prince truly Great and Wise. The Characters of all those Vices which are immediately taken notice of in common Conversation, are admirably drawn by *Theophrastus*. Nothing can give a clearer *Idea* of one that has lived in Difficult Times, than the Writings of *Tacitus*; in whose Histories, almost every Thing is told in that very Way, which (we find by our own Experience) Ill Usage and Disappointments leads Men to censure and mis-
report

derstood by the ancient *Aegyptians*, *Greeks* and *Romans*, in as great Perfection as the Things themselves were capable of. The Arts of Governing of Kingdoms and Families; of Managing the Affections and Fears of the unconstant Multitude; of Ruling their Passions, and Discoursing concerning their several Ways of Working; of Making prudent Laws, and Laying down wise Methods by which they might be the more easily and effectually obeyed; of Conversing each with other; of Giving and Paying all that Respect which is due to Men's several Qualities: In short, all that is commonly meant by knowing the World, and understanding Mankind; all Things necessary to make Men Wise in Counsel, Dexterous in Business, and Agreeable in Conversation, seem to have been in former Ages thoroughly understood, and successfully practised.

There is, indeed, great Reason to fear, that in the Arts of Knavery and Deceit, the present Age may have refined upon the foregoing; but that is so little for its Honour, that common Decency does almost as much oblige me to throw a Veil over this Reproach, as common Interest does all Mankind to put an effectual Stop to its Encrease. But since we are enquiring into Excellencies, not Blemishes and Imperfections, there seems to be great Reason to affirm, that

Idea's, and labouring to express those Sounds, by which he perceived his Mother and Nurse made themselves be understood. We should then see the true Gradations by which Knowledge is acquired. We should judge, perhaps, what is in it self hard, and what easie, and also what it is that makes them so; and thereby make a better Estimate of the Force of Men's Understandings, than can now be made. But this Reminiscence of our first Idea's it is in vain to lament for, since it can never be had. Yet it may in general be observed, that the first Thoughts of Infants are concerning Things immediately necessary for Life. That Necessity being in some measure satisfied, they spend their Childhood in Pleasure, if left to their own liberty, till they are grown up. Then they begin to reflect upon the Things that relate to Prudence and Discretion, and that more or less, according as their Circumstances oblige them to carry themselves more or less warily towards those with whom they converse. This is, and ever was, general to all Mankind; whereas they would not take so much pains to cultivate the Arts of Luxury and Magnificence, if they were not spurr'd on by Pride, and a Desire of not being behind other Men. So that it is reasonable to suppose, that all those Things which relate to Moral Knowledge, taken in its largest Extent, were understood done something more than Copy from their Teachers, and that there is no absolute necessity of making all those melancholy Reflections upon (a) *the Sufficiency and Ignorance of the present Age*, which he, moved with a just Resentment and Indignation, has thought fit to bestow upon it.

(a) Pag. 5, 55, 56.

How far these Things *can* or *cannot* be proved, shall be my Business in these following Papers to enquire. And in these Enquiries I shall endeavour to act the part of a Mediator as nicely as I can, that so those who may not perhaps be satisfied with the Force of my Reasonings, yet may acknowledge the Impartiality of him that makes use of them. But First, Of those Things wherein, if the Ancients have so far excelled as to bring them to Perfection, it may be thought that they did it because they were born before us.

CHAP. II.

Of the Moral and Political Knowledge of the Ancients and Moderns.

I Have often thought that there could not be a pleasanter Entertainment to an inquisitive Man, than to run over the first Reasonings which he had in his Infancy, whilst he was gathering his Collection of

Idea's,

Men's Understandings, who are able to make such Improvements; so in those very Things, such, and so great Discoveries have been made, as will oblige impartial Judges to acknowledge, that there is no probability that the World decays in Vigour and Strength, if (according to Sir *William Temple's* Hypothesis.) we take our Estimate from the Measure of those Men's Parts, who have made these Advancements in these later Years; especially, if it should be found that the Ancients took a great deal of Pains upon these very Subjects, and had able Masters to instruct them at their first setting out: And, Secondly, If it should be proved, that there are other curious and useful Parts of Knowledge, wherein the Ancients had as great Opportunities of advancing and pursuing their Enquiries, as the Moderns, which were either slightly passed over, or wholly neglected, if we set the Labours of some few Men aside: And, Lastly, If it should be proved, that by some great and happy Inventions, wholly unknown to former Ages, new and spacious Fields of Knowledge have been discovered, and, pursuant to those Discoveries, have been viewed, and searched into, with all the Care and Exactness which such noble Theories required. If these Three Things should be done, both Questions would be at once resolved, and Sir *William Temple* would see that the Moderns have

done

Performances; yet the good Fortune of appearing first, added to the Misfortune of wanting a Guide, gives the first Comers so great an Advantage, that though, for instance, the *Fairy Queen*, or *Paradise Lost*, may be thought by some to be better Poems than the *Ilias*; yet the same Persons will not say but that *Homer* was at least as great a Genius as either *Spencer* or *Milton*. And besides, when Men judge of the Greatness of an Inventors Genius barely by the Subtilty and Curiosity of his Inventions, they may be very liable to Mistakes in their Judgments, unless they know and are able to judge of the Easiness or Difficulty of those Methods, or Ratiocinations, by which he arrived at, and perfected these his Inventions; which, with due Allowances, is equally applicable to any Performances in Matters of Learning of any sort.

It will however be some Satisfaction to those who are concerned for the Glory of the Age in which they live, if, in the first place it should be proved, That as there are some parts of real and useful Knowledge, wherein not only great Strictness of Reasoning, but Force and Extent of Thought is required thoroughly to comprehend what is already invented, much more to make any considerable Improvements, so that there can be no Dispute of the Strength of such Men's to Perfection, (in case they did so,) not because they excelled those that came after them in Understanding, but because they got the Start by being born first. (2.) Whether there are any Arts or Sciences which were more perfectly practised by the Ancients, though all imaginable Care hath been since used to equal them. (3.) Whether there may not be others wherein they are exceeded by the Moderns, though we may reasonably suppose that both Sides did as well as they could.

When such Enquiries have once been made, it will be no hard matter to draw such Inferences afterwards, as will enable us to do Justice to both Sides.

It must be owned, that these Enquiries do not immediately resolve the Question which Sir *William Temple* put, for he confounds two very different Things together; namely, *Who were the Greatest Men, the Ancients, or the Moderns?* and, *Who have carried their Enquiries farthest?* The first is a very proper Question for a Declamation, though not so proper for a Discourse, wherein Men are supposed to reason severely; because, for want of Mediums whereon to found an Argument, it cannot easily be decided: For, though there be no surer Way of judging of the Comparative Force of the Genius's of several Men, than by examining the respective Beauty or Subtilty of their

World, and of the Equal Force of Mens Understandings absolutely considered in all Times since Learning first began to be cultivated amongst Mankind, I resolved to make some Enquiry into the Particulars of those Things which are asserted by some to be Modern Discoveries, and vindicated to the Ancients by others.

The General Proposition which Sir *William Temple* endeavours to prove in his *Essay*, is this, " That if we reflect upon the
" Advantages which the Ancient *Greeks* and
" *Romans* had, to improve themselves in
" Arts and Sciences, above what the Mo-
" derns can pretend to; and upon that Na-
" tural Force of Genius, so discernible in
" the earliest Writers, whose Books are still
" exstant, which has not been equalled in
" any Persons that have set up for Promo-
" ters of Knowledge in these latter Ages;
" and compare the Actual Performances of
" them both together, we ought in Justice
" to conclude, that the Learning of the pre-
" sent Age, is only a faint, imperfect Copy
" from the Knowledge of former Times,
" such as could be taken from those scat-
" ter'd Fragments which were saved out of
" the general Shipwreck.

The Question that arises from this Proposition will be fully understood, if we enquire, (1.) Into those Things which the Ancients may have been supposed to bring
to

The Hypothesis which Sir *William Temple* appears for, is received by so great a Number of Learned Men, that those who oppose it, ought to bring much more than a positive Affirmation; otherwise, they cannot exspect, that the World should give Judgment in their Favour. The Question now to be asked, has formerly been enquired into by few, besides those who have chiefly valued Oratory, Poesie, and all that which the *French* call the *Belles Lettres*; that is to say, all those Arts of Eloquence, wherein the Ancients are of all hands agreed to have been truly excellent. So that Monsieur *de Fontenelle* took the wrong Course to have his Paradox be believed; for he asserts all, and proves little; he makes no Induction of Particulars, and rarely enters into the Merits of the Cause: He declares, that he thinks Love of Ease to be the reigning Principle amongst Mankind; for which Reason, perhaps, he was loth to put himself to the trouble of being too minute. It was no wonder therefore if those to whom his Proposition appeared entirely New, condemned him of *Sufficiency*, *the worst Composition out of the Pride and Ignorance of Mankind.*

However, since his Reasonings are, in the main, very just, especially where he discourses of the Comparative Force of the Genius's of Men in the several Ages of the World,

Society, the Comparative Excellency of the Old and New Philosophy was eagerly debated in *England*. But the Disputes then managed between *Stubbe* and *Glanville*, were rather Particular, relating to the Royal Society, than General, relating to Knowledge in its utmost extent. In *France* this Controversie has been taken up more at large: The *French* were not satisfied to argue the Point in Philosophy and Mathematics, but even in Poetry and Oratory too; where the Ancients had the general Opinion of the Learned on their Side. Monsieur *de Fontenelle*, the celebrated Author of a Book concerning the *Plurality of Worlds*, began the Dispute about six Years ago, in a little Discourse annexed to his *Pastorals*. He is something shy in declaring his Mind; at least, in arraigning the Ancients, whose Reputations were already established; though it is plain, he would be understood to give the Moderns the Preference in Poetry and Oratory, as well as in Philosophy and Mathematics. His Book being received in *France* with great Applause, it was opposed in *England* by Sir *William Temple*, who, in the Second Part of his *Miscellanea*, has printed an *Essay* upon the same Subject. Had Monsieur *de Fontenelle*'s Discourse passed unquestion'd, it would have been very strange; since there never was a New Notion started in the World, but some were found who did as eagerly contradict it. The

cients, as our present Learned Men, do now? They would, without question, could they have had any Colour for it. It was the Work of one Age to remove the Rubbish, and to clear the Way for future Inventors. Men seldom strive for Mastery, where the Superiority is not in some sort disputable; then it is that they begin to strive. Accordingly, as soon as there was a fair Pretense for such a Dispute, there were not wanting those who made the most of it, both by exalting their own Performances, and disparaging every Thing that had been done of that kind by their Predecessors. Till the New Philosophy had gotten ground in the World, this was done very sparingly; which is but within the compass of XL or L Years. There were but few before, who would be thought to have exceeded the Ancients, unless it were some Physicians, who set up *Chymical* Methods of Practice, and Theories of Diseases, founded upon *Chymical* Notions, in opposition to the *Galenical*: But these Men, for want of conversing much out of their own Laboratories, were unable to maintain their Cause to the general Conviction of Mankind: The Credit of the Cures which they wrought, not supporting them enough against the Reasonings of their Adversaries.

Soon after the Restauration of King *Charles* II. upon the Institution of the *Royal Society,*

tisfaction that he has done it. This is not only visible in particular Persons, but in the several Ages of Mankind, (which are only Communities of particular Persons, living at the same time,) as often as their Humours, or their Interests, lead them to pursue the same Methods. This Emulation equally shews it self, whatsoever the Subject be, about which it is employed; whether it be about Matters of Trade, or War, or Learning, it is all one: One Nation will strive to out-do another, and so will one Age too, when several Nations agree in the pursuit of the same Design; only the Jealousie is not so great in the Contest for Learning, as it is in that for Riches and Power; because these are Things which enable their Possessors to do their Neighbours greater mischief proportionably as they possess them, so that it is impossible for bordering Nations to suffer with any patience that their Neighbours should grow as great as they in either of them, to their own prejudice; though they will all agree in raising the Credit of the Age they live in upon the Account of these Advantages, that being the only Thing wherein their Interests do perfectly unite.

If this Way of Reasoning will hold, it may be asked how it comes to pass, that the Learned Men of the last Age did not so generally pretend that they out-did the Ancients;

REFLECTIONS UPON *Ancient and Modern* LEARNING.

CHAP. I.

General Reflections upon the State of the Question.

THE present State of the Designs and Studies of Mankind is so very different from what it was CL. Years ago, that it is no Wonder if Men's Notions concerning them vary as much as the Things themselves. This great Difference has arisen from the Desire which every Man has, who believes that he can do greater Things than his Neighbours, of letting them see how much he does excel them: For that will necessarily oblige him to omit no Opportunity that offers it self to do it, and afterwards to express his Sa-

tisfaction

CONTENTS.

Chap. XVIII. *Of the Circulation of the Blood,* p. 210

Chap. XIX. *Farther Reflections upon Ancient and Modern Anatomy,* p. 222

Chap. XX. *Of Ancient and Modern Natural Histories of Elementary Bodies and Minerals,* p. 240

Chap. XXI. *Of Ancient and Modern Histories of Plants,* p. 258

Chap. XXII. *Of Ancient and Modern Agriculture and Gardening,* p. 272

Chap. XXIII. *Of Ancient and Modern Histories of Animals,* p. 288

Chap. XXIV. *Of Ancient and Modern Astronomy and Optics,* p. 300

Chap. XXV. *Of Ancient and Modern Music,* p. 307

Chap. XXVI. *Of Ancient and Modern Physic and Surgery,* p. 314

Chap. XXVII. *Of Ancient and Modern Natural Philosophy,* p. 341

Chap. XXVIII. *Of the Philological Learning of the Moderns,* p. 352

Chap. XXIX. *Of the Theological Learning of the Moderns,* p. 363

Chap. XXX. *Reflections upon the Reasons of the Decay of Modern Learning, assign'd by Sir William Temple,* p. 381

ERRATA.

PAge 129. Line 18. *read* Reason. p. 144. l. 20. r. know. p. 187. l. 24. r. with. p. 224. l 1. r. glandulous. l. 25. r Mesentery. p. 225 l. 18. r. Glandulous. p. 241. l. 31. r. Plants, p 247. l 13 r of such. p. 276. l. 1 r. comes. p. 309. Margin, r. *ducere*. p 317 l. 2. r and. p. 377. l. 30. r. Geography. p 394 l 7. for as r. than, p. 420. Margin, r. *Xenoph* p. 431. l. 19. r νὺν. p. 446. Margin, r. ἐοίκασιν. p. 469. Marg. for l. xi ult. r. II.9. p. 474. l. 16. r. methinks. p. 481. l. 6 r. Sir Isaac. p 485. l. 25. r Commerce. p. 493. l. 27. r this our. p. 495. l. 13. r. Paolo's. p. 496. Marg r. *haveva* and *Vita* p 511 l. 17. r. Chushan-Rishathaim. p. 513. l 12 r MDCLXXXIV.

CONTENTS.

Chap. I. General Reflections upon the State of the Question, Page 1

Chap. II. Of the Moral and Political Knowledge of the Ancients and Moderns, p. 10

Chap. III. Of Ancient and Modern Eloquence and Poesie, p. 18

Chap. IV. Reflections upon Monsieur Perrault's Hypothesis, That Modern Orators and Poets are more excellent than Ancient, p. 42

Chap. V. Of Ancient and Modern Grammar, p. 53

Chap. VI. Of Ancient and Modern Architecture, Statuary and Painting, p. 59

Chap. VII. General Reflections relating to the following Chapters: With an Account of Sir William Temple's Hypothesis of the History of Learning, p. 74

Chap. VIII. Of the Learning of Pythagoras, and the most Ancient Philosophers of Greece. p. 87

Chap. IX. Of the History and Geometry of the Ancient Aegyptians, p. 98

Chap. X. Of the Natural Philosophy, Medicine and Alchemy of the Ancient Aegyptians, p. 110

Chap. XI. Of the Learning of the Ancient Chaldaeans and Arabians, p. 129.

Chap. XII. Of the Learning of the Ancient Indians and Chineses, p. 137

Chap. XIII. Of Ancient and Modern Logic and Metaphysics, p. 157

Chap. XIV. Of Ancient and Modern Geometry and Arithmetic, p. 162

Chap. XV. Of several Instruments invented by the Moderns, which have helped to advance Learning, p. 172

Chap. XVI. Of Ancient and Modern Chymistry, p. 186

Chap. XVII. Of Ancient and Modern Anatomy, p. 195

Chap.

themselves in some other Parts of Natural and Mathematical Learning, it would have met with as proportionable an Encrease; unless we should say, that it is already come to its highest Perfection; which, whether it be or no, I cannot pretend to decide.

The Entire Discourses which are added, are printed by themselves, for the Satisfaction of those who have bought the First Edition, and have no Curiosity to compare that with the Second. But I have not re-printed those lesser Additions which are interwoven into the Body of the Book, both because they would appear only like a parcel of loose Scraps, and because something was to be done in compliance to the Bookseller, who, (having once more, at a time when Printing labours under so great Discouragements, adventured to publish so large a Book which so few People will care to read) desired that this Second Edition might be made as Valuable to him as well it cou'd.

April 30. 1697.

POSTSCRIPT.

It was not enough to tell the World I was of no Side, the contrary was taken for granted, since in so many Particulars I actually gave them the Pre-eminence, when Sir *W.T.* had given it them almost in nothing. I must own, I was glad it could be proved that the World has not actually lost its Vigour, but that a gradual Improvement is plainly visible; which this Instance that Mr. *Bernard* has so incontestably made out, does by no means contradict. For *Surgery*, tho' it is the certainest, yet it is the simplest part of *Medicine*: There the Operator is more let into his Work, which does not depend so much upon Conjecture as *Physic*. The reproach therefore of its comparatively small Proficiency, is to be laid upon the *Men*, not the *Art*; it has been for these last Ages esteemed too Mechanical for Men of Liberal Education, and fine Parts, to busie themselves about: So that I question not but if as many Learned Men had cultivated *Surgery* for these last CCC Years, as have employed
'them-

that he went no farther; tho' at the same time I cannot but heartily congratulate the Felicity of my own Country, which produced the Man that first saw the Importance of these noble Hints, which he improved into a Theory, and thereby made them truly useful to Mankind.

Before I conclude this *Postscript*, it will be exspected, perhaps, that I should say something concerning this New Edition. I have taken the liberty which all Men have ever allowed, to Alter and Add where I thought any thing was faulty or deficient, and now and then I omitted some few Passages that did not so immediately relate to the design of the Book.

By one of these Additions, that of *Surgery*, which Mr. *Bernard* put in at my request, it will be yet farther seen, that I would have nothing allowed to the Moderns, where the Case will not strictly bear it. I had yielded so much to them before, that it was generally thought I was biass'd on their behalf:
It

'*Vital*, it begins to become *Animal*,
'and approaches to the proper Nature
'of the Rational Soul.

This he reasons long upon, to prove, that the Blood is the Soul of Man, and seems to allow no other but what is thus made; first elaborated in the Liver, thence carried by the Veins into the right Ventricle of the Heart, and so into the Lungs; where being mix'd with Air, it becomes Vital; and afterwards being carried by the Arteries into the Brain, it is there farther sublimed, till it receives its last Perfection, so as to be fit to perform the noblest Operations of the Animal Life.

If we compare now this Notion thus explained by *Servetus*, with Dr. *Harvey*'s *Theory of the Circulation of the Blood*, we shall plainly see that he had imperfect Glimmerings of that Light which afterwards Dr. *Harvey* communicated with so bright a Lustre to the Learned World: Which Glimmerings, since they were so true, having nothing in them of a False Fire, I much wonder

'been only for their Nourishment:
'nor would the Heart have been this
'way serviceable to the Lungs, since
'the *Foetus* in the Womb are other-
'wise nourished, by reason of the close-
'ness of the Membranes of the Heart,
'which are never opened till the Birth
'of the Child, as *Galen* teaches.' So
that the whole Mixture of Fire and
'Blood is made in the Lungs where
there is a (d) 'Transfusion out of the
'*Arterious Vein* into the *Venous Artery*,
'which *Galen* took no notice of.

(d) *Trans-fusio à Venâ arteriosâ ad Arteriam venosam propter spiritum, à Galeno non animadversa.*

Afterwards he says, (e) 'That this
'*Vital Spirit* is transmitted from the left
'Ventricle of the Heart into the Arte-
'ries of the whole Body, so that the
'more subtile Parts get upwards, where
'they are yet more refined, especially
'in the *Plexus Retiformis*, which lies in
'the Base of the Brain, where, from

(e) *Ille itaque Spiritus vitalis à sinistro cordis ventriculo in arterias totius corporis deinde transfunditur, ita ut qui tenuior est, superiora petat, ubi magis adhuc elaboratur, praecipue in plexu retiformi sub basi cerebri sito, ubi ex vitali fieri incipit animalis ad propriam rationalis animae rationem accedens.*

Vital,

'tile Blood is very artificially agitated
' by a long passage through the Lungs
' from the right Ventricle of the Heart,
' and is prepared, made florid by the
' Lungs, and transfused out of the *Ar-*
' *terious Vein* into the *Venous Artery*, and
' at last in the *Venous Artery* it self it is
' mixed with the inspired Air, and by
' exspiration purged from its Dregs.
' And thus at length the whole Mix-
' ture is attracted, by the *Diastole* of
' the Heart, into the left Ventricle, be-
' ing now a fit Substance out of which
' to form the Vital Spirit.

' Now that this Communication
' and Preparation is made by the Lungs,
' is evident from the various Conjun-
' ction and Communication of the *Ar-*
' *terious Vein* with the *Venous Artery* in
' the Lungs; the remarkable largeness
' of the *Arterious Vein* does likewise con-
' firm it: since it would never have
' been made of that Form and Bulk,
' nor would it have emitted so great a
' quantity of very pure Blood out of
' the Heart into the Lungs, if it had
' been

Confirmat hoc magnitudo insignis venae arteriosae, quae nec talis nec tanta facta esset, nec tantam à corde ipso vim purissimi sanguinis in pulmones emitteret ob solum eorum nutrimentum, nec cor pulmonibus hac ratione serviret, cum praesertim antea in embryone solerent pulmones ipsi aliunde nutriri ob membranulas seu—— Cordis usque ad horam nativitatis nondum apertas, ut docet Galenus.

'ration of the Vital Spirit, which is
'compounded of, and nourished by
'Inspired Air, and the subtilest part
'of the Blood: The *Vital Spirit* has
'its Original in the left Ventricle of
'the Heart, by the assistance of the
'Lungs, which chiefly contribute to
'its generation. It is a *subtile* Spirit (so
'I render *tenuis* here) wrought by the
'force of Heat; of a florid Colour, ha-
'ving the power of Fire: so that it is
'a sort of shining Vapour made of the
'purer part of the Blood, containing
'within it self the substance of Water,
'Air and Fire. It is made in the
'Lungs, by the mixture of Inspired
'Air with that Elaborated Subtile
'Blood, which the Right Ventricle of
'the Heart communicates to the Left.
'Now this Communication is not
'made through the *Septum* of the Heart,
'as is commonly believed, but the subtile

'therefore is *First*, whose Seat is in
'the Liver and Veins: The *Vital Spi-*
'*rit* is *Second*, whose Seat is in the
'Heart and Arteries: The *Animal Spi-*
'*rit* is *Third*, which is like a Ray of
'Light, and has its Seat in the Brain
'and Nerves.' So that he makes the
beginning of the whole Operation to
be in the Liver; which, according to
him, is the Original Work-house of
the Blood, which he calls the *Soul* or
Life, as it is called in the Old Testament.

Now to understand how the Blood is the Life, he says, (*c*) 'We must 'first understand the substantial Gene-

(*c*) *Ad quam rem est prius intelligenda substantialis Generatio ipsius Vitalis Spiritus, qui ex Aëre inspirato & subtilissimo sanguine componitur & nutritur Vitalis Spiritus in sinistro cordis Ventriculo suam originem habet, juvantibus maxime pulmonibus ad ipsius generationem. Est spiritus tenuis, caloris vi elaboratus, flavo colore, igneâ potentiâ, ut sit quasi ex puriore sanguine lucens vapor, substantiam continens aquae, aeris & ignis: generatur ex factâ in pulmone mixtione inspirati aeris cum elaborato subtili sanguine, quem dexter ventriculus sinistro communicat. Fit autem communicatio haec non per parietem cordis medium, ut vulgo creditur, sed magno artificio à dextro cordis ventriculo longo per pulmones ductu, agitatur sanguis subtilis: à pulmonibus praeparatur, flavus efficitur, & à venâ arteriosâ in arteriam venosam transfunditur; deinde in ipsâ arteriâ venosâ inspirato aëri miscetur, & exspiratione à fuligine repurgatur: atque ita tandem à sinistro cordis ventriculo totum mixtum per Diastolen attrahitur, apta supellex ut fiat spiritus vitalis.*
Quod ita per pulmones fiat communicatio & praeparatio, docet conjunctio varia & communicatio venae arteriosae cum arteriâ venosâ in pulmonibus.

'ration

Servetus says of the Passage of the Blood through the Lungs be in the former Edition, the Discovery has so much the greater Antiquity. The Passages now in question, are in the *Fifth Book of the Trinity*, where he treats *of the Holy Ghost*: There he takes pains to prove, (a) that the *Substance of the Created Spirit of Jesus Christ is Essentially joined to the Substance of the Holy Ghost*. To explain this, he talks much of God's Breathing the Soul into Man, which, by his manner of Explication, it is plain, he believed to be Material. The Way he proceeds is this: 'He sup-
'poses Three Spirits in Man's Body,
'*Natural, Vital,* and *Animal*; which (says
'he) are (b) really not Three, but Two
'distinct Spirits. The *Vital* is that
'which is communicated by *Anastomo-*
'*ses* from the Arteries to the Veins, in
'which it is called *Natural*. The Blood

(a) He says he introduces this Disputation, *ut inde intelligas ipsi Spiritûs Sancti Substantiae esse essentialiter adjunctam creati Spiritûs Christi Substantiam.*

(b) *Qui vere non sunt tres, sed duo Spiritus distincti. Vitalis est spiritus qui per Anastomoses ab Arteriis communicatur Venis, in quibus dicitur Naturalis. Primus ergo est Sanguis, cujus sedes est in hepate & Corporis Venis. Secundus est, Spiritus vitalis, cujus sedes est in corde, & corporis arteriis. Tertius est spiritus animalis, quasi lucis radius, cujus sedes est in cerebro & corporis nervis.*

'there-

POSTSCRIPT.

I am obliged also to take notice, that I have lately got a sight of *Servetus's Christianismi Restitutio*, out of which that famous Passage *concerning the Circulation of the Blood*, which I set down at length, *p.* 230. was copied long ago by that worthy Member of the *Royal Society*, Mr. *Abraham Hill*, from whom Mr. *Bernard* had it. My Lord Bishop of *Norwich*, whose incomparable Library contains every thing that is rare and excellent, did me the honour to show it me. His Manuscript Copy is a Transcript of that Printed one which is preserved in the *Landtgrave* of *Hesse*'s Library at *Cassels*; the very Book that was perused by *Sandius*, who gives an Account of it in his *Bibliotheca Antitrinitariorum*. The Book it self was Printed (at *Basil*, says *Sandius*) in MDLIII. and is a Collection of all *Servetus's Theological Tracts*, though considerably enlarged: Some of which, and particularly his *Discourses concerning the Trinity*, had been publifhed XX Years before. This I mention, because, if what

Servetus

Philosophus ac Medicus Doctissimus dum Neopolitano in Gymnasio publicè Anatomen doceret: And a little after; *Deus tamen gloriosus scit Ingrassiae fuisse inventum; atque cum Stapedis aut Staffae nostrorum Patrum effigiem gestet, merito Stapedis nomine ab eodem fuisse donatum.* Had *Ingrassias*'s Book been printed in his Lifetime, there had never been room for a Dispute; though his Right was so well known, that *Bartholomaeus Eustachius*, who wrote soon after *Columbus*, and put in his Claim to the Glory of the Discovery, mentions *Ingrassias*'s Pretences, which *Columbus* does not.

Some, perhaps, will think this Enquiry into the Author of this Discovery, to be a needless Affectation of Exactness. But 'tis so much the Duty of all Writers, not to mis-lead their Readers in the smallest Particular, that they are obliged to rectifie their own Mistakes where-ever they find them, and not to be afraid of being accused of Negligence; since Truth, and not Glory, ought to be the ultimate End of all our Labours and Enquiries. I

POSTSCRIPT.

Pag. 220. I have, upon his own Authority, given *Columbus* the Credit of Discovering that little Bone in the Inner Cavity of the Ear, which, from its figure, is commonly call'd the *Stirrup*: And indeed, he being the first that ever gave any Account of it in a System of Anatomy, and pretending that it was his own Invention, seems to have the fairest Plea to the Honour of it. But *Philippus Ingrassias*, who wrote some time before *Columbus*, certainly knew it: For, in his Commentary upon *Galen de Ossibus*, he expresly mentions it; and for that Reason, *Falloppius*, who could not want Opportunity of being truly inform'd, and was a right honest Man, and a judicious Anatomist, and one to whom many Discoveries are owing, ascribes it to him in such Terms as put the Controversie beyond Dispute. *Tertium* (says *Falloppius*, speaking of the little Bones in the Inner Cavity of the Ear) *si nolumus debitâ laude quenquam defraudare, invenit & promulgavit primus Johannes Philippus ab Ingrassia Siculus*

Phi-

POSTSCRIPT.

Since the *Second Edition* of my Book was Printed off, we have had an Account in the *Journal des Sçavans*, that Monsieur *Perrault* has Published a THIRD PART of his *Parallel between the Ancients and the Moderns*; in which he undertakes to prove, that the Skill of the Moderns in *Geography, Philosophy, Medicine, Mathematics, Navigation*, &c. is preferrible to that of the Ancients. The Book is not yet, that I know of, in *England*, and possibly may not be procurable in some time. I thought it necessary, however, to take notice, that I have had a bare Intimation of such a Book, and no more; that so if in any Material Things we should happen to Agree, (as writing upon the same Argument, 'tis very probable we may,) I might not hereafter be thought a Plagiary. There was no danger hitherto, since as far as he had gone before, I either openly dissented from him, or directly abridged his Words.

PREFACE.

that I might have been accused of betraying my Cause, if, whilst I endeavoured throughout the whole Controversie to act the Part of a Mediator, and to give to every Side its just due, I had omitted what these two elegant Advocates had severally alledged for their respective Hypotheses.

What Censure the World will pass upon my Performance, I know not; only I am willing to think, that those who shall not agree to what I say, will grant that I have represented the Opinions of other Men with Impartiality and Candour, and that I have not discovered any Bigottry or Inclination to any one particular Side; which will be a good Step to make them believe, that I shall not obstinately defend any one Position, which may hereafter be proved to be Erroneous.

June 11. 1694.

very dear to me, and which in the present Case was a great deal more. One, for whose Sence and Judgment, all that know him have so very particular a Regard, that I resolved at last, rather to hazard my own Reputation, than to deny his Request; especially, since I hoped that it might, perhaps, give some Body else an Opportunity to compleat that, of which this Treatise is a very imperfect Essay.

I hope I need make no Apology, that a great Part of this Discourse may seem too Polemical for a Writing of this kind: For that could not be well avoided, because the Argument it self has been so much debated. The ablest Men of the two opposite Parties, are, Sir *William Temple*, and Monsieur *Perrault*: They are two great Men, and their Writings are too well known, and too much valued, to be over-looked. They cloath their Thoughts in so engaging a Dress, that a Man is tempted to receive all they say, without Examination; and therefore I was afraid

that

PREFACE

I had also a fresh Inducement to this Search, when I found to how excellent Purpose my most Learned and Worthy Friend, Dr. *Bentley*, had, in his late incomparable Discourses *against Atheism*, shewn what admirable Use may be made of an accurate Search into Nature, thereby to lead us directly up to its Author, so as to leave the unbelieving World without Excuse.

But, after all that I have alledged for my self, I must acknowledge, that I soon found that I did not enough consider *Quid valeant Humeri, aut quid ferre recusent.* The Subject was too vast for any one Man, much more for me, to think to do it Justice; and therefore, as soon as I had drawn up a rude Scheme of the Work, I intended to have given it over, if the importunate Sollicitations of my very Ingenious Friend, *Anthony Hammond*, Esq; had not at last prevailed upon me to try what I could say upon it: And it was so difficult a Thing to me to refuse what was so earnestly pressed by a Person who was so

very

to engage me to this Undertaking; which was, the Pleasure and Usefulness of those Studies to which it necessarily led me: For Discoveries are most talked of in the Mechanical Philosophy, which has been but lately revived in the World. Its Professors have drawn into it the whole Knowledge of Nature, which, in an Age wherein Natural Religion is denied by many, and Revealed Religion by very many more, ought to be so far known at least, as that the Invisible Things of the Godhead may be clearly proved by the Things that are seen in the World. Wherefore I thought it might be Labour exceedingly well spent, if, whilst I enquired into what was anciently known, and what is a new Discovery, I should at the same time furnish my Mind with new Occasions of admiring the boundless Wisdom and Bounty of that Almighty and Beneficent Essence, in and by whom alone this whole Universe, with all its Parts, live, and move, and have their Being.

I had

PREFACE.

lapsed to their old Barbarity of themselves, when once they had been weary of those Arts, and of that Learning (such as it was) which then they had? Men are not such stupid Creatures, but if an Invention is at any time found out, which may do them great and eminent Service, they will learn it, and make use of it, without enquiring who it is they learn it of; or taking a Prejudice at the Thing, because, perhaps, they may be indebted to an Enemy for it. *Barbarous* and *Polite* are Words which rather referr to Matters of *Breeding* and *Elegance*, than of *Sound Judgment*, or *Good Sense*; which first shew themselves in making Provision for Things of Convenience, and evident Interest, wherein Men scarce ever commit palpable Mistakes. So that it is unaccountable that the History of Learning and Arts should be of so confessedly late a Date, if the Things themselves had been many Ages older; much more if the World had been Eternal.

Besides these, I had a Third Reason

as Gods, if their Cruelties had not foon led thefe harmlefs People to take them to be fomething elfe, becaufe they taught them the Ufe of *Iron* and *Looking-Glaſſes*? (Whence we may be fure that this innocent and honeſt Nation never had Learning amongſt them before.) Do not we find, that they and the *Mexicans*, in the compafs of Four or Five Hundred Years, which is the utmoſt Period of the Duration of either of their Empires, went on ſtill Improving? (As the whole *New World* would, probably, have done in not many Ages, if thefe two mighty Nations had extended their Conqueſts, or if New Empires had arifen, even though the *Spaniards* had never come among them; fince thofe two Empires of *Mexico* and *Peru*, which were the only confiderable Civilized Governments in *America*, got conſtant Ground of their Enemies; having the fame Advantages over them, as formed Troops have over a loofe Militia.) Or, can we think that they would again have relapfed

PREFACE.

general Use has come in the room of it, or the Conquerors took it away, for some Political Reason, either letting it totally die, or supplying it with something else, which to them seemed a valuable Equivalent. Have any of these Conquerors, since *Tubal-Cain*'s Time, once suffered the Use of Metals, of Iron for instance, or Gold, to be lost in the World? Hath the Use of Letters been ever intermitted since the Time of that *Cadmus*, whoever he was, that first found them out? Or, was Mankind ever, that we know of, put to the trouble of Inventing them a second time? Have the Arts of Planting, of Weaving, or of Building, been at any time, since their first Invention, laid aside? Does any Man believe that the Use of the *Load-stone* will ever be forgotten? Are the *Turks* so barbarous, or so spightful to themselves, that they will not use Gun-powder, because it was taught them by *Christians*? Does not *Garçilasso de la Vega* inform us, that the *Peruvians* would have worshipped the *Spaniards*

either work themselves, or employ others that shall; which, to the present Purpose, is all one. The *Tartars* have, since their Conquest, incorporated themselves with the *Chineses*, and are now become one People, only preserving the Authority still in their own Hands.

In all these Instances one may observe, that how barbarous soever these several Conquerors were when first they came into Civilized Countries, they, in time, learnt so much at least of the Arts and Sciences of the People whom they subdued, as served them for the necessary Uses of Life; and thought it not beneath them to be instructed by those to whom they gave Laws. Wherefore there is Reason to believe, that since Mankind has always been of the same Make, former Conquests would have produced the same Effects, as we see later ones have done. In short, We cannot say that ever any one Invention of considerable Use has been laid aside, unless some other of greater and more

general

fugees, who planted themselves in *Ireland*, and from thence, by the Way of *Scotland*, came by degrees back again into their own Country, had as much, if not more Learning than any of their *Europaean* Neighbours. The *Saracens* applied themselves to Learning in earnest, as soon as the Rage of their first Wars was over; and resolving to make theirs a compleat Conquest, robb'd the *Greeks* of their Knowledge, as soon as they had possessed themselves of the most valuable Parts of their Empire. The *Turks* have learnt enough, not to be thought Illiterate, though less proportionably than any of the fore-mentioned Conquerors: They can Write and Read; they preserve some rude Annals of their own Exploits, and general Memorials, it matters not how imperfect, of precedent Times: They have Mathematics enough to make an Almanac; and they have lost none of the Mechanical Arts that they had occasion for, which they found in the Countries where they came, since they

either

PREFACE.

Barbarous Enemies were anciently of the same Nature, as they have been since; that is, they might possibly make entire Conquests of the Countries which were so invaded; but we cannot suppose that any of these pretended *Ante-Mosaical* Conquests, of which we are now speaking, made a greater Alteration than that which the *Goths* and *Vandals* made in the *Roman* Empire; that which the *Saracens* first, and the *Turks* afterwards made in the *Greek*; or that of the *Tartars* in *China*. The *Goths* and *Vandals* had scarce any Learning of their own; and if we consider Politeness of Manners, and nothing else, they seem truly to have deserved the Name of *Barbarous*: They therefore took some of the *Roman* Learning, as much as they thought was for their Turn, the Memory whereof can never be said to have been quite extinct during the whole Course of those ignorant Ages which succeeded, and were the Effects of their Conquests. The *Saxons* in *England*, being taught by the *British* Refugees

PREFACE.

Scriptures assure us *Noah* was, who then would preserve the Memory of their own Deliverance, which destroys our *Libertines* Hypothesis. Now, partial Deluges are not sufficient: If one Country be destroyed, another is preserved; and if the People of that Country have Learning among them, they will also have a Tradition, that it once was in the other Countries too, which are now dis-peopled.

Upwards, as far as the Age of *Hippocrates*, Knowledge may be traced to its several Sources: But of any Histories older than the *Mosaical*, there are no sort of Foot-steps remaining, which do not, by their Contradictions, betray their Falshood; setting those aside which *Moses* himself has preserved. If any should pretend to solve the Difficulty, by supposing Invasions of Barbarous Enemies, which may have destroy'd the Memory of all past Knowledge, they will soon see new Difficulties arise, instead of having the old ones removed. There is Reason to suppose that Invasions of

Bar-

PREFACE.

Thing besides; I did at last please my self, that I had found these Circumstances; and in setting them down, I took what care I could, neither to be deceived my self, nor to deceive any Body else.

But what shall be said to those numerous Deluges, which, no Body knows how many Ages before that of *Noah*, are said to have carried away all Mankind, except here and there a Couple of ignorant Salvages, who got to some high Mountain, and from thence afterwards replenish'd the Earth? This Hypothesis (as these Men call it) is so very precarious, that there needs nothing to be replied to it, but only that it is as easily dis-proved by Denying, as defended by Asserting, since no Records nor Traditions of the Memory of the Facts are pretended; and something easier, because it may be demonstrably proved, that a General Flood cannot be effected without a Miracle, and if it could, that it must destroy the whole Race of Mankind, unless some few should be preserved, as the Holy
Scrip-

improve, even tho' in some Particulars they should go back, and fall short of the Perfection which once they had.

There is no question but these Excellencies of the Ancients might be accounted for, without hurting the *Mosaical* History, by resolving them into a particular Force of Genius, evidently discernible in former Ages, but exstinct long since. But this seems to be of very ill Consequence, since it does, as it were, suppose that Nature were now worn out, and spent; and so may tempt a *Libertine* to think that Men, as Mushrooms are said to do, sprang out of the Earth when it was fresh and vigorous, impregnated with proper Seminal Atoms, now, of many Ages, no longer seen.

When nothing therefore appear'd to be so likely to take off the Force of the main Objection, as the finding of particular Circumstances which might suit with those Ages that did exceed ours, and with those things wherein they did exceed us, and with no other Age nor Thing

But upon Examination of this Question, several Difficulties appear'd, which were carefully to be remov'd. The greatest was, That some Sciences and Arts, of a very compounded Nature, seem really to have been more perfect anciently, than they are at present; which does, as it were, directly overthrow my Position. Therefore I was obliged, first, to enquire whether the Thing were true in Fact, or not: Next, If true, whether it proceeded from a particular Force of Genius, or from the Concurrence of some accidental Circumstances; and also, whether, in case such Circumstances did concurr, in other Things, where those Accidents could have no place, the Moderns have not out-done the Ancients as much, as, allowing the World to be no older than the *Mosaical* Account, it were reasonably to be exspected they should. For then, if all these Questions could be satisfactorily resolved, the Objection would be no Objection at all; and Mankind might still be supposed to
im-

PREFACE.

The Fabulous Histories of the *Aegyptians*, *Chaldaeans* and *Chineses* seem to countenance that Assertion. The seeming Easiness of solving all Difficulties that occurr, by pretending that sweeping Floods, or general and successive Invasions of Barbarous Enemies, may have, by Turns, destroyed all the Records of the World, till within these last Five or Six Thousand Years, makes this Scheme very desirable to those whose Interest it is, that the *Christian Religion* should be but an empty Form of Words, and yet cannot swallow the *Epicurean* Whimsies of Chance and Accident. Now the Notion of the Eternity of Mankind, through Infinite Successive Generations of Men, cannot be at once more effectually and more popularly confuted, than by shewing how the World has gone on, from Age to Age, Improving; and consequently, that it is at present much more Knowing than it ever was since the earliest Times to which History can carry us.

But

DEDICATORY.

Cause, by this Dedication. For those that consider that the Vertues which make up a Great Character, such as Magnanimity, Capacity for the Highest Employments, Depth of Judgment, Sagacity, Elocution, and Fidelity, are united in as eminent a Degree in Your Lordship, as they are found asunder in the true Characters of the Ancient Worthies; that all this is rendred yet more Illustrious by Your Exemplary Piety and Concern for the Church of England, and Your Zeal for the Rights and Honour of the English Monarchy; and last of all, that these Vertues do so constantly descend from Father to Son in Your Lordship's Family, that its Collateral Branches are esteemed Public Blessings to their Age and Country; will readily confess that the World does still Improve, and will go no further than Your Lordship, to silence all that shall be so hardy as to dispute it.

Justice therefore, as well as Gratitude, oblige me to present these Papers to Your Lordship; Though, since I have taken the Freedom, in several Particulars, to dissent

from

The EPISTLE, &c.

from a Gentleman, whose Writings have been very kindly received in the World, I am bound to declare, that the principal Reason which induced me to make this Address, was, not to interest Your Lordship in my small Disputes, but to let the World see, that I have a Right to Subscribe my self,

May it please Your Lordship,

Your Lordship's

Most obliged,

And Most Dutiful

Servant and Chaplain,

WILLIAM WOTTON.

PREFACE.

THE Argument of these following Papers seems, in a great measure, to be so very remote from that Holy Profession, and from those Studies, to which I am, in a more particular manner, obliged to dedicate my self, that it may, perhaps, be exspected I should give some Account of the Reasons which engaged me to set about it.

In the first place therefore, I imagined, that if the several Boundaries of *Ancient and Modern Learning* were once impartially stated, Men would better know what was still unfinished, and what was, in a manner, perfect; and consequently what deserved the greatest Application, upon the score of its being imperfect: which might be a good Inducement to set those Men, who, having a great Genius, find also in themselves an Inclination to promote Learning, upon Subjects wherein they might, probably

PREFACE.

bably, meet with Success answerable to their Endeavours: By which means, Knowledge in all its Parts, might at last be compleated. I believed likewise, that this might insensibly lead Men to follow such, and only such, for their Guides, as they could confide in for the Ablest and Best in those several kinds of Learning to which they intended to apply their Thoughts. He that believes the Ancient *Greeks* and *Romans* to have been the greatest Masters of the *Art of Writing* that have ever yet appeared, will read them as his Instructors, will copy after them, will strive to imitate their Beauties, and form his Stile after their Models, if he purposes to be excellent in that Art himself: All which Things will be neglected, and he will content himself to read them in their Translations, to furnish his Mind with Topicks of Discourse, and to have a general Notion of what these Ancient Authors say, if he thinks he may be equally Excellent a nearer Way. To read *Greek* and *Latin* with Ease, is a thing not soon learn'd;

PREFACE.

learn'd, those Languages are too much out of the common Road; and the Turn, which the *Greeks* and *Romans* gave to all their Thoughts, cannot be resembled by what we ordinarily meet with in Modern Languages; which makes them tedious, till master'd by Use. So that, constant Reading of the most perfect Modern Books, which does not go jointly on with the Ancients, in their Turns, will, by bringing the Ancients into Dis-use, cause the Learning of the Men of the next Generation to sink; by reason that they, not drawing from those Springs from whence these excellent Moderns drew, whom they only propose to follow, nor taking those Measures which these Men took, must, for want of that Foundation which these their Modern Guides first carefully laid, fail in no long Compass of Time.

Yet, on the other hand, if Men who are unacquainted with these things, should find every thing to be commended because it is *oldest*, not because

it

PREFACE.

it is *best*; and afterwards should perceive that in many material and very curious Parts of Learning, the Ancients were, comparatively speaking, grosly ignorant, it would make them suspect that in all other things also they were equally deficient; grounding their general Conclusion upon this common, tho' erroneous Principle, that because a man is in an Error in those things whereof we can judge, therefore he must be equally mistaken in those things where we cannot. Now, this Extream can be no way more easily avoided, than by stating the due Limits of *Ancient* and *Modern Learning*; and shewing, in every Particular, to which we ought to give the Pre-eminence.

But I had another, and a more powerful Reason, to move me to consider this Subject; and that was, that I did believe it might be very subservient to Religion it self. Among all the Hypotheses of those who would destroy our most Holy Faith, none is so plausible as that of the *Eternity of the World.*

The

plauses, which were certainly unbiassed, because, not being led by the Rewards which it proposes, nor deterred by the Punishments which it threatens, they could have no Motive to commend them but their own native Excellency.

It is evident therefore, that though in some sence, the Moderns may be said to have learned their *Politicks* and *Ethics* from the Ancients, yet there is no convincing Argument that can be brought from those Sciences, singly considered, that the Ancients had a greater Force of Genius than the wise and prudent Men of these later Generations. If, indeed, in all other Sciences, Mankind has for MD Years been at a full Stop, the Perfection of the Ancient *Politics* and *Ethics* may be justly urged, amongst other Arguments, for the comparative Strength of their Parts; otherwise not.

But there are other Parts of Learning, that may seem capable of farther Improvement; of which, the Advocates for the Ancients do not only pretend that they were the Inventors, but that their Performances have never since been equalled, much less out-done; though within these last CC Years all imaginable Pains have been taken to do it; and great Rewards have been given to those who have, *licet non passibus æquis*, laboured to come near the Copies which were already set them. From whence

these

these Men think it probable, that all Modern Learning is but Imitation, and that faint and flat, like the Paintings of those who draw after Copies at a Third or Fourth Hand from the Life. Now, as this can only be known by an Induction of Particulars, so of these Particulars there are Two sorts: One, of those wherein the greatest part of those Learned Men who have compared Ancient and Modern Performances, either give up the Cause to the Ancients quite, or think, at least, that the Moderns have not gone beyond them. The other of those, where the Advocates for the Moderns think the Case so clear on their Side, that they wonder how any Man can dispute it with them. *Poesie, Oratory, Architecture, Painting,* and *Statuary,* are of the *First* Sort: *Natural History, Physiology,* and *Mathematics,* with all their Dependencies, are of the *Second.*

C H A P. III.

Of Ancient and Modern Eloquence and Poesie.

IT is universally acknowledged, that he who has studied any Subject, is a better Judge of that Subject than another Man who did never purposely bend his Thoughts

that

that way, provided they be both Men of equal Parts. Yet we see there are many Things, whereof Men will, at first sight, pass their Judgment, and obstinately adhere to it, though they not only know nothing of those Matters, but will confess that it requires Parts, and Skill, and Exercise, to be excellent in them. This is remarkably visible in the Censures which are passed upon Pieces of *Oratory* and *Poesie* every Day, by those who have but little of that sort of Learning themselves; and to whom all that is said of critical Skill in those Things, and of a true Relish of what is really fine, is Jargon and Cant. And in the mean time, these Men do in other Things shew great Accuracy and Judgment, even in Subjects which require quick Apprehension, nice Observation, and frequent Meditation. If one should ask why such Men so frequently mistake and differ in those other Matters, the Answer, I think, is this: (1.) The Foundations of Eloquence of all sorts lying in Common Sence, of which every Man is in some degree a Master, most ingenious Men have, without any Study, a little Insight into these Things. This little Insight betrays them immediately to declare their Opinions, because they are afraid, if they should not, their Reputation would be in danger. On the contrary, where the Subject is such, that every Man finds he can

frame

frame no *Idea* of it in his own Mind, without a great number of Premises, which cannot be attained by common Conversation, all wise Men hold their Tongues, suspect their own Abilities, and are afraid that they cannot fathom the Depth of his Knowledge with whom they converse; especially if he has a Name for Skill in those Matters. And therefore, talk with such Men of a Law-Case, or a Problem in Geometry, if they never studied those Things, they will frankly tell you so, and decline to give their Opinion. Whereas if you speak to them of a Poem, a Play, or a Moral Discourse upon a Subject capable of Rhetorical Ornaments, they will immediately pass their Censure, right or wrong; and Twenty Men, perhaps, shall give Twenty different Opinions; whilst, in the other Cases, scarce Two of the Twenty shall disagree, if they are conscious to themselves that they have Skill enough to judge without another's help. (2.) In most of these Things our Passions are some way or other concerned; at least, being accustomed to have them moved, we exspect it, and think our selves disappointed when our Exspectation is deceived. Now, when a Man is to judge in Matters of this kind, he generally before-hand is pre-possessed with such Passions as he would willingly have raised, or confirmed; and so speaks as his Exspectation is answered. But when

when our Passions do not move in these Matters, as they seldom do upon Subjects a great way off, then our Censures are more unanimous. For as the Poet says,

Securus licet Aeneam Rutulumque ferocem
Committas; nulli gravis est percussus Achilles.

So that there is no great Wonder why Men should receive the Writings of the Ancients with so great Respect: For the Distance of Time takes off Envy; and the being accustomed from our Childhood to hear them commended, creates a Reverence. Yet though due Allowances ought to be made for these Pre-possessions, one has Reason to believe, that this Reverence for the ancient Orators and Poets is more than Prejudice. (By Orators, I understand all those Writers in Prose who have taken pains to beautifie and adorn their Stile.) Their Works give us a very solid Pleasure when we read them. The best in their kind among the Moderns have been those who have read the Ancients with greatest Care, and endeavoured to imitate them with the greatest Accuracy. The Masters of Writing in all these several Ways, to this Day, appeal to the Ancients, as their Guides; and still fetch Rules from them, for the Art of Writing. *Homer*, and *Aristotle*, and *Terence*, and *Virgil*, and *Horace*, and *Ovid*, are now studied

studied as Teachers, not barely out of Curiosity, by Modern Poets. So likewise are *Demosthenes*, *Aristotle*, *Cicero*, *Quinctilian*, and *Longinus*, by those who would write finely in Prose. There is reason therefore to think that in these Arts the Ancients may have out-done the Moderns; though neither have they been neglected in these later Ages, in which we have seen extraordinary Productions, which the Ancients themselves, had they been alive, would not have been ashamed of.

If this be so, as I verily believe it is, sure now (it will be objected) it is evident that the Ancients had a greater Force of Genius than the Moderns can pretend to. Will it be urged, that here also they had an Advantage by being born first? Have these Arts a fixed Foundation in Nature; or were they not attained to by Study? If they come by Nature, why have we heard of no Orators among the Inhabitants of the Bay of *Soldania*, or eminent Poets in *Peru*? If they are got by Study, why not now, as well as formerly, since Printing has made Learning cheap and easie? Can it be thought harder to Speak and Write like *Cicero* or *Virgil*, than to find out the Motions of the Heavens, and to calculate the Distances of the Stars? What can be the Reason of this Disparity?

The Reasons are several, and scarce one

of

of them, of such a Nature as can now be helped, and yet not conclusive against the Comparative Strength of Understanding, evidently discernible in the Productions of the Learned Men of the present, and immediately foregoing Ages; to which I would here be understood strictly to confine my Notion of the word *Modern*. These Reasons I shall examine at large, because, if they are valid, they quite take away the Force of Sir *William Temple*'s Hypothesis; and by removing the blind Admiration now paid to the Ancient Orators and Poets, set it upon such a Foot as will render the Reading of their Books more useful, because less superstitious. They are of several sorts; some relating to *Oratory*, some to *Poesie*, and some in common to both.

I shall first speak of those which relate more particularly to *Poetry*, because it was much the ancientest way of Writing in *Greece*; where their Orators owned, that they learned a great deal of what they knew, even in their own, as well as in other Parts of Learning, from their Poets. And here one may observe, that no Poetry can be Charming that has not a Language to support it. The *Greek* Tongue has a vast Variety of long Words, wherein long and short Syllables are agreeably intermixed together, with great Numbers of Vowels and Diphthongs in the Middle Syllables, and

those

those very seldom clogged by the joining of harsh-sounding Consonants in the same Syllable: All which Things give it a great Advantage above any other Language that has ever yet been cultivated by Learned Men. By this Means all manner of Tunable Numbers may be formed in it with Ease; as still appears in the remaining *Dramatic* and *Lyric* Composures of the *Greek* Poets. This seems to have been at first a lucky Accident, since it is as visible in *Homer*, who liv'd before the Grammarians had determined the Analogy of that Language by Rules; which Rules were, in a very great measure, taken from his Poems, as the Standard: as in those Poets that came after him. And that this peculiar Smoothness of the *Greek* Language was at first Accidental, farther appears, because the *Phoenician* or *Hebrew* Tongue, from whence it was formed, as most Learned Men agree, is a rough, unpolished Tongue, abounding with short Words, and harsh Consonants: So that if one allows for some small Agreement in the Numbers of Nouns, and Variations of Tenses in Verbs, the two Languages are wholly of a different Make. That a derived Language should be sweeter than its Mother-Tongue, will seem strange to none that compares the Modern *Tuscan* with the Ancient *Latin*; where, though their Affinity is visible at first sight, in every Sentence,

yet

yet one sees that that derived Language actually has a Sweetness and Tunableness in its Composition, that could not be derived from its Parent; since nothing can impart that to another, which it has not it self. And it shews likewise, that a Barbarous People, as the *Italians* were when mingled with the *Goths* and *Lombards*, may, without knowing or minding Grammatical Analogy, form a Language so exceedingly Musical, that scarce any Art can mend it. For in *Boccace*'s Time, who liv'd above CCC Years ago, in the earliest Dawnings of Polite Learning in these Western Parts of the World, *Italian* was a formed Language, endued with that peculiar Smoothness which other *European* Languages wanted; and it has since suffered no fundamental Alterations; not any, one should think, for the better, since in the *Dictionary* of the Academy *della Crusca*, *Boccace*'s Writings are constantly appealed to, as the Standards of the Tongue. Nay, it is still disputed among the Critics of the *Italian Language*, whether (c) *Dante*, *Boccace*, *Petrarch*, and *Villani*, who were all Contemporaries, are not the Valuablest as well as the Ancientest Authors they have.

Now, when this Native Smoothness of the *Greek* Tongue was once discovered to common Ears, by the sweetness of their Verses, which depended upon a Regular

Compo-

(c) See li *Pensieri diversi di Tassoni*, lib. ix. cap 15.

Composition of Long and Short Syllables, all Men paid great Respect to their Poets, who gave them so delightful an Entertainment. The wiser Sort took this Opportunity of Civilizing the rest, by putting all their Theological and Philosophical Instructions into Verse; which being learn'd with Pleasure, and remembred with Ease, help'd to heighten and preserve the Veneration already, upon other Scores, paid to their Poets. This encreased the Number of Rivals, and every one striving to out-doe his Neighbour; some by varying their Numbers, others by chusing Subjects likely to please, here and there some, one or two at least of a sort, proved excellent: And then those who were the most extraordinary in their several Ways, were esteemed as Standards by succeeding Ages; and Rules were framed by their Works, to examine other Poems of the same sort. Thus *Aristotle* framed Rules of *Epic* Poesie from *Homer*: Thus *Aristophanes, Menander, Sophocles* and *Euripides* were looked upon as Masters in *Dramatic* Poesie; and their Practice was sufficient Authority. Thus *Mimnermus, Philetas* and *Callimachus* were the Patterns to following Imitators for *Elegy* and *Epigram*. Now, *Poetry* being a limited Art, and these Men, after the often-repeated Trials of others, had proved successless; finding the true Secret of pleasing their Country-men,

partly

partly by their Wit and Sence, and partly by the inimitable Sweetness of their Numbers, there is no wonder that their Successors, who were to write to a pre-possessed Audience, though otherwise Men of equal, perhaps greater Parts, failed of that Applause of which the great Masters were already in possession; for Copying nauseates more in Poetry, than any thing: So that *Sannazarius* and *Buchanan*, tho' admirable Poets, are not read with that Pleasure which Men find in *Lucretius*, and *Virgil*, and *Horace*, by any but their Country-men; because they wrote in a dead Language, and so were frequently obliged to use the same Turns of Thought, and always the same Words and Phrases, in the same Sence in which they were used before by the Original Authors; which forces their Readers too often to look back upon their Masters; and so abates of that Pleasure which Men take in *Milton*, *Cowley*, *Butler*, or *Dryden*, who wrote in their Mother-Tongue, and so were able to give that unconstrained Range and Turn to their Thoughts and Expressions that are truly necessary to make a compleat Poem.

It may therefore be reasonably believed, that the natural Softness, Expressiveness and Fulness of the *Greek* Language gave great Encouragement to the *Greek* Poets to labour hard, when they had such manageable Matter to work upon, and when such Rewards

con-

constantly attended their Labours. This likewise was a great help to their Orators, as well as their Poets; who soon found the Beauties of a numerous Composition, and left nothing undone, that could bring it to its utmost Perfection. But this was not so important a Consideration, as alone to have encouraged the *Greeks* to cultivate their Eloquence, if the Constitution of their Governments had not made it necessary; and that Necessity had not obliged great Numbers of ingenious Men to take Pains about it.

Most part of *Greece*, properly so called, and of *Asia the Less*, the Coasts of *Thrace*, *Sicily*, the Islands in the *Mediterranean*, and a great part of *Italy*, were long divided into very many Kingdoms and Commonwealths; and many of these small Kingdoms, taking Example by their Neighbouring Cities that had thrown off their imperious Masters, turned, in time, to Commonwealths, as well as they. These, as all little Governments that are contiguous, being well nigh an even Match for each other, continued for many Ages in that Condition. Many of the chiefest were Democracies; as the Republics of *Athens, Syracuse, Thebes* and *Corinth*; where it was necessary to complement the People upon all Occasions: So that busie, factious Men had Opportunities enough to shew their Skill in Politics. Men of all Tempers, and all Designs, that would accuse or defend,

fend, that would advise or consult, were obliged to address themselves in set Harangues to the People. Interest therefore, and Vanity, Motives sometimes equally powerful, made the Study of Rhetoric necessary; and whilst every Man followed the several Bias of his own Genius, some few found out the true Secret of Pleasing, in all the several Ways of Speaking well, which are so admirably and so largely discoursed of by the ancient Rhetoricians. *Demosthenes* being esteem'd beyond all his Predecessors, for the Correctness of his Stile, the Justness of his Figures, the Easiness of his Narrations, and the Force of his Thoughts; his Orations were look'd upon as Standards of Eloquence by his Country-men: Which Notion of theirs effectually dampt future Endeavours of other Men, since here, as well as in Poetry and Painting, all Copiers will ever continue on this side of their Originals. And besides, the great End of Oratory being to persuade, wherein Regard must be had to the Audience, as well as to the Subject, if there be but one Way of doing best at the same time in both, as there can be but one in all limited Arts or Sciences, they that either first find it out, or come the nearest to it, will unquestionably, and of Right, keep the first Station in Men's Esteem, though perhaps they dare not, for fear of disgusting the Age they live in, follow those Methods

which

which they admire so much, and so justly, in those great Masters that went before them.

That these Accidents, and not a particular Force of Genius, raised the *Græcian* Poesie and Oratory, will farther appear, if we reflect upon the History of the Rise and Encrease of both those Arts amongst the *Romans*: Their Learning, as well as their Language, came originally from *Greece*; they saw what was done to their Hands, and *Greek* was a living Language; and so, by the help of Masters, they could judge of all its Beauties. Yet, with all their Care, and Skill, and Pains, they could not, of a long time, bring their Poetry to any Smoothness; they found their Language was not so ductile, they owned it, and complained of it. It had a Majestick Gravity, derived from the People themselves who spoke it; which made it proper for Philosophical and Epical Poems; for which Reason, *Lucretius* and *Virgil* were able to do so great Things in their several Ways, their Language enabling them to give the most becoming Beauties to all their Thoughts. But there not being that Variety of Feet in the *Latin*, which Language, for the most part, abounds in *Dactyles*, *Spondees* and *Trochees*; nor that Sprightliness of Temper, and inbred Gaiety in the *Romans*, which the *Greeks* are to this Day famous for, even to a Proverb, in many parts of Poetry they yielded,
though

though not without Reluctancy, to a People whom they themselves had conquered: Which shews, that there are some Imperfections which cannot be overcome: And when these Imperfections are accidental, as the Language is which every Man speaks at first, though he has equal Parts, and perhaps greater Industry; yet he shall be thrown behind another Man who does not labour under those Inconveniences; and the Distance between them will be greater, or less, according to the Greatness or Quality of these Inconveniences.

If we look into the chiefest Modern Languages, we shall find them labouring under much greater. For, the Quantities of Syllables being in a great measure neglected in all Modern Languages, we cannot make use of that Variety of Feet, which was anciently used by the *Greeks* and *Romans*, in Modern Poems. The Guide of Verses is not now Length of Syllable, but only Number of Feet, and Accent. Most of the *French* Accents are in the last Syllable; Ours, and the *Italian*, in the fore-going. This fits *French* for some sorts of Poems, which *Italian* and *English* are not so proper for. Again, All Syllables, except the Accented one in each Word, being now common in Modern Languages, we Northern People often make a Syllable short that has two or three Consonants in it, because we

abound

abound in Consonants: This makes *English* more unfit for some Poems, than *French* and *Italian*; which having fewer Consonants, have consequently a greater Smoothness and Flowingness of Feet, and Rapidity of Pronunciation.

I have brought these Instances out of Modern Languages, whereof Sir *William Temple* is so great a Master, to prove my first Assertion; namely, That though a very great deal is to be given to the Genius and Judgment of the Poet, which are both absolutely necessary to make a good Poem, what Tongue soever the Poet writes in; yet the Language it self has so great an influence, that if *Homer* and *Virgil* had been *Polanders*, or *High-Dutch-men*, they would never, in all probability, have thought it worth their while to attempt the Writing of Heroick Poems; *Virgil* especially (d), who began to write an Historical Poem of some great Actions of his Country-men; but was so gravell'd with the Roughness of the *Roman* Names, that he laid it aside.

(d) *Cum res Romanas inchoasset, offensus materiâ & nominum asperitate, ad Bucolica transiit.* Donatus *in Vit.* Virgilii.

Now, as the *Roman* Poetry arrived to that Perfection which it had, because it was supported by a Language, which, tho' in some Things inferiour to the *Greek*, had several noble and charming Beauties, not now to be found in Modern Languages; so the

Roman

Roman Oratory was owing to their Government: Which makes the Parallel much more perfect. And all those Reasons alledged already for the Growth of the *Attic* Eloquence, are equally applicable to the History of the *Roman*; so that there is no necessity of Repeating them. To which we may add, That when the *Romans* once lost their Liberty, their Eloquence soon fell: And *Tacitus* (or *Quinctilian*) needed not have gone so far about to search for Reasons of the Decay of the *Roman* Eloquence. *Tully* left his Country and Profession, after his Defence of *S. Roscius Amerinus*, resolving to give over Pleading, if *Sylla*'s Death had not restored that Freedom which only gave Life to his Oratory: And when the Civil Wars between *Pompey* and *Caesar* came on, he retired, because his Profession was superseded by a rougher Rhetoric, which commands an Attentive Audience in all Countries where it pleads.

When Orators are no longer Constituent Parts of a Government, or, at least, when Eloquence is not an almost certain Step to arrive at the chiefest Honours in a State, the Necessity of the Art of Speaking, is, in a great measure, taken off; and as the Authority of Orators lessens, which it will insensibly do, as Tyranny and Absolute Power prevail, their Art will dwindle into Declamation, and an Affectation of Sentences,

D and

and Forms of Wit. The Old Men, who outlive their former Splendour, will, perhaps, set their own Scholars and Auditors right, and give them a true Relish of what is Great and Noble; but that will hardly continue above one or two Generations. Which may be superadded as another Reason why there were no more *Demosthenes's* or *Cicero's*, after the *Macedonian* and *Roman* Emperors had taken away the Liberty of the *Graecian* and *Roman* Commonwealths. It is Liberty alone which inspires Men with Lofty Thoughts, and elevates their Souls to a higher Pitch than Rules of Art can direct. Books of Rhetoric may make Men Copious and Methodical; but they alone can never infuse that true Enthusiastic Rage which Liberty breaths into their Souls who enjoy it; and which, guided by a Sedate Judgment, will carry Men farther than the greatest Industry, and the quickest Parts can go without it.

When Private Members of a Commonwealth can have Foreign Princes for their Clients, and plead their Causes before their Fellow-Citizens; when Men have their Understandings enlarged, by a long Use of public Business, for many Years before they speak in public; and when they know that their Auditory are Men, not only of equal Parts, and Experience in Business; but also many of them Men of equal, if not greater Skill in Rhetoric than themselves: Which was the Case of the Old *Romans*. These Men, inflamed with the mighty Honour of being Patrons to Crowned Heads, having Liberty to speak any Thing that may advantage their Cause, and being obliged to take so great Pains to get up to, or to keep above so many Rivals, must needs be much more excellent Orators, than other Ages, destitute of such concurrent Circumstances, though every thing else be equal, can possibly produce.

Besides all this, the Humour of the Age in which we live is exceedingly altered: Men apprehend or suspect a Trick in every Thing that is said to move the Passions of the Auditory in *Courts of Judicature*, or in the *Parliament-House*. They think themselves affronted when such Methods are used in Speaking, as if the Orator could suppose within himself, that they were to be catched by such Baits. And therefore, when Men have spoken to the Point, in as few Words as the Matter will bear, it is expected they should hold their Tongues. Even in the Pulpit, the Pomp of Rhetoric is not always commended, especially here in *England*; and very few meet with Applause, who do not confine themselves to speak with the Severity of a Philosopher, as well as with the Splendour of an Orator; two Things, not always consistent. What a Difference in the Way of Thinking must this needs create in the World? Anciently, Orators made their Employment the Work of their whole Lives; and as such, they followed it. All their Studies, even in other Things, were, by a sort of Alchemy, turned into Eloquence. The Labour which they thought requisite, is evident to any Man that reads *Quinctilian's Institutions*, and the Rhetorical Tracts of *Cicero*. This exceedingly takes off the Wonder. Eloquence may lie in common for Ancients and Moderns; yet those only shall be most Excellent that cultivate it most, and give it the greatest Encouragement, who live in an Age that is accustomed to, and will bear nothing but Masculine, unaffected Sence; which likewise must be cloathed with the most splendid Ornaments of Rhetoric.

Sir *William Temple* will certainly agree with me in this Conclusion, That former Ages produced greater *Orators*, and nobler *Poets*, than these later ones have done; tho' perhaps he may disagree with me about the Way by which I came to my Conclusion; since hence it will follow, that the present Age, with the same Advantages, under the same Circumstances, might produce a *Demosthenes*, a *Cicero*, a *Horace*, or a *Virgil*; which, for any thing hitherto said to the contrary, seems to be very probable.

But, though the Art of Speaking, assisted by all these Advantages, seems to have been

been at a greater height amongst the *Greeks* and *Romans* than it is at present; yet it will not follow from thence, that every Thing which is capable of Rhetorical Ornaments, should for that sole Reason, be more perfect anciently than now; especially if these be only Secondary Beauties, without which, that Discourse wherein they are found may be justly valuable, and that in a very high Degree. So that, though, for the purpose, one should allow the Ancient Historians to be better Orators than the Modern; yet these last may, for all that, be much better, at least, equally good Historians; those among them especially, who have taken fitting Care to please the Ears, as well as instruct the Understandings of their Readers. Of all the Ancient Historians before *Polybius*, none seems to have had a right Notion of writing History, except *Thucydides*: And therefore *Polybius*, whose first Aim was, to instruct his Reader, by leading him into every Place whither the Thread of his Narrative carried him, makes frequent Excuses for those Digressions, which were but just necessary to beget a thorough Understanding of the Matter of Fact of which he was then giving an Account. These Excuses shew that he took a new Method; and they answer an Objection, which might otherwise have been raised from the small Numbers of exstant Histories that were written before his Time; as if we could make no Judgment of those that are lost, from those that are preserved. For, the Generality of those who wrote before him, made Rhetoric their chief Aim; and therefore All Niceties of Time, and Place, and Person, that might hurt the Flowingness of their Stile, were omitted; instead whereof, the Great Men of their *Drama's*, were introduced, making long Speeches; and such a Gloss was put upon every Thing that was told, as made it appear extraordinary; and whatsoever was wonderful and prodigious, was mentioned with a particular Emphasis.

This Censure will not appear unjust to any Man who has read Ancient Historians with ordinary Care; *Polybius* especially: Who, first of all the Ancient Historians now exstant, fixes the Time of every great Action that he mentions: Who assigns such Reasons for all Events, as seem, even at this distance, neither too great, nor too little: Who, in Military Matters, takes Care, not only to shew his own Skill, but to make his Reader a Judge, as well as himself: Who, in Civil Affairs, makes his Judgment of the Conduct of every People from the several Constitutions of their respective Governments, or from the Characters and Circumstances of the Actors themselves: And last of all, Who scrupulously avoids saying any Thing that might appear incredible to Posterity;

sterity; but represents Things in such a manner, as a wise Man may believe they were transacted: And yet he has neglected all that Artful Eloquence which was before so much in fashion.

If these therefore be the chiefest Perfections of a just History, and if they can only be the Effects of a great Genius, and great Study, or both; at least, not of the last, without the first; we are next to enquire whether any of the Moderns have been able to attain to them: And then, if several may be found, which in none of these Excellencies seem to yield to the noblest of all the Ancient Historians, it will not be difficult to give an Answer to Sir *William Temple's* Question; *Whether* (e) *D'Avila's and Strada's Histories be beyond those of Herodotus and Livy?* I shall name but two; *The Memoirs of* Philip Commes, *and* F. Paul's *History of the Council of* Trent.

(e)Pag 57.

Philip Commines ought here to be mention'd, for many Reasons: For, besides that he particularly excells in those very Vertues which are so remarkable in *Polybius*, to whom *Lipsius* makes no scruple to compare him; he had nothing to help him but Strength of Genius, assisted by Observation and Experience; He owns himself, that he had no Learning; and indeed, the thing it self is evident to any Man that reads his Writings. He flourished in a barbarous Age, and

and died just as Learning had crossed the *Alpes*, to get into *France*. So that he could not, by Conversation with Scholars, have those Defects which Learning cures, supplied. This is what cannot be said of the *Thucydides*'s, *Polybius*'s, *Sallusts*, *Livies*, and *Tacitus*'s of Antiquity. Yet, with all these Disadvantages, (to which this great one ought also to be added, That by the Monkish Books then in vogue, he might sooner be led out of the Way, than if he had had none at all to peruse,) his Stile is Masculine and significant; though diffuse, yet not tedious; even his Repetitions, which are not over-frequent, are diverting. His Digressions are wise, proper, and instructing. One sees a profound Knowledge of Mankind in every Observation that he makes; and that without Ill Nature, Pride, or Passion. Not to mention that peculiar Air of Impartiality, which runs through the whole Work; so that it is not easie to withdraw our Assent from every thing which he says. It is no wonder then if his History never tires, though immediately read after *Livy* or *Tacitus*.

In F. *Paul*'s History one may also find the Excellencies before observed in *Polybius*; and it has been nicely examined by dexterous and skilful Adversaries, who have taken the Pains to weigh every Period, and rectifie every Date. So that, besides the Satisfaction

tisfaction which any other admirable History would have afforded us, we have the Pleasure of thinking that we may safely rely upon his Accounts of Things, without being mis-guided in any one leading Particular of great moment, since Adversaries, who had no Inclination to spare him, could not invalidate the Authority of a Book which they had so great a desire to lessen. I should have taken notice of no Modern Historians besides *D'Avila* and *Strada*, if there were as much Reason to believe their Narratives, as there is to commend their Skill in Writing. *D'Avila* must be acknowledged to be a most Entertaining Historian; one that wants neither Art, Genius, nor Eloquence, to render his History acceptable. *Strada* imitates the old *Romans* so happily, that those who can relish their Eloquence, will be always pleased with his.

Upon the whole Matter, one may positively say, That where any Thing in which Oratory can only claim a Share, has been equally cultivated by the Moderns, as by the Ancients; they have equalled them at least, if not out-done them, setting aside any particular Graces, which might as well be owing to the Languages in which they wrote, as to the Writers themselves.

CHAP.

CHAP. IV.

Reflections upon Monsieur Perrault's Hypothesis, That Modern Orators and Poets are more Excellent than Ancient.

Whatever becomes of the Reasons given in the last Chapter, for the Excellency of Ancient Eloquence and Poetry, the Position it self is so generally held in *England*, that I do not fear any Opposition here at home. It is almost an Heresie in Wit, among our Poets, to set up any Modern Name against *Homer* or *Virgil*, *Horace* or *Terence*. So that though here and there, one should in Discourse preferr the Writers of the present Age, yet scarce any Man among us, who sets a Value upon his own Reputation, will venture to assert it in Print. Whether this is to be attributed to their Judgment or Modesty, or both, I will not determine; though I am apt to believe, to both, because in our Neighbour-Nation, (some of whose Writers are remarkable for a good deal of what Sir *William Temple* calls *Sufficiency*,) some late Authors have spoken much more openly.

For

For one of the Members of the *French Academy*, which, since the Cardinal *de Richelieu*'s time, has taken so much Pains to make the *French* Language capable of all those Beauties which are so conspicuous in Ancient Authors, will not allow me to go so far as I have done. Monsieur *Perrault*, the famous Advocate of Modern Orators and Poets, in Oratory sets the Bishop of *Meaux* against *Pericles*, (or rather, *Thucydides*,) the Bishop of *Nismes* against *Isocrates*, F. *Bourdaloue* against *Lysias*, Monsieur *Voiture* against *Pliny*, and Monsieur *Balzac* against *Cicero*. In Poetry likewise he sets Monsieur *Boileau* against *Horace*, Monsieur *Corneille* and Monsieur *Moliere* against the Ancient *Dramatic* Poets. In short, though he owns that some amongst the Ancients had very exalted Genius's, so that it may, perhaps, be very hard to find any Thing that comes near the Force of some of the Ancient Pieces, in either kind, amongst our Modern Writers; yet he affirms, that Poetry and Oratory are now at a greater height than ever they were, because there have been many Rules found out since *Virgil*'s and *Horace*'s Time; and the old Rules likewise have been more carefully scanned than ever they were before. This Hypothesis ought a little to be enquired into; and therefore I shall offer some few Considerations about this Notion. Sir

William

William Temple, I am sure, will not think this a Digression; because the Author of the Plurality of Worlds, (f) *by censuring of the Old Poetry, and giving Preference to the New, raised his Indignation; which no Quality among Men was so apt to raise in him as Sufficiency, the worst Composition out of the Pride and Ignorance of Mankind.*

(f) Pag. 5.

(1.) Monsieur *Perrault* takes it for granted, that *Cicero* was a better Orator than *Demosthenes*; because, living after him, the World had gone on for above Two Hundred Years, constantly improving, and adding new Observations, necessary to compleat his Art: And so by Consequence, that the Gentlemen of the Academy must out-doe *Tully*, for the same Reasons. This Proposition, which is the Foundation of a great part of his Book, is not very easie to be proved; because Mankind loves Variety in those Things wherein it may be had so much, that the best Things, constantly re-iterated, will certainly disgust. Sometimes the Age will not bear Subjects, upon which an Orator may display his full Force; he may often be obliged to little, mean Exercises. A Thousand Accidents, not discoverable at a distance, may force Men to stretch their Inventions to spoil that Eloquence, which left to it self, would do admirable Things. And that there is such a Thing

Thing as a Decay of Eloquence in After-Ages, which have the Performances of those that went before constantly to recurr to, and which may be supposed to pretend to Skill and Fineness, is evident from the Writings of *Seneca*, and the Younger *Pliny*, compared with *Tully's*: And from a Discourse written in *Tacitus's* Time, upon this very Subject, wherein the Author, taking it for granted that the *Roman* Eloquence was sunk, enquires, with a World of Wit and Spirit, into the Reasons of its Decay. One great Instance which Monsieur *Perrault* alledges of his supposed want of Art in the Ancients, is want of Method in setting down their Thoughts, even when one would think they should have taken the greatest Care. This Accusation is, in my Opinion, very groundless. Let *Tully's Pleadings* and *Quinctilian's Institutions* be examined, and then let the Controversie be decided by that Examination. And if Panegyricks and Funeral-Orations do not seem so regular, it is not because Method was little understood, but because in those Discourses it was not so necessary. Where Men were to reason severely, Method was strictly observed: And the Vertues discoursed upon in *Tully's Offices* are as judiciously and clearly digested under their proper Heads, as the Subject-Matter of most Discourses written by any Modern Author, upon any Subject whatsoever.

ever. It does not seem possible to contrive any Poem, whose Parts can have a truer, or more artful Connexion, than *Virgil's Æneis*. And though it is now objected by Monsieur *Perrault*, as a Fault, that he did not carry on his Poem to the Marriage of *Æneas* and *Lavinia*, yet we may reasonably think, that he had very good Reasons for doing so; because in *Augustus's* Court, where those sort of Things were very well understood, it was received with as great Veneration as it has been since; and never needed the Recommendation of Antiquity, to add to its Authority. But we need not recurr to an Excuse, or to any thing that may look like one, in this Matter: It is a Fault in Heroic Poetry, to fetch Things from their first Originals: And to carry the Thread of the Narrative down to the last Event, is altogether as dull. As *Homer* begins not with the Rape of *Helen*, so he does not go so far as the Destruction of *Troy*. Men should rise from Table with some Appetite remaining: And a Poem should leave some View of something to follow, and not quite shut the Scenes; especially if the remaining part of the Story be not capable of much Ornament, nor will admit of Variety. The Passion of Love, with those that always follow upon its being disappointed, had been shewn already in the Story of *Dido*. But Monsieur
Perrault

Perrault seems to have had his Head possessed with the *Idea* of *French* Romances; which, to be sure, must never fail to end in a general Wedding.

(10.) Another of Monsieur *Perrault*'s Arguments, to prove that the Ancients did not perfect their Oratory and Poesie, is this; That the Mind of Man, being an inexhaustible Fund of new Thoughts and Projects, every Age added Observations of its own to the former Store; so that they still encreased in Politeness, and by consequence, their Eloquence of all sorts, in Verse or Prose, must needs have been more exact. And as a Proof of this Assertion, he instances in Matters of Love; wherein the Writings of the best bred Gentlemen of all Antiquity, for want of Modern Gallantry, of which they had no Notion, were rude and unpolish'd, if compared with the Poems and Romances of the present Age. Here Monsieur *Perrault*'s Skill in Architecture seems to have deceiv'd him: For there is a wide Difference between an Art that, having no Antecedent Foundation in Nature, owes its first Original to some particular Invention, and all its future Improvements to Superstructures raised by other Men upon that first Ground-work; and between such Operations of the Mind, as are Congenial with our Natures; where Conversation will polish them, even without

out previous Intentions of doing so; and where the Experience of a few Ages, if assisted by Books that may preserve particular Cases, will carry them to as great an Height as the Things themselves are capable of. And therefore, he that now examines the Writings of the Ancient Moral Philosophers, *Aristotle* for instance, or the *Stoics*, will find, that they made as nice Distinctions in all Matters relating to Vertue and Vice; and that they understood Humane Nature, with all its Passions and Appetites, as accurately as any Philosophers have done since. Besides, it may be justly question'd, whether what Monsieur *Perrault* calls *Politeness*, be not very often rather a vicious Aberration from, and Straining of Nature, than an Improvement of the Manners of the Age: If so, it may reasonably be supposed, that those that medled not with the Niceties of Ceremony and Breeding, before unpractised, rather contemned them as improper or unnatural, than omitted them through Ignorance occasioned by the Roughness of the Manners of the Ages in which they lived. *Ovid* and *Tibullus* knew what Love was, in its tenderest Motions; they describe its Anxieties and Disappointments in a manner that raises too too many Passions, even in unconcerned Hearts; they omit no probable Arts of Courtship and Address; and keep-

keeping the Mark they aim at still in view, they rather chuse to shew their Passion than their Wit. And therefore they are not so formal as the Heroes in *Pharamond* or *Cassandra*; who, by pretending to Exactness in all their Methods, commit greater Improbabilities than *Amadis de Gaule* himself. In short, (g) *D'Urfe*, and (h) *Calprenede*, and the rest of the *French* Romancers, by overstraining the String, have broke it: And one can as soon believe that *Varillas* and *Maimbourg* wrote the Histories of great Actions just as they were done, as that Men ever made Love in such a way as these *Love-and-Honour Men* describe. That Simplicity therefore of the Ancients, which Monsieur *Perrault* undervalues, is so far from being a Mark of Rudeness, and Want of Complaisance, that their Fault lay in being too Natural, in making too lively Descriptions of Things, where Men want no Foreign Assistance to help them to form their *Idea's*; and where Ignorance, could it be had, is more valuable than any, much more than a Critical Knowledge. But,

(g) The Author of *Astrea*.
(h) The Author of *Cleopatra*.

(3.) Since,
By that loud Trumpet which our Courage aids,
We learn, that Sound, as well as Sense, persuades;

the Felicity of a manageable Language, when improv'd by Men of nice Ears, and true Judgments, is greater, and goes farther to make Men Orators and Poets, than Monsieur *Perrault* seems willing to allow; though there is a plain Reason for his Unwillingness: The *French* Language wants Strength to temper and support its Smoothness for the nobler Parts of Poesie, and perhaps of Oratory too; though the *French* Nation wants no Accomplishments necessary to make a Poet, or an Orator. Therefore their late Critics are always setting Rules, and telling Men what must be done, and what omitted, if they would be Poets. What they find they cannot do themselves, shall be so clogg'd where they may have the Management, that others shall be afraid to attempt it. They are too fond of their Language, to acknowledge where the Fault lies; and therefore the chief Thing, they tell us, is, that Sence, Connexion and Method are the principal Things to be minded. Accordingly, they have translated most of the Ancient Poets, even the *Lyrics*, into *French* Prose; and from those Translations they pass their Judgments, and call upon others to do so too. So that when (to use Sir *J. Denham*'s Comparison) by pouring the Spirits of the Ancient Poetry from one Bottle into another, they have lost the most Volatile Parts, and the rest loses all its relish;

these

these Critics exclaim against the Ancients, as if they did not sufficiently understand Poetical Chymistry. This is so great a Truth, that even in Oratory it holds, though in a less degree. *Thucydides* therefore has hard Measure to be compar'd with the Bishop of *Meaux*, when his Orations are turned into another Language, whilst Monsieur *de Meaux*'s stands unaltered; for, though Sence is Sence in every Tongue, yet all Languages have a peculiar Way of expressing the same Things; which is lost in Translations, and much more in Monsieur *D' Ablancourt*'s, who professed to mind two very different Things at once; to Translate his Author, and to Write elegant Books in his own Language; which last he has certainly done; and he knew that more Persons could find fault with his Stile, if it had been faulty, than find out Mistakes in his Rendring of *Thucydides's Greek*. Besides, the Beauty of an Author's Composition, is, in all Translations, entirely lost, whilst a new Composition suitable to that Language into which the Translation is made is introduced: Yet that was a Thing about which the Ancients were superstitiously exact, (*i*) and in their elegant Prose, as much almost as in their Verse. So that a man can have but half an *Idéa* of the ancient Eloquence, and that not always faithful, who judges of it without such a Skill in *Greek* and *Latin*

(*i*) Vid. *Quinctil. Inst. Orat* lib ix c 4 *de Compositione.*

as can enable him to read Histories, Ora[ti]
ons and Poems in those Languages, w[ith]
Ease and Pleasure; Especially if he is [al]
so well acquainted with the History, Lea[rn]
ing and Customs of the Ages in which [the]
great Men of Antiquity wrote, as to be a[ble]
to discern the Force of the Allusions wh[ich]
they continually make, and which eve[ry]
Reader of their own Age easily understo[od,]
though their Beauty was soon lost, wh[en]
once the Matters of Fact there tacitly [re]
ferred to, were forgotten.

But these are Qualifications which M[on]
sieur *Perrault* extremely wants, who (if [we]
will believe Monf. *Boileau*) has neit[her]
Greek nor *Latin* enough to undertake [to]
make a Parallel between Ancient and M[o]
dern Orators and Poets. But a particu[lar]
Enquiry into his Mistakes would lead [me]
too far out of the way; and besides, [the]
World would think me very vain, to [at]
tempt any thing of this kind, after wh[at]
the Excellent Monsieur *Despreaux* has d[one]
already in his *Critical Reflections upon L*[*on*]
ginus: For there he has given so just a V[in]
dication of those Great Men, whom he [so]
well knows how to imitate, that what[so]
ever I can say after him, will appear f[lat]
and insipid. I shall therefore rather ch[use]
to return to my Subject.

CHA[P.

CHAP. V.

Of Ancient and Modern Grammar.

Grammar is one of the Sciences which Sir *William Temple* says, (k) no Man (k) P. 44. ever disputed with the Ancients.

As this Assertion is expressed, it is a little ambiguous: It may be understood of the Skill of the Moderns in the Grammatical Analogy of *Latin* and *Greek,* or of their Skill in the *Grammar* of their Mother-Tongues: Besides, *Grammar* may either be considered *Mechanically,* or *Philosophically.* Those consider it *Mechanically,* who only examine the Idiotisms and Proprieties of every particular Language, and lay down Rules to teach them to others. Those consider it as *Philosophers,* who consider Language, with the Nature of Grammatical Analogy in general, and then carry down their Speculations to those particular Languages of which they are to discourse; who run over the several Steps, by which every Language has altered its *Idiom*; who enquire into the several Perfections and Imperfections of those Tongues with which they are acquainted, and (if they are living Languages) propose Methods how to remedy them, or, at least, remove those

Obscurities which are thereby occasioned in such Discourses where Truth is only regarded, and not Eloquence.

Now, this *Mechanical Grammar* of *Greek* and *Latin* has been very carefully studied by Modern Critics. *Sanctius*, *Scioppius*, and *Gerhard Vossius*, besides a great number of others, who have occasionally shewn their Skill in their Illustrations of Ancient Authors, have given evident Proofs how well they understood the *Latin* Tongue; So have *Caninius*, *Clenard*, *Gerhard Vossius*, and abundance more, in *Greek*: Wherein they have gone upon sure Grounds, since, besides a great Number of Books in both Languages, upon other Subjects, abundance of Grammatical Treatises, *such as Scholia upon Difficult Authors, Glossaries, Onomasticons, Etymologicons, Rudiments of Grammar*, and the like, have been preserved, and published by skilful Men (most of them at least) with great Care and Accuracy. From all which there seems to be Reason to believe, that some Modern Critics may have understood the Grammatical Construction of *Latin*, as well as *Varro*, or *Caesar*; and of *Greek*, as well as *Aristarchus*, or *Herodian*. But this cannot be pretended to be a new Invention; for the Grammar of dead Languages can be only learned by Books: And since their Analogy can neither be encreased nor diminished, it must be left as we find it. So

So that when Sir *William Temple* says, *That no Man ever disputed Grammar with the Ancients*; if he means, that we cannot make a new Grammar of a dead Language, whose Analogy has been determined almost MM Years, it is what can admit of no Dispute. But if he means, that Modern Languages have not been Grammatically examined, at least, not with that Care that some Ancient Tongues have been; that is a Proposition which may, perhaps, be very justly questioned. And he, of all Men, ought not to have arraign'd the Modern Ignorance in *Grammar*, who puts *Delphos* for *Delphi*, every where in his *Essays*, tho' he knows that Proper Names borrow'd from *Latin* and *Greek* are always put in the Nominative-Case, in our Language. For those who find fault with others, ought to be critically exact in those Things at least themselves. But without making Personal Digressions, in the first place, it ought to be considered, that every Tongue has its own peculiar Form, as well as its proper Words; not communicable to, nor to be regulated by the Analogy of another Language: Wherefore, he is the best *Grammarian*, who is the perfectest Master of the Analogy of the Language which he writes about; and gives the truest Rules, by which another Man may learn it. Next, To apply this to our own Tongue, it may be cer-

certainly affirmed, That the *Grammar* of *English* is so far our own, that Skill in the Learned Languages is not necessary to comprehend it. *Ben. Johnson* was the first Man, that I know of, that did any Thing considerable in it: But he seems to have been too much possessed with the Analogy of *Latin* and *Greek*, to write a perfect Grammar of a Language whose Construction is so vastly different; tho' he falls into a contrary Fault, when he treats of the *English Syntax*, where he generally appeals to *Chaucer* and *Gower*, who lived before our Tongue had met with any of that Polishing, which, within these last CC Years, has made it appear almost entirely New. After him, came Dr. *Wallis*; who examined the *English* Tongue like a Grammarian and a Philosopher at once, and shewed great Skill in that Business: And of his *English Grammar*, one may venture to say, That it may be set against any Thing that is extant of the Ancients, of that kind: For, as Sir *William Temple* says upon another Occasion, there is *a Strain of Philosophy, and curious Thought*, in his previous *Essay of the Formation of the Sounds of Letters*; and of *Subtilty*, in his *Grammar*, in the reducing of our Language under Genuine Rules of Art, that one would not expect in a Book of that kind.

The Care which the *Modern Italians* have taken to cultivate and refine their Language, is hardly to be believed by a People who have been so careless of their own as the *English* have been, till within these last XXX or XL Years. Volumes have been written against the use of some Letters, and in favour of others (*l*). Cardinal *Bembo* drew up such large and exact Rules for the *Italian*, that one would have imagined they could not have received any Additions; and yet *Castelvetro* made an Enlargement which was bigger than the *Cardinal's* Original Work, to which *Salviati* thought it necessary to add an *Appendix* (*m*). The Academy *della Crusca* have been above these C Years *sifting* their Language; and with how great Accuracy and Pains they have examined it, their *Vocabulary*, which has had several Impressions, with vast Augmentations, from what it was at first, is a convincing Proof.

In *France*, since the Institution of the *French Academy*, the *Grammar* of their own Language has been studied with great Care. *Isocrates* himself could not be more nice in the Numbers of his Periods, than these *Academicians* have been in setling the Phraseology, in fixing the Standard of Words, and in making their Sentences, as well as they could, numerous and flowing. Their *Dictionary*, which is come out at last; *Vaugelas's*

(*l*) H. and Z.

(*m*) Vid. li Pensieri diversi di Tassoni, l.x. c. 2.

gelas's, *Bouhours*'s and *Menage*'s *Remarks upon the French Tongue*, *Richelet*'s and *Furetiere*'s *Dictionaries*, with abundance of other Books of that kind, which, though not all written by Members of the *Academy*, yet are all Imitations of the Patterns which they first set, are Evidences of this their Care. This Sir *William Temple* somewhere owns: And though he there supposes, that these *Filers* and *Polishers* may have taken away a great part of the Strength of the Tongue, (which, in the main, is true enough,) yet that is no Objection against their Critical Skill in *Grammar*; upon which Account only their Labours are here taken notice of. So much for the *Mechanical* Part of *Grammar*.

Philosophical Grammar was never, that we know of, much minded by the Ancients. So that any great Performances of this sort, are to be looked upon as Modern Additions to the Commonwealth of Learning. The most considerable Book of that kind, that I know of, is Bishop *Wilkin*'s *Essay towards a Real Character, and Philosophical Language*: A Work, which those who have studied, think they can never commend enough. To this one ought to add, what may be found relating to the same Subject, in the Third Book of Mr. *Locke*'s *Essay of Humane Understanding*.

CHAP.

CHAP. VI.

Of Ancient and Modern Architecture, Statuary, and Painting.

Hitherto the *Moderns* seem to have had very little Reason to boast of their Acquisitions and Improvements; Let us see now what they may have hereafter. In those Arts, sure, if in any, they may challenge the Preference, which depending upon great Numbers of Experiments and Observations, that do not every Day occurr, cannot be supposed to be brought to Perfection in a few Ages. Among such, doubtless, *Architecture, Sculpture* and *Painting* may and ought here to be reckoned; both because they were extremely valued by the *Ancients*, and do still keep up their just Price. They are likewise very properly taken notice of in this Place, because they have always been the Entertainments of Ingenious and Learned Men, whose Circumstances would give them Opportunity to lay out Money upon them, or to please themselves with other Men's Labours. In these Things, if we may take Men's Judgments in their own Professions, the Ancients have far out-done the Moderns. The *Italians*, whose Performances
have

have been the most considerable in this kind, and who, as Genuine Successors of the Old *Romans*, are not apt to undervalue what they do themselves, have, for the most part, given the uncontested Pre-eminence to the Ancient *Greek* Architects, Painters and Sculptors. Whose Authority we ought the rather to acquiesce in, because *Michael Angelo* and *Bernini*, two wonderful Masters, and not a little jealous of their own Honour, did always ingenuously declare, that their best Pieces were exceeded by some of the Ancient Statues still to be seen at *Rome*.

Here therefore I at first intended to have left off; and I thought my self obliged to resign what I believed could not be maintained, when Monsieur *Perrault*'s *Parallel of the Ancients and Moderns* came to my Hands. His Skill in *Architecture* and *Mechanics*, may, in all probability, be relied upon; since the *French King*, who is said to be not over-apt to conferr Employments upon Men that do not understand how to manage them, has made him (*n*) *Chief Surveyor of his Buildings*. And his long Conversation with the finest Pieces of Antiquity, and of these Latter Ages, which his Employment necessarily led him to, fitted him for judging of these Matters better than other Men. So that, though there might be great Reason not to agree to his Hypo-

(*n*) *Premier Commis de la Surintendance des Batimens de France*

Hypothesis *of the State of Ancient and Modern Eloquence and Poesie*; yet in Things of this Nature, where the *Mediums* of Judging are quite different, and where Geometrical Rules of Proportion, which in their own Nature are unalterable, go very far to determine the Question, his Judgment seemed to be of great weight. I shall therefore chuse rather to give a short View of what he says upon these Subjects, than to pass any Censure upon them of my own.

Of *Architecture*, he says; 'That though Pag. 88. 'the Moderns have received the Knowledge of the Five Orders from the Ancients, yet if they employ it to better 'Purposes, if their Buildings be more useful, and more beautiful, then they must 'be allowed to be the better Architects: 'For it is in Architecture, as it is in Oratory; as he that lays down Rules, when 'and how to use *Metaphors, Hyperbole's, Apostrophe's,* or any other Figures of *Rhetoric*, may very often not be so good an 'Orator as he that uses them judiciously 'in his Discourses: So he that teaches 'what a *Pillar*, an *Architrave* or a *Cornice* 'is, and that instructs another in the Rules 'of Proportion, so as to adjust all the 'Parts of each of the several Orders a-'right, may not be so good an Architect 'as he that builds a magnificent Temple, 'or a noble Palace, that shall answer all
'those

'those Ends for which such Structures are
'designed. That the chief Reason why
'the *Doric*, the *Ionic*, or the *Corinthian*
'Models have pleased so much, is, partly
'because the Eye has been long accustom-
'ed to them, and partly because they have
'been made use of by Men who under-
'stood and followed those other Rules
'which will eternally please, upon the
'score of real Usefulness; whereas the
'Five Orders owe their Authority to Cu-
'stom, rather than to Nature. That these

Pag. 95. 'Universal Rules are; To make those
'Buildings which will bear it, lofty and
'wide: In Stone-work, to use the largest,
'the smoothest, and the evenest Stones:
'To make the Joints almost imperceptible:
'To place the Perpendicular Parts of the
'Work exactly Perpendicular, and the Ho-
'rizontal Parts exactly Horizontal: To
'support the weak Parts of the Work by
'the strong: To cut Square Figures per-
'fectly Square, and Round Figures per-
'fectly Round: To hew the whole exact-
'ly true; and to fix all the Corners of the
'Work evenly, as they ought to be. That
'these Rules, well observ'd, will always
'please even those who never understood
'one single Term of Art: Whereas the
'other accidental Beauties, such as he sup-
'poses *Doric*, *Ionic*, or *Corinthian* Work to
'be, please, only because they are found
'together

'together with these, though their being
' the most conspicuous Parts of a Build-
' ing, made them be first observ'd: From
' whence Men began to fansie Inherent
' Beauties in that, which owes the greatest
' part of its Charms to the good Company
' in which it is taken notice of, and so in
' time delighted, when it was seen alone.
' That otherwise it would be impossible Pag. 97,
' that there should be so great a Variety in 99.
' the Assigning of the Proportions of the
' several Orders; no two eminent Archi-
' tects ever keeping to the same Measure,
' though they have neither spoiled nor les-
' sened the Beauty of their Works. That
' if we go to Particulars, we shall not find
' (for the purpose) in the *Pantheon* at *Rome*,
' which is the most regular, and the most
' magnificent ancient Building now extant,
' two Pillars of a like thickness. That
' (*o*) the Girders of the arched Roof do (*o*) *Ban-*
' not lie full upon the great Columns or *deaux de la*
' Pilasters; but some quite over the Cavi- *Temple,*
' ties of the Windows which are under- Pag. 111,
' neath; others half over the Windows, and Pag. 113.
' half upon the Columns or Pilasters. That Pag. 114.
' the Modillons of the Cornice are not ex-
' actly over the Middle of the Chapiters
' of the Pillars. That in the Fronts of
' the Piazza's, the Number of the Modil-
' lons in Sides of equal length is not alike:
' With several Instances of Negligence,
                                    ' which

‘ which would now be thought unpardon-
‘ able. That, generally speaking, in o-
‘ ther Buildings, their Floors were twice as
‘ thick as their Walls; which loaded them
‘ exceedingly, to no purpose. That their
Pag. 115. ‘ way of Laying Stones in Lozenges, was
‘ inconvenient, as well as troublesome;
‘ since every Stone so placed, was a Wedge
‘ to force those asunder on which it leaned.
Pag. 117. ‘ That they did not understand the nicest
‘ Thing in Architecture, which is, the Art
‘ of Cutting Stones in such a manner, as
‘ that several Pieces might be jointed one
‘ into another; for want of which, they
‘ made their Vaults of Brick plaister'd
‘ over; and their Architraves of Wood,
‘ or of one single Stone; which obliged
‘ them to set their Pillars closer to one ano-
‘ ther than otherwise had been necessary:
‘ Whereas, by this Art of Cutting Stone,
‘ Arches have been made almost flat: Stair-
‘ Cases of a vast height have been raised,
‘ where the Spectator is at a loss to tell
‘ what supports them; whilst the Stones
‘ are jointed into each other in such a man-
‘ ner, that they mutually bear up them-
‘ selves, without any Rest but the Wall,
‘ into which the innermost Stones are fa-
Pag. 118. ‘ stened. That they had not Engines to
‘ raise their Stones to any considerable
‘ height; but if the Work was low, they
‘ carried them upon their Shoulders; if
‘ high,

' high, they raised sloping Mounts of
' Earth level with their Work, by which
' they rolled up their Stones to what height
' they pleased: For, as for the Engines
' for raising of Stones, in *Vitruvius*, those
' who understand Mechanics, are agreed,
' that they can never be very serviceable.
' That it is not the Largeness of a Build-
' ing, but the well executing of a Noble
' Design, which commends an Architect;
' otherwise the *Aegyptian* Pyramids, as they
' are the greatest, would also be the finest
' Structures in the World. And last of all;
' That the *French King*'s Palace at *Versailles*, Pag 119,
' and the Frontispiece of the *Louvre*, disco- 120
' ver more true Skill in Architecture of all
' sorts, than any thing which the Ancients
' ever performed, if we may judge of
' what is lost, by what remains.

What Monsieur *Perrault* says of the Ancients Way of Raising their Stone, may be
confirmed by the Accounts which *Garçilasso de la Vega*, and others, give of the
vast Buildings of massy Stone which the
Spaniards found in *Peru*, upon their first
Arrival. It is most certain, that the *Peruvians* knew not the Use of Iron; and by
consequence, could make no Engines very
serviceable for such a purpose. They
ground their Stones one against another,
to smooth them; and afterwards they raised them with Leavers: And thus, with

F   Mul-

Multitude of Hands they reared such Structures as appeared wonderful even to Men acquainted with Modern Architecture.

Of *Sculpture*, he says; 'That we are to
'distinguish between entire Statues, and
'*Basso Relievo's*; and in entire Statues, be-
'tween Naked and Cloathed Pieces. The
'Naked Images of the Ancients, as *Her-*
'*cules*, *Apollo*, *Diana*, the *Gladiators*, the
'*Wrestlers*, *Bacchus*, *Laocoon*, and some few
'more, are truly admirable: They shew

Pag. 125 'something extremely Noble, which one
'wants Words for, that is not to be found
'in Modern Work: Though he cannot tell
'whether Age does not contribute to the
'Beauty. That if some of the most excel-
'lent of the Modern Pieces should be pre-
'served MD or MM Years; or ting'd with
'some Chymical Water, that could in a
'short time make them appear Antique, it
'is probable they would be viewed with
'the same Veneration which is now payed
'to Ancient Statues. That the Naked

Pag. 129. 'Sculpture of single Figures is a very noble
'Art indeed, but the simplest of any that
'has ever charmed Mankind; not being
'burthen'd with a Multiplicity of Rules,
'nor needing the Knowledge of any other
'Art to compleat it; since a Man that has
'a Genius and Application, wants only a
'beautiful Model in a proper Posture, which
'he is faithfully to copy: And therefore,

'That

'That in the Cloathed Statues of the Anci- Pag. 121, 122, 123.
'ents, the Drapery wants much of that Art
'which is discernible in some Modern Pie-
'ces; they could never make the Cloaths
'fit loose to the Bodies, nor manage the
'Folds so as to appear easie and flowing,
'like well-made Garments upon living Bo-
'dies. That the *Basso Relievo's* of the An- Pag. 129.
'cients plainly shew, that the Statuaries in
'those Days did not understand all the Pre-
'cepts that are necessary to compleat their
'Art; because they never observed the
'Rules of Perspective, they did not lessen
'their Figures gradually, to make them sui-
'table to the Place where they stood, but
'set them almost all upon the same Line;
'so that those behind were as large, and as
'distinguishable, as those before; as if they
'had been purposely mounted upon Steps,
'to be seen over one another's Heads. That
'this is visible in the *Columna Trajana*, at Pag. 130.
'this Day, though that is the noblest anci-
'ent Performance in *Basso Relievo* still re-
'maining; wherein, together with some ve-
'ry beautiful Airs of some of the Heads, Pag. 132
'and some very happy Postures, one may
'discern that there is scarce any Art in the
'Composition of the whole, no gradual
'lessening of the *Relievo* in any part, with
'great Ignorance in Perspective in the whole.
'That the ancient Works in *Basso Relievo* Pag. 133
'did not truly deserve that Name, being

F 2 'pro-

'properly entire Statues, either sawed down
'perpendicularly, from Head to Foot, with
'the fore-part fasten'd or glued to a flat
'Ground, or sunk half way in: Whereas

Pag. 134. 'the true Art consists in raising the Figures
'so from their Ground, which is of the
'same Piece, that with two or three Inches
'of *Relievo*, they may appear like distinct
'Images sunk into the Ground, some more,
'some less, according to the several Distan-
'ces in which they ought to be placed.

Pag. 143. Of *Painting*, he says; 'That Three
'Things are necessary to make a perfect
'Picture; *To represent the Figures truly;*
'*To express the Passions naturally; and, To put*
'*the whole judiciously together.* For the *First*,
'it is necessary that all the Out-Lines be
'justly Drawn, and that every Part be pro-
'perly Coloured. For the *Second*, It is ne-
'cessary that the Painter should hit the dif-
'ferent Airs and Characters of the Face,
'with all the Postures of the Figures, so as
'to express what they do, and what they
'think. *The whole is judiciously put together,*
'when every several Figure is set in the Place
'in which we see it, for a particular Pur-
'pose; and the Colouring gradually weaken-
'ed, so as to suit that part of the Plain in
'which every Figure appears. All which is
'as applicable to the several Parts of a Pi-
'cture that has but one Figure, as to the se-
'veral Figures in a Picture that has more.
                                                        'That

'That if we judge of Ancient and Modern Pag 135.
' Paintings by this Rule, we may divide
' them into Three Classes: The First takes
' in the Age of *Zeuxis, Apelles, Timanthes,*
' and the rest that are so much admir'd in
' Antiquity. The Second takes in the Age
' of *Raphaël, Titian, Paul Veronese,* and
' those other great Masters that flourished in
' *Italy* in the last Age. The Third contains
' the Painters of our own Age, such as *Pous-*
' *sin, Le Brun,* and the like. That if we may
' judge of the Worth of the Painters of the
' First Classe, by the Commendations which
' have been given them, we have Reason to
' say, either that their Admirers did not un-
' derstand Painting well, or that themselves
' were not so valuable, or both. That Pag 136.
' whereas *Zeuxis* is said to have painted a
' Bunch of Grapes so naturally, that the
' Birds peck'd at them; Cooks have, of Pag 138.
' late Years, reached at Partridges and Ca-
' pons, painted in Kitchins; which has
' made By-standers smile, without raising
' the Painter's Reputation to any great
' height. That the Contention between *Pro-* Pag 139.
' *togenes* and *Apelles* shewed the Infancy of
' their Art: *Apelles* was wonderfully ap-
' plauded for Drawing a very fine Stroke
' upon a Cloth: *Protogenes* drew a Second
' over that, in a different Colour; which
' *Apelles* split into two, by a Third. Yet Pag 141.
' this was not so much as what *Giotto* did,

F 3 ' who

'who lived in the Beginning of the Resto-
'ration of Painting in *Italy*, who drew,
'without Compasses, with a single Stroke
'of a Pencil, upon a Sheet of Paper, an O,
'so exquisitely round, that it is still Prover-
'bial among the *Italians*, when they would
'describe a Man that is egregiously stupid,
'to say, *That he is as round as the O of Gi-*

Pag. 142. '*otto.* That when *Poussin*'s Hand shook so
'much, that he could scarce manage his
'Pencil, he painted some Pieces of inesti-
'mable Value; and yet very indifferent
'Painters would have divided every Line
'that he drew, into nine or ten parts. That
'the *Chineses*, who cannot yet express Life
'and Passion in their Pieces, will draw the
'Hairs of the Face and Beard so fine, that
'one may part them with the Eye from
'one another, and tell them. Though the

Pag 150. 'Ancients went much beyond all this; for
'the Remains of the Ancient Painting dis-
'cover great Skill in Designing, great Judg-
'ment in Ordering of the Postures, much
'Nobleness and Majesty in the Airs of the
'Heads; but little Design, at the same
'time, in the Mixing of their Colours, and
'none at all in the Perspective, or the Pla-
'cing of the Figures. That their Colouring
'is all equally strong; nothing comes for-
'ward, nothing falls back in their Pictures;
'the Figures are almost all upon a Line:
'So that their Paintings appear like Pieces

'in

'in *Basso-Relievo*, coloured; all dry and un-
'moveable, without Union, without Con-
'nexion; and that living Softness which di-
'stinguishes Pictures from Statues in Mar-
'ble or Copper. Wherefore, since the Paint-
'ings of these Ancient Masters were justly
'design'd, and the Passions of every several
'Figure naturally expressed, which are the
'Things that the generality of Judges most
'admire, who cannot discern those Beauties
'that result from a judicious Composition
'of the whole, so well as they can the di-
'stinct Beauties of the several Parts, there
'is no wonder that *Zeuxis* and *Apelles*, and
'the other Ancient Masters, were so fa-
'mous, and so well rewarded. For, of the
'Three Things at first assigned, as necessa-
'ry to a Perfect Painter, true Drawing,
'with proper Colouring, affect the Senses;
'natural Expressing of the Motions of the
'Soul, move the Passions; whereas a Judi- Pag 146.
'cious Composition of the whole, which is
'discernible in an Artful Distribution of
'Lights and Shades, in the gradual Lessen-
'ing of Figures, according to their respe-
'ctive Places, in making every Figure an-
'swer to that particular Purpose which it is
'intended to represent, affects the Under-
'standing only; and so, instead of Charm-
'ing, will rather disgust an unskilful Spe-
'ctator. Such a Man, and under this Head Pag 147
'almost all Mankind may be comprehended,

F 4 will

'will contentedly forgive the grossest Faults
'in Perspective, if the Figures are but ve-
'ry prominent, and the View not darken-
'ed by too much Shade; which, in their
'Opinion, spoils all Faces, especially of
'Friends, whose Images chiefly such Men
'are desirous to see.

When he compares the Paintings of *Raphaël* and *Le Brun* together, he observes,
Pag. 159. 'That *Raphaël* seems to have had the
'greater Genius of the two; that there is
'something so Noble in his Postures, and
'the Airs of his Heads; something so just
'in his Designs, so perfect in the Mixture
'of his Colours, that his St. *Michael* will
'always be thought the first Picture in the
'World, unless his *H. Family* should dis-
'pute Precedency with it. In short, he
Pag. 160 'says, That if we consider the Persons of
'*Raphaël* and *Le Brun*, *Raphaël* perhaps
'may be the greater Man: But if we con-
'sider the Art, as a Collection of Rules,
'all necessary to be observed to make it
'perfect, it appears much more compleat
'in Monsieur *Le Brun*'s Pieces; For *Raphaël* understood so little of the gradual
'Lessening of Light, and Weakening of
'Colours, which is caused by the Inter-
'position of the Air, that the hindermost
'Figures in his Pieces appear almost as
'plain as the foremost; and the Leaves of
'distant Trees, almost as visible as of those
'near

'near at hand; and the Windows of a
'Building four Leagues off, may all be
'counted as eafily as of one that is within
'twenty Paces. Nay, he cannot tell whe-
'ther fome part of that Beauty, now fo pe-
'culiar to *Raphael*'s Pieces, may not, in a
'great meafure, be owing to Time, which
'adds a real Beauty to good Paintings.
'For, in the Works of this kind, as in
'New-kill'd Meat, or New-gather'd Fruit,
'there is a Rawnefs and Sharpnefs, which
'Time alone concocts and fweetens, by
'mortifying that which has too much Life,
'by weakening that which is too ftrong,
'and by mixing the Extremities of every
'Colour entirely into one another. So Pag. 161.
'that no Man can tell what will be the
'Beauty of *Le Brun*'s *Family of Darius,*
'*Alexander*'s *Triumph, the Defeat of Porus,*
'and fome other Pieces of equal Force,
'when Time fhall have done her Work,
'and fhall have added thofe Graces which
'are now fo remarkable in the *St. Michael,*
'and the *H. Family.* One may already
'obferve, that Monfieur *Le Brun*'s Pieces
'begin to foften; and that Time has, in
'part, added thofe Graces which It alone
'can give, by fweetning what was left on
'purpofe, by the judicious Painter, to a-
'mufe its Activity, and to keep it from
'the Subftance of the Work. Thus far
Monfieur *Perrault.*

Whe-

Whether his Reasonings are just, I dare not determine: Thus much may very probably be inferred, That *in these Things also the World does not Decay so fast as Sir William Temple believes;* and that *Poussin, Le Brun* and *Bernini* have made it evident by their Performances in Painting and Statuary, (*p.*) *That we have had Masters in both these Arts, who have deserved a Rank with those that flourished in the last Age, after they were again restored to these Parts of the World.*

(p) P. 52.

CHAP. VII.

General Reflections relating to the following Chapters: With an Account of Sir William Temple's Hypothesis of the History of Learning.

IF the bold Claims of confident and numerous Pretenders, might, because of their Confidence and Numbers, be much relied on, it were an easie Thing to determine upon the remaining Parts of Learning, hereafter to be discoursed of. The generality of the Learned have given the *Ancients* the Preference in those Arts and Sci-

Sciences which have hitherto been considered: But for the Precedency in those Parts of Learning which still remain to be enquired into, the *Moderns* have put in their Claim, with great Briskness. Among this sort, I reckon *Mathematical* and *Physical Sciences*, considered in their largest Extent. These are Things which have no Dependence upon the Opinions of Men for their Truth; they will admit of fixed and undisputed *Mediums* of Comparison and Judgment: So that, though it may be always debated, who have been the best Orators, or who the best Poets; yet it cannot always be a Matter of Controversie, who have been the greatest *Geometers, Arithmeticians, Astronomers, Musicians, Anatomists, Chymists, Botanists,* or the like; because a fair Comparison between the Inventions, Observations, Experiments and Collections of the contending Parties, must certainly put an End to the Dispute, and give full Satisfaction to all Sides.

The Thing contended for, is, the *Knowledge of Nature*; what the Appearances are which it exhibits, and how they are exhibited; thereby to shew how they may be enlarged, and diversified, and Impediments of any sort removed. In order to this, it will be necessary, (1.) To find out all the several Affections and Properties of Quantity, abstractedly considered; with the
Pro-

Proportions of its Parts and Kinds, either severally considered, or compared and compounded with one another; either as they may be in Motion, or at Rest: This is properly the *Mathematician's* Business. (2.) To collect great Numbers of Observations, and to make a vast Variety of Experiments upon all sorts of Natural Bodies. And because this cannot be done without proper Tools, (3.) To contrive such Instruments, by which the Constituent Parts of the Universe, and of all its Parts, even the most minute, or the most remote, may lie more open to our View; and their Motions, or other Affections, be better calculated and examined, than could otherwise have been done by our unassisted Senses. (4.) To range all the several Species of Natural Things under proper Heads; and assign fit Characteristics, or Marks, whereby they may be readily found out, and distinguished from one another. (5.) To adapt all the Catholic Affections of Matter and Motion to all the known Appearances of Things, so as to be able to tell how Nature works; and, in some particular Cases, to command her. This will take in *Astronomy, Mechanics, Optics, Music,* with the other *Physico-Mathematical* and *Physico-Mechanical* Parts of Knowledge; as also, *Anatomy, Chymistry,* with the whole Extent of *Natural History*. It will help us

to

to make a just Comparison between the *Ancient* and *Modern Physics*; that so we may certainly determine who Philosophized best, *Aristotle* and *Democritus*, or Mr. *Boyle* and Mr. *Newton*.

In these Things therefore the Comparison is to be made, wherein one can go no higher than the Age of *Hippocrates*, *Aristotle* and *Theophrastus*; because the Writings of the Philosophers before them are all lost. It may therefore be plausibly objected, That this is no fair Way of Proceeding, because the *Aegyptians* and *Chaldæans* were Famous for many Parts of real Learning long before; from whom *Pythagoras*, *Thales*, *Plato*, and all the other *Græcian* Philosophers, borrow'd what they knew. This Sir *William Temple* insists at large upon; so that it will be necessary to examine the Claims of these Nations to Universal Learning: In doing of which, I shall follow Sir *William Temple*'s Method; first I shall give a short Abstract of his Hypothesis, and then enquire how far it may be relied on.

Sir *William Temple* tells us, That the chiefest Argument that is produced in behalf of the Moderns, is; (*q*) ‘ That ‘ they have the Advantage of the Anci- ‘ ents Discoveries to help their own: So ‘ that, like Dwarfs upon Giants Shoulders, ‘ they must needs see farther than the Gi- ‘ ants

(*q*) Pag. 5.

'ants themselves.' To weaken this, we are told, (*r*) 'That those whom we call Ancients, are Moderns, if compared to those who are ancienter than they: And that there were vast Lakes of Learning in *Aegypt, Chaldæa, India* and *China*; where it stagnated for many Ages, till the *Greeks* brought Buckets, and drew it out.

(*r*) Pag. 6——10.

The Question therefore which is first to be asked here, is, *Where are the Books and Monuments wherein these Treasures were deposited for so many Ages?* And because they are not to be found, Sir *William Temple* makes a doubt, (*s*) *Whether Books advance any other Science, beyond the particular Records of Actions, or Registers of Time.* He may resolve it soon, if he enquires how far a Man can go in Astronomical Calculations, for which the *Chaldæans* are said to be so Famous, without the Use of Letters. The *Peruvian* Antiquities, which he there alledges, for Twelve or Thirteen Generations, from *Mango Capac*, to *Atahualpa*, were not of above D Years standing. The *Mexican* Accounts were not so old; and yet these, though very rude, needed Helps to be brought down to us. The *Peruvian* Conveyances of Knowledge, according to *Garçilasso de la Vega*, were not purely Traditionary, but were Fringes of Cotton, of several Colours, tied and woven with a vast Variety of Knots, which had all determi-

(*s*) Pag 8.

terminate Meanings; and so supplied the Use of Letters, in a tolerable degree: And the *Mexican* Antiquities were preserved, after a sort, by Pictures; of which we have a Specimen in *Purchas's Pilgrim*. So that when Sir *William Temple* urges the Traditions of these People, to prove that Knowledge may be conveyed to Posterity without Letters, he proves only what is not disputed, namely, That Knowledge can be imperfectly conveyed to Posterity without Letters; not that Tradition can preserve Learning as well as Books, or something equivalent.

But since Sir *William Temple* lays no great Weight upon this Evasion, I ought not to insist any longer upon it. He says therefore, (*t*) 'That it is a Question, whether (*t*) Pag. 6.
' the Invention of Printing has multiplied
' Books, or only the Copies of them;
' since, if we believe that there were Six
' Hundred Thousand Books in the *Ptole-*
' *mæan* Library, we shall hardly pretend to
' equal it by any of ours, nor perhaps by
' all put together; that is, we shall scarce
' be able to produce so many *Originals* that
' have lived any Time, and thereby given
' Testimony of their having been thought
' *worth preserving.*' All this, as it is urged by Sir *William Temple*, is liable to great Exception. For, (1.) If we should allow that there is no Hyperbole in the Number

of Books in the *Ptolemœan* Library, yet we are not to take our Estimate by the common Way of Reckoning. Every Oration of *Demosthenes* and *Isocrates*, every Play of *Aeschylus* or *Aristophanes*, every Discourse of *Plato* or *Aristotle*, was anciently called a Volume. This will lessen the Number to us, who take whole Collections of every Author's Works in one Lump; and accordingly give Names to them in our Catalogues, if printed together, under one Title. (2.) Sir *William Temple* seems to take it for granted, that all these Books were *Originals*; that is to say, Books *worth preserving*; which is more than any Man can now prove. I suppose he himself believes that there were Ancients of all Sorts and Sizes, as well as there are Moderns now. And he that raises a Library, takes in Books of all Values; since bad Books have their Uses to Learned Men, as well as good ones. So that, for any thing we know to the contrary, there might have been in this *Alexandrian* Library a great Number of (*u*) Scribbles, that, *like Mushrooms or Flies, are born and die in small Circles of Time*. (3.) The World can make a better Judgment of the Value of what is lost, at least, as far as it relates to the present Enquiry, than one at first View might perhaps imagine. The lost Books *of the Antiquities of several Nations, of their Civil History, of the Limits of their seve-*

(*u*) Ibid.

ral *Empires* and *Commonwealths*, of their *Superstitious Rites and Ceremonies*, of their *Laws and Manners*, or of any Thing immediately relating to any of these, are not here to be considered; because it cannot be pretended that the Moderns could know any of these Things, but as they were taught. So neither is what may have related to *Ethics, Politics, Poesie* and *Oratory* here to be urged, since in those Matters, the Worth of Ancient Knowledge has already been asserted. So that we are only to enquire what and how great the Loss is of all those Books upon *Natural* or *Mathematical Arguments*, which were preserved in the *Alexandrian, Asiatic* and *Roman* Libraries, or mentioned in the Writings of the Ancient Philosophers and Historians. By which Deduction, the former Number will be yet again considerably lessened.

Now a very true Judgment of Ancient Skill in Natural History may be formed out of *Pliny*, whose Extracts of Books, still exstant, are so particular for the present Purpose, that there is Reason to believe they were not carelesly made of those that are lost. *Galen* seems to have read whatever he could meet with relating to Medicine, in all its Parts: And the Opinions of Abundance of Authors, which are no where else preserved, may be discovered out of his Books; of the famous ones especially;

G whom,

whom, at every turn, he either contradicts, or produces to fortifie his own Affertions. *Ptolomee* gives an Account of the Old Aſtronomy, in his *Almageſt*. Very many Particulars of the Inventions and Methods of Ancient Geometers are to be found in the *Mathematical Collections* of *Pappus*. The Opinions of the different Sects of Philoſophers are well enough preſerved in the entire Treatiſes of the ſeveral Philoſophers who were of their Sects; or in the Diſcourſes of others, who occaſionally or expreſly confute what they ſay. So that I am apt to think, that the *Philoſophical* and *Mathematical Learning* of the Ancients is better conveyed to us than the *Civil*; the Books which treated of thoſe Subjects ſuiting better the Genius of ſeveral Men, and of ſeveral Nations too: For which Reaſon the *Arabs* tranſlated the moſt conſiderable *Greek* Books of this kind; as, *Euclid, Apollonius, Ariſtotle, Epictetus, Cebes*, and Abundance more, that had written of Philoſophy or Mathematics, into their own Language; whilſt they let Books of Antiquity and Civil Hiſtory lie unregarded.

Sir *William Temple*'s next Enquiry, is, From whence both the Ancients and Moderns have received their Knowledge? His Method does not ſeem to be very natural, nor his Queſtion very proper; ſince, if Diſcoveries are once made it is not ſo material

terial to know who taught the several Discoverers, as what these Discoverers first taught others. But setting that aside, the Sum of what he says, in short, is this:

(w) 'The Moderns gather all their Learn- (w) Pag. 11, 12.
'ing out of Books in Universities; which
'are but dumb Guides, that can lead Men
'but one Way, without being able to set
'them right, if they should wander from
'it. These Books, besides, are very few;
'the Remains of the Writings of here and
'there an Author, that wrote from the
'Time of *Hippocrates*, to *M. Antoninus*,
'in the compass of Six or Seven Hundred
'Years: Whereas *Thales* and *Pythagoras*
'took another sort of a Method; *Thales*
'acquired his Knowledge in *Aegypt*, *Phœ-*
'*nicia*, *Delphos*, and *Crete*; (x) *Pythago-* (x) Pag.
'*ras* spent Twenty-Two Years in *Aegypt*, 13, 14, 15.
'and Twelve Years more in *Chaldæa*, and
'then returned, laden with all their Stores;
'and not contented with that, went into
'*Aethiopia*, *Arabia*, *India*, and *Crete*; and
'visited *Delphos*, and all the renowned O-
'racles in the World.

(y) 'Lest we should wonder why *Py-* (y) Pag.
'*thagoras* went so far, we are told, that 16, 17.
'the *Indian Brachmans* were so careful to
'educate those who were intended for
'Scholars, that as soon as the Mothers
'found themselves with Child, much Thought
'and Diligence was employed about their

G 2 'Diet

'Diet and Entertainment, to furnish them
' with pleasant Imaginations, to compose
' their Mind and their Sleeps with the best
' Temper, during the Time that they car-
' ry'd their Burthen. It is certain, that
' they must needs have been very Learn-
' ed, since they were obliged to spend
' Thirty Seven Years in getting Instructi-
' on: Their Knowledge was all Traditio-
' nal; they thought the World was Round,
' and made by a Spirit; they believed the
' Transmigration of Souls; and they
' esteemed Sickness such a Mark of In-
' temperance, that when they found them-
' selves indisposed, they died out of Shame
' and Sullenness, though some lived an
' Hundred and Fifty, or Two Hundred
(z) Pag. ' Years. (z) These *Indians* had their
22, 23. ' Knowledge, in all probability, from *Chi-*
' *na*, a Country where Learning had been
' in request from the Time of *Fohius*, their
' first King. It is to be presumed, that
' they communicated of their Store to
' other Nations, though they themselves
' have few Foot-steps of it remaining, be-
' sides the Writings of *Confucius*, which
' are chiefly Moral and Political; because
' one of their Kings, who desired that the
' Memory of every thing should begin
' with himself, caused Books of all sorts,
' not relating to Physic and Agriculture,
' to be destroyed.

(a) ' From

(*a*) 'From *India*, Learning was carried (*a*)Pag.21
'into *Aethiopia* and *Arabia*; thence, by
'the Way of the *Red Sea*, it came into
'*Phœnicia*; and the *Aegyptians* learn'd it
'of the *Aethiopians*.

This is a short Account of the History of Learning, as Sir *William Temple* has deduced it from its most ancient Beginnings. The Exceptions which may be made against it are many, and yet more against the Conclusions which he draws from it. For, though it be certain that the *Aegyptians* had the Grounds and Elements of most parts of real Learning among them earlier than the *Greeks*, yet that is no Argument why the *Græcians* should not go beyond their Teachers, or why the Moderns might not out-doe them both.

Before I examine Sir *William Temple*'s Scheme, Step by Step, I shall offer, as the Geometers do, some few Things as *Postulata*; which are so very plain, that they will be assented to as soon as they are proposed. (1.) That all Men who make a Mystery of Matters of Learning, and industriously oblige their Scholars to conceal their Dictates, give the World great Reason to suspect that their Knowledge is all Juggling and Trick. (2.) That he that has only a Moral Persuasion of the Truth of any Proposition, which is capable of Natural Evidence, cannot so properly be esteemed the Inventor, or the Discoverer rather, of that Proposition, as another Man, who, though he lived many Ages after, brings such Evidences of its Certainty, as are sufficient to convince all competent Judges; especially when his Reasonings are founded upon Observations and Experiments drawn from, and made upon the Things Themselves. (3.) That no Pretenses to greater Measures of Knowledge, grounded upon Accounts of Long Successions of Learned Men in any Country, ought to gain Belief, when set against the Learning of other Nations, which made no such Pretenses, unless Inventions and Discoveries answerable to those Advantages, be produced by their Advocates. (4.) That we cannot judge of Characters of Things and Persons at a great Distance, when given at Second-hand, unless we knew exactly how capable those Persons, from whom such Characters were first taken, were to pass a right Judgment upon such subjects; and also the particular Motives that biassed them to pass such Censures. If *Archimedes* should, upon his own Knowledge, speak with Admiration of the *Aegyptian* Geometry, his Judgment would be very considerable: But if he should speak respectfully of it, only because *Pythagoras* did so before him, it might, perhaps, signifie but very little. (5.) That excessive Commendations of any Art or Science whatsoever, as also of the Learning of any particular Men or Nations, only prove that the Persons who give such Characters never heard of any Thing or Person that was more excellent in that Way; and therefore that Admiration may be as well supposed to proceed from their own Ignorance, as from the real Excellency of the Persons or Things, unless their respective Abilities are otherwise known.

CHAP. VIII.

Of the Learning of Pythagoras, *and the most Ancient Philosophers of* Greece.

IN my Enquiries into the Progress of Learning, during its obscurer Ages, or those, at least, which are so to us at this Distance, I shall begin with the Accounts which are given of the Learning of *Pythagoras,* rather than those of the more Ancient *Graecian* Sages; because his School made a much greater Figure in the World, than any of those which preceded *Plato* and *Aristotle.* In making a Judgment upon the Greatness of his Performances, from the Greatness of his Reputation, one ought to con-

consider how near to his Time those lived, whose express Relations of his Life are the oldest we have.

Diogenes Laërtius is the ancientest Author exstant, that has purposely written the Life of *Pythagoras*: According to *Menagius*'s Calculations, he lived in *M. Antoninus*'s Time: And all that we learn from *Diogenes*, is only, that we know very little certainly about *Pythagoras*. He cites, indeed, great Numbers of Books; but those so very disagreeing in their Relations, that a Man is confounded with their Variety. Besides, the *Graecians* magnified every Thing that they commended, so much, that it is hard to guess how far they may be believed, when they write of Men and Actions at any Distance from their own Time. *Graecia Mendax* was almost Proverbial amongst the *Romans*. But by what appears from the Accounts of the Life of *Pythagoras*, he is rather to be ranked among the Law-givers, with *Lycurgus* and *Solon*, and his own two Disciples, *Zaleucus* and *Charondas*, than amongst those who really carried Learning to any considerable height. Therefore, as some other Heathen Legislators pretended to have, Super-natural Assistances, that they might create a Regard for their Laws in the People to whom they gave them; so *Pythagoras* found out several Equivalents, which did him as much Service. He is said, indeed,

deed, to have lived many Years in *Aegypt*, and to have conversed much with the Philosophers of the *East*; but if he invented the XLVII*th* Proposition in the First Book of *Euclid*, which is unanimously ascribed to him by all Antiquity, one can hardly have a profound Esteem for the Mathematical Skill of his Masters. It is, indeed, a very noble Proposition, the Foundation of Trigonometry, of universal and various Use in those curious Speculations about Incommensurable Numbers; which his Disciples from him, and from them the *Platonists*, so exceedingly admired. But this shews the Infancy of Geometry in his Days, in that very Country which claims the Glory of Inventing it to her self. It is probable, indeed, that the *Aegyptians* might find it out; but then we ought also to take notice, that it is the only very considerable Instance of the real Learning of *Pythagoras* that is preserved. Which is the more observable, because the *Pythagoreans* paid the greatest Respect to their Master, of any Sect whatsoever; and so we may be sure that we should have heard much more of his Learning, if much more could have been said: And though the Books of *Hermippus* and *Aristoxenus* (*b*) are lost, yet *Laërtius*, who had read them, and *Porphyry* and *Jamblichus*, Men of great Reading, and diffuse Knowledge, who, after *Diogenes*, wrote the Life

(*b*) Two very considerable Writers of *Pythagoras* his Life.

Life of the same *Pythagoras*, would not have omitted any material Thing of that kind, if they had any where met with it.

Amongst his other Journeys, Sir *William Temple* mentions *Pythagoras*'s Journey to *Delphi* (c). What that Voyage of his is here remembred for, it is not easie to guess. *Apollo*'s Priestesses are not famous for discovering Secrets in Natural or Mathematical Matters; and as for Moral Truths, they might as well be known, without going to *Delphi* to fetch them. *Van Dalen*, in his Discourses of the Heathen Oracles, has endeavoured to prove, that they were only Artifices of the Priests, who gave such Answers to Enquirers as they desired, when they had either Power or Wealth to back their Requests. If *Van Dalen*'s Hypothesis be admitted, it will strengthen my Notion of *Pythagoras* very much; since, when he did not care to live any longer in *Samos*, because of *Polycrates*'s Tyranny, and was desirous to establish to himself a lasting Reputation, for Wisdom and Learning, amongst the ignorant Inhabitants of *Magna Graecia*, where he setled upon his Retirement, he was willing to have them believe that *Apollo* was of his Side. That made him establish the Doctrine of Transmigration of Souls, which he brought with him out of *India*, that so those *Italians* might think that he had a certain Reminiscence of

Things

(c) Pag 15.

Things paſt, ſince his firſt Stage of Life, and the Beginning of the World; and upon that Account admire him the more: For *Laërtius* (*d*) ſays, that he pretended to remember every Thing that he had done formerly, whilſt he was in thoſe other Bodies; and that he received this as an eſpecial Favour from *Mercury*, who gave him his Choice of whatſoever he deſired, except Immortality. (*e*) For theſe Reaſons alſo he obliged his Scholars to go through a Trial of Five Years, to learn Obedience by Silence: And that afterwards it was granted to ſome few, as a particular Favour, to be admitted into his Preſence. Theſe Things tended very much to impreſs a Veneration of his Perſon upon his Scholars, but ſignified nothing to the Advancement of Learning; yea, rather hindred it. Thoſe that live in the End of the World, (*f*) when every Thing, according to Sir *William Temple*, is in its Declenſion, know no Way ſo effectual to promote Learning, as much Converſation and Enquiry; and, which is more, they have no *Idea* how it can be promoted without them. The Learned Men of the preſent Age pretend to no Acquaintance with *Mercury* or *Apollo*, and can do as little in Natural Knowledge by ſuch a Sham-Revelation, as they can by Reminiſcence. If a Man ſhould, for Five Years together, read Lectures, to one that

(*d*) *Vit. Pythag.* §. 4.

(*e*) *Ibid.* §. 10.

(*f*) Pag. 53.

was

was not allowed to make Pauses, or ask Questions; another Man, in the ordinary Road, by Books and Professors, would learn more, at least to much better purpose, in Six Months, than he could in all that Time.

Pythagoras was, without question, a wise Man, well skill'd in the Arts of Civil Prudence; by which he appeased great Disturbances in those *Italian* Commonwealths: He had probably much more Knowledge than any Man of that Age in *Italy*, and knew how to make the most of it. He took great Delight in Arithmetical Speculations, which, as *Galileo* (g), not improbably, guesses, he involved in Mysteries, that so ignorant People might not despise him, for busying himself in such abstruse Matters, which they could not comprehend; and if they could have comprehended, did not know to what Use to put them. He took a sure Way to have all his Studies valued, by obliging his Scholars to resign up their Understandings to his Authority and Dictates. The great Simplicity of his Manners, with the Wisdom of his Axioms and Symbols, charmed an ignorant Age, which found real Advantages, by following his peaceful Measures; much above those that were formerly procured by Rapin and Violence. This seems to be a true Account of *Pythagoras*, in the History

(g) *System. Cosmic.*

ſtory of whoſe Reputation, there is nothing extraordinary, ſince Civilizers of Nations have always been as much magnify'd as the Inventors of the moſt uſeful Arts: But one can no more conclude from thence, That *Pythagoras* knew as much as *Ariſtotle* or *Democritus*, than that Friar *Bacon* was as great a Mathematician as Dr. *Barrow*, or Mr. *Newton*, becauſe he knew enough to be thought a Conjurer in the Age in which he lived, and no deſpicable Perſon in any other.

But it may not be amiſs to give a Taſt of ſome of the *Pythagorean* Notions; ſuch, I mean, as they firſt ſtarted in *Europe*, and chiefly valued themſelves upon. Of this ſort, were their Arithmetical Speculations: By them they pretended to explain the Cauſes of Natural Things. The following Account of their Explication of Generation, is taken out of *Cenſorinus* and *Ariſtides*:

'Perfect Animals are generated in two
'diſtinct Periods of Time; ſome in Seven
'Months, ſome in Nine. Thoſe Genera-
'tions that are compleated in Seven
'Months, proceed in this Order: In the
'firſt Six Days after Conception, the Hu-
'mour is Milky; in the next Eight it is
'turned into Blood; which Number 8
'bears the Proportion of $1\frac{1}{3}$ to 6; in Nine
'Days more it becomes Fleſh; 9 is in a
'Seſcuple Proportion to 6; in Twelve
'Days

'Days more the Embryo is form'd; 12 is
'double to 6: Here then are these Stages,
'6, 8, 9, 12; 6 is the first perfect Num-
'ber, because it is the Summ of 1, 2, 3,
'the only Numbers by which it can be
'divided: Now, if we add these Four
'Numbers, 6, 8, 9, 12, together, the
'Summ is 35; which multiply'd by 6,
'makes 210, the Number of Days from
'the Conception to the Birth; which is
'just Seven Months, allowing 30 Days to
'a Month. A like Proportion must be
'observed in the larger Period of Nine
'Months; only 10, the Summ of 1,2,3,4,
'added together, must be added to 35,
'which makes 45; that multiply'd by 6,
'gives 270; or Nine times 30, the Num-
'ber of Days in larger Births.

If these fine Notions be compar'd with Dr. *Harvey*'s upon the same Subject, no doubt but we shall all be Converts to Sir *William Temple*'s Opinion, and make a vast Difference between the poor Observations of these later Ages, and the sublime Flights of the Ancients.

Now, though abstracted Mathematical Theories, which cannot be relished by one that has not a tolerable Skill in Mathematics before, might, perhaps, prudently be concealed from the Vulgar, by the *Pythagorean* School; and in their stead, such grave Jargon as this imposed upon them; yet
even

even that shews how little Knowledge of Nature they could pretend to. Men that aim at Glory, will omit no probable Methods to gain it, that lie in their Way; and solid Discoveries of a real Insight into Nature, would not only have been eternally true, but have charm'd Mankind at another Rate, than such dry sapless Notions as seem at first View to have something of Subtilty; but upon a Second Reflection, appear vain and ridiculous.

From *Pythagoras*, I shall go on to the Ancient Sages (*h*), who were so learned in Natural Philosophy, that they Foretold not only Eclipses in the Heavens, but Earthquakes at Land, and Storms at Sea, great Droughts, and great Plagues, much Plenty or much Scarcity of certain sorts of Fruits or Grains, not to mention the Magical Powers attributed to several of them, to allay Storms, to raise Gales, to appease Commotions of People, to make Plagues cease.

(*h*) Pag. 28

One of the ancientest of these was *Thales*: He was so deeply skill'd in Astronomy, that by the Sun's Annual Course he found out the Equinoxes and Solstices: He is said also first to have foretold Eclipses; some Geometrical Properties of Scalene Triangles are ascribed to him, and challenged by *Euphorbus*: Nice we are sure they were not, because the Theorem of *Pythagoras* was not then found out.

When

When Sir *William Temple* extolled the Skill of these *Ancient Sages*, in foretelling Changes of Weather, he seems to have forgotten that he was in *England*, and fansied that these Old Philosophers were there too. The Climates of *Asia Minor*, and *Greece*, are not so various as ours; and at some stated Times of the Year, of which the recurrent Winds give them constant Warning, they are often troubled with Earthquakes, and always with violent Tempests: So that by the Conjectures that we are here able to make of the Weather at some particular Seasons, though we labour under so great Disadvantages, we may easily guess how much certainer Predictions may be made by curious Men in serener and more regular Climates; which will take off from that Admiration that otherwise would be paid to those profound Philosophers, even though we should allow that all those Stories which are told of their Skill, are exactly true.

Besides, there is Reason to believe that we have the Result of all the Observations of these Weather-wise Sages in *Aratus's Diosemia*, and *Virgil's Georgics*; such as those upon the Snuffs of Candles, the Croaking of Frogs, and many others quite as notable as the English Farmer's *Living Weather-Glass*, his *Red Cow that prick'd up her Tail*, an Infallible Presage of a coming Shower.

Sir *William Temple*'s Method leads me now to consider, what Estimate ought to be made of the Learning of those Nations, from which he derives all the Knowledge of these Ancient *Greeks*: I shall only therefore give a short Specimen of those Discoveries, with which these Ancient Sages enriched the Ages in which they lived, as I have already done of the *Pythagoreans*, and then proceed.

Diogenes Laërtius informs us of *Empedocles*'s (*i*) Skill in Magic, by the Instance of his stopping those pestilential Vapours that annoy'd his Town of *Agrigentum*. He took some Asses, and flea'd them, and hung their Hides over those Rocks that lay open to the *Etesian* Winds, which hindred their Passage, and so freed the Town. He tells another Story of *Democritus* (*k*), That he was so nice in his Observations, that he could tell whether a Young Woman were a Virgin, by her Looks, and could find it out, though she had been corrupted but the Day before; and he knew, by looking upon it, that some Goat's Milk that was brought him, was of a Black Goat that had had but one Kid.

These are Instances very seriously recorded by grave Authors of the *Magical Wisdom* of the Ancients; that is, as Sir *William Temple* defines it, of that (*l*) *excelling Knowledge of Nature, and the various*

(*i*) *Vit. Empedoclis*, §. 60.

(*k*) *Vit. Democriti*, §. 42.

(*l*) Pag 46.

Powers

Powers and Qualities in its several Productions, and the Application of certain Agents to certain Patients, which, by Force of some peculiar Qualities, produce Effects very different from what fall under Vulgar Observation and Comprehension.

CHAP. IX.

Of the History and Geometry of the Ancient Aegyptians.

FRom these *Ancient Sages*, Sir *William Temple* goes to the Nations from which they received their Knowledge, which are *Aegypt, Chaldaea, Arabia, India,* and *China;* only he seems to invert the Order, by pretending that *China* and *India* were the Original Fountains from which Learning still ran Westward. I shall speak of them in the Order in which I have named them; because the Claims of the *Aegyptians* and *Chaldaeans* having a greater Foundation in Ancient History, deserve a more particular Examination.

It must be owned, That the Learning which was in the World before the *Graecian* Times was almost wholly confined to the *Aegyptians,* excepting what was amongst the *Israelites:* And whosoever does

but

but consider how difficult it is to lay the First Foundations of any Science, be they never so small, will allow them great Commendation; which if their Advocates had been contented with, there had been an End of the Controversie. Instead of that, all that has since been added to their Foundations, has been equally challenged as originally due to them, or at least once known by them, by (m) *Olaus Borrichius*, and several others long before Sir *William Temple* wrote upon this Argument.

(m) *In Hermete Aegyptio.*

Before I enter upon this Question, I shall desire that one Thing may be taken Notice of; which is, that the *Aegyptians* anciently pretended to so great Exactness, that every Failure is more justly imputable to them, than to other Nations; not only their History was so carefully look'd after, that there was a College of Priests set up on purpose, whose chief Business it was successively to preserve the remarkable Matters of Fact that occurred in their own Ages, and transmit them undisputed to Posterity, but also, there was answerable Care taken to propagate and preserve all other Parts of useful Learning: All their Inventions in *Physic*, in *Geometry*, in *Agriculture*, in *Chymistry*, are said to have been inscribed on Pillars, which were preserved in their Temples; whereby not only the Memory of the Things themselves was less

H 2 liable

liable to be loſt, but Men were farther encouraged to uſe their utmoſt Diligence in making Diſcoveries that might be of Public Advantage, when they were certain of getting Immortality by ſuch Diſcoveries. This generous Cuſtom was the more to be applauded, becauſe every Man was confined to one particular Part of Learning, as his chief Buſineſs; that ſo nothing might eſcape them. One was Phyſician for the *Eyes*, another for the *Heart*, a third for the *Head* in general, a fourth for *Chirurgical* Applications, a fifth for *Womens Diſeaſes*, and ſo forth. *Anatomy*, we are told, was ſo very much cultivated by the Kings of *Aegypt*, that they particularly ordered the Bodies of dead Men to be opened, that ſo Phyſic might be equally perfect in all its parts. Where ſuch Care has been uſed, proportionable Progreſſes may be exſpected; and the World has a Right to make a Judgment, not only according to what is now to be found, but according to what might have been found, if theſe Accounts had been ſtrictly true.

In the firſt Place therefore, we may obſerve, That *the Civil Hiſtory of* Aegypt is as lamely and as fabulouſly recorded, as of any Nation in the Univerſe: And yet the *Aegyptians* took more than ordinary Care to pay all poſſible Honours to the Dead, eſpecially their Kings; by preſerving their
Bodies

Bodies with Bitumen and resinous Drugs, and by building sumptuous Monuments to lay them in: This certainly was done to perpetuate their Memories, as well as to pay them Respect: It was at least as Ancient as *Joseph*'s time (*n*); how much older we know not. The *Jews*, who for another and a more sacred Reason, took Care of their Dead, took equal Care to preserve their Genealogies, and to draw an Uniform Thread of their History from *Abraham*, down to the Destruction of the Second Temple. Herein they acted consistently, and their History is a standing Instance of this their Care; whereas the *Aegyptian* History is so very inconsistent a Business, that it is impossible to make a coherent Story out of it: Not for Want of Materials, but because their Materials neither agree with themselves, nor with the History of any other Nation in the World.

(*n*) Gen. 50. 2.

A more certain Proof of the Deficiency of the *Aegyptian* History cannot be produced, than that the *Time of the building of the Pyramids* was lost when *Herodotus* was in *Aegypt*; as also the *Aera* of the only great Conqueror of that Nation, *Sesostris*. The first of these is not slightly to be passed over. Such vast Fabricks could not be raised without Numbers of Hands, and a great Expense of Time and Money, or something equivalent. The *Traditions* of their Erection are indeed minutely enough set down in *Herodotus*, but then they are set down as *Traditions*; and, which is more, they are solely to be found in him, though he is not the only ancient Writer that mentions the Pyramids; he only names the Kings that Erected them, *Cheops* and *Mycerinus*, who are also differently named by other Historians; and the Time when they lived, is as little agreed upon, as the Names by which they are called. The History of a Nation can sure be worth very little, that could not preserve the Memory of the Names at least, if not the Time, of those Princes, who were at so much Pains to be remembred, in a Place where their Monuments were so visible, that no Person could sail up and down the *Nile*, to or from their Capital City *Memphis*, without taking notice of them; and every Man, upon his first seeing of them, would naturally ask, what they were, by whom, and for what Intent erected. To which we may add, That these very Buildings are more exactly described in Mr. *Greaves*'s *Pyramidographia*, than in any ancient Author now extant.

The Difficulty of determining the Age when *Sesostris* lived, is another Instance of the Carelesness of the *Aegyptian* Historians. Either he was the same with *Sheshak*, who

Invaded *Judaea* in *Rehoboam's* Time, (as Sir *John Marsham* (o) asserts after *Josephus*) or not: If he was, his Time is known indeed; but then the Authority of *Manetho*, and of those Pillars from which *Manetho* pretended to transcribe the Tables of the several Dynasties of the *Aegyptian* Kings, is at an End: Besides, it contradicts all the *Greek* Writers that mention *Sesostris*, who place him in their fabulous Age, and generally affirm, that he lived before the Expedition of the *Argonauts*, which preceded the War of *Troy*. If he was not that *Sheshak*, then the Time when the only famous Conqueror of the *Aegyptian* Nation lived is uncertain, and all that they know of him is, that *once upon a time* there was a mighty King in *Aegypt*, who conquer'd *Aethiopia*, *Arabia*, *Assyria*, and up to *Colchis*, with *Asia the Less*, and the Islands of the *Aegaean* Sea, where having left Marks of his Power, he returned home again to reap the Fruits of his Labours: A Tradition which might have been preserved without setting up a College at *Heliopolis* for that purpose.

(o) *In Canone Chronico*

The very Learned Mr. *Dodwell*, in his Discourse *concerning the Phaenician History of Sanchoniathon*, advances a Notion which may help to give a very probable Account of those vast Antiquities of the *Aegyptians* pretended to by *Manetho*. He thinks that after the History of *Moses* was translated into *Greek*, and so made common to the Learned Men of the neighbouring Nations, that they endeavoured to rival them by pretended Antiquities of their own, that so they might not seem to come behind a People, who till then had been so obscure. This, though particularly applied by that Excellent Person to *Sanchoniathon*'s History, seems equally forcible in the present Controversie: For *Manetho* dedicated his History to *Ptolemee Philadelphus*, at whose Command it was written, and wrote it about the Time that the LXXII Interpreters translated the *Pentateuch*. The great Intercourse which the *Aegyptians* and *Israelites* formerly had each with other, made up a considerable part of that Book, and occasion'd its being the more taken notice of; so that this History being injurious to the vain Pretences of that People, might very probably provoke some that were jealous for the Honour of their Nation, and *Manetho* among the rest, to set up an Anti-History to that of *Moses*; and to dedicate it to the same Prince who employ'd the *Jews* to translate the *Pentateuch*, and who ordered *Manetho* himself to bring him in an Account of the *Aegyptian* Antiquities, that so any Prejudices which *Ptolemee*, who was of another Nation himself, might entertain against their Country, might be effectually removed. This

This Notion is the more probable in our Case, because it equally holds, whether we follow Sir *John Marsham*'s Accounts, who has made the *Aegyptian* Antiquities intelligible; or whether they are left in the same Confusion that they were in before. That most Learned Gentleman has reduced the wild Heap of *Aegyptian* Dynasties into as narrow a Compass as the History of *Moses*, according to the *Hebrew* Account, by the help of a Table of the *Theban* Kings, which he found under *Eratosthenes*'s Name, in the Chronography of *Syncellus*. For, by that Table, he (1.) Distinguished the Fabulous and Mystical part of the *Aegyptian* History, from that which seems to look like Matter of Fact. (2.) He reduced the Dynasties into Collateral Families, reigning at the same time, in several Parts of the Country; which, as some Learned Men saw before, was the only Way to make those Antiquities consistent with themselves, which till then were confused and incoherent. But it seems evident, by the Remains that we have of *Manetho* in *Eusebius*, and by the Accounts which we have of the *Aegyptian* History in *Josephus*'s Books against *Apion*, and in the Ancient *Christian* Writers, that the *Aegyptians* in *Ptolemee*'s Time did not intend to confine themselves within the Limits set by *Moses*, but resolved to go many Thousand Years beyond them. If therefore

fore *Eratosthenes*'s Table be genuine, not only *Manetho*'s Authority sinks, but the Pillars from whence he transcribed his Tables of the Kings of their several Dynasties are Impostures, since they pretend to give successive Tables of vast Numbers of Kings reigning in several Families, for many Ages; which ought to be contracted into a Period of Time, not much exceeding MM Years. If the Table of *Eratosthenes* be not the true Rule by which the *Aegyptian* Antiquities are to be squared, then the former Prejudices will return in full force; and one cannot value *Tables*, and *Pillars*, and *Priests*, that could not fix *the Time of the Erection of the Pyramids*, and the *Age of Sesostris*, so certainly, as that when *Herodotus* was in the Country, they might have been able to inform him a little better than they did.

This long Enquiry into the *Aegyptian* History, will not, I hope, be thought altogether a Digression from my Subject, because it weakens the *Aegyptians* Credit in a most sensible Part: For, if their Civil History is proved to be egregiously fabulous, or inconsistent, there will be no great reason to value their mighty Boasts in any thing else; at least, not to believe them upon their own Words, without other Evidence.

In

In *Geometry*, the *Aegyptians* are, of all hands, allowed to have laid the first Foundations: The Question therefore is, How far they went? Before this can be answer'd satisfactorily, one ought to enquire whether *Pythagoras* and *Thales*, who went such long Voyages to get Knowledge, would not have learn'd all that the *Aegyptians* could teach them? Or, whether the *Aegyptians* would willingly impart all they knew? The former, I suppose, no body questions: For the latter, we are to distinguish between Things that are concealed out of Interest, and between other Things, which, for the same Interest, are usually made public. The *Secrets of the* Aegyptian *Theology* were not proper to be discovered, because by those Mysteries they kept the People in awe: The *Philosopher's Stone* likewise, if they had been Masters of it, might, for Gain, have been concealed: And *Medicinal Arcana* are of Advantage often-times to the Possessors, chiefly because they are *Arcana*. But *Abstracted Mathematical Theories*, which bring Glory to the Inventors, when they are communicated to those that can relish them, and which bring no Profit when they are locked up, are never concealed from such as shew a Desire to learn them; provided that by such a Discovery the first Inventors are not deprived of the Glory of their Inventions; which is encreased by publishing, if they have

have before-hand taken care to secure their Right. So that since *Pythagoras* is commended for no famous Invention in Geometry, except the XLVII*th* Proposition of the First Book of *Euclid*: And since, *Thales* is said to have sacrificed an Oxe, for finding out how to inscribe a Rectangled Triangle within a Circle, which implies, that he learn'd it not of the *Aegyptians*, we may reasonably conclude, that these Two *Graecian* Philosophers brought nothing of more Moment, in that Way, with them, out of *Aegypt*; and therefore, either the farther Discoveries that were made in Geometry, were made by the *Aegyptians* afterwards; or, which is more probable, they were *Graecian* Superstructures upon *Aegyptian* Foundations. Besides, though a Man travelled into *Aegypt*, yet it does not follow from thence, that he learn'd all his Knowledge there. Though *Archimedes* and *Euclid* were in *Aegypt*, yet they might, for all that, have been Inventors themselves of those noble Theorems which are in their Writings. In *Archimedes*'s Time, the *Greeks* were setled in *Alexandria*, under the *Ptolemee*'s, who were then, and long before, Lords of *Aegypt*; and the Learning of *Aegypt*, at that Time, could no more be attributed to those Old *Aegyptians*, who lived before the *Graecian* Conquest, than the Learning of Archbishop *Usher*, Sir *James Ware*, and Mr. *Dod-*

Mr. *Dodwell*, can be attributed to a Succession of those Learned *Irish-men* who were so considerable in the *Saxon* Times.

This last Consideration is of very great Moment; for few of the *Greeks*, after *Plato*, went into *Aegypt* purely for Knowledge: And though *Plato* brought several of his Notions out of *Aegypt*, which he interwove into his Philosophy, yet the Philosophers of the *Alexandrian* School, who, for the most part, were *Platonists*, shew, by their Way of Writing, and by their frequent Citations out of *Plato's* Books, that they chose to take those Things from the *Graecians*, which, one would think, might have been had nearer Home, if they had been of the Original Growth of the Country. The most considerable Propositions in *Euclid's Elements* were attributed to the *Greeks*; and we have nothing confessedly *Aegyptian*, to oppose to the Writings of *Archimedes*, *Apollonius Pergaeus*, or *Diophantus*: Whereas, had there been any Thing considerable, it would most certainly have been produced, or, at least, hinted at, by some of those very Learned *Aegyptians*, or rather later *Greeks* born in *Aegypt*, whose Writings that treat of the Extent of the *Aegyptian* Knowledge, are still extant.

Having now examined the *History* and *Geometry* of the *Aegyptians*, it will be much easier to go through their Pretences, (or rather

rather the Pretences of their Advocates) to Superiority in other Parts of Learning. The *Aegyptians* seem to have verified the Proverb, *That he that has but one Eye, is a Prince among those that have none.* This was Glory enough; for it is always exceedingly Honourable to be the First, where the Strife is concerning Things which are worth contending for.

CHAP. X.

Of the Natural Philosophy, Medicine and Alchemy of the Ancient Aegyptians.

THE *Aegyptian Natural Philosophy* and *Physic* shall be joined together, because there is so great an Affinity between them, that true Notions in either Science assist the other. Their *Physic*, indeed, was very famous in *Homer's* Time; and wonderful Things are told of *Hermes*, the pretended Father of the Chymical Art. But one ought to distinguish between Particular Medicines, how noble soever, and General Theories founded upon a due Examination of the Nature of those Bodies from whence such

such Medicines are drawn, and of the Constitution and Fabric of the Bodies of the Patients to whom they are to be applied, and of the incidental Circumstances of Time and Place; which are necessary to be taken in by a wise Physician. The Stories of the *West-Indian* Medicines are many of them very astonishing, and the *American* Salvages knew perfectly how to use them before ever the *Europaeans* came among them, and yet they were never esteemed able Physicians. This Instance is applicable to the present Question: *Galen* often mentions *Aegyptian* Remedies, in his Treatises *of Medicines*, which are numerous and large, though he seldom mentions any of their Hypotheses, from which only a Man can judge whether the *Aegyptians* were well-grounded Physicians, or Empirics. This is the more remarkable, because *Galen* had lived long at *Alexandria*, and commends the Industry of the *Alexandrians* in cultivating Anatomy, which is so necessary a Part of a Physician's Business.

In General therefore we may find, that all the *Aegyptian Notions of Physical Matters* were built *upon Astrological and Magical Grounds:* Either the Influence of a Particular Planet, or of some Tutelar Dæmon, were still considered. These Foundations are precarious and impious, and they put a stop to any Encrease of real Knowledge,

which

which might be made upon other Principles. He that minds the Position of the Stars, or invokes the Aid of a Dæmon, will rarely be follicitous to examine nicely into the Nature of his Remedies, or the Constitution of his Patients, without which, none of the ancient Rational Physicians believed that any Man could arrive at a perfect Knowledge of their Art. So that if *Hippocrates* learn'd his Skill in *Aegypt*, as it is pretended, the *Aegyptian* Physicians afterwards took a very stupid Method to run so far upon Imaginary Scents, as even to lose the Memory that they had ever pursued more Rational Methods. Those that would be further satisfy'd of the Truth of this Matter of Fact, may find it abundantly proved in *Conringius*'s Discourse (*p*) of the Old *Aegyptian* Medicine.

(*p*) *De Hormetica Aegyptiorum vetere & Paracelsicorum nova Medicina.*

But we are told, that there was *a particular sort of Physic*, used only *amongst the* Aegyptian *Priests*, which was kept secret, not only from the *Greeks* that came into their Country for Knowledge, but from the Generality of the Natives themselves; wherein by the help of the *Grand-Elixir*, they could do almost any thing but restore Life to the Dead. This *Elixir*, which was a Medicine made with the Philosophers-Stone, was a Chymical Preparation; and, if if we may believe *Olaus Borrichius* (*q*), the Great and Learned *Advocate* of the *Chymical* and *Adept Philosophers*, was the Invention of *Hermes*, who was Contemporary with *Isis* and *Osiris*, whose Age none ever yet determined. If these Claims are true, there is no question but the *Aegyptians* understood Nature, at least that of Metals, in a very high degree. This is *an Application of Agents, to Patients* (*r*); which if made good, will go farther than any Assertion commonly brought to prove the Extent of *Aegyptian* Knowledge. And therefore, I presume, I shall not be thought tedious, if I enlarge more particularly upon this Question, than I have done upon the rest; especially since there has not been, that I know of, any direct Answer ever printed to *Borrichius*'s Book upon this Argument, which he wrote against the foremention'd Discourse of *Conringius*.

(*q*) *De Ortu & Progressu Chemiæ, as also Hermetis Aegyptiorum & Chemicorum sapientia ab Herm. Conringii Animadversionibus vindicata.*

(*r*) Pag. 46.

One may justly wonder that there should have been so noble an Art as that of turning baser Metals into Gold and Silver, so long in the World, and yet that there should be so very little, if any thing, said of it in the Writings of the Ancients. To remove this Prejudice therefore, all the fabulous Stories of the *Greeks*, have, by Men of fertile Inventions, been given out to be disguised Chymical *Arcana*. *Jason's* Golden

I Fleece,

Fleece, which he brought from *Colchis*, was only *a Receipt to make the Philosopher's-Stone*; and *Medea* restored her Father-in-Law, *Aeson*, to his Youth again by the *Grand Elixir*. *Borrichius* is very confident that the *Aegyptian* Kings built the Pyramids with the Treasures that their Furnaces afforded them; since, if there were so many Thousand Talents expended in Leeks and Onions, as *Herodotus* tells us there were, which must needs have been an inconsiderable Summ, in comparison of the whole Expense of the Work, one cannot imagine how they could have raised Money enough to defray the Charge of the Work any other Way. And since *Borrichius*, *Jacobus Tollius* has set out a Book called *Fortuita*, wherein he makes most of the old Mythology to be Chymical Secrets.

But though *Borrichius* may believe that he can find some obscure Hints of this *Great Work* in the Heathen Mythologists, and in some scatter'd Verses of the Ancient Poets, which, according to him, they themselves did not fully understand when they wrote them; yet this is certain, That the ancientest Chymical Writers now exstant, cannot be proved to have been so old as the Age of *Augustus*. *Conringius* believes that *Zosimus Panopolita* is the oldest Chymical Author that we have, whom he sets lower than *Constantine the Great*. That

perhaps

perhaps may be a Mistake; for *Borrichius*, who had read them both in MS. in the *French King*'s Library, brings very plausible Arguments to prove that *Olympiodorus*, who wrote Commentaries upon some of the Chymical Discourses of *Zosimus*, was CL Years older than *Constantine*; because he mentions the *Alexandrian* Library in the Temple of *Sarapis*, as actually in being, which, in *Ammianus Marcellinus*'s Time, who was Contemporary with *Julian the Apostate*, was only talk'd of, as a thing destroyed long before. I don't mean that which was burnt in *Julius Caesar*'s Time, but one afterwards erected out of the scatter'd Remains that were saved from that great Conflagration, which is mentioned by *Tertullian*, under the Name of *Ptolemee*'s Library at *Alexandria*. If this *Zosimus* is the same whom *Galen* mentions, for a Remedy for Sore Eyes, in his IVth Book *of Topical Medicines*, then both he and *Olympiodorus* might have been considerably older, and yet have lived since our Blessed Saviour's Time. However, be their Age what it will, they wrote to themselves, and their Art was as little known afterwards as it was before: *Julius Firmicus* is the First Author that has mention'd *Alchemy*, either by Name, or by an undisputed Circumlocution; and he dedicated his Book *of Astrology* to *Constantine the Great*. *Manilius* indeed (who is suppos'd to have

liv'd

liv'd in *Augustus*'s Time) in the IVth Book of his *Astronomicon*, where he gives an Account of those that are born under *Capricorn*, has these words,

———————*scrutari cæca metalla,
Depositas & opes, terræque exquirere venas,
Materiemque manu certâ duplicarier arte.*

which last Verse seems to be a Description of *Alchemy*: But, besides that the Verse is suspected to be spurious; even the Age of *Manilius* himself is not without Controversie; some making him Contemporary with the Younger *Theodosius*, and consequently later than *Firmicus* himself. We may expect to have this Question determined, when my most Learned Friend, Dr. *Bently*, shall oblige the World with his *Censures* and *Emendations* of that Elegant Poet.

But if these *Graecian* Chymists should have the utmost Antiquity allowed them that *Borrichius* desires, it would signifie little to deduce their Art from *Hermes*; since Men might pretend that their Art was derived from him in *Zosimus*'s Days, and yet come several Thousand Years short of it, if we follow the Accounts of *Manetho*. Wherefore, though this is but a Negative Argument, yet it seems to be unanswerable; because if there had been such an Art, some of the *Greeks* and *Romans*, who were successive cessively Masters of *Aegypt*, would have mention'd it, at least, before *Zosimus*'s Time. Such a Notice, whether with Approbation, or Contempt, had been sufficient to ascertain the Reality of such a Tradition. *Tacitus* (s) tells us, that *Nero* sent into *Africa* to find some Gold, that was pretended to be hid under Ground; This would have been an excellent Opportunity for him to have examined into this Tradition, or to have punished those, who either falsly pretended to an Art which they had not, or would not discover the true Secret; which, in his Opinion, would have been equally criminal; and had *Nero* done it, *Pliny* would have told us of it, who was very inquisitive to collect all the Stories he could find of every thing that he treats about, whereof Gold (t) is one that is not slightly passed over; and besides, he never omits a Story because it appears strange and incredible, if we may judge of what he has left out, by what he has put in, but often ranges the wonderful Qualities of Natural Bodies under distinct Heads, that they might be the more observed.

(s) Anna. Lib XVI

(t) Nat. Hist Lib XXXIII. capp 1, 2, 3, 4

To evade the Force of this Argument, *Borrichius* (u) says that the *Aegyptians* were afraid of their Conquerors, and therefore industriously concealed their Art. But there is a wide Difference between concealing the Rules and Precepts of an Art, and concealing

(u) H. m Ægypt.

cealing the Memory that ever there was such an Art. If it was ever known before the *Perfian* Conqueſt, as by his Account of the Erection of the Pyramids, which were built many Ages before *Cambyſes*'s Time, it is plain he believes it was, though we ſhould allow it to have been in few Hands, it is not credible that this Art of Making Gold ſhould never have been pretended to before *Diocletian*'s Time, who is reported by *Suidas* to have burnt great Numbers of Chymical Books, which gave an Account of the Proceſs. Whereas afterwards, every now and then, Footſteps of cheating *Alchemiſts* are to be met with in the *Byzantine* Hiſtorians. It was not poſſible to pretend to greater Secrecy in the Manner of their Operations, than is now to be found in all the Writings of Modern *Adept Philoſophers* (as they call themſelves.) And yet theſe Men, who will not reveal their Proceſs, would think themſelves affronted, if any Man ſhould queſtion the real Exiſtence of their Art.

But the Hypotheſis of thoſe who find Chymical Secrets in *Homer*, *Virgil*, and the reſt of the ancient Poets, is liable to ſeveral Exceptions taken notice of neither by *Conringius* nor *Borrichius*.

(1.) They ſay, that when *Jaſon* heard that the King of *Colchis* had a Book written upon a Ram's-ſkin, wherein was the Proceſs

cess of the Philosophers-Stone, he went with the *Argonauts* to fetch it. Here it may be objected, (1.) That it is not likely that *Sesostris*, who conquer'd *Colchis*, would ever suffer the *Aegyptian* Priests to reveal such a Secret to that conquered People. *Diocletian*, according to them, burnt all the Chymical Books that he could find in *Aegypt*, that the *Aegyptians* might not rebel, when they were deprived of that Fund, which supported their Wars. And *Borrichius* supposes that the *Aegyptian* Priests used this Art chiefly to supply the Expenses of their Kings. (2.) How came *Jason* and the *Argonauts* not to grow richer by this Fleece? It cannot be pretended that it was concealed from them, upon the Account of its being (like the Books of the Modern *Adepti*) written in so obscure a Stile, that it was unintelligible for want of a Master; since *Medea* was with *Jason*, who had the Secret, what or how great soever it was. (3.) Since the *Graecians* were not tied to Secrecy, how came their Traditions to be so obscure, that those Passages in *Apollonius Rhodius's Argonauticks* which are supposed to be meant of the *Grand Elixir*, were never applied to a Chymical Sense, till the Writings of *Synesius*, *Zosimus*, and the other old *Graecian* Chymists appeared? Especially since, (4.) *Apollonius Rhodius* himself was an *Alexandrian Greek*, born in *Aegypt*, and so could easily acquaint himself with the Traditions of that Country, which he, originally of another Nation, was under no Obligation to conceal.

(2.) The Chymists, at least *Borrichius* for them, own *Democritus*'s Books to be genuine, upon the Credit of *Zosimus* who quotes them: If they are, this pretended Secrecy falls to the ground: For *Democritus* affirms, That he learn'd his Art from *Ostanes* or *Otanes* a *Mede*, who was sent by the Kings of *Persia* into *Aegypt*, as Governor of the *Aegyptian* Priests. Then the Secret was divulged to some of the Conquerors of their Country. If so, why no more Tradition of it? If not the Process it self, yet at least the Memory that once there was such a Process? Which would have been enough for this Purpose. The same Question may be asked of *Democritus*, to whom *Ostanes* revealed it. This will weaken *Zosimus*'s Credit as an Antiquary, upon whose Assertion most of this pretended Antiquity is founded. Since at the same time that he objects the Secrecy of the Ancient *Aegyptian* Priests, as a Reason why the Memory of this Art was so little known, he owns himself obliged to a *Greek*, who had it from the *Aegyptians* at Second Hand.

But how will these Pretenders to remote Antiquity, who tell us, that *Moses*, by his Skill

Skill in Chymistry, ground the Golden Calf to Powder, reconcile a Passage in *Theophrastus* to their *Pretensions*? He speaking of Quick-silver (*w*), says, that the Art of Extracting it from *Cinnabar* was not known till XC Years before his Time, when it was first found out by *Callias* an *Athenian*. Can we think that the *Aegyptians* could hinder these inquisitive *Graecians*, who staid so long in their Country, from knowing that there was such a Metal as *Mercury*? Or could these *Aegyptians* make Gold without it? If they could, they might reasonably suppose that the *Israelites* could make Brick without Straw, since they could make Gold and Silver without that, which Modern *Adepti* affirm to be the Seed of all Metals. *Theophrastus*'s Words are too general, to admit of an Objection, as if he believed that *Callias*'s Invention ought to be limited to his own Country. This, join'd to the great Silence of the Ancients (especially *Herodotus* and *Diodorus Siculus*, who dwell so long upon the *Aegyptian* Arts and Learning) concerning most of the wonderful *Phaenomena* of that extravagant Metal, plainly shews that there were no Traditions of such mighty things to be done by it, as the *Alchemist*'s Books are full of. *Borrichius* therefore recurs to his old Subterfuge, *Aegyptian* Secrecy, and finds some doubtful at least,

(*w*) Lib. *de Lapidibus*.

least, if not fabulous, Stories of *Daedalus* and *Icarus*, and the Poetical Age, which he opposes to the positive Testimony of *Theophrastus*. Perhaps my urging the late Discovery of *Mercury*, may be thought to be begging the Question, since some who have written of the Philosophers-Stone, have taught that their *Mercury* has no Affinity with common *Mercury*: Which has led many Persons to try several extravagant Processes to find it out. But *Eirenaeus Philalethes*, who is look'd upon as one of the clearest Writers that has ever written upon this Subject, says expresly, that (*x*) Natural Mercury *Philosophically prepared, is the Philosophical Menstruum, and the Dissolvent* Mercury.

(*x*) *Enarratio Methodica trium Gebri Medicinarum, p. 18.*

After so long an Enquiry into the Antiquity of this Art of Transmuting Metals, it will be asked perhaps, what may be thought of the Art it self. I must needs say, I cannot tell what Judgment to make of it: The Pretenses to Inspiration, and that Enthusiastic Cant which run through the Writings of almost all the *Alchemists*, seem so like Imposture, that one would be tempted to think that it was only a Design carried on from Age to Age, to delude Mankind; and it is not easie to imagine why God should hear the Prayers of those that desire to be Rich. If, as they pretend, it was Zeal for the Good of Mankind

kind that made them take such Pains to find out such noble Medicines as should free Men from the most obstinate Diseases to which our Natures are subject, why do they not communicate them, and leave the Process in Writing plainly to Posterity, if they are afraid of Danger for themselves? Concern for the Welfare of Mankind, and affected Secrecy, seem here inconsistent Things: Men of such mortified Tempers, and public Spirits, ought not to be concerned, though Gold or Silver were made as common as Lead or Tin, provided that the *Elixir* which should remove all Diseases were once known.

Though these are reasonable Prejudices against the Belief of the Truth of this Operation, yet one can hardly tell how to contradict a Tradition so general, and so very well attested (*y*). So many Men, methinks, could not have cheated the World successfully for so many Ages, if some had not been sincere: And, to use a Proverb in their own way, *So much Smoak could scarce have lasted so long without some Fire.* Till the Seminal Principles from which Metals are compounded are perfectly known, the Possibility of the Operation cannot be disproved; Which Principles, as all other Real Essences of Things, are concealed from us.

(*y*) Vid. Borrichium *de Ortu & Progressu Chemiæ,* & Morhosii *Epistolam de Transmutatione Metallorum ad Joelem Langelottum.*

But

But as a wife Man cannot, perhaps, without Rashness disbelieve what is so confidently asserted, so he ought not to spend much Time and Cost about Trying whether it will succeed, till some of the *Adepti* shall be so kind as to give him the Receipt.

By what has been said, it is evident, what Opinion one ought to have of the Chymical Skill of the Ancient *Aegyptians*; Though it is most probable that the Art owes its Original to them from whom it receives its Name: But this Original is much too late to do Sir *William Temple's* Hypothesis any Service.

But it is high time to leave the *Aegyptian Physic*, and therefore I shall only add One or Two Instances of their *Skill in Anatomy*, and so pass on. *Gellius* (z) and *Macrobius* (a) observe; the one from *Apion*, who wrote of the *Aegyptians*; the other from the *Aegyptian* Priests themselves, that there is a particular *Nerve* that goes from the Heart to the Little-Finger of the Left-Hand, for which Reason they always wore Rings upon that Finger; and the Priests dipped that Finger in their perfumed Ointments: This being ridiculed by *Conringius*, *Borrichius* (b) assures us, that he always found something to countenance this Observation, upon cutting of his Nails to the quick. *Pliny* (c) and *Censorinus* (d) give this following Reason from *Dioscorides* the

(z) *Noct. Attic.* Lib X cap. 10
(a) *Saturnal.* l. 7. cap. 13.

(b) *Herm. Aegypt. Praefat*
(c) *Hist. Nat* lib xi. cap. 37
(d) *De Die Natali* cap. 17.

the Astrologer, why a Man cannot live above a Hundred Years, because the *Alexandrian* Embalmers observed a constant Encrease and Diminution of Weight of the Hearts of those sound Persons whom they opened, whereby they judged of their Age. They found that the Hearts of Infants of a Year old weighed two Drachms, and this Weight encreased Annually by two Drachms every Year, till Men came to the Age of Fifty Years: At which time they as gradually decreased till they came to an Hundred, when, for want of a Heart, they must necessarily die.

To these Two Instances of the *Criticalness of Aegyptian Anatomy*, I shall add one of *their Curiosity in Natural Enquiries*; and that is, *their Knowledge of the Cause of the Annual Overflowing of the Nile*. This, which was the constant Wonder of the Old World, was a *Phaenomenon* seldom over-looked by the *Greek* Philosophers: Seven of whose Opinions are reckoned up by *Plutarch*, in the First Chapter of the Fourth Book *of his Opinions of the Philosophers*. If Curiosity generally attends a Desire of Knowledge, and grows along with it, then the *Aegyptian* Priests were inexcusably negligent, that they did not very early know that the Swelling of the *Nile* proceeded from the Rains that fell in *Aethiopia*, which raising the River at
cer-

certain Seasons, made that Overflowing of the Flats of *Aegypt*. One would think that in *Sesostris*'s Time the *Aegyptian* Priests had Access enough into *Aethiopia*; and whoever had once been in that Countrey, could have resolved that Problem, without any Philosophy. It was known indeed in *Plato*'s Time, for then the Priests told it to *Eudoxus*; but *Thales*, *Democritus*, and *Herodotus*, who had all enquired of the *Aegyptians*, give such uncouth Reasons, as shew that they only spoke by guess. *Thales* thinks that the *Etesian* Winds blew at that Time of the Year against the Mouths of the River, so that the fresh Water finding no Vent, was beaten back upon the Land. *Democritus* supposes that the Northern Snows being melted by the Summer Heats, are drawn up in Vapours into the Air; which Vapours circulating towards the South, are, by the Coldness of the *Etesian* Winds, condensed into Rain, by which the *Nile* is raised. *Herodotus* thinks that an equal Quantity of Water comes from the Fountains in Summer and Winter, only in Summer there are greater Quantities of Water drawn up by the Sun, and in Winter less, and so by consequence all that time it overflowed. *Democritus*'s Opinion of the *Phaenomenon* seems not amiss, though his Hypothesis of the Cause of it is wrong in all probability; yet it is plain, That

Plutarch did not believe it to be the same with that which the *Aegyptian* Priests gave to *Eudoxus*, which is the only true one, because he sets them both down apart. The Cause of this wonderful *Phaenomenon* could not be pretended to be a Secret; no Honour could be got by concealing a Thing, the pretended Ignorance whereof was rather a Disgrace. Those *Aegyptian* Priests, whose Business it was to gather Knowledge, must have had an extraordinary Love for a Sedentary Life, or have been averse to inform themselves from others, more than the rest of Mankind, who would not be at the Pains either to learn what *Sesostris*'s Soldiers could have told them, or to go CC or CCC Miles Southward to search for that, which they must certainly have often *reasoned about*, if they were such Philosophers as they pretended to be.

Nay, by the Curiosity of the *Greeks*, we are sure they did *reason about* it; they thought it as much a Wonder as we can do now; rather more, because they knew of no other Rivers that overflow at periodical Seasons like it, as some are now known to do in other Parts of *Africa*, and the *East-Indies*.

Upon the whole Matter, after a particular Search into the whole Extent of *Aegyptian* Learning, there seems to be no Reason to give the *Aegyptians* the Preeminence
in

in point of Knowledge above all Mankind. However, considering the great Labour which is requisite to form the First Notions of any part of Learning, they deserve great Applause for what they discovered, and ought to have proportionable Grains of Allowance for what they left unfinished: Wherefore, when the Holy Scriptures (e) assure us, that *Moses* was skill'd in all the Learning of the *Aegyptians*, they give him the greatest Character for Humane Knowledge that could then be given to any Man. The *Aegyptian* Performances in Architecture were exceedingly wonderful, (f) and the Character which *Hadrian* the Emperor gives them, that they found Employments for all sorts of Persons, the Blind, the Lame, the Gouty, as well as the Strong and Healthy, shews that it was natural to the *Aegyptians* to be always busied about something useful. The Art of Brewing Mault-Drinks was long ago ascribed (g) to the *Aegyptians* as the first Inventors, for which these Northern Nations are not a little beholding to them. Their Laws have, by those who have taken the greatest Pains (h) to destroy the Reputation of their Learning in other things, been acknowledged to be very wise, and worth going so far as *Pythagoras*, *Solon* and *Lycurgus* did to fetch them. So that if their Modern Advocates had extolled their Learning

(e) Acts vii. 22.

(f) Vid. Herodoti Euterpen.

(g) Herodotus: Columella, Lib. X.

(h) Conringius in Medicinâ Hermetica.

ing with any other Design than that of Disparaging the Knowledge of the present Age, there would have been no Reason to oppose their Assertions.

CHAP. XI.

Of the Learning of the Ancient Chaldaeans and Arabians.

THE *Chaldaeans* and the *Arabs* are the People that lie next in Sir *William Temple*'s Road. Though it is not easie to separate what is Fabulous from what is Genuine in the Antiquities of these Nations, yet we may pronounce with some Certainty,

(1.) That the *Chaldaean* Astronomy could not be very valuable, since, as we know from *Vitruvius*, and others, they had not discovered that the Moon is an Opake Body. For which Reasons, possibly, with several others, some of their Learnedest Champions have confessed, that they believed that the Ancient *Chaldaean* Observations, were rather Registers of the *Phaenomena* of Heavenly Bodies, after they had appeared, than Predictions of their future Appearance. Whether their Astronomical Observations were older than their Mo-

narchy

narchy, is uncertain: If they were not, then in *Alexander the Great's* Time they could not challenge an Antiquity of above D or DC Years. I mention *Alexander*, because he is said to have sent vast Numbers of Observations from *Babylon*, to his Master *Aristotle*. The *Assyrian* Monarchy, of which the *Chaldaean* might not improperly be called a Branch, pretends, indeed, to great Antiquity: Mighty Things are told of *Ninus* and *Semiramis*, who is more than once mentioned by Sir *William Temple*, in these *Essays*, for her Victories, and her Skill in Gardening. But these Accounts are very probably fabulous, for the following Reasons.

Till the Time of *Tiglath-Pileser* and *Pul*, we hear no News of any *Assyrian* Monarchs in the *Jewish* History. In *Amraphel's* Time, who was overthrown by *Abraham* and his Family, in the Vale of *Siddim*, the Kings of *Chaldaea* seem to have been no other than those of *Canaan*, Captains of *Hords*, or Heads of *Clans*: And *Amraphel* was Tributary to *Chedorlaomer* King of *Elam*, whose Kingdom lay to the East of *Babylon*, beyond the River *Tigris*. *Chushan Rishathaim*, King of *Mesopotamia*, who was overthrown some Ages after by *Othoniel* the *Israelitish* Judge, does not seem to have been a powerful Prince: It may be said, indeed, that he was General to some *Assyrian* Monarch;

but

but that is begging the Question, since there is nothing which can favour such an Assertion in the Book of *Judges*.

But when the *Assyrians* and *Babylonians* come once to be mentioned in the *Jewish* History, they occur in almost every Page of the *Old Testament*. There are frequent Accounts of *Pul, Tiglath-Pileser, Shalmanezer, Sennacherib, Esar-haddon, Nebuchadnezzar, Evil-merodach, Belshazzar,* and who not? But these Kings lived within a narrow Compass of Time; the oldest of them but a few Ages before *Cyrus*. This would not suit with that prodigious Antiquity which they challenged to themselves. The Truth is, *Herodotus*, who knew nothing of the Matter, being silent, *Ctesias* draws up a new Scheme of History much more pompous; and from him, or rather, perhaps, from *Berosus*, who was Contemporary with *Manetho*, and seems to have carried on the the same Design for *Chaldaea*, which *Manetho* undertook for *Aegypt*, *Diodorus Siculus, Pompeius Trogus, Eusebius, Syncellus,* and all the Ancients that take notice of the *Assyrian* History, have afterwards copied.

Ctesias knew he should be straitned to find Employment for so many Kings for MCCC Years; and so he says, they did little memorable after *Semiramis's* Time. As if it were probable that a great Empire could lie still for above a M Years; or that no Popular Generals should wrest the Reins out of the Hands of such drowzy Masters in all that time. No History but this can give an Instance of a Family that lasted for above a M. Years, without any Interruption: And of all its Kings, not one is said to Reign less than XIX, but some LV Years. The Healthiest Race that ever was heard of; of whom, in MCCC Years, not one seems to have died an untimely Death. If any thing can be shewed like this in any other History, Sacred or Profane, it will be easie to believe whatsoever is asserted upon this Subject.

If therefore the *Chaldaean* Learning was no older than their Monarchy, it was of no great standing, if compared with the *Aegyptian*. The Account of *Nebuchadnezzar*'s Dream, in the II^{d.} Chapter of *Daniel*, shews the *Chaldaean* Magic to have been downright Knavery; since *Nebuchadnezzar* might reasonably exspect that those should tell him what his Dream was, who pretended to interpret it when it was told them; both equally requiring a Super-natural Assistance: Yet there lay their chiefest Strength; or, at least, they said so: Their other Learning is all lost. However, one can hardly believe that it was ever very great, that considers how little there remains of real Value, that was learn'd from the *Chaldaeans*. The History of Learn-

Learning is not so lamely conveyed to us, but so much would, in all probability, have escaped the general Ship-wreck, as that, by what was saved, we might have been able to guess at the real value of what was lost.

(2.) That if the *Learning* of these *Ancient Chaldaeans* came as near *that of the Arabs* as their *Countries* did; one may give as good a Judgment of the Extent of the *Arabian* Learning, as of the *Chaldaean*. Sir *William Temple* rightly observes, that Countries little exposed to Invasions, preserve Knowledge better than others that are perpetually harassed by a Foreign Enemy; and by consequence, whatsoever Learning the *Arabs* had, they kept; unless we should suppose that they lost it through Carelesness. We never read of any Conquests that pierced into the Heart of *Arabia the Happy*, *Mahomet's* Country, before the Beginning of the *Saracen* Empire. It is very strange therefore, if, in its Passage through this noble Country, inhabited by a sprightly, ingenious People, Learning, like Quick-silver, should run through, and leave so few of its Influences behind it. It is certain that the *Arabs* were not a Learned People when they overspread *Asia*: So that when afterwards they translated the *Graecian* Learning into their own Language, they had but little of their own, which was not taken from those Fountains. Their *Astro-*

nomy and *Astrology* was taken from *Ptolomee*, their *Philosophy* from *Aristotle*, their *Medics* from *Galen*, and so on: *Aristotle* and *Euclid* were first translated into *Latin*, from *Arabic* Copies; and those Barbarous Translations were the only Elements upon which the *Western School-men* and *Mathematicians* built. If they learn'd any thing considerable elsewhere, it might be *Chymistry* and *Alchemy* from the *Aegyptians*; unless we should say that they translated *Synesius*, or *Zosimus*, or some other *Graecian Chymists*.

Hence it follows, that the *Arabs* borrowed the greatest part, at least, of their Knowledge from the *Greeks*, though they had much greater Advantages of Communicating with the more Eastern Parts of the World, than either *Greeks* or *Romans* ever had. They could have acquainted us with all that was rare and valuable amongst those Ancient Sages. The *Saracen* Empire was under one Head in *Almanzor*'s Time, and was then almost as far extended Eastward as ever afterwards. His Subjects had a free Passage, from the *Tagus* to the *Ganges*; and being united by the common Bond of the same Religion, the *Brachmans*, some of whom did, in all probability, embrace the *Mahometan* Faith, would not be shy of revealing what they knew, to their *Arabian* Masters. By this means, the Learning of the *Aegyptians*, *Chaldaeans*, *Indians*, *Greeks*, and *Arabs*,

ran

ran in one Common Channel. For several Ages, Learning was so much in fashion amongst them, and they took such care to bring it all into their own Language, that some of the learnedest *Jews, Maimonides* in particular, wrote in *Arabic,* as much as in their own Tongue. We might reasonably therefore have exspected to have found greater Treasures in the Writings of these learned *Mahometans,* than ever were discovered before: And yet those that have been conversant with their Books, say, that there is little to be found amongst them, which any Body might not have understood as well as they, if he had carefully studied the Writings of their *Graecian* Masters. There have been so many Thousands of *Arabic* and *Persic* MSS. brought over into *Europe,* that our learned Men can make as good, nay, perhaps, a better Judgment of the Extent of their Learning, than can be made, at this distance, of the *Greek.* There are vast Quantities of their Astronomical Observations in the *Bodleian* Library, and yet Mr. *Greaves* and Dr. *Edward Bernard,* two very able Judges, have given the World no Account of any Thing out of them, which those *Arabian* Astronomers did not, or might not have learn'd from *Ptolemee's Almagest,* if we set aside their Observations which their *Graecian* Masters taught them to make; which, to give them their due, Dr. *Bernard*
com-

commends, as much more valuable than is commonly believed, in a Letter to Dr. *Huntingdon*, printed in the *Philosophical Transactions*, containing their Observations of the Latitudes of Twenty of the most eminent of the Fixed Stars. We owe, indeed, to them alone the Way of Counting by Ten Cyphers, ascending byond Ten in a Decuple Proportion; which is of unspeakable Use in *Astronomical* and *Algebraical* Calculations, and indeed, in all Parts of *Arithmetic*. The Use of *Chymistry* in *Physic*, together with some of the most considerable Chymical Preparations, which have led the Way to most of the late Discoveries that have been made in that Art, and in *Natural Philosophy* by its means, have been unanimously ascribed to the *Arabs* by those Physicians that have studied their Books(z). Though in strictness, the whole *Arabian* Learning, with all their Inventions, what, and how great soever they were, may be reckoned as Modern, according to Sir *William Temple*'s Computation. But I have in this whole Dispute confined my self to *Moderns*, in the strictest sence of the word, and have only argued from what has been done by the Learned Men of these two last Ages, after the *Greeks* brought their Learning along with them into *Italy*, upon the Taking of *Constantinople* by the *Turks*. So that the *Arabs* are Ancients here; and what has

(z) Vid. Morhofii Epist ad Langlelotium.

has been said already, evidently proves that the old *Arabian* Learning could never be any one of those Fountains from whence the *Graecian* might have been drawn, and consequently can never be urged as such by those who give an Account of the History of Learning.

CHAP. XII.

Of the Learning of the Ancient Indians *and* Chineses.

WE are now arrived in our Passage Eastward as far as the *Indies*, where, according to Sir *William Temple*, the first Springs of that Learning which afterwards flow'd always Westward, arose. Thither *Pythagoras* is said to have gone, and to have fetch'd from thence his celebrated Doctrine of the *Transmigration of Souls*, which he taught, and is now believed by the Modern *Bramines* as it was the Opinion of the *Brachmans* of old.

We have very little if any Account of these *Indian* Philosophers before *Alexander the Great*, who extended his Conquests as far as the River *Indus*. His Historians acquaint us with a Set of Philosophers in that

Countrey, who practised great Austerities themselves, and taught others that Wisdom lay in living upon a little, in Abstaining from almost all sorts of Natural Pleasures, and Promoting the Prosperity and Welfare of the rest of Mankind. The Description that *Strabo* gives us of them, out of *Megasthenes*, *Onesicritus* and *Aristobulus*, which is very well Abridged by Sir *W. T.* is the Fullest and most Authentic that we have. And that the Body of it may be True, is probable from the Accounts of their Successors the *Bramines*, which are given us by Monsieur *Bernier*, and *Abraham Roger*, who lived many Years among them, and made it their Business to collect their Opinions with all the Exactness they could.

The superstitious Care which these People take to follow the Customs, and propagate the Opinions of their Ancestors, be they never so absurd and senseless, plainly shews that they would have preserved their Learning with equal Care, had there been any of it to preserve. They keep a Collection of the wise Sayings of one *Barthrouherri*, which Monsieur *Roger* has given us a Tast of, but such miserable Stuff for the generality, that one cannot read them without smiling at the Simplicity of those that can admire them. They wou'd not shew Monsieur *Roger* their Book of the Law, which they pretend to be sent from God;

God; but by the Account which his *Bramine* Doctor gave of it, it is only an abſurd Hiſtory of the fabulous Succeſſions of their Deities, and as abſurd a Collection of ſuperſtitious Ceremonies, by which they were to be worſhipped. Their Doctrine of the *Tranſmigration of Souls*, which *Pythagoras* firſt taught in the Weſt, is a precarious idle Notion, which theſe beſotted *Indians* do ſo blindly believe, that they are afraid of killing a Flea or a Louſe, for fear of diſturbing the Soul of one of their Anceſtors. Though at the ſame time they ſcruple not to force Multitudes of poor ſilly Women, and ſometimes too, full ſore againſt their Wills, to burn themſelves alive with their deceaſed Husbands Bodies, under a Pretence of their being ſerviceable to them in another World, though they are far from having any Aſſurance that their Husbands will there ſtand in need of them. Can we believe that there is a generous Spirit reſiding in a People, who have now for MM or MMM Years placed the higheſt degrees of Sanctity and Prudence in half-ſtarving themſelves, and depriving themſelves of the lawful Conveniencies of Life? Yet theſe were the chiefeſt Employments of the Ancient *Brachmans*, as they are ſtill of the Modern *Bramines*.

So that there is Reaſon to fear that the Stories of the extraordinary Wiſdom

of

of the Ancient *Brachmans* are in a great meafure fabulous, becaufe in the idle and bigotted part of the Narrative they do fo particularly agree with the Modern *Bramines*; and alfo, becaufe if one confults what the Ancients have recorded of the *Brachman*'s in *Alexander*'s time, which is all gathered into a Body by Sir *Edward Byfhe* (*k*), he will find that the Accounts which come the nearest to the Fountain, have lefs in them of the Romance (*l*) and that their Hiftorians have exfpatiated and flourifh'd more, as they were at the greater diftance. For, upon comparing what all thofe Authors there quoted have faid, I am enclinable to believe, that all we know of the Ancient *Brachmans*, is due to the Accounts which *Alexander*'s Companions have given us.

But let us enter into Particulars. Sir *William Temple* tells us, out of *Strabo*, (*m*) "That their Opinions in Natural Philofo-
"phy, were, that the *World* was *Round*;
"that it had a Beginning, and would have
"an End, but reckoned both by immenfe
"Periods of Time; that the Author of it
"was a Spirit, or a Mind that pervaded
"the whole Univerfe, and was diffufed
"through all the Parts of it; and that they
"held

(*k*) *Palladius de Gentibus Indiae, & Bragmanibus*, Edit. *Biffaei*, Lond 1665.

(*l*) Let but any Man compare *Strabo* and *Palladius* together, and he will fee the difference, though 'tis plain they relate to the fame Time.

(*m*) Lib. 15.

"held the Transmigration of Souls, and
"some used Discourses of Infernal Man-
"sions, in many things like those of *Pla-
"to.*" (*n*) Whether *Megasthenes*, from
whom *Strabo* takes all this Account, has
not made it a little more beautiful than he
ought, I very much question, since Monsieur *Bernier* says, (*o*) That the *Bramines*
believe, "That the *Earth* is *Flat*, and
"*Triangular*, with several Stories, all dif-
"fering in Beauty, Perfection, and Inha-
"bitants, each of which is encompassed,
"they say, by its Sea; that one of these
"Seas is of Milk, another of Sugar, the
"third of Butter, the fourth of Wine,
"and so forth: So that after one Earth
"there comes a Sea, and after a Sea an
"Earth, and so on to seven,
"beginning from *Someire* (*p*)
"which is in the midst of these
"Stories: That the first Story,
"which is at the foot of *So-*
"*meire*, hath *Deuta's* (*q*) for
"its Inhabitants which are ve-
"ry Perfect; that the second contains
"likewise *Deuta's*, but less perfect; and
"so of the rest, still lessening the Perfe-
"ction to the seventh, which, they say,
"is ours, that is, of Men far less Perfect
"than all the *Deuta's*: And, lastly, That
"this whole Mass is sustained upon the
"Heads of divers Elephants, which, when
"they

(*n*) *Essay.* pag. 17.

(*o*) *Voyages* Tom. 3. pag. 168. Edit. Eng.

(*p*) An Imaginary Mountain, which they place in the midst of the Earth.

(*q*) The Semi-Gods of the *Bramines*.

"they stir, cause an Earthquake." Upon all this, and abundance more of the like nature in *Astronomy, Anatomy, Medicine,* and *Physic's,* which seems to be the true Oriental Doctrine, consonant to those noble Discoveries which are in (r) Monsieur *Roger's History of the Lives and Manners of the Bramines,* Monsieur *Bernier* makes this Remark; (s) "All these strange Impertinencies, which I have had the patience to relate, have often made me think, that if *they* be those famous Sciences of the Ancient *Brachmans* of the *Indies,* very many have been deceived in the great Opinion they entertained of them. For my part, I can hardly believe it, but that I find the Religion of the *Indians* to be from immemorial Times; that 'tis written in the *Hanscrit* Language, which cannot but be very ancient, since its Beginning is unknown, and 'tis a *dead* Language, not understood but by the Learned; that *all* their Books are only written in that Tongue: All which are as many Marks of a very great Antiquity." This, by the way, confutes the Opinion of those (t) who make the *Indian* Learning to be all Traditionary; for not only their Religious, but their Profane Knowledge too, is all written in this *Hanscrit* Dialect.

(r) *Histoire de la Vie & des Mœurs des Bramines.*

(s) Pag. 169.

(t) Sir W. T. his *Essay,* p. 17.

Yet

Yet one Notion of these *Bramines* I cannot but take notice of, because it is a very Philosophichal one, and has been with probability started and defended by some of the most curious Anatomists of the present Age, who built their Hypothesis upon the latest Discoveries which have been made in their admirable Art: I shall set it down in Monsieur *Bernier*'s words; (*u*) "The Seeds of Plants and Animals are "not formed anew, but were contrived in "the first Production of the World, and "dispensed abroad every where, and mix-"ed in all things; and they are not only "potentially but actually the very and en-"tire Plants, and Animals, though so "small, that their Parts cannot be distin-"guisht, but when put into a convenient "Womb, and there nourisht, they extend "themselves and encrease: So that the "Seeds of an Apple and Pear-Tree, are a "little, entire, and perfect Apple and "Pear-Tree, having all its Essential Parts; "And so the Seeds of an Horse, an Ele-"phant, a Man, &c. are a little Horse, a "little Elephant, a little Man, in which "there wants nothing but the Soul and "Nourishment to make them appear what "they are.

(*u*) Pag 175, 17

This Opinion seems rather to have been maintained by a *Leeuwenhoek*, or a *Malpighius*, than by an *Indian*, who, as Mon-

sieur

(w) Pag. 166.

sieur *Bernier* assures us, (w) *understands nothing at all of Anatomy, and can speak nothing upon that Subject but what is impertinent.* Had it been the Result of Thought and Meditation, founded upon proper Premises, which must be the Effects of many and repeated Observations, one *might* justly have looked for, and *would* infallibly have found many other Notions of equal Subtilty, among these *Bramines*; which though erroneous, (and so, perhaps, may this be,) yet could not have been made by any but Skilful Men. Such Discoveries likewise would have obliged us to have entertained a very honourable Notion of the Learning of the Ancient *Brachmans*; because, though they *might* have been Modern, in comparison of those Ancient Times, yet they *might not* also, for ought we knew, and consequently might have been challenged to those Ancient Philosophers by their Modern Champions. But when, amidst a vast variety of wild and phantastical Opinions, a Man meets with one or two which stand alone by themselves, without any thing that appears to have raised or confirmed them, he ought not presently to conclude, that the Philosophers who maintain them are Wise and Learned Men, though once, perhaps, or twice, *Quod nequit Ingenium, Casus fecit.*

By

By this time, I am afraid I shall be thought as Tedious as an *Irish Tale-teller*, fit only to lull my Reader asleep: But there is but one Stage more left; and though it is a great way off, yet it may be easily reached upon Paper, and then will be as easily dispatched. For *China*, we are told, is a charming Countrey, and therefore most proper to be thought upon at the End of a tedious Discourse.

Sir *William Temple* knows very well, that the whole *Chinese* History depends upon the sole Authority of *Martinius*, and those Missionaries who published *Confucius* lately at *Paris*. *Martinius* (*x*) tells his Reader, that he was obliged to learn Sixty Thousand independent Characters before he could read the *Chinese* Authors with ease. This is, without all doubt, an excellent Method to propagate Learning, when Eight or Ten of the best Years of a Man's Life must be spent in learning to Read. The most considerable Specimen of *Chinese* Learning that we have, is in the Writings of *Confucius*; which, if F. *Couplet* and his Companions had printed under their own Names, (*y*) *those Rules and Instructions discoursed of with great Compass of Knowledge, Excellence of Sense, Reach of Wit, illustrated with Elegance of Stile, and Aptness of Similitudes and Examples,* would soon have been called an incoherent Rhapsody

(*x*) *Hist. Sinic. Praefat.*

(*y*) Pag. 178.

sody of Moral Sayings, with which good Sense and tolerable Experience might have furnished any Man, as well as *Confucius*.

If the *Chineses* think every part of Knowledge, but their own *Confucian* Ethics, ignoble and mechanical, why are the *Europaean* Missionaries so much respected for their Skill in Medicine and Mathematics? So much Knowledge in Mathematics as will but just serve an Almanack-maker, will do their Business. F. *Verbiest* says, in a Letter printed some Years since in the *Philosophical Transactions*, That the Honours which were paid him in the Emperor's Court, were in a great measure owing to his Teaching the Emperor to find the Time of the Night by the Fixed Stars, and an Astrolabe: This shews that the *Chineses* were but meanly skilled in these Things; and it is probable, that those who are ignorant of such ordinary Matters, seldom carry their Speculations to a much greater Height.

Martinius and *Trigautius*, who lived long in *China*, were able fully to inform the World of the Extent of the *Chinese* Knowledge; and the Pains which *Martinius* has taken to write the History, and to state the Geography of that mighty Empire, is a sufficient Indication of his great Willingness to advance its Reputation in *Europe*. The *Chineses* are certainly a sagacious

ous and industrious People, and their Skill in many Mechanical Arts shew them to be so; so that if they had ever applied themselves to Learning in good earnest, and that for near so long a Time, as their History pretends to, there is no Question but we should have heard much more of their Progress. And therefore, whatsoever can be said of *Chinese* Knowledge, can never be of any weight, as long as small Skill in *Physic* and *Mathematics* shall be enough to protect the *Europaean* Missionaries in a Court where they themselves are esteemed the greatest Scholars, and honoured accordingly.

But the *Chinese Physic* is wonderfully commended by Dr. *Vossius* and Sir *William Temple* (z): *The Physicians excel in the Knowledge of the Pulse, and of all simple Medicines, and go little further: Neither need they; for in the first, they are so skilful, that they pretend not only to tell by it, how many Hours or Days a sick Man may last; but how many Years a Man in* perfect seeming *Health may live, in case of no Accident or Violence; and by Simples, they pretend to relieve all Diseases that Nature will allow to be cured.* What this boasted Skill is, may be seen in the little Tracts of the *Chinese Physic,* published by *Andrew Cleyer* (a); but because few will, in all probability, have patience to go through with them,

(z) Pag. 179, 180.

(a) Specimen Medicinae Sinicae Francof 1682. Quarto.

since

since they are not very pleasant to read, I shall give a short Specimen of them, by which one may judge of the rest.

The most Ancient *Chinese* Discourse of Physic, entituled, *Nuy Kim* (*b*), gives this Account of the Production of our Bodies, and of the Relation of the several Parts, with the Five Elements:

(*b*) Ibid. Pag. 85, 86, 87.

' Out of the Eastern Region arises the
' Wind, out of the Wind Wood, or Plants,
' out of Wood Acidity, from thence the
' Liver, from the Liver the Nerves, from
' them the Heart: The Liver is genera-
' ted the Third in Order, and perfected
' the Eighth: The Spirits of the Liver,
' as they relate to the Heaven (the Air)
' are Wind; as Wood in the Earth, as the
' Nerves in our Bodies, so is the Liver in
' the Limbs: Its Colour is Blue, and its
' Use and Action is to move the Nerves:
' The Eyes are the Windows of the Liver;
' its Tast is acid, its Passion or Affection is
' Anger: Anger hurts the Liver, but Sor-
' row and Compassion conquer Anger, be-
' cause Sorrow is the Passion of the Lungs,
' and the Lungs are Enemies to the Liver:
' Wind hurts the Nerves, but Drought,
' the Quality of the Lungs, conquers
' Wind: Acidity hurts the Nerves, but
' Acrimony, or that sharp Tast which is
' proper to the Lungs, conquers Acidity,
' or Metal conquers Wood.

' Out

'Out of the Southern Region arises
'Heat, out of Heat Fire, out of Fire Bit-
'ternefs: From it the Heart is generated,
'thence the Blood; out of Blood comes
'the Spleen, or Earth out of Fire; the
'Heart governs the Tongue; that which
'is Heat in Heaven, Fire upon Earth,
'Pulfation in the Body, is the Heart in the
'Members: Its Colour is Red, has the
'Sound of Laughing; its Viciffitudes are
'Joy and Sorrow; the Tongue is its Win-
'dow, its Taft Bitternefs, its Paffion Joy;
'too much Joy hurts the Heart; but
'Fear, the Paffion of the Reins, which
'are Enemies to the Heart, conquers Joy:
'Heat hurts the Spirits, but Cold con-
'quers Heat: Bitternefs hurts the Spirits,
'but Saltnefs of the Reins conquers Bit-
'ternefs, or Water quenches Fire. The
'Heart is generated the Second in Order,
'and is perfected the Seventh.

'Out of the Middle Region arifeth
'Moifture; out of that Earth; out of
'Earth Sweetnefs; from Sweetnefs com-
'eth the Spleen, Flefh from that, and the
'Lungs from Flefh: The Spleen governs
'the Mouth; that which is Moifture in
'the Heaven, is Earth in Earth, Flefh in
'the Body, and the Spleen in the Mem-
'bers: Its Colour is Yellow; it has the
'Sound of Singing; its Window is the
'Mouth, its Taft is fweet, its Paffion is
'much

'much Thoughtfulness: Thoughtfulness hurts the Spleen, but Anger conquers Thoughtfulness: Moisture hurts Flesh, but Wind conquers Moisture: Sweetness hurts Flesh, but Acidity conquers Sweetness: In a word, Wood conquers Earth, or the Liver the Spleen. The Spleen is generated the Fifth in Order, and is perfected the Tenth.

'Out of the Western Region arises Drought: Thence come Metals, from them comes Sharpness, out of that are the Lungs, out of the Lungs comes Skin and Hair, out of Skin and Hair come the Reins; the Lungs govern the Nostrils; That which is Drought in the Heaven (or Air) is Metal in the Earth, Hair and Skin in the Body, and Lungs in the Members: Its Colour is Whitish, has the Sound of Weeping; its Windows are the Nostrils, its Taft is sharp, its Passion is Sorrow: Sorrow hurts the Lungs, but Joy conquers Sorrow: Heat hurts the Skin and Hair, but the Cold of the Reins conquers Heat: Sharpness hurts the Skin and Hair, but Bitterness conquers Sharpness. The Lungs are generated the Fourth in Order, and are perfected the Ninth.

'Out of the Northern Region arises Cold, out of Cold comes Water, thence Saltness, thence the Reins, thence the

'Mar-

'Marrow of the Bones, thence the Liver.
'The Reins govern the Ears; that which
'is Cold in the Air, Water in the Earth,
'Bones in the Body, is Reins in the Mem-
'bers: Its Colour is Blackish, has the
'Sound of Sobbing; its Windows are the
'Ears, its Taſt is Saltneſs, its Paſſion is
'Fear: Fear hurts the Reins, but Thought-
'fulneſs conquers Fear: Cold hurts the
'Blood, but Drought conquers Cold:
'Saltneſs hurts the Blood, but Sweetneſs
'conquers Saltneſs. The Reins are gene-
'rated the Firſt in Order, and perfected
'the Sixth.

The Miſſionary who ſent this Account to *Cleyer* a Phyſician at *Batavia*, was afraid (*c*) that it would be thought ridiculous by *Europaeans*; which Fear of his ſeems to have been well grounded. Another who lived long in *China*, wrote alſo an Account of the *Chineſe* Notions of the Nature and Difference of Pulſes, which he (*d*) profeſſes that he would not undertake to prove by *Europaean* Principles. One may judge of their Worth by the following Specimen (*e*):

'The *Chineſes* divide the Body into
'Three Regions: The Firſt is from the
'Head to the Diaphragm: The Second
'from thence to the Navel, containing
'Stomach, Spleen, Liver and Gall, and
'the Third to the Feet, containing the

(*c*) *Riſum forte plus movebit Europaeo, quam plauſum* ibid. pag 87

(*d*) *Haud-quaquam ſuſcipiam principia iſta principiis noſtratibus pro-banda* ib. pag 2
(*e*) Ibid. pag 3, 4

'Blad-

'Bladder, Ureters, Reins and Guts. To
'these Three Regions, they assign Three
'sorts of Pulses in each Hand. The up-
'permost Pulse is governed by the radical
'Heat, and is therefore in its own Nature
'overflowing and great. The lowermost
'is governed by the Radical Moisture,
'which lies deeper than the rest, and is
'like a Root to the rest of the Branches:
'The middlemost lies between them both,
'partakes equally of Radical Heat and
'Moisture, and answers to the middle Re-
'gion of the Body, as the uppermost and
'lowermost do to the other two. By
'these Three sorts of Pulses, they pre-
'tend to examine all sorts of Acute Dis-
'eases, and these also are examined Three
'several Ways: Diseases in the Left-Side
'are shewn by the Pulses of the Left-
'Hand, and Diseases in the Right-Side by
'the Pulses of the Right.

It would be tedious to dwell any longer upon such Notions as these, which every Page in *Cleyer*'s Book is full of: The Anatomical Figures annexed to the Tracts, which also were sent out of *China*, are so very whimsical, that a Man would almost believe the whole to be a Banter, if these Theories were not agreeable to the occasional Hints that may be found in the Travels of the Missionaries. This, however, does no Prejudice to their Simple Medicines.

cines, which may, perhaps, be very admirable, and which a long Experience may have taught the *Chineses* to apply with great success; and it is possible that they may sometimes give not unhappy Guesses in ordinary Cases, by feeling their Patients Pulses: Still this is little to Physic, as an Art; and however, the *Chineses* may be allowed to be excellent Empiricks, as many of the *West-Indian* Salvages are, yet it cannot be believed that they can be tolerable Philosophers; which, in an Enquiry into the Learning of any Nation, is the first Question that is to be considered.

Thus I have taken a short View of the Learning of the East. Sir *William Temple* is not the only Man who has asserted great things concerning it. Other Men, to strengthen their particular Hypotheses, have exalted it as much as he: Of all these, few have taken greater Pains than Dr. *Burnet* (*f*), who having given us a new Theory of the Creation and the Deluge, was obliged to examine into the Traditions of the oldest Nations, especially those which pretended most to ancient Monuments of their own Extraction, and the Origination of Mankind. If his Enquiries have not proved what he particularly designed they should, which was, the attesting to the Truth of his own Hypotheses: yet they have proved an almost universal Tradition of the World's

(*f*) *Archaeolog. Philosoph.*

World's being once made out of a Chaos, with many other Points, which do exceedingly strengthen our Belief of the *Mosaical History*. He ingenuously owns, that when once the Business came to downright Reasoning, to raising Principles, and drawing Conclusions from those Principles, the *Greeks* went very much beyond their Teachers; and he does as good as confess, that all the *Barbaric Philosophy* was either *Traditionary* or *Superstitious*. His Authority is of great Moment here, because his Design led him to make an Accurate Enquiry into these Things; which Design he has very carefully executed.

Now, if the Philosophy of the Eastern Nations was all *Traditionary*, 'tis plain their other Learning could not be profound. For great Skill in *Geometry*, *Astronomy*, *Natural History*, the *Experimental* part of *Physic's*, or *Medicine*, will naturally lead Men into Enquiries into the Causes of the *Phaenomena* which daily occur. Those Enquiries will necessarily produce Principles and Hypotheses; which Principles and Hypotheses, though for want of sufficient Light, they may be precarious and groundless, yea, sometimes, possibly, absurd and phantastical, yet will evidently shew, that the Philosophers who devised them, were Men of Search and Reasoning, of Knowledge and Experience.

The

The several Hypotheses of Ancient and Modern Philosophers, since Hypotheses have first been introduced to account for the *Phaenomena* of *Nature*, do plainly prove this Matter. The *Aristotelians*, who solve all by a Mixture of the Four Elements, go uppon Observations and Experiments, such as they are. The *Ancient Chymists*, who found Salt, Sulphur and Mercury in all Mix'd Bodies, prove (as they think) their Hypothesis by Matter of Fact. So the more Modern ones; some of whom compound every thing out of Acids and *Alkali*'s; others join with the Corpuscularians, who solve all by the various Motions of Minute Bodies. Still all these Sects pretend Observation and Experience: and the successive Alteration of their Hypotheses, shews that their Stock of Knowledge did proportionably encrease. Wherefore, since this has been the Constant, and is the Natural Method, we ought to conclude, that if the *Barbaric Philosophy* had been built upon such Foundations, it would have produced like Effects.

Whereas *Tradition*, the Fountain of all their Knowledge, is only the Effect of Memory: And as it shews, that there is no Inquisitive Genius (the Mother of all Knowledge) in the People who content themselves with it, so all Acquiescence in it is utterly inconsistent with great Progresses in Natu-

Natural Learning, of any sort, unless, perhaps, we should except Abstracted Mathematics; which too, whether they need be excepted, may be justly questioned.

If, indeed, the Traditions of the East had comprehended a System of Natural Knowledge, had given an Account of the leading *Phaenomena* of the Universe, had, in short, been any thing else but bare Memorials, and those short, imperfect and obscure, of what the World once was, and what it should hereafter be, they would be much more valuable for the present purpose, than any Conclusions made by the exactest Reasoning possible. They would then, as they ought, be esteemed as Revelations made by Him that made the World, and consequently, could best tell in what Manner, and for what Ends and Purposes he has created, and does preserve this Planetary System in which we live. But since this is not pretended to, and if it were, could not be made good, I cannot possibly see how those who allow the *Greeks* to have been the chief Advancers of *Science* as opposed to *Tradition* amongst the Ancients, can deny that Natural Learning, in every Particular, was carried to a greater height by them, than by any of the Oriental Nations.

It is therefore now high time to leave those Countries, in some of which there seems never to have been any solid Learning origi-

originally, and in the rest but the beginnings of it, to come to *Greece*, as it stood in the Age of *Aristotle, Theophrastus, Euclid*, and those other Great Men, who, about the Time of *Alexander the Great*, and afterwards, made such mighty Progresses in almost all Parts of real Learning. If, upon Enquiry, it shall be found, that a Comparison may be made between these Ancients and the Moderns, upon any Heads wherein Learning is principally concerned, which will not be to the Disadvantage of the latter, then there needs not any thing to be said farther. Whether it can or no, is now to be enquired.

CHAP. XIII.

Of Ancient and Modern Logic and Metaphysics.

Since all that has been said in the Second and Third Chapters, concerning the *Ethics, Politics, Eloquence* and *Poesie* of the Ancient *Graecians*, belongs to them in their most flourishing Ages, a great part of the Subject Matter of this Enquiry has already been dispatched. The remaining Parts of their knowledge may be reduced to these

Four

Four Heads: *Logic, Metaphysics, Mathematics* and *Physiology*. *Logic* is the *Art of Reasoning*; but by it Men commonly understand the Art of Disputing, and making Syllogisms; of Answering an Adversary's Objections dexterously, and making such others as cannot easily be evaded: In short, of making a plausible Defense, or starting probable Objections, for or against any Thing. As this is taught in the Schools, it is certainly owing to the Ancients: *Aristotle's Organum* is the great Text by which Modern *Logicians* have framed their Systems; and nothing, perhaps, can be devised more subtle in that captious Art (g), than the Sophisms of the Ancient *Stoics*. But as *Logic* is truly the Art of Reasoning justly, so as not only to be able to explain our own Notions, and prove our own Assertions, clearly and distinctly, but to carry our Speculations farther than other Men have carried theirs, upon the same Arguments; it has not only been much cultivated by Modern Philosophers, but as far pursued as ever it was by the Ancients: For hereby have the late Enquiries been made into *Physical, Metaphysical* and *Mathematical* Matters, the Extent whereof is hereafter to be examined. Hereby the Ancient *Mathematicians* made their Discoveries, and when they had done, they concealed their Art; for, though we have many noble Propositions

(g) Vid. *A. Gellii Noct Attic.* lib. 1. cap 2.

tions of theirs, yet we have few Hints how they found them out; since the Knowledge of the fore-going Books in *Euclid's Elements* is necessary to explain the Subsequent; but is of little or no use to help us to find out any Propositions in the subsequent Books, (which are not immediate Corollaries from what went before) in case those Books had been lost. Whether the Moderns have been deficient in this noble Part of *Logic*, may be seen by those who will compare *Des Cartes's Discourse of Method*, Mr. *Lock's Essay of Humane Understanding*, and *Tschirnhaus's Medicina Mentis*, with what we have of the Ancients concerning the *Art of Thinking*. Such a Comparison would not be to the Disadvantage of these Modern Authors; for, though it may be pretended, that their Thoughts and Discoveries are not entirely new in themselves, yet to us, at least, they are so, since they are not immediately owing to ancient Assistances, but to their own Strength of Thinking, and Force of Genius. And since this Art is, indeed, the Foundation of all Knowledge, I ought to take notice, that my Lord *Bacon* and *Des Cartes* were the two Great Men, who both found fault with the *Logic* of the Schools, as insufficient of it self for the great Design of *Logic*, which is the Advancement of real Learning; and got Authority enough to persuade the World, in a very great degree, that other Methods must be taken, besides making Syllogisms, and ranking the Sorts of Things under Predicaments and Predicables, by those who would go much farther than their Predecessors went before them. The true Use of the common *Logic*, being rather to explain what we know already, and to detect the Fallacies of our Adversaries, than to find that out, of which we before were ignorant. So that the Moderns have enlarged its Bottom; and by adding that *Desideratum* which the Ancients either did not perfectly know, or, which is worse, did invidiously conceal, namely, *the Method of Discovering Unknown Truths*, as Monsieur *Tschirnhaus* calls it, have, if not made it perfect, yet put it into such a Posture, as that future Industry may very happily compleat it.

Metaphysics is properly that Science which teaches us those Things that are out the Sphere of Matter and Motion, and is conversant about God, and Spirits, and Incorporeal Substances. Of these Things *Plato* and his Disciples wrote a great deal: They plainly saw, that something beyond Matter was requisite to create and preserve the August Frame of the World. If we abstract from Revelation, the *Cartesians* discourse more intelligibly concerning them, than any of the Ancients. So that though very

very many of their particular Notions, as also of F. *Mallebranche's*, and other Modern *Metaphysicians*, are justly liable to exception, yet the main Foundations upon which they reason, are, for the most part, real; and so, by consequence, the Superstructures are not entirely fantastical: And therefore they afford a vast Number of Hints to those who love to apply their Thoughts that way, which are useful to enlarge Men's Understandings, and to guide their Manners. This, which is strictly true of the Modern *Metaphysics*, is as much as can be said of the Ancient: And because a Comparison cannot be made without reading their several Writings, the surest way to try the Truth of this Proposition, will be to read *Plato* and his Commentators; and along with them, *Des Cartes's Meditations*, *Velthuysius de Initiis primae Philosophiae*, *Mallebranche's Recherche de la Verité*, and Mr. *Lock's Essay of Humane Understanding*, already mentioned. This may be done, without undervaluing what the Ancients wrote upon these noble Subjects: And the Question is not, *Whether they were Great Men*; But, *Whether the Moderns have said any thing upon these Matters, without Copying out of other Men's Writings?* Which, unless we will do them Wrong, we are bound to say they have.

CHAP. XIV.

Of Ancient and Modern Geometry and Arithmetic.

IN the Method which I set to my self in these *Reflections*, I chose to begin with an Enquiry into those Sciences whose Extent is more liable to be contested, and so onwards, to those in which the Controversy may more easily be determined. Monsieur *Perrault*, who has not finished his *Parallel*, that I know of, took it for granted, that if the Prize were allowed to the Moderns in *Eloquence*, in *Poesie*, in *Architecture*, in *Painting*, and in *Statuary*, the Cause would be given up in every thing else; and he, as the declared Advocate for the Moderns, might go on triumphantly with all the rest. Wherein, possibly, he was not, in the main, much mistaken. How he intends to manage the remaining Part of his *Parallel*, I know not. I shall begin with *Abstracted Mathematics*; both because all its Propositions are of Eternal Truth, and besides, are the Genuine Foundations upon which all real *Physiology* must be built.

The

The Method which I shall follow is this: (1.) I shall enquire into the State of Ancient and Modern *Mathematics*, without any particular Application of the Properties of the several Lines and Numbers, Surfaces and Solids, to Physical Things. (2.) I shall enquire what New Instruments have been invented, or Old ones improved, by which the Knowledge of Nature of any sort has been, or may be, farther enlarged. (3.) I shall enquire whether any Improvements have been actually made of *Natural History*, and of any *Physico-Mathematical* or *Physical Sciences*, such as *Astronomy, Music, Optics, Medics*, and the like. (4.) From all this, I shall endeavour to pass a Judgment upon the Ancient and Modern Ways of *Philosophizing* concerning Nature in general, and its principal *Phaenomena*, or *Appearances*.

I begin with *Geometry* and *Arithmetic*, because they are general Instruments whereby we come to the Knowledge of many of the abstrusest Things in Nature; since, as *Plato* said of old, *God always Geometrizes in all his Works*. That this Comparison might be the more exact, I desired my Learned and Worthy Friend, Mr. *John Craig*, to give me his Thoughts upon this Matter; His own learned Writings upon the most difficult Parts of *Geometry*, for such are the *Quadratures of Curve Lines*, will be sufficient Vouchers for his Skill in these Things. I shall set down what he says, in his own Words:

'If we take a short View of the *Geo-*
'*metry* of the Ancients, it appears, that
'they considered no *Lines*, except *Streight*
'*Lines*, the *Circle*, and the *Conic Sections*:
'As for the *Spiral*, the *Quadratrix*, the
'*Conchoid*, the *Cissoid*, and a few others,
'they made little or no Account of them.
'It is true, they have given us many ex-
'cellent and useful Theorems concerning
'the Properties of these others, but far
'short of what has been discovered since.
'Thus, to instance in the *Quadrature* of
'the *Circle*, which did so much exercise
'and perplex the Thoughts of the Anci-
'ents; How imperfect is that of *Archime-*
'*des*, in comparison of that exhibited by
'*Van Ceulen?* And every body knows how
'this is exceeded by the later Performances
'of Mr. *Newton*, and Monsieur *Leibnitz*.
'*Archimedes*, with a great deal of La-
'bour, has given us the exact *Quadrature*
'of the *Parabola*; but the Rectification
'of the *Parabolic Line*, depending on the
'*Quadrature* of the *Hyperbola*, is the In-
'vention of this last Age. The rare Pro-
'perties of the *Conic Sections*, in the *Re-*
'*flexion* and *Refraction* of *Light*, are the
'undoubted Discoveries of these later
'Times. It were easie to give more In-
'stances

'ſtances of this nature, but theſe are ſuf-
'ficient to ſhew how far the Modern Ma-
'thematicians have out-done the Ancients,
'in diſcovering the nobleſt and uſefulleſt
'Theorems, even of thoſe few Figures
'which they chiefly conſidered.

'But all this is nothing, in compariſon
'of that boundleſs Extent which the Mo-
'dern Mathematicians have carried Geo-
'metry on to: Which conſiſts in their re-
'ceiving into it all the *Curve Lines* in Na-
'ture, together with the *Area's* and *Solids*
'that reſult from them; by diſtinguiſhing
'them into certain *Kinds* and *Orders*; by
'giving general Methods of deſcribing
'them, of determining their *Tangents*,
'their *Lengths*, their *Area's*, and the *Solids*
'made by the Rotation of them about their
'Axes. Add to all this, the general Me-
'thods that have been invented of late for
'finding the Properties of a great Number
'of theſe *Curves*, for the Advancement of
'*Optics, Mechanics*, and other Parts of *Phi-*
'*loſophy*: And let any Man of Senſe give
'the Preference to the Ancient Geometry
'if he can.

'That the Ancients had general Me-
'thods of Conſtructing all plain Problems
'by a ſtreight Line and a Circle, as alſo all
'Solid Problems by the help of a Conic
'Section, is moſt certain. But it is as certain
'that here they ſtopped, and could go no
'farther,

'farther, because they would not receive
'any Order of Curves beyond the Conic
'Sections, upon some nice Scrupulosity in
'multiplying the Number of the *Postulata*,
'requisite to the describing of them.
'Whereas the Modern Geometers, parti-
'cularly the Renowned *Des Cartes*, have
'given general Rules for Constructing all
'Problems of the Vth or VIth Degree.
'Which Method, if rightly understood, is
'applicable to all Problems of any Superi-
'or Order.

'How deficient the Geometry of the
'Ancients was in that Part which related
'to the *Loca Geometrica*, is manifest from
'the Account that *Pappus* gives us of that
'Question, about which *Euclid* and *Apollo-*
'*nius* made so many ineffectual Attempts:
'The Solution whereof we owe entirely
'to Mr. *Isaac Newton* (h). For it is evi-
'dent, that *Des Cartes* mistook the true
'Intent of the Ancients in this Matter. So
'that the *Loca Solida* is now one of the
'perfectest Parts of Geometry that we have,
'which before was one of the most confu-
'sed and defective.

'From comparing the Ancient and Mo-
'dern Geometry, I proceed to the Com-
'parison of those Arts to which we owe
'the Improvements both of the one and
'the other. These are chiefly Two, *Al-*
'*gebra*, and the *Method of Indivisibles*. As

(h) Philos. P. 74, 75.

'to the latter of these, I shall not stand to
'enquire whether *Cavallerius* was the first
'Inventor, or only the Restorer of it. I
'know Dr. *Wallis* (i) is of Opinion, that (i) *Hist. of*
'it is nothing but the Ancients *Method of* *Algebra,* p. 285
'*Exhaustions,* a little disguised. It is enough
'for your Purpose, that by the help of
'*Cavallerius*'s Method, Geometry has been
'more promoted in this last Age, than it
'was in all the Ages before. It not only
'affords us neat and short Demonstrations,
'but shews us how to find out the abstru-
'sest Theorems in Geometry. So that there
'has hardly been any considerable improve-
'ment of late, which does not owe its Rise
'to it; as any Man may see, that consi-
'ders the Works of *Cartes*, *Fermat*, *Van*
'*Heuraet*, *Huygens*, *Neil*, *Wallis*, *Barrow*,
'*Mercator*, *Leibnitz*, and *Newton*. *Archi-*
'*medes*'s Propositions of the Properties of
'a Sphere, and a Cylinder, are some of the
'easiest Examples of this Method. How
'vastly more curious and more useful The-
'orems have been since added to Geome-
'try, is known to every one that is conver-
'sant in the afore-mentioned Authors; es-
'pecially Mr. *Newton*, *Leibnitz*, and *Huy-*
'*gens*: To instance in particulars, were to
'transcribe their whole Books and Treatises.
  'Let us, in the next place, compare the
'*Ancient* and *Modern Algebra*. That the
'Ancients had some kind of *Algebra* like

M 4 'unto

'unto ours, is the Opinion of several learn-
'ed Writers of late: And it is evident from
'the Seven remaining Books of *Diophantus*,
'that it was brought to a considerable
'Length in his Time. But how infinitely
'short this was of that *Algebra* which we
'now have, since *Vieta*'s Time, will ap-
'pear to any one that considers the diffe-
'rent Process of both. For, though *Dio-
'phantus* has given us the Solution of a
'great many hard and knotty Arithmeti-
'cal Problems, yet the last Step of his
'Resolution serves only for one particular
'Example of each Problem: So that for
'every new Example of the same Questi-
'on, there must be a new Process made of
'the whole *Analysis*. Whereas by our Mo-
'dern *Algebra*, the *Analysis* of any one
'Case gives a general Canon for all the in-
'finite Cases of each Problem; whereby
'we discover many curious Theorems a-
'bout the Properties of Numbers, not to
'be attained by *Diophantus*'s Method; this
'being the peculiar Advantage of *Specious
'Algebra*, first introduced by *Vieta*, and
'wonderfully promoted by several worthy
'Mathematicians since. Beside this into-
'lerable Imperfection of the Ancient *Al-
'gebra*, used by *Diophantus*, which requi-
'red as many different Operations as the
'Problem had different Examples, that is,
'infinite: all which are included in one
'ge-

'general Solution by the Modern *Algebra*;
'there is this great Defect in it, that in
'*Undetermined Questions*, which are capa-
'ble of innumerable Solutions, *Diophan-*
'*tus's Algebra* can seldom find any more
'than one; whereas, by the Modern *Al-*
'*gebra*, we can find innumerable, some-
'times all in one Analysis; tho' in many
'Problems we are obliged to re-iterate the
'Operation for every new Answer. This
'is sufficient to let you see, that (even in
'the Literal Sence) our *Algebra* does infi-
'nitely exceed that of the Ancients. Nor
'does the Excellency of our *Algebra* ap-
'pear less in the great Improvements of
'Geometry. The reducing all Problems to
'Analytical Terms, has given Rise to those
'many excellent Methods whereby we
'have advanced Geometry infinitely be-
'yond the Limits assigned to it by the An-
'cients. To this we owe, (1.) The Expres-
'sing all Curves by Equations, whereby we
'have a View of their Order, proceeding
'gradually on *in infinitum*. (2.) The
'Method of Constructing all Problems
'of any Assignable Dimension; whereas
'the Ancients never exceeded the Third.
'Nay, from the Account which *Pappus*
'gives us of the afore-mentioned Que-
'ition, it is evident, that the Ancients
'could go no further than Cubic Equa-
'tions: For he says expresly, they knew

'not

'not what to make of the continual Mul-
'tiplication of any Number of Lines more
'than Three; they had no Notion of it.
'(3.) The Method of Measuring the
'*Area's* of many Infinities of Curvilinear
'Spaces; whereas *Archimedes* laboured
'with great Difficulty, and wrote a par-
'ticular Treatise of the Quadrature of on-

(k) The Parabola.

'ly one (k), which is the simplest and
'easiest in Nature. (4.) The Method of
'Determining the Tangents of all Geome-
'tric Curve Lines; whereas the Ancients
'went no further than in Determining the
'Tangents of the Circle and Conic Secti-
'ons. (5.) The Method of Determining
'the Lengths of an infinite Number of
'Curves; whereas the Ancients could ne-
'ver measure the Length of one. If I
'should descend to Particulars, the Time
'would fail me. As our *Algebra*, so also
'our *Common Arithmetic* is prodigiously
'more perfect than theirs; of which, *De-
'cimal Arithmetic* and *Logarithms* are so
'evident a Proof, that I need say no more
'about it.

'I would not be thought, however, to
'have any Design to sully the Reputation
'of those Great Men, *Conon*, *Archimedes*,
'*Euclid*, *Apollonius*, &c. who, if they had
'lived to enjoy our Assistance, as we now
'do some of theirs, would, questionless,
'have been the greatest Ornaments of this
'Age,

'Age, as they were deservedly the greatest Glory of their own." Thus far Mr. *Craig*.

Those that have the Curiosity to see some of these Things proved at large, which Mr. *Craig* has contracted into one View, may be amply satisfied in Dr. *Wallis*'s *History of Algebra*, joined with *Gerhard Vossius*'s *Discourses De Scientiis Mathematicis*.

It must not here be forgotten, that Abstracted Mathematical Sciences were exceedingly valued by the ancientest Philosophers: None, that I know of, expressing a Contempt of them but *Epicurus*, though all did not study them alike. *Plato* is said to have written over the Door of his Academy, *Let no Man enter here, who does not understand Geometry.* None of all the Learned Ancients has been more extolled by other Learned Ancients, than *Archimedes*. So that, if in these Things the Moderns have made so great a Progress, this affords a convincing Argument, that it was not want of Genius which obliged them to stop at, or to come behind the Ancients in any thing else,

CHAP.

CHAP. XV.

Of several Instruments invented by the Moderns, which have helped to advance Learning.

HAving now enquired into the State of *Mathematics*, as they relate to *Lines* and *Numbers* in *general*, I am next to go to those Sciences which consider them as they are applied to *Material Things*. But these being of several Sorts, and of a vast Extent, taking in no less than the whole Material World, it ought to be observed, that they cannot be brought to any great Perfection, without Numbers of Tools, or Arts, which may be of the same Use as Tools, to make the Way plain to several Things, which otherwise, without their Help, would be inaccessible.

Of these Tools, or Instruments, some were anciently invented, and those Inventions were diligently pursued: Others are wholly new. According to their Uses, they may be ranged under these Two General Heads: (1.) Those which are useful to all Parts of Learning, though perhaps not to all alike. (2.) Those which are particularly subservient to a Natural Philo-

Philosopher, and a Mathematician. Under the first Head one may place *Printing*, *Paper of Rags*, and *Engraving*. Under the latter come *Telescopes*, *Microscopes*, *Thermometers*, the *Baroscopes*, the *Air-Pumps*, *Pendulum-Clocks*, *Chymistry*, and *Anatomy*. All these, but the two last, were absolutely unknown to the Ancient *Greeks* and *Romans*. *Chymistry* was known to the *Greeks*, and from them carried to the *Arabs*. *Anatomy* is, at least, as old as *Democritus* and *Hippocrates*; and doubtless, among the exact *Aegyptians*, something older.

The Benefit of *Printing* has been so vast, that every thing else wherein the Moderns have pretended to excell the Ancients, is almost entirely owing to it: And withal, its general Uses are so obvious, that it would be Time lost to enlarge upon them; but it must be taken notice of, because Sir *William Temple* has question'd (*l*) whether Printing *has multiplied Books, or only the Copies of them*; from whence he concludes, that we are not to suppose that the Ancients had not equal Advantages by the Writings of those that were ancient to them, as we have by the Writings of those that are ancient to us. But he may easily solve his own Doubt, if he does but reflect upon the Benefit to Learning which arises from the *multiplying Copies* of good Books: For though it should be allowed, that there

(*l*) Pag. 6.

there were anciently as many Books as there are now, which is scarce credible; yet still the Moderns have hereby a vast Advantage, because, (1.) Books are much cheaper, and so come into more Hands. (2.) They are much more easily read: and so there is no Time lost in poring upon bad Hands, which weary the Readers, and spoil their Eyes. (3.) They can be printed with Indexes, and other necessary Divisions, which, though they might be made in MSS. yet they would then make them so voluminous and cumbersome, that not one in forty who now mind Books, because they love Reading, would then apply themselves to it. (4.) The Notice of new and excellent Books is more easily dispersed. (5.) The Text is hereby better preserved entire, and is not so liable to be corrupted by the Ignorance or Malice of Transcribers; this is of great Moment in Mathematics, where the Alteration of a Letter, or a Cypher, may make a Demonstration unintelligible.

Paper made of *Linnen Rags*, may, in a larger sence, be reckoned also amongst Modern Inventions; the Improvement of which to the present Fineness and Cheapness, is almost of as great Advantage to Learning, as *Printing* it self: And if we were, with the Old *Greeks* and *Romans*, obliged to Write upon *Barks of Plants*, smooth-

smoothed Wood, Wax, or *Parchment*, we should soon think so; since Instruments easily got, even though they should in some things be inferior to others, do, by making Men's Labours easie and pleasant, exceedingly contribute to encrease their Industry, and excite their Emulation. But to say more upon these Subjects, would be to abuse Men's Patience, since these things are so plain, that they need no Proof.

Engraving upon Wood, or *Copper*, is of great Use in all those Parts of Knowledge where the Imagination must be assisted by sensible Images. For want of this noble Art, the *Ancient Books* of *Natural History*, and *Mechanical Arts*, are almost every where obscure, in many places unintelligible. *Mathematical Diagrams*, which need only a Ruler and a Pair of Compasses, could be drawn with more Ease, which has been a means of their being better preserved: But in *Anatomy*, in *Mechanics*, in *Geography*, in all Parts of *Natural History*, *Engraving* is so necessary, and has been so very advantageous, that without it, many of those Arts and Sciences would to this hour have received very little Encrease. For when the Images, the Proportions, and the Distances of those Things wherein a Writer intends to instruct his Reader, are fully and minutely engraven

in

in Prints, it not only saves abundance of Words, by which all Descriptions must of necessity be obscured, but it makes those Words which are used, full and clear; so that a skilful Reader is thereby enabled to pass an exact Judgment, and can understand his Authors without a Master, which otherwise it would be impossible to do, so as to be able to discern all, even the minutest Mistakes and Oversights in their Writings, which puts an end to Disputes, and encreases Knowledge.

These are general Instruments, and more or less serviceable to all sorts of Learned Men in their several Professions and Sciences: Those that follow, are more particular: I shall begin with those that assist the Eye, either to discern Objects that are too far off, or too small.

The *Imperfections* of *Distance* are remedied in a great measure by *Telescopes*, whose chief Use, that comes under our Consideration, is to discern the Stars, and other Celestial Bodies.

To find out the first Inventor of these sorts of Glasses, it will be necessary to learn who first found out the Properties of Convex and Concave Glasses in the Refraction of Light. Dr. *Plot* has collected a great deal concerning F. *Bacon*, in his *Natural History of Oxfordshire*; which seems to put it out of doubt, that he knew

that

that great Objects might appear little, and small Objects appear great; that distant Objects would seem near, and near Objects seem afar off, by different Applications of Convex and Concave Glasses; upon the Credit of which Authorities, Mr. *Molineux* (m) attributes the Invention of Spectacles to this learned Friar, the Time to which their earliest Use may be traced, agreeing very well with the Time in which he lived; but how far F. *Bacon* went, we know not: So that we must go into *Holland* for the first Inventors of these excellent Instruments, and there they were first found out by one *Zacharias Joannides* (n), a Spectacle-maker (o) of *Middleburgh*, in *Zeland*; in MDXC he (p) presented a Telescope of Two Glasses to Prince *Maurice*, and another to Arch-Duke *Albert*, the former of whom apprehending that they might be of great Use in War, desired him to conceal his Secret. For this Reason, his Name was so little known, that neither *Des Cartes* (q) nor *Gerhard Vossius* (r) had ever heard any thing of him, when they attributed the Invention of Telescopes to *Jacobus Metius* of *Alkmaer*. However, the Invention taking Air, *Galileo Galilei* pursued the Hint, and made several Telescopes, with which he made Observations upon Heavenly Bodies, that got him immortal Honour. Thereby

(m) *Dioptric.* p 256, 257, 258.

(n) *Borel. de vero Inventore Telescopii*, p. 30.
(o) Ibid. p. 35.
(p) Ibid. p. 30.

(q) *Dioptric.*
(r) *De Scientiis Mathemat.* p. 70.

N (s) he

(s) he discovered Four Planets moving constantly round *Jupiter*, from thence usually called his *Satellits*, which afterwards were observed to have a constant, regular, and periodical Motion. This Motion is now so exactly known, that Mr. *Flamsteed*, who is one of the most accurate Observers that ever was, has been able to calculate Tables of the Eclipses of the several Satellits, according to which, Astronomers in different Quarters of the World, having Notice of the precise Time when to look for them, have found them to answer to his Predictions, and published their Observations accordingly. This is an effectual Answer to all that Rhapsody which *Stubbe* (t) has collected in his Brutal Answer to Mr. *Glanvile*'s *Plus Ultra*, about the Uncertainty of all Observations made by Telescopes; since it is impossible to calculate the Duration of any Motion justly by fallacious and uncertain Methods. By the Eclipses of *Jupiter*'s Satellits, Longitudes would soon be exactly determined, if Tubes of any Length could be managed at Sea. (u) But *Jupiter* is not the only Planet about which Things anciently unknown have been revealed by this noble Instrument. The Moon has been discovered to be an Earth endued with a libratory Motion, of an uneven Surface which has something analogous to Hills

(s) Vide *Galilaei Nuntium sidereum primo ni fallor, impressum, A D.* MDCVIII

(t) *Plus Ultra* reduced to a *Non plus*, p 28, 36

(u) Vid *Philosoph. Transact* n 177.

and Dales, Plains and Seas; and a New Geography, (if one may use that Word without a Blunder) with accurate Maps, has been Published by the Great *Hevelius* (w), and Improved by *Ricciolus* (x), by which Eclipses may be observed much more nicely than could be done formerly: The Sun has been found to have Spots at some times; the Planets to move round their Axes; *Saturn* to have a Luminous Ring round about his Body, which in some Positions appears like two Handles, as they are commonly called, or large Prominencies on opposite Parts of his Limb, carried along with him, beside Five Planets moving periodically about him, as those others do about *Jupiter*: The milky Way, to be a Cluster of numberless Stars; the other Parts of the Heaven, to be filled with an incredible Number of Fixed Stars, of which, if *Hevelius*'s Globes are ever published, the World may hope to see a Catalogue. These are some of the remarkable Discoveries that have been made by *Telescopes*: And as New Things have been revealed, so Old ones have been much more nicely observed, than formerly it was possible to observe them.

But I need not enlarge upon particular Proofs of that, which every Astronomical Book, printed within these L-Years, is full of; if I should, it would be said, perhaps,

(w) *Selenograph.*
(x) *Almagest.*

haps, that I had only copied from the *French* Author *of the Plurality of Worlds,* so often mentioned already.

As some Things are too far off, so others are too small to be seen without help. This last Defect is admirably supplied by *Microscopes,* Invented by the same *Zacharias Joannides* (*y*); which have been made useful in *Anatomical* and *Physical* Enquiries by *Malpighius, Leeuwenhoek, Grew, Havers,* and several others. The first considerable Essay to shew what might be discovered in Nature, by the help of *Microscopes,* was made by Dr. *Hook,* in his *Micrography;* wherein he made various Observations upon very different sorts of Bodies. One may easily imagine what Light they must needs give to the understanding of the nicer Mechanism of most kinds of Bodies, when Monsieur *Leeuwenhoek* has plainly proved, that he could, with his Glasses, discern Bodies several Millions of times less than a Grain of Sand. This Assertion of his, how incredible soever it may seem to those who are unacquainted with Physical Matters, may in all probability be believed, because Dr. *Hook,* who examined what *Leeuwenhoek* says of the little Animals which he discerned in Water, of which he tells the most wonderful Things, does, in his *Microscopium,* attest the Truth of *Leeuwenhoek*'s Observations.

Besides

(*y*) Borellus, *ubi supra,* p. 35.

Besides these that are of more universal Use, several other *Instruments* have been invented, which have been very serviceable to find out the Properties of Natural Bodies; and by which several Things of very great moment, utterly unknown to the Ancients, have been detected, As,

(1.) The *Thermometer*, invented (z) by *Sanctorius*, an eminent Physician of *Padua*. Its immediate Use is, to determine the several Degrees of Heat and Cold; of which our Senses can give us but uncertain Notices, because they do not so much inform us of the State of the Air in it self, as what its Operations are at that time upon our Bodies. But *Sanctorius* used only Vessels open at each end, which are of small Use, since Liquors may rise or fall in the Tubes, as well from the Encrease or Diminution of the Weight of the Air, as of Heat and Cold. That Defect was remedied by Mr. *Boyle* (a), who sealed up the Liquors in the Tubes, Hermetically, so that nothing but Heat and Cold could have any Operation upon them. The Uses to which they have been applied, may be seen at large in Mr. *Boyle's History of Cold*, and the Experiments of the Academy del Cimento.

(2.) The *Baroscope*, or *Torricellian Experiment*, so called from its Inventor, *Evangelista Torricelli*, a *Florentine* Mathematician,

(z) Borellus *de Motu Animalium*, Part II. Propos. clxxv.

(b) See his *Thermometrical Thoughts*, prefixed to his *History of Cold*.

tician, who, about the Year MDCXLIII, found that Quick-silver would stand erect in a Tube, above XXVIII Inches from the Surface of other Quick-silver into which the Tube was immersed, if it was before well purged of Air. This noble Experiment soon convinced the World, that the Air is an actually heavy Body, and gravitates upon every Thing here below. This Gravitation being found unequal at several times, Mr. *Boyle* applied this Instrument to Mechanical Uses (*b*), and shewed how it might teach us to know the Differences and changes of Weather; when dry, and when wet; since, by a vast Number of Observations, he had learn'd, that in dry Weather the Air drove up the *Mercury*, and in wet Weather let it fall again; though never lower than XXVIII Inches, and scarce ever higher than XXXII.

(*b*) *Philos. Transact.* n. 9, 10, 11,—55.

(3.) These Observations, with other Collateral Experiments, induced him to believe that the Air was, in truth, a Springy Body, which expanded or contracted it self in a Reciprocal Proportion, to the Encrease or Lessening of the Compression of the Ambient Bodies. For which he invented an Instrument to draw the Air out of Vessels that were filled with it, by Suction. The first Essays of that kind seem to have been made some Years before his appeared, by *Otto Guerick* of *Magdebourg*:

bourg: but as he applied them chiefly to the Gravitation of the Air, without taking any notice of its Spring; so they were very imperfect, when compared to Mr. *Boyle's.* By this *Air-Pump,* as it is usually called, he discovered abundance of Properties in the Air, before never suspected to be in it. What they are, either considered singly, or in their Operations upon all sorts of Bodies, may be seen at large in his *Physico-Mechanical Experiments concerning the Weight and Spring of the Air,* and in several of his other Discourses upon the same Argument, some of which are printed by themselves, and others in the (*c*) *Philosophical Transactions.* How far they may be relied upon, appears from this; That though *Hobbes* and *Linus* have taken a great deal of Pains to destroy Mr. *Boyle's* Theory, yet they have had few or no Abettors: Whereas the Doctrine *of the Weight and Spring of the Air,* first made thoroughly intelligible by Mr. *Boyle,* has universally gained Assent from Philosophers of all Nations who have, for these last XXX Years, busied themselves about Natural Enquiries.

(*c*) *Numb.* 62, 63, 122 *Vid* Catalogue of Mr *Boyle*'s Works, at the end of the First Part of the *Medicinal Experiments,* printed MDCXCII in *Twelves.*

(4.) The Invention of *Pendulum-Clocks* ought here to be remembred, because, it being certain from Astronomical Principles, and Observations, that the Diurnal Motion of the Earth is not so exactly Periodical, as that a true Equation of Time can thereby be obtained: By this Instrument, the Measure of the Variation being once adjusted, the true Time of the Earth's Diurnal Motion, can, at all Seasons of the Year, be more exactly known. Its Usefulness in making Astronomical Observations is also very obvious; for they could not anciently be so minute as they are at present, for want of such nice Sub-Divisions of an equable Motion as it affords. The Invention of this noble Instrument is attributed, by the Publisher of the Experiments of the Academy *del Cimento*, to *Galileo Galilei*, who found out so many excellent Theorems of the Nature and Proportions of the Motions of Projected and Vibrating Bodies. He says that *Galileo* first applied the *Pendulum* to *Clock-work*; and that his Son *Vincenzio* put it in practice in the Year MDCXLIX (*d*). It was little taken notice of, however, in these Parts, till Monsieur *Huygens* revived or invented it a-new; to whom, for that Reason, the Glory of finding out this useful Instrument is commonly attributed. Upon this Occasion, I ought not to omit, that great Improvement of Watches, by adding a Second Spring to balance the First, (as the *Pendulum* in a Clock does the Weights) which also is attributed to Monsieur *Huygens*.

(*d*) Experiments of the Academy del Cimento, p. 12 Eng. Edit.

gens, though he and Dr. *Hook* have both contended for the Honour of this useful Invention. It appears by the *Philosophical Transactions*, and by Dr. *Hook's Lectures*, that he had a right Notion of this Matter, and that he had made several Essays to reduce it to Practice, some Years before any of Monsieur *Huygens*'s Watches were produced; but that Monsieur *Huygens* first made *Pendulum-Watches* (so they are commonly call'd) that proved thoroughly serviceable. These will not be disputed to be Modern Inventions, since the whole Business of Clocks and Watches was unknown to all, even the (e) *Arabian* Antiquity: Their Astronomers measured their Time by Hour-Glasses of Water, or Vibrating Strings of several Lengths; which would, indeed, serve them, in most cases, to measure Time nicely by, whilst they were observing; though they were of no Use upon other Occasions, and even then were liable to great Hazards.

(e) See Dr. *Edw. Bernard*'s Letter to Dr. *Huntingdon*, about the Latitude of Twenty Fixed Stars, from *Arabian* Observations. *Philosoph. Transact.* n. 159.

CHAP.

CHAP. XVI.

Of Ancient and Modern Chymistry.

Chymistry, or the Art of Dividing Bodies by Fire, comes next to be considered. So great Things have thereby been discovered in Nature, that would have been utterly unknown without it, that it may justly be esteemed as one of the chiefest Instruments whereby Real Knowledge has been advanced. It has been cultivated by three sorts of Men, for very different Reasons; by *Refiners*, *Alchemists*, and *Chymists* properly so called. The *Refiner's* Art, which is older than the Flood, is, in *Holy Scripture*, ascribed to *Tubal-Cain*, as its first Inventor (*f*). The early Use of Gold and Silver, as Instruments of Exchange in Trade, and of Copper and Iron for Mechanical Uses, in the Eastern Parts, shews, that Men soon knew how to separate Metals from their Dross, to a great degree. And as frequent Purifications are necessary for that Work, so we find that the Necessity of them was long ago commonly known, since *David* compared a Righteous Man to Silver Seven times purified in the Fire (*g*). But though

(*f*) Gen. iv. 22.

(*g*) Psal. xii 6.

the *Ancients* knew pretty well how to Refine their Metals, and to Extract them from their Ores, in common Cases, where but one sort of Metal lay in the same Lump, or where the different Metals were easily separable; yet in nicer Cases, where many different Sorts were blended in the same Mass, and where the Metal was obstinately mixed in Stones, over which the Fire could have but small Power, both which Cases do not unfrequently occurr, they were often at a loss; and besides, being wholly ignorant of the Use of *Quick-silver* in separating Metals from their Ores, and of *Aquae-Fortes*, and the *Cupel*, by which all manner of Metals are with Ease parted from one another, their Work was laborious, bungling, and many times imperfect. Gold, indeed, which is generally found alone, might be thoroughly purified; which Silver could not be, without great Difficulty and Loss: Whereas now, since the Property of Quick-silver's incorporating will all Metals but Copper and Iron is universally known, every Workman in the *Peruvian* Mines understands that when once his Ore is duly prepared, every Particle of the Silver will *amalgamate* (as the Chymists call it) with the Mercury, and so make a Past that gives him all his Metal without any trouble; and if it is mixed with Gold, *Aqua-Regis*, will part them; if

with

with Copper, *Aqua-Fortis*; if with Lead, the *Cupel*. Nor ought we to forget that useful Invention of turning Copper into Brass with *Lapis Calaminaris*, by which its Weight is considerably augmented, its Lustre heightned, and its Usefulness for many Mechanical Purposes encreased.

It must be own'd, that Skill in *Fossils*, and particularly in *Metals*, has not been cultivated by the *Moderns* proportionably with other Parts of *Natural History*. Yet what a Difference there must arise between their Knowledge, and that of the Ancients from these few Things alone, is evident to any Man who has the least insight into these Matters. The *Ancients* were so grosly ignorant of the commonest Properties of Mercury, that they only knew that it would incorporate with Gold. We know, from *Vitruvius* and *Pliny*, that this Property of Mercury was formerly observed; and *Pliny* (*h*) adds, *That every thing swims upon Mercury but Gold; that only it draws to it self*. And how well they were skill'd in the Specific Weight of Metals, appears from their believing (*i*) that *Lead was heavier, and more ductile than Gold*. The Use and Composition of *Aquae-Fortes* is ascribed to the *Arabs*, by the Learned (*k*) in these Matters; and

(*h*) *Omnia ei* [Mercurio] *innatant praeter Aurum; id unum ad se trahit.* Plin. Nat. Hist. l. xxxiii. c. 6.

(*i*) *Nec pondere aut facilitate materiae praelatum est* [Aurum] *caeteris metallis, cum cedat per utrumque Plumbo.* Plin Nat Hist. l. xxxiii. c. 3.

(*k*) Borrichius *de Ortu & Progressu Chemiae.*

and the *Cupel* is notoriously known to be a Modern Invention. So that I think we may boldly compare the Modern Writers of Metals with the best of the Ancients, of whose Skill in these Things *Pliny* gives us a good Account, whose Writings may be set against what *Georgius Agricola, Alonso Barba, Lazarus Erckern*, and our Countryman *Webster*, have said upon these Subjects; in whose Writings, Skill in Distinguishing, Purifying, Separating and Assaying Ores and Metals, is what is chiefly to be regarded. These Things depend upon Observation and Experience, which is certain, and consequently will admit of comparison, since it may easily be decided, whose Trials and Observations of any sort have been the most Exact. It signifies nothing whose Hypotheses of the Nature, Texture, Growth, and Possibility of the Transmutation of Metals, be rightest, in the Dispute before us. Men may eternally, and will dispute *pro* and *con* about those Things which will, in all probability, lie undetermined, till either we know the Essences of Things, (which, perhaps, are not to be known in this Life,) or till Mankind be furnished with a larger stock of Experiments and Observations than yet they are. So that though several of the Modern Writers of Metals that might be named, if Show and Ostentation were proper, give very poor Accounts

of

of the Physical Nature of Minerals, yet their Experiments and Observations are never a whit the less valuable; and others who seem to Philosophize much nearer the Truth, yet are not here to be esteemed Advancers of the Stock of Knowledge upon the score of their Hypotheses; because what is still contested, is not to be given in as Evidence, especially when the Cause does not want it.

I have spoken already of *Alchemy*, or the Art of Making Gold; and so I shall pass on to the *Chymist's Art*, which consists in making such Analyses of Bodies by Fire, or other Agents, Chymically prepared, as may reduce them into more simple Substances than those out of which they were before compounded. I make a difference between the *Chymist* and the *Refiner*; because the Operations of the *Chymist* are employ'd about making useful Medicines, or Philosophical Experiments; whereas the Disquisitions of the *Refiner* terminate altogether in finding out ways how to part his Metals from their Ores, and from one another, and to purifie them from their Dross. The Discoveries therefore which have been made by *Chymistry* properly so called, are so much later than those Ages which Sir *William Temple* contends for, that those who thought they had a great deal to say for the other Parts of *Chymistry*, do here give up

the

the Controverſie. *Borrichius* himſelf owns, that *Hippocrates, Ariſtotle* and *Galen* knew ſo little of *Chymiſtry*, that they could not ſo much as make *Roſe-Water*. Now, tho' he ſays this, with a deſign to Diſparage their Skill in Phyſic, when compared with the *Aegyptian*, yet therein he deſtroys his own Hypotheſis; becauſe, in ſeveral Places of his *Vindication of the Hermetical and Chymical Philoſophy and Medicine*, againſt *Conringius*'s Book *de Medicina Hermetica*, he takes Pains to prove, that the Knowledge of theſe very Men was originally owing to the *Aegyptians*. But the Thing ſpeaks it ſelf: The Inward Uſe of Antimonial, Vitriolic and Mercurial Preparations in Phyſic, was but little known before the Time of *Baſilius Valentinus*, and *Paracelſus*: What was ancienter, was taken from the *Arabs*, who are Moderns againſt Sir *William Temple*, (*l*) They may be looked upon as the firſt Inventors of Chymical Medicine: (*l*) They firſt extracted Vinous Spirits from Fermented Liquors: Not to mention abundance of other Preparations, which *Arnoldus de Villa Nova, Raymund Lully* his Scholar, and F. *Bacon* learned from them. I will not deny but ſome Chymical Experiments were very anciently known. *Solomon* (*m*) hints at the diſagreement of *Vinegar* and *Nitre*; which, though not intelligible of common *Nitre*, yet as Mr. *Boyle* (*n*) found

(*l*) Borrichius *de Ortu & Prog Chem.* Morhofius *ad Langelottum.*

(*m*) Prov xxv 20
(*n*) Boyle' Producibleneſs of Chymical Principles p. 30, 31.

found by his own Experience, it is certainly true of *Aegypt Nitre*; which, as being a natural *Alkali*, will cause an Ebullition, when joined with any Acid Salt.

Some Passages likewise are produced by *Borrichius*, to prove that the Ancients understood something of Calcinations, and the Use of Lixiviate Salts: But these things are very few, very imperfect, and occasional. Chymistry was not esteemed as a distinct Art; or the Analyses thereby produced, worthy a Philosopher's notice; though the Industry of later Ages have found them to be so regular and remarkable, that many Persons have thought that the Constituent Principles of Mixed Bodies are no other way so certainly to be found out. Hence have the *Hypotheses* of the *Paracelsians* taken their Beginning, who held, that *Salt*, *Sulphur* and *Mercury* were the Active Principles of Composition of all Mixed Bodies. Hence several others have been led to believe, that the Primary Constituents of most Bodies were *Acid* and *Alkalizate Salts*. Which Hypotheses, though liable to many Exceptions, as Mr. *Boyle* (o) has fully proved, are founded upon such a variety of surprizing Experiments, that those who first started them, were not so unadvised, as one that is wholly unacquainted with the Laboratories of the *Chymists*, might, at first view, suspect. For it is

(o) *Sceptical Chymist* and *Producib. of Chymical Principles.*

certain

certain, that Five distinct and tolerably uniform Substances may be drawn from most Vegetable and Animal Substances, by Fire; *Phlegm, Fixed Salt, Oil, Earth,* and *Spirit,* or *Volatile Salt* dissolved in *Phlegm.* So that here is a new Field of Knowledge, of which the Ancients had no sort of Notion.

The great and successful Change hereby made (*p*) in the *Pharmaceutical* Part of Physic, shews that these Philosophers by Fire, have spent their Time to very good purpose. Those Physicians who reason upon *Galenical* Principles, acknowledge, that in many Cases, the *Tinctures, Extracts, Spirits, Volatile Salts,* and *Rosins* of Vegetables and Animals, are much more efficacious Remedies than the *Galenical* Preparations of those self-same Medicines. Nay, though they are not easily reconciled to Mineral Preparations, because the Ancients not knowing how to separate them from their grosser *Faeces,* durst seldom apply them to any but Chirurgical Uses; yet they themselves are forced to own, that some Diseases are of so malignant a Nature, that they cannot be dispelled by milder Methods. The Use of *Mercury* in Venereal Distempers, is so great, and so certain, that if there be such a Thing as a Specifical Remedy in Nature, it may justly deserve that Title. The Unskilfulness of those who have prepared and administred *Antimonial* Medicines, has made

(*p*) See Mr *Boyle's Usefulness of Experimental Philosophy.*

them

them infamous with many Persons, though many admirable Cures have been, and are wrought by them, skilfully corrected, every Day. And it is well known, that the Inward Use of *Steel* has been so successful, that in many Diseases, where the nicest Remedies seem requisite, whether the Constitution of the Patients, or the Nature of the Distempers, be considered, it is, without Fear, made use of; though its Medicinal Vertues, in these Cases, have been found out by Chymical Methods.

Upon the whole Matter, it is certain, that here is a new and gainful Acquisition made: The old *Galenical Materia Medica* is almost as well known, in all probability, as ever it was; since there are so great Numbers of Receipts preserved in the Writings of the old Physicians. The Industry of Modern Naturalists has, in most, at least in all material Cases, clearly discovered what those Individual Remedies are, which are there described. So that whatsoever Enlargement is made, is a clear Addition; especially, since these Minerals and Metals were then as free and common as they are now. Besides, vast Numbers of *Galenical* Medicines, Chymically prepared, are less nauseous, and equally powerful; which is so great an Advantage to Physic, that it ought not to be over-looked.

CHAP

CHAP. XVII.

Of the Ancient and Modern Anatomy.

Anatomy is one of the most necessary Arts to open to us Natural Knowledge, of any that was ever thought of. Its Usefulness to Physicians was very early seen; and the *Greeks* took great Pains to bring it to perfection. Some of the first Dissectors (*q*) tried their Skill upon living Bodies of Men, as well as Brutes. This was so inhumane and barbarous a Custom, that it was soon left off: And it created such an abhorrence in Men's Minds of the Art it self, that in *Galen*'s time, even dead Bodies were seldom opened; and he was often obliged (*r*) to use Apes, instead of Men, which sometimes led him into great Mistakes.

It may be said, perhaps, that because there is not an ancient System of Anatomy extant, therefore the Extent of their Knowledge in this Particular cannot be known. But the numerous Anatomical Treatises of *Galen* do abundantly supply that Defect. In his elaborate Work *of the Uses of the Parts of Humane Bodies,* he gives so full an Idea of ancient Anatomy, that if no other

(*q*) *Vide* Corn. Celsum *in* Praefatione.

(*r*) *Anatom. Administ passim.*

ancient Book of Anatomy were exstant, it alone would be sufficient for this Purpose. He is very large in all his Writings of this kind, in taking Notice of the Opinions of the Anatomists that were ancienter than himself, especially when they were mistaken, and had spent much time and Pains in Opening Bodies of Brutes, of which he somewhere promises to write a Comparative Anatomy. So that his Books not only acquaint us with his own Opinions, but also with Reasonings and Discoveries of *Hippocrates*, *Aristotle*, *Herophilus* and *Erasistratus*, whose Names were justly Venerable, for their Skill in these Things. Besides, he never contradicts any body, without appealing to Experience, wherein though he was now and then mistaken, yet he does not write like a Pedant, affirming a thing to be true or false, upon the Credit of *Hippocratres*, or *Herophilus*, but builds his Arguments upon Nature, as far as he knew her. He had an excellent Understanding, and a very piercing Genius; so that the false Uses which he frequently assigns to several Parts, do certainly shew that he did not understand the true Texture of those Parts; because where his Anatomy did not fail him, his Ratiocinations are, generally speaking, exact: Wherefore, in this Particular, his Mistakes instruct us as effectually in the Ancients Ignorance,

as

as his true Notions do in their Knowledge. This will appear at large hereafter, where it will be of mighty use to prove, That the Ancients cannot be supposed to have known many of the most eminent Modern Discoveries; since if they had known them, they would not have assigned such Uses to those Parts, as are not reconcilable to those Discoveries. If *Galen* had known that the *Pancreas* had been a Heap of small Glands, which all emit into one common Canal, a particular Juice carried afterwards through that Canal into the Guts, which there meeting with the Bile, goes forward, and assists it in the making of the Chyle, he would never have said (*s*) that Nature made it for a Pillow to support the Veins, which go out of the Liver in that Place, where they divide into several Branches, lest if they had been without a Rest, they should have been hurt by the violent Eruption of the Blood; and this too, without assigning any other Use for it.

(*s*) *De Usu Partium,* lib. v. c 2.

By *Anatomy*, there is seldom any thing understood but the Art of laying open the several Parts of the Body with a Knife, that so the Relation which they severally bear each to other may be clearly discerned. This is generally understood of the *containing* Parts, Skin, Flesh, Bones, Membranes, Veins, Arteries, Muscles, Tendons, Ligaments, Cartilages, Glands, Bowels, wherein the Ancients chiefly busied themselves: As for the Examination of the Nature and particular Texture of the *contained* Parts, Blood, Chyle, Urine, Bile, Serum, Fat, Juices of the Pancreas, Spleen and Nerves, Lympha, Spittle, Marrow of the Bones, Mucilages of the Joints, and the like; they made very few Experiments, and those too, for want of Chymistry and Microscopes, very imperfect. The Discoveries therefore which have been made in that nobler Part, which are numerous and considerable, are in a manner wholly owing to later Ages. In the other, a great deal was anciently done, though a great deal more was left for Posterity to do.

I shall begin with the Body in general. It is certain, that all the great Divisions of the Bones, Muscles, Veins and Arteries, most of the visible Cartilages, Tendons and Ligaments were exactly known in *Galen*'s time; the Positions of the Muscles, their several Originations, the Insertions of their Tendons, and investing Membranes, were, for the most part, traced with great Nicety and Truth; the more conspicuous Pairs of Nerves which arise either from the Brain or Spinal Marrow, were well known, and carefully followed; most of the great Branches of the Veins and Arteries, almost all the Bones and Cartilages, with very many Muscles, have still old *Greek* Names imposed

posed upon them by the Old Anatomists, or *Latin* Names translated from the *Greek* ones: So that, not only the easie things, and such as are discernible at first sight, were thoroughly known; but even several Particulars, especially in the Anatomy of the Nerves, were discovered, which are not obvious without great Care, and a good deal of Practical Skill in Dissecting. So much in general; from which it is evident, that as far as Anatomy is peculiarly useful to a Surgeon, to inform him how the Bones, Muscles, Blood-Vessels, Cartilages, Tendons, Ligaments and Membranes, lie in the Limbs, and more conspicuous Parts of the Body, so far the Ancients went: And here, there is very little that the Moderns have any Right to pretend to, as their own Discovery; though any Man that understands these things, must own, that these are the first things which offer themselves to an Anatomist's View.

Here I shall beg leave to descend to Particulars, because I have not seen any Comparison made between *Ancient and Modern Anatomy*, wherein I could acquiesce; whilst some; as Mr. *Glanvile* (*t*), and some others who seem to have copied from him, have allowed the Ancients less than was their Due; others, as *Vander Linden*, and *Almeloveen* (*u*), have attributed more to them than came to their Share; especially since

(*t*) Essay of Modern Improvements of Useful Knowledge.

(*u*) *Inventa Nov-Antiqua.*

(though

(though perhaps it may be a little tedious, yet) it cannot be called a Digression.

Hippocrates (w) took the Brain to be a Gland. His Opinion was nearer to the Truth than any of his Successors; but he seems to have thought it to be a similar Substance, which it evidently is not. And therefore, when several Parts of it were discovered not to be glandulous, his Opinion was rejected. *Plato* took it to be Marrow, such as nourishes the Bones; but its Weight and Texture soon destroyed his Notion, since it sinks in Water wherein Marrow swims; and is hardened by Fire, by which the other is melted. *Galen* (x) saw a little farther, and he asserts it to be of a Nervous Substance, only something softer than the Nerves in the Body. Still they believed that the Brain was an Uniform Substance, and as long as they did so, they were not like to go very far. The first Anatomist who discovered the true Texture of the Brain, was *Archangelus Piccolhomineus* (y) an *Italian*, who lived in the last Age. He found that the Brain properly so called, and *Cerebellum*, consist of Two distinct Substances, an outer Ash-coloured Substance, through which the Blood-Vessels, which lie under the *Pia Mater* in innumerable Folds and Windings, are disseminated; and an inner every where united to it, of a Nervous Nature, that joins this *Bark* (as it is usually call'd)

(w) *De Glandulis*, pag 418 § 7 Edit *Lander Linden*.

(x) *De Usu Partium*, lib viii cap 6.

(y) Malpighius *Epist de Cerebro ad Fracassatum*, p. 2.

call'd to the *Medulla Oblongata*, which is the Original of all the Pairs of Nerves that issue from the Brain, and of the Spinal Marrow, and lies under the Brain and *Cerebellum*. After him, Dr. *Willis* (z) was so very exact, that he traced this Medullar Substance through all its Insertions into the Cortical, and the *Medulla Oblongata*, and examined the Rises of all the Nerves, and went along with them into every Part of the Body with wonderful Curiosity. Hereby not only the Brain was demonstrably proved to be the Fountain of Sense and Motion, but also by the Courses of the Nerves, the manner how every Part of the Body conspires with any others to procure any one particular Motion, was clearly shewn; and thereby it was made plain, even to Sence, that where-ever many Parts joined at once to cause the same Motion, that Motion is caused by Nerves that go into every one of those Parts, which are all struck together. And tho' *Vieuffens* and *du Verney* have in many things corrected Dr. *Willis's Anatomy of the Nerves*; yet they have strengthened his general Hypothesis, even at the time when they discovered his Mistakes, which is the same thing to our present purpose. *Galen* (a) indeed, had a right Notion of this Matter, but he traced only the larger Pairs of Nerves, such as could not escape a good Anatomist.

(z) *Anat. Cerebri.*

(a) De U.P. l.8. c 4.

But

But the manner of the forming of the *Animal Spirit* in the Brain, was wholly unknown. In order to the Discovery whereof, *Malpighius* (*b*), by his Microscopes, found that the Cortical Part of the Brain consists of an innumerable Company of very small Glandules, which are all supplied with Blood by Capillary Arteries; and that the Animal Spirit, which is separated from the Mass of the Blood in these Glandules, is carried from them into the *Medulla Oblongata* thorough little Pipes, whereof one belongs to every Gland, whose other End is inserted into the *Medulla Oblongata*, and that these Numberless Pipes, which in the Brain of some Fishes look like the Teeth of a small Ivory Comb (*c*), are properly that which all Anatomists after *Piccolhomineus* have called the *Corpus Callosum*, or the Medullar Part of the Brain. This Discovery destroys the Ancient Notions of the Uses of the Ventricles of the Brain, and makes it very probable, that those Cavities are only Sinks to carry off excrementitious Humours, and not Storehouses of the Animal Spirit: It shews likewise how little they knew of the Brain, who Believed that it was an uniform Substance. Some of the Ancients disputed (*d*) whether the Brain were not made to cool the Heart. Now, though these are ridicul'd by *Galen*, so that their Opinions are not imputable to those who

(*b*) *De Cerebri Cortice*

(*c*) *De Cerebro,* pag 4.

(*d*) Galen *de U P.* l. VIII. c. 2.

who never held them; yet they shew, that these famous Men had examined these things very superficially: For no Man makes himself ridiculous if he can help it; and now, since Mankind are satisfied, by Ocular Demonstration, that the Brain is the Original of the Nerves, and the Principle of Sense and Motion, he would be thought out of his Wits, that should doubt of this Primary Use of the Brain; though formerly, when things had not been so experimentally proved, Men might talk in the dark, and assign such Reasons as they could think of, without the Suspicion of being ignorant or impertinent.

The *Eye* is so very remarkable a Member, and has so many Parts peculiar to it self, that the Ancients took great Notice of it. They found its Humours, the Watry, Crystalline, and Glassy, and all its Tunicles, and gave a good Description of them; but the Optic Nerve, the Aqueous Ducts which supply the Watry Humour, and the Vessels which carry Tears, were not sufficiently examined. The first was done by Dr. *Briggs* (e), who has found, that in the *Tunica Retiformis*, which is contiguous to the Glassy Humour, the Filaments of the Optic Nerve there expanded, lie in a most exact and regular Order, all parallel one to another; which when they are united afterwards in the Nerve, are not shuffled confusedly

(e) Theory of Vision. *Grew's* Transact. numb. 6. and Philos. Transact. numb. 147.

sedly together, but still preserve the same Order till they come to the Brain. The Crystalline Humour had already been discovered to be of a Double-Convex Figure, made of Two unequal Segments of Spheres, and not perfectly Spherical, as the Ancients thought. So that this farther Discovery made by Dr. *Briggs*, shews evidently why all the Parts of the Image are so distinctly carried to the Brain, since every Ray strikes upon a several Filament of the Optic Nerve; and all those Strings so struck, are moved equably at the same time. For want of knowing the Nature and Laws of Refraction, which have been exactly stated by Modern Mathematicians, the Ancients discoursed very lamely of Vision. This made *Galen* think that the Crystalline Humour (*f*) was the Seat of Vision, whereas its only Use is, to refract the Rays; as the common Experiment of a dark Room, with one only Hole to let in Light, plainly proves: For if one puts a Convex Glass within it, so as to suffer no light to be let in but thorough that Glass, a most exact Land-skip of every thing without, in their proper Colours, Heights and Distances, will be represented upon a Paper placed in the Focus of the Glass: And it is well known, that the same thing will appear, if the Crystalline Humour taken out of an Oxe's or a Man's Eye, be placed in the Hole, instead

(*f*) *De Usu Partium*, lib. viii. cap. 6.

of the Glass. The Way how the Watry Humour of the Eye, when by Accident lost, may be and is constantly supplied, was first found out and described by Monsieur *Nuck* (g), who discovered a particular Canal of Water arising from the internal Carotidal Artery, which creeping along the Sclerotic Coat of the Eye, perforates the Cornea near the Pupil, and then branching it self curiously about the Iris, enters into and supplies the Watry Humour. As to the Vessels which moisten the Eye, that it may move freely in its Orbit, the Ancients knew in general, that there were Two Glands in the Corners of the Eyes; (h); but the Lympheducts, through which the Moisture is conveyed from those Glands, were not fully traced till *Steno* (i) and *Briggs* (k) described them; so that there is just the same difference between our Knowledge and the Ancients in this Particular, as there is between *his* Knowledge who is sure there is some Road or other from this Place to that, and *his* who knows the whole Course, and all the Turnings of the Road, and can describe it on a Map.

(g) *De Ductibus novis Aquosis.*

(h) *Galen de U P. lib. 10. c xi.*
(i) *Observat. Anatomica de Oris Oculorum & Narium Vasis.*
(k) *Ophthalmographia.*

The Instruments by which Sounds are conveyed from the *Drum* to the *Auditory Nerves* in the inner Cavities of the *Ear*, were very little, if at all, known to the Ancients. In the First Cavity there are Four small Bones, the *Hammer*, the *Anvil*, the

the *Stirrup*, and a small flattish Bone just in in the Articulation of the *Anvil* and the *Stirrup*. It is now certainly known, that when the Drum is struck upon by the external Air, these little Bones, which are as big in Infants, as in adult Persons, move each other; the Drum moves the Hammer, That the Anvil, That the Stirrup, which opens the Oval Entrance into the Second Cavity: None of these Bones were ever mentioned by the Ancients, who only talked of Windings and Turnings within the *Os Petrosum*, that were covered by the large Membrane of the Drum. *Jacobus Carpus*, one of the first Restorers of Anatomy in the last Age, found out the *Hammer* and the *Anvil*; *Realdus Columbus* discovered the *Stirrup*; and *Franciscus Silvius*, the little flattish Bone by him called *Os Orbiculare*, but mistook its Position: He thought it had been placed Sideways of the Head of the *Stirrup*, whereas Monsieur *du Verney* (*l*) found that it lies in the *Head* of the *Stirrup*, between that and the *Anvil*. The other inner Cavities were not better understood, the Spiral Bones of the *Cochlea*, that are divided into Two distinct Cavities, like Two Pair of Winding-Stairs parallel to one another, which turn round the same Axis, with the Three Semicircular *Canals* of the *Labyrinthus*, into which the inner Air enters, and strikes upon the small Twigs of the Auditory

(*l*) Traité del' Organe de l' Ouye. Paris, 1683.

tory Nerves inserted into those small Bones, were things that they knew so little of, that they had no Names for them; and indeed, till Monsieur *du Verney* came, those Mazes were but negligently, at least unsuccessfully, examined by Moderns, as well as Ancients; it being impossible so much as to form an Idea of what any former Anatomists asserted of the wonderful Mechanism of those little Bones, before he wrote, if we set aside Monsieur *Perrault*'s (m) *Anatomy* of those Parts, which came out a Year or two before, who is not near so exact as Monsieur *du Verney*.

(m) *Essays de Physique*. Part II.

The other Parts of the Head and Neck, wherein the *Old Anatomy* was the most defective, were the *Tongue*, as to its Internal Texture; and the *Glands of the Mouth, Jaws* and *Throat*. The Texture of the *Tongue* was but guessed at, which occasioned great Disputes concerning the Nature of its Substance, (n) some thinking it to be Glandulous, some Muscular, and some of a peculiar Nature, not to be matched in any other Part of the Body. This therefore *Malpighius* examined with his Glasses, and discovered, that it was cloathed with a double Membrane; that in the inner Membrane there are abundance of small *Papillæ*, which have extremities of Nerves inserted into them by which the Tongue discerns Tasts, and that

(n) *Vide Malpighium de Linguâ*.

that under that Membrane it is of a Muscular Nature, consisting of numberless Heaps of Fibres, which run all manner of ways, over one another, like a Mat.

The general Uses of the *Glands of the Mouth, Jaws* and *Neck*, were anciently known; it was visible that the Mouth was moistened by them, and the Mass of the Spittle supplied from them; and then, having named them from the Places near which they lie, as the *Palate*, the *Jaws*, the *Tongue*, the *Ears*, the *Neck*, they went no further; and there was little, if any thing, more done, till Dr. *Wharton* and *Nicolaus Steno* examined these *Glands*. And upon an exact Enquiry, Four several Salival Ducts have been discovered, which from several Glands discharge the Spittle into the Mouth. The first was described by Dr. *Wharton* (*o*) near Forty Years ago; it comes from the *Conglomerate Glands* that lie close to the inner side of the lower Jaw, and discharges it self near the middle of the Chin into the Mouth. The Second was found out by *Steno* (*p*), who published his Observations in MDCLXII; this comes from those Glands that lie near the Ears, in the inside of the Cheek, and the outside of the Upper Jaw. The Third was

(*o*) *Adenograph.c* 21.

(*p*) *Observat. Anat de Oris Vasis.*

found

found out by (*q*) *Thomas Bartho-* (*q*) Nuck
lin, who gave an Account of it in Sialograph.
MDCLXXXII, and about the same time
by one *Rivinus* a *German:* It arises from
the Glands under the Tongue, and going
in a distinct Canal to the Mouth of *Wharton*'s Duct, there, for the most part, by
a common Orifice, opens into the Mouth.
The Fourth was discovered by Monsieur
Nuck (*r*); he found a Gland within the (*r*) Ibid.
Orbit of the Eye, from which, not far
from the Mouth of *Steno*'s Duct, Spittle
is supplied to the Mouth by a peculiar
Canal. Besides these, the same Monsieur *Nuck* found some smaller Glands
near the last, but lower down, which,
by Four distinct Pipes, carry some Spittle
into the Mouth; so careful has Nature
been to provide so many Passages for that
necessary and noble Juice, that if some
should fail, others might supply their
Want.

P CHAP.

CHAP. XVIII.

Of the Circulation of the Blood.

FRom the *Head*, we are to look into the *Thorax*, and there to consider the *Heart* and the *Lungs*. The *Lungs*, as most of the other *Viscera*, were believed to be of a *Parenchymous* Substance, till *Malpighius* found by his Glasses (*s*) that they consist of innumerable small Bladders, that open into each other, as far as the outermost; which are covered by the outer Membrane, that incloses the whole Body of the *Lungs*: And that the small Branches of the *Wind-Pipe* are all inserted into these Bladders; about every one of which the *Veins* and *Arteries* are entwined, in an unconceivable Number of Nets and Mazes; that so the inspired Air may press upon, or mix with the Mass of Blood, in such small Parcels as the Ancients had no Notion of. The *Wind-Pipe* also it self is nourished by an *Artery* that creeps up the Back-side, and accompanies it in all its Branchings: Which was first found out by *Frederic Ruysch*, a a *Dutch* Professor of *Anatomy* at *Leyden*, about Thirty Years ago.

(*s*) *Epist de Pulmonibus.*

But

But the great Discovery that has been made of the *Lungs*, is, That the whole Mass of Blood is carried out of the Right Ventricle of the Heart, by the *Arteria Pulmonaris*, called anciently *Vena Arteriosa*, thorough all the small Bladders of the *Lungs*, into the *Vena Pulmonaris*, (or *Arteria Venosa*;) and from thence, into the Left Ventricle of the Heart again. So that the Heart is a strong Pump, which throws the Blood, let in from the Veins, into the Lungs; and from the Lungs, afterwards, into the Arteries; and this by a constant rapid Motion, whereby the Blood is driven round several times in an Hour. This Discovery, first made perfectly intelligible by Dr. *Harvey*, is of so very great Importance to shew the Communication of all the Humours of the Body, each with other, that as soon as Men were perfectly satisfied that it was not to be contested, which they were in a few Years, a great many put in for the Prize, unwilling that Dr. *Harvey* should go away with all the Glory. *Vander Linden*, who published a most exact Edition of *Hippocrates*, in *Holland*, about XXX Years ago, has taken a great deal of Pains to prove that *Hippocrates* knew the *Circulation of the Blood*, and that Dr. *Harvey* only revived it. The Substance of what has been said in this Matter, is this; That

Hippocrates speaks (*t*) in one place, *of the Usual and Constant Motion of the Blood:* That, in another place, he calls (*u*) the *Veins and Arteries, the Fountains of Humane Nature, the Rivers that water the whole Body, and convey Life; and which, if they be dried up, the Man dies:* That, in a third place, he says, (*w*) *That the Blood-Vessels, which are dispersed over the whole Body, give Spirit, Moisture and Motion, and all spring from one; which one* (Blood-Vessel) *has no Beginning, nor no End, that I can find; for where there is a Circle, there is no Beginning.* These are the clearest Passages that are produced, to prove, that *Hippocrates* knew the *Circulation of the Blood*; and it is plain from them, that he did believe it as an *Hypothesis*; that is, in plain *English*, that he did suppose the Blood to be carried round the Body by *a constant accustomed Motion:* But that he did not know what this *constant accustomed Motion* was, and that he had not found that Course which, in our Age, Dr. *Harvey* first clearly demonstrated, will appear evident from the following

(*t*) Παραφρονέεσιν ἐν τῇ νόσῳ διὰ παντὸς, ἅτε τε αἵματος ἐφθαρμένε τε κ᾽ ἐκκεκινημένε τ᾽ εἰωθυΐαν κίνησιν. De Morbis, lib. 1. §. 30. Edit. Vand.

(*u*) Αὗται πηγαὶ φύσιος ἀνθρώπε, κ᾽ οἱ ποταμοὶ ἐνταῦθα ἀνὰ τὸ σῶμα τοῖσιν ἄρδει τὸ σκῆνος· ἔτοι δ᾽ κ᾽ ζώην φέρεσι τῷ ἀνθρώπῳ κἢν αὐανθέωσιν ἀπέθανεν ὁ ἄνθρωπος. De Corde, §. 5.

(*w*) Αἱ φλέβες διὰ τῇ σώματος κεχύνδαι, πνεῦμα, κ᾽ ῥεῦμα κ᾽ κίνησιν παρέχονται, ἀπὸ μιῆς πολλαὶ διαβλαστάνεσαι, κ᾽ ἀρχή μὲν ἡ μίη, ὅθεν ἤρξατο κ᾽ ἡ τετελεύτηκεν, ἐκ οἶδα κύκλε γεγραμμένε ἀρχὴ ἐκ εὑρέθη. De Venis, §. 17.

ing Considerations. (1.) He says nothing of the *Circulation of the Blood*, in his Discourse *of the Heart*, where he Anatomizes it as well as he could, and speaks of the (*x*) Ventricles, and the Valves (*y*), which are the immediate Instruments by which the Work is done. (2.) He believes that the Auricles of the Heart (*z*) are like Bellows, which receive the Air to cool the Heart. Now, there are other Uses of them certainly discovered, since they assist the Heart in the Receiving of the Blood from the *Vena Cava*, and the *Vena Pulmonaris*. This, no Man that knows how the Blood circulates, can be unacquainted with; and accordingly, would have been mentioned by *Hippocrates*, had he understood it. (3.) *Hippocrates* (*a*) speaks of Veins, as receiving Blood *from* the Heart, and going *from* it: Which also was the constant way of Speaking of *Galen*, and all the Ancients. Now, no Man that can express himself properly, will ever say, That any Liquors are carried away *from* any Cistern, as from a Fountain or Source, through *those* Canals which, to his Knowledge, convey Liquors *to* that Cistern. (4.) *Hippocrates* says, the Blood is carried into the Lungs, from the Heart, for the Nourishment of the Lungs; without assigning any other Reason (*b*). These seem to be positive Arguments, that *Hippocrates*

(*x*) *De Corde* §. 4.
(*y*) Ibid. §. 7, 8.
(*z*) Ibid. §. 6.

(*a*) *Arteriae quidem purum sanguinem & spiritum à corde recipiunt, Venae autem & ipsae à corde sanguinem sumunt, per quas corpori distribuitur.* De Structura Hominis, §. 2.
(*b*) *De Corde,* §. 10.

pocrates knew nothing of this Matter; and accordingly, all his Commentators, Ancient and Modern, before Dr. *Harvey*, never interpreted the former Passages of the *Circulation of the Blood*: Neither would *Vander Linden*, in all probability, if Dr. *Harvey* had not helped him to the Notion; which he was then resolved to find in *Hippocrates*, whom he supposed to be not the Father only, but the Finisher also of the whole Medical Art. It is pretended to by none of the Ancients, or rather their Admirers for them, after *Hippocrates*. As for *Galen*, any Man that reads what he says of the Heart and Lungs, in the Sixth Book of his *De Usu Partium*, must own, that he does not discourse as if he were acquainted with Modern Discoveries; and therefore it is not so much as pretended that he knew this Recurrent Motion of the Blood. Which also farther shews, that if *Hippocrates* did know it, he explained himself so obscurely, that *Galen* could not understand him; who, in all probability, understood *Hippocrates*'s Text as well as any of his Commentators, who have written since the *Greek* Tongue, and much more, since the *Ionic* Dialect has ceased to be a living Language.

Since the Ancients have no Right to so noble a Discovery, it may be worth while to enquire, to whom of the Moderns the
Glory

Glory of it is due; for this is also exceedingly contested. The first Step that was made towards it, was, the finding that the whole Mass of the Blood passes thorough the Lungs, by the Pulmonary Artery and Vein.

The first that I could ever find, who had a distinct *Idea* of this Matter, was *Michael Servetus*, a *Spanish* Physician, who was burnt for *Arianism*, at *Geneva*, near CXL Years ago. Well had it been for the *Church of Christ*, if he had wholly confined himself to his own Profession! His Sagacity in this Particular, before so much in the dark, gives us great Reason to believe, that the World might then have had just Cause to have blessed his Memory. In a Book (*c*) of his, entituled, *Christianismi Restitutio*, printed in the Year MDLIII. (*d*) he clearly asserts, that the Blood passes thorough the Lungs, from the Left to the Right Ventricle of the Heart; and not thorough the *Partition* which divides the two Ventricles, as was at that Time common-

(*c*) *Vitalis Spiritus in sinistro cordis ventriculo suam Originem habet, juvantibus maximè pulmonibus ad ipsius generationem. Est spiritus tenuis, caloris vi elaboratus, flavo colore, ignea potentia, ut sit quasi ex puriore sanguine lucidus vapor: generatur ex facta in pulmone mixtione inspirati aeris cum elaborato subtili sanguine, quem dexter ventriculus sinistro communicat. Fit autem communicatio haec non per parietem cordis medium ut vulgo creditur, sed magno artificio à dextro cordis ventriculo, longo per pulmones ductu, agitatur sanguis subtilis; à pulmonibus praeparatur, flavus efficitur, & à venâ arteriosâ in arteriam venosam transfunditur; deinde in ipsâ arteriâ venosâ inspirato aeri miscetur & exspiratione à fuligine repurgatur; atque ita tandem à sinistro cordis ventriculo totum mixtum per diastolen attrahitur, apta supellex ut fiat spiritus vitalis* Servet. Christian Restit.

(*d*) Vid. *Sandii Bibliothecam Anti-Trinitariorum,* p. 13.

ly believed. How he introduces it, or in which of the Six Discourses, into which *Servetus* divides his Book, it is to be found, I know not, having never seen the Book my self. Mr. *Charles Bernard*, a very Learned and Eminent Chirurgeon of *London*, who did me the Favour to communicate this Passage to me, (set down at length in the Margin) which was transcribed out of *Servetus*, could inform me no further, only that he had it from a Learned Friend of his, who had himself copied it from *Servetus*.

Realdus Columbus, of *Cremona*, was the next that said any thing of it, in his *Anatomy*, printed at *Venice*, MDLIX. in *Folio*; and at *Paris*, in MDLXXII. in *Octavo*; and afterwards elsewhere. There he asserts the same (e) Circulation thorough the Lungs, that *Servetus* had done before; but says, that no Man had ever taken notice of it before him, or had written any thing about it: Which shews that he did not copy from *Servetus*; unless one should say, that he

(e) *Duae insunt cordi cavitates*, h. e. *ventriculi duo, ex his alter a dextris est, à sinistris alter; dexter sinistro multo est major; in dextro sanguis adest naturalis, ac vitalis in sinistro illud autem observatu perpulcrum est, substantiam cordis dextrum ventriculum ambientem tenuem satis esse, sinistram vero crassam; & hoc tum aequilibrii causâ factum est, tum ne sanguis vitalis, qui tenuissimus est, extra resudaret. Inter hos ventriculos septum adest, per quod fere omnes existimant sanguini à dextro ad sinistrum aditum patefieri; id ut fiat facilius, in transitu ob vitalium spirituum generationem tenuem reddi. Sed longa errant viâ. nam sanguis per arteriosam venam ad pulmonem fertur, ibique attenuatur; deinde cum aëre unà per arteriam venalem ad sinistrum cordis ventriculum defertur; quod nemo hactenus aut animadvertit, aut scriptum reliquit.* Reald. Columb. Anat. lib. vii. p 325. Edit. Lut.

ſtole the Notion, without mentioning *Servetus*'s Name; which is injurious, ſince in theſe Matters the ſame thing may be, and very often is obſerved by ſeveral Perſons, who never acquainted each other with their Diſcoveries. But *Columbus* is much more particular; (*f*) for he ſays, That the Veins lodge the whole Maſs of the Blood in the *Vena Cava*, which carries it into the Heart, whence it cannot return the ſame Way that it went; from the Right Ventricle it is thrown into the Lungs by the Pulmonary Artery, where the Valves are ſo placed, as to hinder its Return that Way into the Heart, and ſo it is thrown into the Left Ventricle, and by the *Aorta* again, when enliven'd by the Air, diffuſed thorough the whole Body.

(*f*) *Idcirco quando dilatatur, ſanguinem a cavâ venâ in dextrum ventriculum ſuſcipit, nec non ab arteriâ venoſâ ſanguinem paratum ut diximus unàcum aëre in ſiniſtrum: propterea membranae illae demittuntur & ingreſſui cedunt. nam cum cor coarctatur, hae clauduntur; ne quod ſuſciperetur per eaſdem vias retrocedat; eodémque tempore membranae tum magnae arteriae, tum venae arterioſae recluduntur, aditumque praebent ſpirituoſo ſanguini exeunti, qui per univerſum corpus funditur, ſanguinique naturali ad pulmones delato Res itaque ſemper habet, cum dilatatur, quas prius memoravimus, recluduntur, clauduntur reliquae, itaque comperies ſanguinem qui in dextrum ventriculum ingreſſus eſt, non poſſe in cavam venam retrocedere.* Ibid. pag. 330. Vide quoque lib. 11. pag. 411.

Some Years after appeared *Andreas Caeſalpinus*, who printed his *Peripatetical Queſtions* at *Venice*, in *Quarto*, in MDLXXI. And afterwards, with his *Medical Queſtions*, at the ſame Place, in MDXCIII. He is rather more particular than *Columbus*, eſpecially in examining how Arteries and

Veins

Veins join at their Extremities; which he supposes to be by opening their Mouths into each other: And he uses the word *Circulation* in his *Peripatetical Questions*, which had never been used in that sence before. He also takes notice, that the Blood swells below the Ligature in Veins, and urges that in Confirmation of his Opinion. Some Hints of this Matter are likewise to be found in *Constantius Varolius*, who printed his *Anatomy* in the Year MDXCI.

At last, Dr. *William Harvey* printed a Discourse on purpose, upon this Subject, at *Francfort*, in MDCXXVIII. This Notion had only been occasionally and flightly treated of by *Columbus* and *Caesalpinus*, who themselves, in all probability, did not know the Consequence of what they asserted; and therefore it was never applied to other Purposes, either to shew the Uses of the other *Viscera*, or to explain the Natures of Diseases: Neither, for any thing that appears at this day, had they made such numbers of Experiments as were necessary to explain their Doctrine, and to clear it from Opposition. All this Dr. *Harvey* undertook to do, and with indefatigable Pains traced the visible Veins and Arteries throughout the Body, in their whole Journey *from* and *to* the Heart, so as to demonstrate, even to the most incredulous

lous, not only that the Blood circulates thorough the Lungs and Heart, but the very Manner how, and the Time in which that great Work is performed. When he had once proved that the Motion of the Blood was so rapid as we now find it is, then he drew such Consequences from it, as shewed that he throughly understood his Argument, and would leave little, at least as little as he could, to future Industry to discover in that particular Part of Anatomy. This gave him a just Title to the Honour of so Noble a Discovery, since what his Predecessors had said before him, was not enough understood, to form just Notions from their Words. One may also observe how gradually this Discovery, as all abstruse Truths of Humane Disquisition, was explained to the World. *Hippocrates* first talked of the *Usual Motion of the Blood*. *Plato* said, That the *Heart* was the *Original* of the *Veins*, and of the *Blood*, that was carried about every Member of the Body. *Aristotle* also, somewhere, speaks of a *Recurrent Motion of the Blood*. Still all this was only *Opinion* and *Belief*: It was Rational, and became Men of their Genius's; but, not having as yet been made evident by Experiments, it might as easily be denied as affirmed. *Servetus* first saw that the Blood passes thorough the Lungs; *Columbus* went farther, and shew'd

the

the Uses of the *Valves*, or *Trap-doors* of the Heart, which let the Blood *in* and *out* of their respective Vessels, but not the self-same Road. Thus the Way was just open when Doctor *Harvey* came, who built upon the First Foundations: To make his Work yet the easier, the Valves of the Veins, which were discovered by F. *Paul* the *Venetian*, had not long before been explained by *Fabricius ab Aqua-Pendente*, whence the Circulation was yet more clearly demonstrated.

There was one thing still wanting to compleat this Theory, and that was, the Knowledge how the Veins received that Blood which the Arteries discharged; first it was believed that the Mouths of each sort of Vessels joined into one another: That Opinion was soon laid aside, because it was found that the Capillary Vessels were so extremely small, that it was impossible with the naked Eye to trace them. This put them upon imagining that the Blood ouzes out of the Arteries, and is absorbed by the Veins, whose small Orifices receive it, as it lies in the Fibres of the Muscles, or in the Parenchyma's of the Bowels: Which Opinion has been generally received by most Anatomists since Dr. *Harvey*'s Time. But Monsieur *Leeuwenhoek* has lately found in several sorts of Fishes (g), which were more manageable by

(g) Letter 65, 66.

by his Glasses than other Animals, that Arteries and Veins are really continued Syphons variously wound about each other towards their Extremities in numberless Mazes, over all the Body: And others have found (h) what he says to be very true, in a Water Newt. So that this Discovery has passed uncontested. And since it has been constantly found, that Nature follows like Methods in all sorts of Animals, where she uses the same sorts of Instruments, it will always be believed, that the Blood circulates in Men, after the same Manner as it does in *Eels, Perches, Pikes, Carps, Bats,* and some other Creatures, in which Monsieur *Leeuwenhoek* tried it. Though the Ways how it may be visible to the Eye, in Humane Bodies, have not, that I know of, been yet discovered. However, this Visible *Circulation of the Blood* in these Creatures, effectually removes Sir *William Temple's* Scruple, who seems unwilling to believe the *Circulation of the Blood*, because he could not see it: His Words are these; (i) *Nay, it is disputed whether* Harvey's *Circulation of the Blood be true or no; for though Reason may seem to favour it more than the contrary Opinion, yet Sense can very hardly allow it; and to satisfie Mankind, both these must concurr.* Sense therefore here allows it, and that this Sense might the sooner *concurr*, Monsieur

(h) Philos. Transact. numb. 177.

(i) Pag. 44, 45.

Leeu-

Leeuwenhoek describes the Method how this Experiment may be tried in his LXVIth. Letter. The Inferences that may be made from this noble Discovery are obvious, and so I shall not stay to mention them.

CHAP. XIX.

Farther Reflections upon Ancient and Modern Anatomy.

IF after this long Enquiry into the First Discovery of the *Circulation of the Blood*, it should be found that the *Anatomy* of the Heart was but slightly known to the Ancients, it will not, I suppose, be a Matter of any great Wonder. The First Opinion which we have of the Texture of the Heart, was that of *Hippocrates* (k), That it is a very strong Muscle. This, though true, was rejected afterwards, for want of knowing its true Use. Its Internal Divisions, its Valves, and larger Visible Fibres, were well known, and distinctly described by the Ancients; only they were mistaken in thinking that there is a Communication between the Ventricles thorough the *Septum*, which is now generally known to be an Errour.

(k) *De Corde*, § 4.

The

The Order of the Muscular Fibres of the Heart was not known before Dr. *Lower*, who discovered them to be Spiral like a Snail-Shell, as if several Skains of Threads of different Lengths had been wound up into a Bottom of such a Shape, hollow, and divided within. By all these Discoveries *Alphonsus Borellus* (*l*) was enabled to give such a Solution of all the Appearances of the Motion of the Heart, and of the Blood in the Arteries, upon Mathematical and Mechanical Principles, as will give a more satisfactory Account of the wonderful Methods of Nature, in dispensing Life and Nourishment to every Part of the Body, than all that had ever been written upon these Subjects before those things were found out.

(*l*) De *Motu Animalium*, Part II. cap. 5.

Below the *Midriff* are several very noble *Viscera*: The *Stomach*, the *Liver*, the *Pancreas* or *Sweet-bread*, the *Spleen*, the *Reins*, the *Intestines*, the *Glands of the Mesentery*, and the *Instruments of Generation of both Sexes*; in the Anatomical Knowledge of all which Parts, the Ancients were exceedingly defective.

The *Coats of the Stomach* have been separated, and the several Fibres of the middle Coat examined by Dr. *Willis* (*m*) with more Exactness than formerly; he also has been very nice in tracing the Blood-Vessels and Nerves that run amongst the Coats, has evidently shewn that its Inside is covered

(*m*) *Pharmaceut. Rational.*

red with a gladulous Coat, whose Glands separate that Mucilage; which both preserves the Fibres from being injured by the Aliments which the Stomach receives, and concurrs with the Spittle to further the Digestion there performed; and has given a particular Account of all those several Rows of Fibres which compose the musculous Coat. To which if we add *Steno*'s Discovery of the Fibres of the Musculous Coat of the Gullet, that they are Spiral in a double Order, one ascending, the other descending, which run contrary Courses, and mutually cross each other in every Winding; with Dr. *Cole*'s (*n*) Discovery of the Nature of the Fibres of the Intestines, that they also move spirally, tho' not, perhaps, in a contrary Order, from the beginning of the *Duodenum*, to the end of the streight Gut, the Anatomy of those Parts seems to be almost compleat.

(*n*) Philos. Transact. n. 125.

The great Use of the *Stomach* and the *Guts*, is to prepare the Chyle, and then to transmit it thorough the Glands of the Mesentry into the Blood. This the Ancients knew very well; the Manner how it was done they knew not. *Galen* (*o*) held, that the Mesaraic Veins, as also those which go from the Stomach to the Liver, carry the Chyle thither; which, by the Warmth of the Liver, is put into a Heat, whereby the Faeculencies are separated

(*o*) De Usu Partium, l. 4 c. 2, 3, 4, 5.

rated from the more spirituous Parts, and by their Weight sink to the Bottom. The purer Parts go into the *Vena Cava*; the Dregs, which are of two sorts, *Choler* and *Melancholy*, go into several Receptacles; the Choler is lodged in the Gall-Bladder, and *Porus Bilarius*: Melancholy is carried off by the Spleen. The Original of all these Notions, was Ignorance of the Anatomy of all these Parts, as also of the constant Motion of the Blood thorough the Lungs and Heart. *Herophilus*, who is commended as the ablest Anatomist of Antiquity, found out (*p*) that there were Veins dispersed quite through the Mesentery, as far as the small Guts reach, which carried the Chyle from the Intestines into several *Glaudulous Bodies*, and there lodged them. These are the *Milky Veins* again discovered by *Asellius* about L Years ago; and those Glands which *Herophilus* spoke of, are probably that great Collection of Glands in the Mesentery, that is commonly called the *Pancreas Asellii*. After *Herophilus*, none of the Ancients had the Luck to trace the Motions of the Chyle any farther, and so these Milky Veins were confounded with the Mesaraics, and 'twas commonly believed, That because all the Mesariacs carry the Blood from the Intestines into the Liver, therefore they carried Chyle also,

(*p*) *Galen. De U P* l 4. c 19.

Q when

when there was any Chyle to carry; and hence, probably, it was that the Liver was believed to be the common Work-House of the Blood. But when *Asellius* had traced the Chyle as far as the great Gland of the Mesentery, it was soon found not to lie there. And *Pecquet*, about XL Years since, discovered the *common Receptacle of the Chyle*, whither it is all brought. Thence he also found that it is carried, by particular Vessels, thorough the Thorax, almost as high as the Left Shoulder, and there thrown into the Left Subclavian Vein, and so directly carried to the Heart. It has also been discovered, that in his Canal, usually call'd *Ductus Thoracicus*, there are numerous Valves, which hinder the Return of the Chyle to the common Receptacle, so that it can be moved forwards, but not backwards.

Since this Passage of the Chyle has been discovered, it has been by some believed, that the *Milk* is conveyed into the Breasts, by little Vessels, from the *Ductus Thoracicus*. The whole Oeconomy of that Affair has been particularly described, very lately, by Mr. *Nuck*, before whose time it was but imperfectly known. He says therefore, that the Breasts are heaps of Glands, supplied with Blood by innumerable Ramifications of the Axillary and Thoracic Arteries; some of which passing thorough the Breastbone,

bone, unite with the Vessels of the opposite Side. These Arteries, which are unconceivably small, part with the Milk in those small Glands, into small Pipes, four or five of which meeting together, make one small Trunk; of these small Trunks, the large Pipes, which terminate in the Nipple, are made up; though before they arrive thither, they straiten into so small a compass, that a stiff Hair will just pass thorough. The Nipple, which is a Fibrous Body, has seven or eight, or more Holes, thorough which every Pipe emits its Milk upon Suction; and lest any one of them being stopp'd, the Milk should stagnate, they all have cross Passages into each other at the bottom of the Nipple, where it joins to the Breast.

The fore-mentioned Discovery of the Passage of the Chyle, obliged Men to re-examine the Notions which, till then, had generally obtained, concerning the Nature and Uses of the *Liver*. Hitherto it had been generally believed, that the Blood was made there, and so dispersed into several Parts, for the Uses of the Body, by the *Vena Cava*. *Erasistratus*, indeed, supposed (*q*) that its principal Use was, to separate the Bile, and to lodge it in its proper Vessels: But, for want of farther Light, his Notion could not then be sufficiently proved; and so it presently fell, and was never revived

(*q*) Galen *de U P.* l. iv. c. 13

revived, till *Asellius*'s and *Pecquet*'s Discoveries put it out of doubt. Till *Malpighius* discovered its Texture by his Glasses, its Nature was very obscure. But he has found out, (1.) That the Substance of the Liver is framed of innumerable Lobules, which are very often of a Cubical Figure, and consist of several little Glands, like the Stones of Raisins; so that they look like Bunches of Grapes, and are each of them cloathed with a distinct Membrane. (2.) That the whole Bulk of the Liver consists of these Grape-stone-like Glands, and of divers sorts of Vessels. (3.) That the small Branches of the *Cava*, *Porta*, and *Porus Bilarius*, run thorough all, even the least of these Lobules, in an equal Number; and that the Branches of the *Porta*, are as Arteries that convey the Blood *to*, and the Branches of the *Cava* are the Veins which carry the Blood *from* all these little Grape-stone-like Glands. From whence it is plain, that the Liver is a Glandulous Body, with its proper Excretory Vessels, which carry away the Gall that lay before in the Mass of the Blood.

Near the Liver lies the *Pancreas*, which *Galen* believed (r) to be a Pillow to support the Divisions of the Veins, as they go out of the Liver; and, for what appears at present, the Ancients do not seem to have concerned themselves any farther about

(r) De U. P. l. v. c 2.

about it. Since, it has been found to be a Glandulous Body, wherein a distinct Juice is separated from the Blood; which by a peculiar Canal, first discovered by *Georgius Wirtsungus*, a *Paduan* Physician, is carried into the *Duodenum*; where meeting with the Bile, and the Aliment just thrown out of the Stomach, assists and promotes the Business of Digestion.

The *Spleen* was as little understood as the *Pancreas*, and for the same Reasons: Its Anatomy was unknown, and its Bulk made it very remarkable; something therefore was to be said about it: And what no Body could positively dis-prove, might the easier be either received or contradicted. The most general Opinion was, that the grosser Excrements of the Chyle and Blood were carried off from the Liver, by the *Ramus Splenicus*, and lodged in the Spleen, as in a common Cistern: But since the *Circulation of the Blood* has been known, it has been found, that the Blood can go from the Spleen to the Liver, but that nothing can return back again into the Spleen. And as for its Texture, (s) *Malpighius* has discover'd, that the Substance of the Spleen, deducting the numerous Blood-Vessels and Nerves, as also the Fibres which arise from its second Membrane, and which support the other Parts, is made up of innumerable little Cells, like Honey-combs, in which there

(s) *De Liene.*

there are vast Numbers of small Glandules, which resemble Bunches of Grapes; and that these hang upon the Fibres, and are fed by Twigs of Arteries and Nerves, and send forth the Blood there purged, into the *Ramus Splenicus*, which carries it into the Liver; to what purpose, not yet certainly discovered.

The Use of the *Reins* is so very conspicuous, that, from *Hippocrates*'s Time, downwards, no Man ever mistook it: But the Mechanism of those wonderful Strainers was wholly unknown, till the so often mentioned *Malpighius* (*t*) found it out. He therefore, by his Glasses, discovered, that the Kidneys are not one uniform Substance, but consist of several small Globules, which are all like so many several Kidneys, bound about with one common Membrane; and that every Globule has small Twigs from the emulgent Arteries, that carry Blood to it; Glands, in which the Urine is strained from it; Veins, by which the purified Blood is carried off to the Emulgent Veins, thence to go into the *Cava*; a Pipe, to convey the Urine into the great Basin in the middle of the Kidney, and a Nipple, towards which several of those small Pipes tend, and through which the Urine ouzes out of them into the Basin. This clear Account of the Structure of the Reins, has effectually

confute

(*t*) *De Renibus.*

confuted several Notions that Men had entertained, of some Secondary Uses of those Parts; since hereby it appears, that every Part of the Kidneys is immediately and wholly subservient to that single Work, of freeing the Blood from its superfluous *Serum*.

What has been done by Modern *Anatomists*, towards the compleating of the Knowledge of the remaining Parts, I shall omit. That the Ancients likewise took Pains about them, is evident from the Writings of *Hippocrates*, *Aristotle* and *Galen*. The Discoveries which have since been made, are so great, that they are, in a manner, undisputed: And the Books which treat of them are so well known, that it will not be suspected that I decline to enlarge upon them, out of a Dread of giving up more to the Ancients in this Particular, than I have done all along.

The Discoveries hitherto mention'd, have been of those Parts or Humours of the Body, whose Existence was well enough known to the Ancients. But, besides them, other Humours, with Vessels to separate, contain, and carry them to several Parts of the Body, have been taken notice of; of which, in strictness, the Ancients cannot be said to have had any sort of Knowledge. These are, the *Lympha*, or Colourless Juice, which is carried to the Chyle and Blood, from separate Parts of the Body: And the *Mucilage of the Joints*, which lubricates them, and the Muscles, in their Motions. The Discovery of the *Lympha*, which was made about XL Years ago, is contended for by several Persons. *Thomas Bartholine*, a *Dane*, and *Olaus Rudbeck*, a *Suede*, published their Observations about the same time: And Dr. *Jolliffe*, an *English-Man*, shewed the same to several of his Friends, but without publishing any thing concerning them. The discoveries being undoubted, and all Three working upon the same Materials, there seems no reason to deny any of them the Glory of their Inventions. The Thing which they found, was, that there are innumerable small, clear Vessels in many Parts of the Body, chiefly in the Lower Belly, which convey a Colourless Juice, either into the common Receptacle of the Chyle, or else into the Veins, there to mix with the Blood. The *Valves* which *Frederic Ruysch* found and demonstrated in them, about the same time, manifestly shewed, that this is its Road; because they prove, that the *Lympha* can go forwards from the Liver, Spleen, Lungs, Glands of the Loins and Neck, or any other Place, whence they arise, towards some Chyliferous Duct, or Vein; but cannot go back from those Chyliferous Ducts, or Veins, to the Place of their Origination.

rigination. What this Origination is, was long uncertain, it not being easie to trace the several Canals up to their several Sources. *Steno* (*u*) and *Malpighius* (*w*) did, with infinite Labour, find, that abundance of Lympheducts passed thorough those numerous *Conglobate Glands* that are dispersed in the *Abdomen* and *Thorax*; which made them think that the Arterious Blood was there purged of its *Lympha*, that was from thence carried off into its proper Place, by a Vessel of its own. But Mr. *Nuck* has since (*x*) found, that the Lympheducts arise immediately from Arteries themselves; and that many of them are percolated thorough those *Conglobate Glands*, in their Way to the Receptacle of the Chyle, or those Veins which receive them. By these, and innumerable other Observations, the Uses of the Glands of the Body have been found out; all agreeing in this one thing, namely, That they separate the several Juices that are discernible in the Body, from the Mass of the Blood wherein they lay before. From their Texture they have of late been divided into *Conglomerate* and *Conglobate*. The *Conglomerate Glands* consist of many smaller Glands, which lie near one another, covered with one common Membrane, with one or more common Canals, into which the separated Juice is poured by little Pipes, coming

(*u*) *Observat. Anatom*
(*w*) *Epist. deGlandul Conglobat.*

(*x*) *Adenograph.*

coming from every smaller Glandule; as in the Liver, the Kidneys, the Pancreas, and Salival Glands of the Mouth. The *Conglobate Glands* are single, often without any Excretory Duct of their own, only perforated by the Lympheducts. Of all which Things, as Essential to the Nature of Glands, the Ancient Anatomists had no sort of Notion.

The *Mucilage of the Joints and Muscles* was found out by Dr. *Havers* (y). He discovered in every Joint, particular Glands, out of which issues a Mucilaginous Substance, whose Nature he examined by Numerous Experiments; which, with the Marrow supplied by the Bones, always serves to oil the Wheels, that so our Joints and Muscles might answer those Ends of Motion, for which Nature designed them. This was a very useful Discovery, since it has made abundance of Things that were obscure in that part of Anatomy, plain, and facile to be understood: And, among other Things, it shews the use of that excellent Oil which is contained in our Bones, and there separated by proper Strainers, from the Mass of the Blood; especially, since, by a nice Examination of the true inward Texture of all the Bones and Cartilages of the Body, he shew'd how this Oil is communicated to the Mucilage, and so united, as to perform their Office.

(y) Osteo-
log.

And

And if one compares what Dr. *Havar*'s says of Bones and Cartilages, with what had been said concerning them before him, his Obfervations about their Frame may well be added to some of the nobleft of all the former Difcoveries.

These are some of the moft remarkable Inftances, how far the Knowledge of the Frame of our Bodies has been carried in our Age. Several Obfervations may be made concerning them, which will be of Ufe to the prefent Queftion. (1.) It is evident, that only the moft vifible Things were anciently known; fuch alone as might be difcovered without great Nicety. Mufcles and Bones are eafily feparable; their Length is foon traced, and their Origination prefently found. The fame may be truly faid of large Blood-Veffels, and Nerves: But when they come to be exquifitely fub-divided, when their Smalnefs will not fuffer the Eye, much lefs the Hand, to follow them, then the Ancients were conftantly at a Lofs: For which Reafon they underftood none of the *Vifcera*, to any tolerable degree. (2.) One may perceive, that every new Difcovery ftrengthens what went before; otherwife the World would foon have heard of it, and the erroneous Theories of fuch Pretenders to new Things would have been exploded and forgotten, unlefs by here and there a curious Man, that
pleafes

pleases himself with reading obsolete Books. *Nullius in Verba* is not only the Motto of the ROYAL SOCIETY, but a received Principle among all the Philosophers of the present Age: And therefore, when once any new Discoveries have been examined, and received, we have more Reason to acquiesce in them, than there was formerly. This is evident in the *Circulation of the Blood*: Several Veins and Arteries have been found, at least, more exactly traced, since, than they were in Dr. *Harvey*'s Time. Not one of these Discoveries has ever shewn a single Instance of any Artery going *to*, or of any Vein coming *from* the Heart. Ligatures have been made of infinite Numbers of Vessels; and the Course of all the Animal Juices, in all manner of living Creatures, has thereby been made visible to the naked Eye; and yet not one of these has ever weakened Dr. *Harvey*'s Doctrine. The Pleasure of Destroying in Matters of this kind, is not much less than that of Building. And therefore, when we see that those Books which have been written against some of the eminentest of these Discoveries, though but a few Years ago, comparatively speaking, are so far dead, that it is already become a Piece of Learning even to know their Titles, we have sufficient Assurance that those Discoverers, whose Writings out-live Opposition, neither deceive themselves nor others.

So

So that whatsoever it might be formerly, yet in this Age, general Consent in Physiological Matters, especially after a long Canvass of the Things consented to, is an almost infallible Sign of Truth. (3.) The more ways are made use of to arrive at any one particular Part of Knowledge, the surer that Knowledge is, when it appears that these different Methods lend Help each to other. If *Malpighius*'s, or *Leeuwenhoek*'s Glasses had made such Discoveries as Men's Reason could not have agreed to; if Objects had appeared confused and disorderly in their Microscopes; if their Observations had contradicted what the naked Eye reveals, then their Verdict had been little worth. But when the Discoveries made by the Knife and the Microscope, disagree only as Twi-light and Noon-day, then a Man is satisfied that the Knowledge which each affords to us, differs only in Degree, not in Sort. (4.) It can signifie nothing in the present Controversie, to pretend that Books are lost; or to say, that, for ought we know, *Herophilus* might anciently have made this Discovery, or *Erasistratus* that; their Reasonings demonstrate the Extent of their Knowledge, as convincingly as if we had a Thousand old Systems of Ancient Anatomy exstant. (5.) In judging of Modern Discoveries, one is nicely to distinguish between *Hypothesis* and *Theory*. The
Anatomy

Anatomy of the Nerves holds good, whether the Nerves carry a Nutritious Juice to the several Parts of the Body, or no. The *Pancreas* sends a Juice into the *Duodenum*, which mixes there with the Bile, let the Nature of that Juice be what it will. Yet here a nice Judge may observe, that every Discovery has mended the Hypotheses of the Modern Anatomists; and so it will always do, till the Theories of every Part, and every Juice, be as entire as Experiments and Observations can make them.

As these Discoveries have made the Frame of our our own Bodies a much more intelligible Thing than it was before, though there is yet a great deal unknown; so the same Discoveries having been applied to, and found in almost all sorts of known Animals, have made the Anatomy of Brutes, Birds, Fishes and Insects, much more perfect than it could possibly be in former Ages. Most of the Rules which *Galen* lays down in his *Anatomical Administrations*, are concerning the Dissection of Apes. If he had been now to write, besides those tedious Advices how to part the Muscles from the Membranes, and to observe their several Insertions and Originations, the Jointings of the Bones, and the like, he would have taught the World how to make Ligatures of all sorts of Vessels, in their proper Places; what Liquors had been most
con-

convenient to make Injections with, thereby to discern the Courses of Veins, Arteries, Chyle-Vessels, or Lympheducts; how to unravel the Testicles; how to use Microscopes to the best Advantage: He would have taught his Disciples when and where to look for such and such Vessels or Glands; where Chymical Trials were useful; and what the Processes were, by which he made his Experiments, or found out his Theories: Which Things fill up every Page in the Writings of later Dissectors. This he would have done, as well as what he did, had these Ways of making Anatomical Discoveries been then known and practised. The World might then have expected such Anatomies of Brutes, as Dr. *Tyson* has given of the *Rattle-Snake*, the *Opossum*, and the *Orang-Outang*; or Dr. *Moulin*, of the *Elephant*: Such Dissections of Fishes as Dr. *Tyson*'s of the *Porpesse*; and *Steno*'s, of a *Shark's Head*: Such of Insects as *Malpighius*'s of a *Silk-Worm*; *Swammerdam*'s, of the *Ephemeron*; Dr. *Lister*'s, of *Snails*, and *Testaceous Animals*; Mr. *Waller*'s of the *Flying Gloeworm*; and the same Dr. *Tyson*'s, of *Long and Round Body-Worms*. All which shew Skill and industry, not conceivable by a Man that is not a little versed in these Matters.

To this *Anatomy of Bodies that have Sensitive Life*, we ought to add the *Anatomy of of Vegetables*, begun and brought to great Perfection in *Italy* and *England* at the same Time, by *Malpighius* and Dr. *Grew*. By their Glasses they have been able to give an Account of the different Textures of all the Parts of Trees, Shrubs and Herbs; to trace the several Vessels which carry Air, Lympha, Milk, Rosin and Turpentine, in those Plants which afford them; to describe the whole Process of Vegetation, from Seed to Seed; and, in a word, though they have left a great deal to be admired, because it was to them incomprehensible; yet they have discovered a great deal to be admired, because of its being known by their Means.

CHAP. XX.

Of Ancient and Modern Natural Histories of Elementary Bodies and Minerals

HAving now finished my Comparison of *Ancient and Modern Anatomy*, with as much Exactness as my little Insight into those Things would give me leave, I am sensible that most Men will think that I have been too tedious. But besides that I had not any where found it carefully done to my my Hands, (though it is probable that it has in Books which have escaped my Notice,) I thought that it would be a very effectual Instance, how little the Ancients may have been presumed to have perfected any one Part of Natural Knowledge, when their own Bodies, which they carried about with them, and which, of any thing, they were the nearlist concerned to know, were, comparatively speaking, so very imperfectly traced. However, in the remaining Parts of my Parallel, I shall be much shorter; which, I hope, may be some Amends for my too great Length in this.

From those *Instruments*, or *Mechanical Arts*, whether Ancient or Modern, by which *Knowledge* has been advanced, I am now to go to the *Knowledge* it self. According to the Method already proposed, I am to begin with *Natural History* in its usual Acceptation, as it takes in the *Knowledge* of the several Kinds of *Elementary Bodies, Minerals, Plants, Insects, Beasts, Birds*, and *Fishes*. The Usefulness and the Pleasure of this Part of Learning, is too well known to need any Proof. And besides, it is a Study, about which the greatest Men of all Ages have employed themselves. Of the very few lost Books that are mentioned in the *Old Testament*, one was an *History of Plants*, written by the Wisest of Men, and he a King. So that there is Reason to believe,

lieve, that *Natural History* was cultivated with abundance of Care by all those who did not place the Perfection of Knowledge in the Art of Wrangling about Questions, which were either useless, or which could not easily be decided.

Before I enter into Particulars, it is necessary to enquire what are the greatest Excellencies of a Compleat History of any one sort of Natural Bodies. This may soon be determined. That History of any Body, is certainly the best, which, by a full and clear Description, lays down all the Characteristical Marks of the Body then to be described; so as that its Specifical Idea may be clearly form'd, and it self certainly and easily distinguish'd from any other Body, though at first View, it be never so like it; which enumerates all its known Qualities; which shews whether there are any more besides those commonly observed; and, last of all, which enquires into the several Ways whereby that Body may be beneficial or hurtful to Man, or any other Body; by giving a particular Account of the several *Phaenomena* which appear upon its Application to, or Combination with other Bodies, of like, or unlike Natures. All this is plainly necessary, if a Man would write a full History of any single Species of Animals, Plants, Insects, or Minerals, whatsoever. Or, if he would draw up a General

neral History of any one of these *Universal Sorts*; then he ought to examine wherein every Species of this *Universal Sort* agrees each with other; or wherein they are discriminated from any other *Universal Sort* of Things: And thus, by degrees, descend to Particulars, and range every Species, not manifestly Anomalous, under its own Family, or Tribe; thereby to help the Memory of Learners, and assist the Contemplations of those who, with Satisfaction to themselves and others, would Philosophize upon this amazing Variety of Things.

By this Test the Comparison may be made. I shall begin with the simplest Bodies first; which as they are the commonest, so, one would think, should have been long ago examined with the strictest Care. By these I mean, *Air, Water, Fire, Earth,* commonly called *Elements.* Three of these are certainly distinct and real Bodies, endued with proper and peculiar Qualities, and so come under the present Question.

Of the *History of Air* the Ancients seem to have known little more than just what might be collected from the Observation of its most obvious Qualities. Its Necessity for the immediate Subsistence of the Life of all sorts of Animate Bodies, and the unspeakable Force of Rapid Winds, or Air forcibly driven all one Way, made it be sufficiently observed by all the World; whilst its Internal Texture, and very few of its remoter Qualities, were scarce so much as dreamt of by all the Philosophers of Antiquity. Its Weight only was known to *Aristotle* (z), (or the Author of the Book *de Coelo*,) who observed, that a full Bladder out-weighed an empty one. Yet this was carried no farther by any of the Ancients, that we know of; dis-believed by his own School, who seemed not to have attended to his Words, opposed and ridiculed, when again revived, and demonstrably proved, by the Philosophers of the present Age. All which are Evidences, that anciently it was little examined into, since Proofs were wanting to evince that, which Ignorance only made disputable. But this has been spoken to already; I shall therefore only add, that, besides what Mr. *Boyle* has written concerning the Air, we may consult *Otto Guerick*'s *Magdebourg-Experiments*; the *Experiments of the Academy del Cimento*; *Sturmius*'s *Collegium Curiosum*; Mr. *Halley*'s *Discourses concerning Gravity, and the Phaenomena of the Baroscope*, in the *Philosophical Transactions*. (a). From all which, we shall find not only how little of the Nature of the Air was anciently known; but also, that there is scarce any one Body, whose Theory is now so near being compleated, as is that of the Air.

The

(z) *De Coelo*, l. 4. c. 4

(a) Num 179, & 181

The *Natural History of Earth and Water* comes under that of *Minerals*: *Fire*, as it appears to our Senses, seems to be a Quality, rather than a Substance; and to consist in its own Nature, in a Rapid Agitation of Bodies, put into a quick Motion; and divided by this Motion, into very small Parts. After this had been once asserted by the *Corpuscularian* Philosophers, it was exceedingly strengthned by many Experimental Writers, who have taken abundance of Pains to state the whole *Doctrine of Qualities* clearly, and intelligibly; that so Men might know the difference between the Existence or Essential Nature of a Body, and its being represented to our Senses under such or such an Idea. This is the Natural Consequence of proceeding upon clear and intelligible Principles; and resolving to admit nothing as conclusive, which cannot be manifestly conceived, and evidently distinguished from every thing else. Here, if in any thing, the old Philosophers were egregiously defective: What has been done since, will appear, by consulting, among others, the Discourses which Mr. *Boyle* has written upon most of the considerable Qualities of Bodies, which come under our Notice; such as his *Histories of Fluidity and Firmness, of Colours, of Cold,* his *Origin of Forms and Qualities, Experiments about the Mechanical Production of divers par-*

ticular Qualities, and several others, which come under this Head; because they are not Notions framed only in a Closet, by the help of a lively Fancy: but genuine Histories of the *Phaenomena* of Natural Bodies; which appeared in vast Numbers, after such Trials were made upon them, as were proper to discover their several Natures.

And therefore, that it may not be thought that I mistake every plausible Notion of a Witty Philosopher, for a new Discovery of Nature, I must desire that my former Distinction between *Hypotheses* and *Theories* may be remembred. I do not here reckon the several *Hypotheses* of *Des Cartes*, *Gassendi*, or *Hobbes*, as Acquisitions to real Knowledge, since they may only be Chimaera's, and amusing Notions, fit to entertain working Heads. I only alledge such Doctrines as are raised upon faithful Experiments, and nice Observations; and such Consequences as are the immediate Results of, and manifest Corollaries drawn from, these Experiments and Observations: Which is what is commonly meant by *Theories*. But of this more hereafter.

That the *Natural History of Minerals* was anciently very imperfect, is evident from what has been said of *Chymistry* already; to which, all the Advances that have ever been made in that Art, unless when

when Experiments have been tried upon *Vegetable* or *Animal Substances*, are properly to be referred. I take *Minerals* here in the largest sense; for all sorts of *Earths, Sulphurs, Salts, Stones, Metals*, and *Minerals* properly so called. For *Chymistry* is not only circumstantially useful, but essentially necessary here; since a great many Minerals of very differing Natures would never have been known to have belonged to several Families, if they had not been examined in the Furnaces of the Chymists. Nay, most *Fossils* are of a such a Nature, that what sort of Minerals they contain, cannot be known, till they be tried in the Fire. Worthless Marcasites cannot any otherwise be distinguisht from rich Lumps of Ore. For this Reason, and because the Subterraneous World is not so easily accessible, the Knowledge of *Fossils*, taken in the general, has received less Advancement than any one Part of Natural Learning. But I shall rather chuse to speak here of the Discoveries which have been made in the Mineral Kingdom without the help of Chymistry: The greatest of which is, of a Stone which the Ancients admired (*b*), without ever examining to what Uses it might be applied; and that is the *Magnet*; the noblest Properties whereof Sir *William Temple* acknowledges to be ancient-

(*b*) Their Opinions are collected by *Gassendi*, in his *Animadversions upon* Laertius's *Life of* Epicurus, *p.* 362, 363.

ly

ly unknown *(c)*: Which is more indeed, than what some do *(d)*, who at the same time, make our Fore-fathers to have been extremely stupid, that could suffer such a Discovery to be ever lost. So that all that can be said of the Advances which, by the Uses of the *Load-stone*, have been made in several Parts of Learning, do not in the least affect Sir *William Temple*. However, I shall mention some of the greatest; because he charges the Moderns with not making all those Uses of so noble an Invention, which he supposes the Ancient *Greeks* and *Romans* would have made, had it fallen into their Hands: Which makes him assert, that the Discoveries hereby made in remote Countries have been rather pursued to accumulate Wealth *(e)*, than to encrease Knowledge. Now, if both these can be done at once, there is no harm done: And since there is no Dispute of the one, I think it will be an easy Matter to prove the other. I shall name but a few Particulars, most of them rather belonging to another Head.

Geography therefore was anciently a very imperfect Study, for want of this Knowledge of the Properties of the *Load-stone*. The Figure of the Earth could formerly only be guess'd at; which Sir *William Temple's*

(c) P. 48.

(d) This they have collected from a Passage in *Plautus*, (*Merc* Act 5 Sc) *Huc Secundus vertus nunc est, cape modo Vorsoriam*; where by *Vorsoria* they understand the *Compass*, because the Needle always points towards the North. Whereas *Vorsoria* is nothing but that Rope with which the Mariners turned their Sails.

(e) P. 49.

ples admired *Epicurus* (*f*) did, for that Reason, deny to be Round; wherein he seems to have been more reasonable, than in many other of his Assertions; because he thought it an Affront to the Understanding of Man, to be determined by bare Conjectures, in a Matter which could at that time be no other way decided. Whereas now, most Parts of the Ocean being made easily accessible, the Latitudes, and respective Bearings of every Place, are commonly known: The Nature and Appearances of Winds and Tides are become familiar, and have been nicely examined by Intelligent Men in all Parts of the World: The Influence of the Moon, joined with the Motion of the Earth, have been taken in upon almost infallible Grounds, to found Theories of the Sea's Motion upon. And there are great Numbers of other noble, pleasant and useful Propositions in *Geography*, *Astronomy* and *Navigation*, which ultimately owe their Original to the Discovery of that single Quality of this wonderful Stone, *that it points towards the North*. If these Sciences have brought to us the Wealth of the *Indies*; if they have enlarged the Commerce and Intercourse of Mankind, it is so far from being a Disparagement to the Industry of the Moderns, who have cultivated them to such useful Pur-

(*f*) Vid. *Gassendi*'s Animadversions upon *Laertius*'s *Epicurus*, p. 672.

Purposes, that it is the highest Character that could be given of those Men, that they pursued their Inventions to such noble Ends. Knowledge, not reduced to Practice, when that is possible, is so far imperfect, that it loses its principal Use. And it is not for acquiring Wealth, but for mis-employing it when it is acquired, that a Man ought to be blamed.

Now, to compleat what I have to say of *Geography* all at once, I shall take notice, that as the Improvements by Navigation, have made all the Sea-Coasts of the Universe known, so the Art of Engraving upon Copper-Plates has made it easie for Men to draw such Charts of every particular Coast, as will imprint lasting and just Idea's of all the extream Parts of the known World. For want of this, the Ancient Descriptions even of those Countries which they knew, were rude, and imperfect: Their Maps were neither exact nor beautiful: The Longitudes and Latitudes of Places, were very little considered; the latter of which can now be exactly determined, and the former may be very nearly adjusted, since the Application of Telescopes to Astronomical Uses has enabled Men to make much nicer Observations of the Moon's Eclipses than could formerly be made; besides those of *Jupiter's* Satellites, to which the Ancients were entirely Strangers. This makes our Maps wonderfully exact; which are not only the Divertisements of the Curious, but of unspeakable Use in Civil Life, at Sea especially; where, by the help of Sea Charts, Sailers know where they are, what Rocks lye near them, what Sands they must avoid; and can as perfectly tell which Way they must steer to any known Port of the Universe, as a Traveller can, upon *Salisbury-Plain*, or *New-Market-Heath*, which Way he must ride to a great Town, which he knows before-hand is not far from the Edge of the Plain, or of the Heath. *Velserus* has printed some ancient Maps (g), that were made for the Direction of the *Roman* Quarter-Masters; and if a Man will compare them with *Sanson*'s, or *Blaeu*'s, he will see the difference; which in future Ages will certainly be vastly greater, if those Countries which are now barbarous, or undiscovered, should ever come into the Hands of a Civilized or Learned People. But I have not yet done with the *Loadstone*.

(g) Commonly called the *Peutingerian* Tables.

Besides these occasional Uses of the *Magnet*, its Nature, abstractedly taken, has been nicely enquired into, thereby to discover both its own Qualities, and its Relation to other Bodies that are round about it. And here, indeed, one may justly wonder,

der, that when *Flavio Amalphi* (*h*) had discovered, that Iron touch'd with a *Magnet*, points towards the North, that all the Philosophers of that Age did not immediately try all manner of Experiments upon that strange Stone, which was found to be so exceedingly useful in Matters of common Life. The *Portugueses*, who first made daring Voyages, by the help of the Compass, into the Southern and South-Eastern Seas, better knew the Value of that rich Discovery: But Philosophy was in those darker Ages divided between the *School-men* and the *Chymists*; the former presently salved the Business with their *Substantial Forms*, and what they could not comprehend, came very properly under the Notion of an *Occult Quality*: The latter found nothing extraordinary in their Crucibles, when they analyzed the *Magnet*; and so they seem soon to have given it over: Besides, in those Days, few Men studied Chymistry with any other Design than that of finding out the Philosopher's Stone, to which the Load-stone could do them no farther service than that of supplying them with another hard

(*h*) To him this Discovery is attributed by *Salmuth* upon *Pancirollus*; others call him *John Goia*, of *Amalphi*; but *Gassendi*, *Animad* pag. 364. says, it was found out by a *Frenchman*, about the Year MCC. since it is mentioned by one *Guyotus Provineus*, a *French* Poet of that time, who calls the Compass *Marineta*; to which *Gassendi* also adds, That it was most probably a *French* Invention, because the *North-Point* is by all Nations marked in their Compasses by a *Flower-de-Luce*, the Arms of *France*.

hard Name to Cant with (*i*). For these Reasons therefore, it lay in a good measure neglected by Men of Letters, till our Famous Country-man, Dr. *Gilbert* of *Colchester*, by a vast number of Experiments, found that the *Earth* was but a *larger Magnet*; and he, indeed, was the first Author of all those Magnetical Speculations which have been made since his had the good fortune to be generally approved. This Great Man, whom *Galileo* and *Kepler* express a great Veneration for in their Writings, deserves here to be mentioned upon another Account; because He, my Lord *Bacon*, and Mr. *Harriot*, all *Englishmen*, are the Three Men to whom Monsieur *Des Cartes* was so very much obliged for the first Hints of the greatest Things, which he has given us in his Philosophical and Mathematical Discourses. For nothing does more convincingly put Things of this Nature out of doubt, than to trace them up to their first Originals, which can be done but in very few. So great have been the Advantages which have accrued to the World, only by Men's Enquiries into the Properties of one single Natural Body.

But the Knowledge of *Minerals* (strictly so called) though infinitely useful to the Life of Man, is not the only thing which may be learn'd in the Subterraneous World. The Bowels of the Earth are wonderfully

Fruit-

(*i*) *Magnesia Nigra*, is one of the hard Words used by *Eyrenæus Philalethes*: and it is ridiculed by *Surly* in *Ben Johnson's Alchemist*.

Fruitful, and afford a Variety, comparatively speaking, not much regarded till these later Ages. Not only *Salts* and *Metals*, *Marble*, *Coal*, and *Amber*, may be, and are dug from thence; but the Inhabitants of the Earth and Sea, have made their Graves in the solidest Rocks, in the profoundest Caverns, in Places, to one's thinking, the most inaccessible, as well as the most unexspected, that could have been imagined. Beds of *Oysters*, *Cockles*, and *Scallops*, have been found in the Bowels of the highest Hills, and the hardest Quarries. Groves of Trees have been taken out of the Ground, in Countries where they have never been seen to grow. In short, by raking into the deepest Places of the Earth, we have seen that Things have once changed their Places; and without the Authority of Writings, or Ancient Tradition, we are assured that the Face of the World is not what it always was.

Men have yet proceeded farther, and made Observations upon the Figures of every Stone which they found; very many of which, Antiquity, and even every other Age before this, did quite overlook. Those, whose Lustre and Colour made them remarkable, which are peculiarly called *Gems*, or those whose Figure had something that was surprizing at first view, were indeed taken notice of, and sufficiently

ently valued; but of them too, very few were then known, in comparison of what have since been discovered. The Ancients *Knowledge of the Species of Stones*, and of the whole *Natural History of the Earth*, is in a manner all contained in the 33^d, 34th, 35th, 36th, and 37th Books of *Pliny's Natural History*; where there is so much Fabulous, that it is not easily distinguishable from what is Real: If this were compared with the Writings of *Fabius Columna* (k), *Agostino Scilla* (l), *Steno* (m), *Ray* (n), *Hooke* (o), *Lister* (p), *Woodward* (q), and *Plot* (r), what new Scenes of Knowledge would appear? What Discoveries has Signior *Scilla* made of the *Petrifactions* (as they are vulgarly esteemed) of the Isle of *Malta* alone? The Ancients were not sufficiently aware of the Treasures which the Earth contains within it. The *Ancients*, did I say? hardly any of the *Moderns*, till within these last Thirty Years. *Gold*, indeed, and *Silver*, have, for very many Ages, been insatiably thirsted after; and the other Metals, *Tin* and *Copper*, *Iron* and *Lead*, whose Uses have long been known, have

(k) *De Purpurâ: Dissertat. de Glossopetris.*

(l) *La Vana Speculazione disingannata dal Senso*, printed at *Naples*, in MDCLXX. and epitomiz'd in the *Philosoph. Transact.* numb. 219.

(m) *In Prodromo*: & *Dissertat. de Cane Carchariæ & Glossopetris.*

(n) *Travels*, p. 113, 131. and *Three Physico-Theological Discourses*, Edit. 2.

(o) *Microgr.* p. 109, 112. *Lecture of Springs*, p. 48, 49, 50.

(p) *Philosoph. Transact.* & *de Cochlitis*

(q) *Essay towards a Natural History of the Earth*

(r) *Nat. Hist.* of Oxfordsh.

have been carefully searched for. But when those Six Metals, and some of the most remarkable Minerals, such as *Mercury, Antimony, Vitriol, Nitre, Sulphur, Sal Gemmæ, Pit-Coal, Amber,* and the like, were once found, the Curiosity of Mankind was pretty much at a stand. Whereas, since so many Learned and Industrious Men have thought it worth their while to make Enquiries after the nicest Varieties, and most minute Productions of their Mother Earth, they have found such incredible Numbers of *formed Stones,* and *Shells as hard as Stones,* upon its Surface, and in its lowermost Recesses that Men have ever dug to, that they have thereby been enabled to raise several Hypotheses (*s*), which may perhaps hereafter, when Men are better acquainted with the Productions of the Subterraneous World, be a means of solving some of the greatest Difficulties in the *Mosaical History.*

(*s*) Vid. *Woodward's Essay towards the Natural History of the Earth,* and *Whiston's Theory of the Earth.*

I have taken notice of this, to justifie those Gentlemen who have laboured in these sort of Enquiries: Some of them who have taken the greatest Pains, have been publicly ridiculed (*t*), as if what they had done, had tended no more to the Advancement of valuable Knowledge, than if they had gather'd Pebbles upon the Shore

(*t*) See the Character of a Virtuoso, in the *Essay in Defense of the Female Sex.*

Shore to throw away again, as *Caligula's* Soldiers did upon the *Batavian* Coast, when they should have been transported into *Britain*. There would have been a stop put to the Progress of Learning long ago, if immediate Usefulness had been the sole Motive of Men's Enquiries. Whatsoever our Great Creator has thought fit to give a Specifical Being to, is, if accessible, certainly worth our searching after. And tho' we do not see the present Advantage that will accrue to Mankind by the Discovery of this or that particular Species of Minerals, Stones, Plants, or Insects, yet Posterity may; and then all the Returns for the Uses that they can ever make of them, will be in a great measure due to him that found them out. He that first pick'd up a *Magnet*, and perceived that it would draw Iron, might then perhaps be laugh'd at, for preserving a Child's Play-thing; and yet the Observation of that noble Quality, was necessarily previous to the succeeding Observations of its pointing towards the North, which have proved so unspeakably useful in Civil Life. So that I think all these excellent Men do highly deserve Commendation for these seemingly useless Labours, and the more, since they run the hazard of being laughed at by Men of Wit and Satyr, who always have their End, if they make their Readers Sport,

whe-

whether the thing which they expose, deserves to be ridiculed or not.

But it is time to leave this Argument, when I have observed, that all that has yet been published concerning the *formed Stones, Shells* and *Petrifactions* found in and upon the Earth, will seem but Gleanings, in comparison of that vast Collection which those excellent Naturalists, Mr. *Edward Lhwyd* of *Oxford*, and Dr. *Woodward* have promised shortly to present the World withal.

CHAP. XXI.

Of Ancient and Modern Histories of Plants.

THE *Natural History of Plants* comes next; which, for Variety and Use, is one of the noblest and pleasantest Parts of Knowledge. Its Mechanical and Medicinal Advantages were early known. Fruits afforded the first Sustenance to Mankind; and the old Heathens esteemed those worthy of Consecration, who taught them to Till their Grounds, Gather their Seed, and Grind their Corn: With Trees they built themselves Houses; afterwards they

found

found that the Bark of some Plants would serve for Cloaths, and others afforded Medicines against Wounds and Diseases. There is no doubt therefore, but this Part of Knowledge was sufficiently cultivated for the Uses of Humane Life; especially when Mankind becoming numerous, those that were inquisitive communicated their Notions together, and Conversation had introduced the Arts of Luxury and Plenty into the World. Even in *America*, where *most* of the Nations which the *Europaeans* discovered were Salvage, and *all* Unlearned, the Natives knew the Oeconomical and Medical Uses of many of their noblest Plants. They made Bread of their *Mayz*, and the Roots of *Yucca*, some smoaked *Tobacco*, some poysoned their Arrows with the Juice of one Plant, others made their *Chocolate* with the Seeds of another, some cloathed themselves with *Cotton*, others cured *Agues* with the *Cortex*, and Venereal Diseases with *Guajacum*, and almost every other sort of Disease to which they were incident with some Specific or other, which Use and Experience had taught them. But whether the *Natural History of Plants* was yet notwithstanding all this, so exactly known formerly, as it is at present, is the Question.

The ancientest Writers of *Plants* now exstant, are *Theophrastus*, *Pliny*, and *Dioscorides*;

scorides; indeed, the only ones who say any thing considerable to the present Purpose. *Theophrastus* describes little; gives abundance of Observations upon several Plants, and the like; but what he says, is rather to be taken notice of when we speak of *Agriculture* and *Gardening*, than in this place. *Pliny* and *Dioscorides*, who lived long after him, give Descriptions indeed of a great many Plants, but short, imperfect, and without Method; they say, for Instance, that a Plant is hairy, has broad Leaves, that its Stalks are knotty, hollow, or square; that its Branches creep upon the Ground, are erect, and so forth; in short, if there is any thing remarkable in the Colour or Shape of the Stalk, Root, Seed, Flower or Fruit, which strikes the Eye at first sight, it may perhaps be taken notice of, but then every thing is confused, and seldom above one or two Plants of a sort are mentioned; though sometimes later *Botanists* have observed some Scores plainly reducible to the same general Head. *Pliny* ranges many of the Plants, which he describes in an Order (*u*) something Alphabetical; others (*w*) he digests according to their Virtues; others (*x*) he puts together, because they were discovered by great Persons, and

(*u*) *N. H.* l. 12 c. 13 and l. 27. throughout

(*w*) The 12th. Book is chiefly of Plants which bear odoriferous Gums, and so on of all the rest.

(*x*) *N. H.* l. 25. c. 6, 7 *& alibi passim*

and called by their Discoverers Names: All which Methods, how much soever they may assist the Memory in remembring hard Names, or in retaining the *Materia Medica* in one View in a Man's Head, signifie nothing to the Understanding the Characteristical Differences of the several Plants; by which alone, and not by accidental Agreements in Virtue, Smell, Colour, Taste, Place of Growth, Time of Sprouting, or any Mechanical Use to which they may be made serviceable, Men may reasonably exspect to become exact *Botanists*: Without such a Method, to which the Ancients were altogether Strangers, the Knowledge of Plants is a confused thing, depending wholly upon an uncommon Strength of Memory and Imagination, and even with the Help of the best Books scarce attainable without a Master, and then too not under a very long Time.

Conradus Gesner, to whose Labours the World has been unspeakably beholden in almost all Parts of Natural History, was the first Man (that I know of) who hinted at the true Way to distinguish Plants, and reduce them to fixed and certain Heads. In a Letter to *Theodorus Zuingerus* (y), he says, that Plants are to be ranged according to the Shape of their Flowers, Fruits and Seeds; having observed that Cultivation, or any accidental Difference of Soil,

(y) *Epist. Medicinal.* p 113 a.

never alters the Shape of these more Essential Parts; but that every Plant has something there peculiar, by which it may be distinguished, not only from others of a remoter *Genus*, but also from those of the same Family.

About the same time, *Andreas Caesalpinus*, and *Fabius Columna*, the first especially, reduced that into an Art, which *Gesner* had hinted at before. The first of these, divided the whole Body of Plants, then known, into Classes, from the Number and Order of their Seeds and Seed-Vessels, and drew up a History accordingly. But his Method was too general; and because it took too little notice of the *Roots*, *Leaves*, *Stalks*, and *Perianthia* of Plants, which in some Tribes ought necessarily to be considered, it was long laid by as useless; though *Clusius*, *Gaspar Bauhinus*, *Parkinson*, *Gerard* and *Johnson*, and *John Bauhinus*, had taken very laudable Pains, not only in describing the more general Sorts taken notice of by the Ancients, but also in observing their several Sub-divisions with great Niceness and Skill. *Gaspar Bauhinus*, who spent Forty Years in compleating his *Pinax*, or *General Index* to all the Botanical Writers, Ancient and Modern, that had appeared before him, ranged the whole System of Plants, then known, into such Classes as he thought properest. Yet though his Method

thod is allow'd to have been the best, setting *Caesalpinus*'s aside, which had till then been made use of, (z) it was far from being Natural, and accordingly has never since been follow'd. *John Bauhinus* also had described every particular Plant then known, in his *General History of Plants*, with great Accuracy; and compared whatsoever had been said by former Botanists, and adjusted old Names to those Plants which Modern Herbarists had gathered, with so much Care, that the Philological part of *Botany* seems by him to have, in a manner, received its utmost Perfection.

(z) Vid. *Morison*. *Prælud. Botanic.* p. 403.

The great Work therefore already begun by *Caesalpinus* and *Columna*, was still imperfect; which, though perhaps not the most Laborious, was yet the most necessary to a Man that would consider those things Philosophically, and comprehend the whole Vegetable Kingdom, as the Chymists call it, under one View. This was, to digest every Species of Plants under such and such Families and Tribes; that so, by the help of a general Method (taken only from the Plants themselves, and not from any accidental Respects, under which they may be considered) once thoroughly understood, a Learner might not be at a loss upon the Sight of every new Plant that he should meet with, but might discern its general Head at first View; and then, by

running

running over the Tables thereunto belonging, might, at laſt, either come to the particular Species which he ſought for, or, which would pleaſe him much better, find that the Plant before him was hitherto undeſcribed, and that by it there would be a new acceſſion made to the old Stock. Mr. *Ray* drew a rough Draught of this Matter, in the *Tables of Plants* inſerted into Biſhop *Wilkins*'s Book, *Of a Real Character, and Philoſophical Language*; and was ſoon followed by Dr. *Morifon*, in his *Hortus Regius Bleſenſis*, who, purſuant to his own Method, (which, indeed, is nothing elſe but *Andreas Caeſalpinus*'s a little alter'd) begun *A General Hiſtory of Plants*; which he not living to finiſh, Mr. *Ray* undertook the whole Work anew, and very happily compleated it.

This great Performance of his, which will be a ſtanding Monument of Modern Induſtry and Exactneſs, deſerves to be more particularly deſcribed. Firſt, therefore, He gives an Anatomical Account, from *Malpighius* and *Grew*, of Plants in general: And becauſe the Ancients had ſaid nothing upon that Subject, of which, for want of Microſcopes, they could have but a very obſcure Notion, all that he ſays upon that Head is Modern. Afterwards, when he comes to particular Plants, he draws up Tables,

bles, to which he reduces the whole Vegetable Kingdom, except some few irregular Plants, which stand by themselves. These Tables are taken from the Shape and Colour of the Flowers, Seeds, Seed-Vessels, Stalks, Leaves and Roots; from the Number or Order of these when determined, and Irregularity when undetermined; from the want, or having of particular Juices, Lympha's, Milks, Oils, Rosins, or the like: In short, from Differences, or Agreements, wholly arising from the Plants themselves. His Descriptions are as exact as *John Bauhine's* every where; since he copy's him where others have not described a Plant, better than he; and always supplies, with great Nicety and Art, what was wanting in their Descriptions: We may be sure therefore that here has been a gradual Improvement; for *John Bauhine's* Descriptions are much better than those of the generality of Botanists that were before him; and there are scarce any of theirs, which are not preferable to those of *Pliny* and *Dioscorides*: He gives the *Synonyma* of the most exact and best known Botanists; the want of adjusting which carefully, had made former Compilers tedious; and by inserting what was already exstant in the *Malabar-garden, Boym's Flora Sinensis, Marcgravius's Natural History of* Brasil, *Hernandez's Account of the Plants of* Mexico, *Cornutus's nutus*'s *History of the Plants of* Canada, and other *Exotic* Accounts of Natural Rarities, into his General History, has shewed, that the Moderns have been as careful to compleat the Natural History of remoter Countries, as to understand the Productions of their own.

Before I quit this Work of Mr. *Ray*'s, which is but one of the many Labours that he has happily gone through to enlarge the Bounds of Natural Knowledge, I must observe what he delights so much to have remembred; That a considerable part of the Debt which Posterity will owe to this excellent Naturalist, will be due to the Assistances which he has for many Years received from my most Learned Friend Dr. *Tancred Robinson*, whose Skill in all Parts of Physical Knowledge have long made him capable of performing whatsoever he should think fit to undertake in that sort of Learning, and consequently of enlarging the Bounds of Natural Knowledge as much as any of those great Men who have been here remembred.

It may be wonder'd at, perhaps, why I should mention Modern Discoveries of Natural Knowledge in the *East* and *West Indies*, since the Ancients were not to be blamed for being ignorant of Things which they had no Opportunity of knowing. But, besides

besides that it proves the Extent of the Knowledge of the Present Age in Natural History, which may be considered, without any regard to the Opportunities of acquiring it; it proves also, against Sir *William Temple*, that the Moderns have done what they could in every Point, to make the greatest Use they were able of every Addition to their former Knowledge, which might accrue to them by the Discovery of the Usefulness of the *Load-stone* in Navigation: His words are these; (a) *The vast Continents of* China, *the* East *and* West-Indies, *the long Extent and Coasts of* Africa, *have been hereby introduced into our Acquaintance, and our Maps; and great Encreases of Wealth and Luxury, but none of Knowledge brought among us, further than the Extent and Situation of Countreys, the Custom and Manners of so many Original Nations.*——— *I do not doubt but many great and more noble Uses would have been made of such Conquests, or Discoveries, if they had fallen to the Share of the* Greeks *and* Romans*, in those Ages, when Knowledge and Fame were in as great Request as endless Gains and Wealth are among us now: And how much greater Discoveries might have been made by such Spirits as theirs, is hard to guess.* Sir *William Temple* here owns, that the *Political* Uses which can be made by such Discoveries, are, comparatively speaking, but inconsiderable; though,

(a) P. 49.

though, at the same time, he confesses, that even those have not been neglected, since he acknowledges that Men have brought from those Barbarous Nations an Account of their *Customs and Manners*, which is the only Political Use, that I know of, that is to be learnt by Travel. What other Advantages might have been made, is hard to tell, unless such as may conduce to the Compleating of Natural History; the Benefits whereof are agreed upon, of all Hands, to be very great. The Subject now before me is *Botanics*, which has been so far from being neglected, that all imaginable Care has been taken to compleat it. Monsieur *Herman* spent several Years in the *East-Indies*, and at the *Cape of Good Hope*, to bring back into *Europe* an Account of the Natural Rarities of those Countries; and his Writings since his return, shew that he did not lose his Time. Monsieur *Van Rheed*, the noble Collector of the Plants that are so magnificently printed in the Eleven Volumes of the *Hortus Malabaricus*, has added more to the Number of those formerly known, than are to be found in all the Writings of the Ancients. As much may be said of that Excellent Collection of Exotic Plants which Dr. *Plukenet* has since given us in his incomparable Tables, besides great Numbers before undescribed, of which he has set down Characteristical Marks in his

Botanical

Botanical Almagest. Nay, this ought farther to be added in his Commendation; That coming after those who had newly done so great Things before him, such a Harvest where small Gleanings were rationally to be expected, is more surprizing and extraordinary. When (*b*) Prince Maurice of *Nassaw* was in *Brasil*, he ordered Pictures and Descriptions to be taken of all the Beasts, Birds, Fishes and Plants that could be found in that Country: They are now in the King of *Prussia*'s Library fit for the Press. But I must not forget Dr. *Sloane*'s *Catalogue of the Plants of* Jamaica, *and the* Caribbee *Islands*, a Specimen only of a larger Work, which when once it appears, will (if we had no other Arguments) effectually confute all those who imagine that *Wealth* and *Luxury* only have been the Motives of *Europæan* Voyages into the *New World.* Since I may venture to say, that there is but a very small Part of the *Old* so well known, after so long study, as those Islands, as to all their Natural Productions, will then be, through the Labour and Skill of that industrious Naturalist. And if Mr. *Banister* had lived to have compleated his Enquiries into the *Natural History* of *Virginia*, we should have had another Instance of our own Nation, how very Laborious and Careful the Men of these later Ages have been to leave no part

(*b*) *Mentzel.* Index Plantar. Multilin. *in Præfatione.*

part of accessible Knowledge uncultivated. Every Day New Additions are made to this Part of Natural History. *Breynius's*, *Plumier's*, *Hermane-Camelli's* Collections, are Modern to those of *Bellonius*, *Clusius*, *Rauwolfius*, and *Prosper Alpinus*; as theirs are to those of *Pliny* and *Dioscorides*. One is also to consider, that this is a much more laborious Business, than the Knowledge of Fowls, Fishes, and Quadrupeds. The Confusion in which the Ancients left *Botanical Knowledge*, shews how little they understood it. And, which is still more remarkable, it is not only in Accounts of Plants peculiar to the *Indies*, or to *China*, that our *Botanical Knowledge* excels theirs, but in the Productions of Countries, equally accessible to them, as to us. There are no new Species in *Europe* or *Asia*, which the Ancient Herbarists could not have discovered; no new Soils to produce them without Seed, in case such a thing were ever naturally possible. Let but a Man compare Mr. *Ray's Catalogue of English Plants*, and those other numerous Catalogues of the Plants of other Countries, drawn up by other Modern Botanists, with the Writings of *Pliny* and *Dioscorides*; let him examine *Ray's General History*, or, if that be not at hand, *Gerard's*, *Parkinson's*, or *John Bauhine's Herbals*, or *Gaspar Bauhine's Pinax*; and deduct every Plant, not growing wild,
with-

within the Limits of the *Roman* Empire, and he will see enough to convince him, that not only this Part of Knowlede is incomparably more exact and large than it was formerly, but also, by comparing the Writings of the first Restorers of the Knowledge of Simples, *Matthiolus*, *Dodonaeus*, *Fuchsius*, *Turner*, and the rest, with the Writings of *Plukenet*, *Ray* and *Morison*, that it has been always growing, and will do so still, till the Subject be exhausted.

It is well known, that Travelling in *Mahometan* Countries is extremely dangerous; that it is what no Man that makes Learning his Aim in Journeying, would willingly undertake, if he were not ardently possessed with the Love of it. So that whatsoever Perils the *Ancient Sages* endured in their Journeys into *Aegypt* for Knowledge, they are equalled at least, if not out-done by our *Modern Sages*; to use that Word in Sir *William Temple*'s sence, for one that goes far and near to seek for Knowledge. Nay, I may safely add, that a few inquisitive and learned Travellers, such as *Rauwolfius*, *Prosper Alpinus*, *Bellonius*, *Guillandinus*, and Sir *George Wheler*, have acquainted the Learned Men of these Parts of the World with the Natural History of the Countries of the *Levant*, not only better than they could have known it by reading the Books of the Ancients, but, in many

Parti-

Particulars, better than the Ancients themselves, Natives of those very Countries, knew it, if the exstant Books can enable us to give a competent Judgment in this Matter. And if Travelling far for Knowledge, be sufficient to recommend the Ancients to our Imitation, I may observe, that Mr. *Edmond Halley*, who went to St. *Helena*, an Island situate in the XVIth. Degree of Southern Latitude, to take an Account of the Fixed Stars in the Southern Hemisphere, which are never visible to us who live in the Northern; and to *Dantzick*, to conferr about Astronomical Matters, with the great *Hevelius*, has taken much larger Journeys than any of the Ancients ever did in the sole Pursuit of Knowledge.

CHAP. XXII.

Of Ancient and Modern Agriculture and Gardening.

THE *Ancients* set so great a Value upon the Country-man's Arts, and we have so many Treatises still exstant concerning them, written by their greatest Philosophers, their ablest Philologers, and their

best

best Poets, that to say nothing of them, may be thought an inexcusable Omission. *Husbandry* and *Gardening* are Subjects upon which *Theophrastus* (*Aristotle*'s Darling Disciple,) *Varro* (who is said to be the learnedest of all the *Romans*,) and *Pliny* (perhaps no-way his inferior) have written large Discourses yet remaining. *Varro* and *Pliny* quote numbers of Authors, some of them no less than Crowned-Heads, since lost. *Hesiod*, whom some of the Ancients make older than *Homer*, and *Virgil* the Prince of *Roman* Poets, have left us Precepts of these Arts. *Columella* says, they are related to Philosophy it self, which those Heathen Sages Priz'd so highly: And the later *Roman* Writers are still upbraiding the Luxury of their own Times, which wholly took off their Minds from these most useful Employments; and sending their effeminate Country-men back to their renowned Ancestors who went from the Plough to the Camp, and having there commanded victorious Armies, returned back again to the Plough, to redeem the Time they had lost.

There is no doubt but great Things were done in these Arts by the Ancients: Had we no Books remaining to acquaint us with their Knowledge, yet the thing shews it self: Countries cannot be peopled by Civilized Nations, nor great Cities filled, nor

Trade carried on by polite and industrious Inhabitants, unless the Arts of Husbandry flourish. Mankind, without them, would be Wild, like the *Negroes*, and *American* Salvages, or must live in movable *Clans* like the *Arabs*. But yet one Nation may be much more knowing in these Things than another, and one Age consequently, though all may have Skill enough to answer the Necessities of Civil Life.

In making my Comparison, I shall comprehend all that the Ancients understood by their *Res Rustica*, as it takes in the *Forester's*, the *Husbandman's*, and the *Gardener's* Business: *Cato*, *Varro* and *Columella* include the *Grasier's* also, thereby compleating the whole Body of *Farming*; but since *his* Work cannot well be made a Science of, I shall omit it.

By a *Forester* here, I understand one that knows how to Plant, Propagate and Encrease all sorts of Timber Trees; what Soils are proper for every sort; how they may best be defended from Dangers in their Growth; to what Uses they are most applicable, when they have arrived to their utmost Perfection; and how they may be best applied: Such a Man, in short, as Mr. *Evelyn* instructs in his *Silva*, where he gives a full System of the *Wood-man's* Skill, what he ought to know, and what to practise. A great part of his Work, and indeed

deed the Nicest part of it, the Ancients were Strangers to, as having less Occasion for it. The World was then, comparatively speaking, in its Infancy; there was no want of Wood, for Fuel, Building, or Ships; and this Plenty made Men less curious in Contriving Methods of Preserving what they had in so great Abundance. *England*, till within a few Ages, was every where over-run with Wood: The *Hercynian* Forest anciently took up what is now the most flourishing Part of *Germany*: And *France*, which is at present so wonderfully Populous, that little Cultivable Ground remains Untill'd, was in *Caesar*'s time overspread with Woods and Forests. As Men encrease, Tillage becomes more and more requisite; the consumption of Wood will be proportionably greater; and its want, and the necessary Uses of Timber, which grow upon Men as they become more numerous, will of consequence, put them upon Ways to preserve and encrease it. Commerce with distant Parts, will shew Men rare and useful Trees, to which their own Soil was before a stranger; and Luxury will soon teach them to transplant them.

No wonder therefore if Modern Writers excel the Ancients, upon a Subject which they had less Occasion for. The *Romans*, indeed, were Curious in Planting Trees for Shade or Fruit; but their Industry in that

Particular come under another Head, as rather belonging to the *Gardener's* Work. It may therefore, perhaps, be esteemed a small Character of Mr. *Evelyn's Discourse of Forest Trees*, to say, that it Out-does all that *Theophrastus* and *Pliny* have left us on that Subject: For it not only does that, and a great deal more, but contains more useful Precepts, Hints and Discoveries upon that now so necessary a Part of our *Res Rustica*, than the World had till then known from all the Observations of former Ages. To name others after him, would be a Derogation to his Performance.

Agriculture properly so called, has been always necessary since *Noah's* time, when the Flood, that *destroy'd the World of the Ungodly*, wrought such a Change upon the Face of the Earth, as made it necessary for all Mankind *in the Sweat of their Brows to eat their Bread*. And the early Populousness of the Eastern Nations, (though I would not bring *Semiramis* and *Zoroaster's* Armies to prove it) shews how much it was followed. For though those Countries should be allowed to be, as they really are, marvellously fruitful; yet even *Aegypt*, and the Plains of *Babylonia*, must be Tilled, to yield a Crop to satisfie the Hunger of their Inhabitants. Westward, as the World was later Peopled, so Tillage

was

was proportionably later; and the *Athenians* tell of one *Triptolemus*, who learn'd the Art of Sowing Corn of the *Aegyptians*, above M Years after *Noah*'s Flood. (*c*). After that, Necessity taught them many Rules; and it is evident from *Theophrastus*, and the *Roman* Writers of *Geoponic*'s, that their Knowledge in this kind was very great. They were thoroughly versed in the Art of Dressing their Grounds, and the Seasons when it was proper to do every Part of a Husbandman's Work; what Compost was fit to meliorate their over-wrought or barren Lands; what Soil was best for this Grain, and what for that. Their Vines and Olives, which were their Farmer's Care, were managed with much Skill and Curiosity; and *Pliny* reckons up a great many sorts of both of them, which the Luxury of that Age had taught them to Cultivate. In a Word; They were Industrious, and Skilful Husbandmen; and perhaps, 'tis not possible to tell, at this distance, whether our Farmers manage their Grounds more judiciously than they did theirs: Since any Improvements particular to one Climate and Soil, do not prove that Age in which they are made, more Knowing than another, wherein such Improvements could take no place: Though at the same time, a Country naturally barren, which has a weak Sun in

(*c*) Vid. *Marshami Chronicon.* pag 249. Edit. *Lond.*

an unkindly Climate, requires more Skill, as well as more Industry, to make it Fertile. And therefore it may be question'd, whether, considering the Natural Felicity of the Soils of *Sicily*, *Africa*, and *Greece*, and much more of *Aegypt*, *Judaea* and *Babylonia*, whose Fertility was anciently, with Reason, so much extolled, the Improvements in *England*, *Scotland* and *Holland* may not justly come into Competition with any ancient Performances, which how great soever in themselves, were yet less upon this Account, that the Husbandmen in those Regions had not such Difficulties to struggle with.

But though the Ancients, probably, understood the Art of Sowing Wheat, and Barly, and Legumes, and Flax, and how to Manage their Vines and Olives, as well as any Age has done since; yet other Things of unspeakable Use they were wholly Strangers to. The Art of making *Cydar*, at least of Chusing the best Apples, and Managing their Orchards and Plantations accordingly, they knew little or nothing of. And here again I must remember to take notice, (which, upon every Opportunity, I gladly do,) that Mr. *Evelyn's Pomona* has taught the present Age many things concerning the way of Ordering Apple-Trees, and Making *Cydar*, to which the World, till then, were wholly Strangers

gers, and for which he ought here to be mentioned with Honour. The *Sugar-Cane* was not anciently unknown, since it grows naturally in *Arabia* and *Indostan*; but so little was the *Greek* or *Roman* World acquainted with the Nature of its delicious Juice, that some of their ablest Men doubted whether it were a Dew like Manna, or the Juice of the Plant it self. All the Arts and Methods therefore of Preparing *Sugar*, which have made it so very Useful to Humane Life, are owing to Modern *Portugezes* and *English*. *Mault Drinks* were used in *Gaul* and *Spain* anciently, as also in *Eegypt*, where probably, they were first invented; but whether they were so accurately made as ours, no Man can tell, unless he knew certainly whether and with what they fermented them. May I not farther instance in *Coffee* and *Tobacco*? The *Romans* drove a greater Trade in *Arabia*, and were better acquainted with its Commodities, than this Part of the World has been at any time since, which no Man that has ever read the XIIIth. Book of *Pliny's Natural History* can possibly doubt of; yet there is no one Syllable of any thing like *Coffee* in his whole Work, nor indeed in any other Ancient Author before the *Arabs*. It is very probable that it grows wild in *Arabia*, since it is known to grow no where else; and that the Prohibition of *Wine* by the *Mohometan*

metan Law, made the *Arabs* find out its Virtues, (whereas before it was a neglected Shrub) to supply the place of the other Liquor. But still its Cultivation is, as to the present Question, Modern; and since the *Arabs* do now bestow great Care and Pains in Managing it, it comes not improperly in among the Augmentations of *Modern Agriculture*. And that *Tobacco* ought here to be mentioned, is question'd by none who know what a Delight and Refreshment it is to so many Nations, so many several Ways. The Accounts of *Virginia* and *Brasil* will inform us what Pains our *Europaean* Planters are at, to make that Herb Palatable to all sorts of Persons. So that without taking notice of any more Particulars, we may be assured, that the *Modern Husbandry* is a *larger*, if not a more *exact* thing than the *Ancient*; and even in those things wherein the Ancients did most excel, in the Management of their Vines and Olives, the comparative Excellency of the later Ages will perhaps be allowed by all those who are acquainted with the Curiosity of the present, in Managing of their Fruit-Trees; which shall be treated of in its proper Place.

I deferred to speak of *Gardening* till the last; because Luxury always comes after Necessity, though, generally, when it is once introduced, it still goes on encreasing,

till

till it is come to the utmoſt pitch to which it can be carried. In the preſent Subject, we ſhall find a gradual Improvement ſo very viſible, that I hope to put it paſt Controverſy, where the real Excellency lies.

The Babylonian *Horti Penſiles*, or Gardens on the tops of Buildings, ought, in moſt Men's Opinion, firſt to be mentioned in point of Antiquity: Theſe, *Joſephus* aſſures us, were only large Walks of Trees planted on the tops of Mounts of Maſons Work, erected in the midſt of the City by *Nebuchadnezzar*, to pleaſe his Wife. If they are no older, *Alcinous*'s Garden, deſcribed by *Homer* (d), was long before them. There one ſees the Simplicity of that Heroical Age very plainly. The Poet thought he did a magnificent Thing, when he made it Four Acres in Circumference: He tells us, it was ſtored with Pear-Trees and Apple-Trees, Pomegranates and Figs, Vines and Olives, which furniſhed him with conſtant ſucceſſions of Fruit; and had two Fountains, one cut into Streams, to water it within, the other flowing from thence, to ſupply the Neceſſities of the Inhabitants of the Town. And this is all he ſays of it: Poets and Romancers deſcribe every thing for their Hero's Uſes, as ſplendidly as they can: what they have ſeen, read, or heard of, is always brought in, as 'tis exſpected it ſhould. Accordingly

(d) *Odyſſ.* lib. viii.

ly the Garden described by *Eustathius* (*e*), in the later times of the *Graecian* Empire, when Luxury was improved into an Art, which it was far from being in old *Homer's* time, is much finer, though far short of the Gardens and *Villa's* of the Princes and Great Men of the present Age. *Eustathius's* Garden has open and arched Walks of Lawrel, Cypress and Mirtle, with Arbors of Vines for the Conveniencies of the Guests, to gather the Grapes as they lay at their Meals by the Fountain-side; with a *Jet d'eau* in the middle of it, spouting Water out of an Eagle's Bill; by which a She-Goat was milked, with the Liquor dropping out of the Nipples into a Pail on purpose: round the Fountain are Swallows and Peacocks, Doves and Cocks, all either Cast or Carved, out of whose Bills the Water flowing, gave a Sound to the several Birds. This indeed is very Pleasant and Poetical, and shews, that *Eustathius* had seen or heard of something of this nature, by which he guided his Fancy.

What the *Roman* Gardens were, we are sufficiently taught by their Writers *of Country Affairs*: (*f*) *Columella's* and (*g*) *Pliny's* Precepts and Descriptions are fit for nothing else but a Kitchin-Garden: They give Directions for Ordering Cucumbers, Melons, Artichokes, Coleworts, Turneps, Radishes, Parsnips, Skirrets, Garlick, Leeks, Onions,

(*e*) *Amorum Ysminiæ & Ysmines*, l. i.

(*f*) Lib. x. tot. & lib. xi. cap 3.
(*g*) Lib. xix.

Asparagus, and a numerous train of Pot-Herbs, with a little Garden-Physic. They both assign this as the Reason why *Virgil* would say nothing of Gardening, in his *Georgic's*, it being a Subject so very poor and jejune, that it would not bear the Ornaments which that Divine Poet gave to all his Works: So they seem to understand his *Spatia iniqua* which he complains of, upon which account he left off where he did.

For if we fansie that the Gardens of *Lucullus*, *Pompey*, *Cicero*, *Maecenas*, *Seneca*, and of all those Great *Romans* which are so highly extolled by the Ancients, were what we ordinarily call Gardens, we are very much mistaken: Their Gardens were spacious Plats of Ground, filled and surrounded with stately Walks of Platan's, and other shady Trees, built round with Xysti, Portico's, finely paved with curiously coloured, and far fetch'd Marble, lay'd in Artificial Figures, noble Ranges of Pillars, adorned within with Fish-Ponds, Aviaries, Fountains and Statues. Such still are the Villa's of the *Italian* Princes at *Frascati*, *Tivoli*, and their other delicious Seats in *Latium* and *Campania*, so celebrated of old, for being the Gardens of the *Europaean* World. Such, in some measure, are the famous Gardens about *Ispahan*, where Shade and Coolness give them their greatest Pleasure,

sure, in a Region where the Soil naturally furnishes its Inhabitants with excellent Fruit, and fragrant Flowers; so that they are at little Pains to cultivate that which they can have without, and which would not afford half that Delight in their Gardens of Pleasure, that they find in lying, in the Cool of the Day, under a shady *Plane*, by a Fountain-side. This made the Ancients, who all lived in warm Climates, admire the *Plane* so exceedingly, that frantic Stories are told of *Xerxes*'s doting upon one in the *Lesser Asia*, when he was bringing down his mighty Armies against *Greece*(*h*). The Walks of *Academus*, and the Gardens of *Epicurus*, were of this sort, Cool and Delicious, but which can give us no Idea of the Artificial Beauties of Modern Gardens. For the Question is not, which is in it self pleasanter, or whether if we lived in *Greece* or *Persia*, we should not rather chuse to imitate the Fashion of those Countries; but, which shews the greatest Skill of him that makes it.

(*h*) *Aelian. Var. Hist.* 2. 14.

The Gardens of this Age are of several sorts, *for the Kitchin for Flowers, for Greens,* and *Shady Walks, for Fruit-Trees,* and *for the Apothecary.*

To the First of these, the Industry of the Ancients (as we have seen already) was in a manner wholly confined. That they knew how to Manage those Kitchin Stores which

which their Gardens yielded, is unquestionable; but their variety was not near so great since neither was the New World known, nor the old so well examined as it has been since. Besides, they knew little of the Art of Raising Summer Plants, in the severest Frosts, and so making all Seasons of the Year unite in one, at Great Men's Tables; the bringing which to the present Perfection, is due to the Industry and Sagacity of the Age we live in; which how much it has enlarged this part of Gardening from what it was anciently, every Man by himself will easily imagine. The *Romans*, indeed, had a Way of Preserving Melons in Winter, by Sowing them in a large Box fill'd with rich Mold and Dung, which they housed in Winter, and exposed in Sun-shiny Days under their *Specularia*, that seem to have been of the Nature of our Glasses; by which contrivance, *Tiberius* the Emperor had Melons all the Year round. That shews what Necessity might have forced them to, had they been put to it.

As for *Flower Gardens*, the Ancients minded them not. They require an open Sun, and a free Air, which in hot Countries would have been Nuisances, rather than Delights. Plants remarkable for their Beauty, or their Smell, had a Place, indeed, in their Plantations; but we find no mention

tion of any great Variety of Species, or Art in Ranging or Managing those they had. There is nothing said in any *Greek* or *Roman* Authors of large Gravel-Walks, surrounding spacious Grass-Plats, edged with beautiful Borders, fill'd with all that Choice of Auricula's, Tulipa's, Carnations, Tuberoses, Jonquilles, Lily's, Hyacinths, Narcissus's, and that almost infinite Diversity of Beautiful and Odoriferous Flowers that now adorn our *Gardens*. They knew not the Art of Diversifying the Colours, Enlarging the Flowers, and giving them all those sickly or luxuriant Beauties which are so commonly to be met with in our Gardens. Some Notion they had of Managing *Dwarf-Trees*, and Clipping other Trees that would bear it into what Form the Garderners please; but they speak so little of it, that we have no reason to think they understood much of that beautiful Furniture which *Dwarfs* and *Ever-greens* afford us.

The Usefulness of *Fruit-Trees* made them be anciently more regarded. The Vines and Olives of the Ancient *Greeks* and *Romans* we have mentioned already. They had several sorts of Apples, Pears, Quinces, Peaches, Pomegranates, Plums, Figs and Nuts: As for Oranges and Limons, and the delicious Fruits of the *East* and *West-Indies*, they were wholly Strangers

to

to them. And they had not near the Variety of those they knew, with which Monsieur *de la Quintinie*, were they now alive could furnish them. Though they had many Precepts concerning Pruning, Setting, Graffing and Inoculating, knew their Usefulness, and could perform all those Operations with Success; yet, comparatively speaking, their Manner was course; and had their Climates been as unkindly, their Success would have been but indifferent. They could Manage Earth, and Air, and Water, pretty tolerably; but how to bring the Sun under Rules, (if I may use so bold an Expression) they knew not; which yet, by their Wall-Plantations, our Gardeners do every Day. That is an Invention the Ancients were entirely unacquainted with; thereby, in Cold Countries, we can command the Warmth of *Italy* and *Spain*, and in kindly Summers have Fruits of a Bigness, and Colour, and Taste, which even at Home they can scarce reach.

It will not be hard now, with due Allowances, to make a just Comparison between *Ancient* and *Modern Horticulture*. Monsieur *de la Quintinie* will give us a full and just Idea of what the Skill of this Age can reach to: Mr. *Evelyn*'s *Kalendarium Hortense* ought to be joined with it, to shew the Difference in a more Northern Clime. What Variety our Florists can
pre-

pretend to; will appear from *Parkinson's Paradise*, *Ferrarius's Flora*, or *Sweertius's Florilegium*. In those Books one may see what Art can do, to beautifie and enlarge Flowers beyond what Nature ordinarily produces. Other Men can only *follow* Nature; the Gardener alone *leads* it, and hastens or slackens its pace according as suits best with his Designs or Inclinations.

I need say nothing of the *Physic-Garden*, since what has been said already in the foregoing Chapter enables every Man to judge there aright. So much for *the Knowledge of Things not endued with Sensible Life*.

CHAP. XXIII.

Of Ancient and Modern Histories of Animals.

INsects seem to be the lowest and simplest Order of Animals; for which Reason I shall begin with them. That some are very beneficial to Man, affording him Food and Rayment; as, the *Bee*, and the *Silk-Worm*: And others, again, exceedingly troublesom; as, *Wasps, Hornets, Gnats, Moths*, and abundance more; was formerly as well known as now. In their Observations about

Bees,

Bees, the Ancients were very curious. *Pliny* (i) mentions one *Aristomachus*, who spent LVIII Years in Observing them: And it is evident from Him, *Aristotle* and *Aelian*, that as far as they could make their Observations, the Ancients did not neglect to digest necessary Materials for the Natural History of this wonderful and useful Insect. They were so particularly careful to collect what they could gather concerning it, that it is to be feared, a great part of what they say, is fabulous. But if they were curious to collect Materials for the History of this single Insect, they were, in the main, as negligent about the rest. They had, indeed, Names for the general Sorts of most of them; and they took notice of some, though but few, remarkable Sub-divisions. The Extent of their Knowledge, in this particular, has been nicely shewn by *Aldrovandus* and *Moufet*. In their Writings one may see, that the Ancients knew nothing of many Sorts; and of those which they mention, they give but indifferent Descriptions; contenting themselves with such Accounts as might, perhaps, refresh the Memories of those who knew them before, though they could signifie little to Persons who had never seen them. But of their Generation or Anatomy they could know nothing considerable, since those things are, in a great measure, owing to

(i) N. H. l. 11. c. 9.

Ob-

Observations made by Microscopes; and having observed few Sub-divisions, they could say little to the Ranging of those Insects which they knew already by distinct Characteristics, under several Heads. For want of observing the several Steps of Nature in all their Mutations, and taking notice of the Sagacity of many sorts of Insects, in providing convenient Lodgings for themselves, and fit Harbours for their young ones, both for Shelter and Food, they often took those to be different, which were only the same Species at different Seasons; and those to be near of Kin, which Chance only, not an Identity of Nature, brought together.

The clearing of all these Things is owing to Modern Industry, since the Time that Sir *William Temple* has set as a Period of the Advancement of Modern Knowledge; even within these last XL Years. It lies, for the most part, in a few Hands, and so is the more easily traced. In *Italy*, *Malpighius* and *Redi* took several Parts. *Redi* (k) examined abundance of general Sorts, those Insects especially which were believed to have been produced from the Putrefaction of Flesh; those he found to grow from Eggs laid by other grown Insects of the same Kinds; But he did not trace the Origination of those which are found upon Leaves, Branches, Flowers, and Roots of Trees.

(k) *Experimenta circà Generationem Insectorum.*

Trees. The Generation of those was nicely examined by *Malpighius*, in his curious Discourse of *Galls*, which is in the II^d Part of his *Anatomy of Plants*; wherein he has sufficiently shewn, that those Excrescencies and Swellings which appear in Summer-time upon the Leaves, tender Twigs, Fruits and Roots of many Trees, Shrubs and Herbs, from whence several sorts of Insects spring, are all caused by Eggs laid there by full-grown Insects of their own Kinds; for which Nature has kindly provided that secure Harbour, till they are able to come forth, and take care of themselves. But *Redi* has gone further yet, and has made many Observations upon Insects that live, and are carried about on the Bodies of other Insects. His Observations have not been weakened by Monsieur *Leeuwenhoek*, whose Glasses, which are said to excel any ever yet used by other People, shewed him the same Animals that Monsieur *Redi* had discovered already; and innumerable sorts of others, never yet thought of.

Besides Monsieur *Leeuwenhoek*, there have been Two Men in *Holland* very eminent for this Business, *Goedartius* and *Swammerdam*. *Goedartius*, who was no Philosopher, but one who, for his Diversion, took great Delight in Painting all sorts of Insects, has given exact Histories of the several Changes of great Numbers of Caterpillars into

Butter-Flies, and Worms or Maggots into Flies; which had never before been taken notice of, as Specifically different. These Changes had long ago been observed in Caterpillars and Maggots, by *Aristotle*, *Theophrastus* and *Pliny*: But they who acquaint us with the greatest part of what has been done in this Matter by the Ancients, content themselves with general Things. They enter not into minute Enquiries about the several Species of these Animals, which are exceedingly numerous: They do not state the Times of their several Changes. So that these Matters being left untouch'd, we have an admirable Specimen of the Modern Advancement of Knowledge, in *Goedartius*'s Papers (*l*).

Still an Anatomical Solution of these Appearances was wholly unknown. What *Ovid* (*m*) says of the Metamorphoses of Insects, is suitable enough to the Design of his Poem: And there we may well allow such a Natural Change of Caterpillars into Butter-Flies, as is not to be accounted for by the Regular Laws of the Growth and Augmentation of Natural Bodies. But a Natural Historian has no need of the Fictions of a Poet. These Difficulties therefore were cleared by *Swammerdam* (*n*), who in his *General History of Insects*, proves, that all the Parts of the full grown-Insect, which first appears in a different Form from what

(*l*) De Insectus, Edit. *Lister*

(*m*) Metam. l. 15.

(*n*) Hist General. Insect.

it assumes afterwards, were actually exiſtent in the *Foetus*, which creeps about as a Caterpillar, or a Maggot, till the Wings, Horns and Feet, which are incloſed in fine Membranes, come to their full growth; at which time, that Membrane which at firſt was only viſible, dries up, and breaks; out of which comes forth the Inſect proper to that Kind; which then gendring with its like, lay ſuch Eggs as in a ſeaſonable Time are Hatched; that ſo the Species, which is not generated by Chance, may always be preſerved.

In *England*, Dr. *Liſter* has done the moſt, to compleat this Part of Natural Hiſtory. His Book *of Spiders*, gives an Account of great Numbers of Species of thoſe Animals, formerly unobſerved. His *Latin and Engliſh Editions of* Goedartius, have not only made that Author more intelligible, by ranging his confuſed Obſervations under certain Heads conformable to Nature, which may ſerve alſo as Foundations to enlarge upon, as more Species ſhall hereafter be diſcovered, but he has taken that Occaſion of ſaying many new Things, pertinent to that Subject, all tending to encreaſe our Knowledge of thoſe ſmall Productions of the Divine Mechanics. His Tables *of Shells*, exhibit to the Eye a ſurprizing Variety of thoſe Inhabitants of the Waters, of which, comparatively ſpeak-

speaking, the World before had no Idea. *Buonanni* publish'd a beautiful Collection of them some Years before, at *Rome*, which when compared with those mentioned in Ancient Books, does as far exceed them, as it self is exceeded by Dr. *Lister's*: And his Anatomical Discourses *of Testaceous Animals*, lately printed, have discovered several curious Things in that wonderful Tribe; some of which, though observed above XXX Years ago by Mr. *Ray*, yet had not been much believed, because not sufficiently illustrated by an able Anatomist.

This is what our Age has seen; and it is not the less admirable, because all of it, perhaps, cannot be made immediately useful to Humane Life: It is an excellent Argument to prove, That it is not Gain alone which biasses the Pursuits of the Men of this Age after Knowledge; for here are numerous Instances of Learned Men, who finding other Parts of Natural Learning taken up by Men, who, in all probability would leave little for After-comers, have, rather than not contribute their Proportion towards the Advancement of Knowledge, spent a World of Time, Pains and Cost, in examining the Excrescencies of all the Parts of Trees, Shrubs and Herbs, in observing the critical Times of the Changes of all sorts of Caterpillars and

Maggots, in finding out, by the Knife and Microscopes, the minutest Parts of the smallest Animals, examining every Crevice, and poring in every Ditch, in tracing every Insect up to its Original Egg; and all this with as great Diligence, as if they had had an *Alexander* to have given them as many Talents, as he is said to have given to his Master *Aristotle*.

I shall put *Fishes*, *Fowls*, and *Quadrupeds* together; because the Question, as it relates to the Natural History of these Animals, may be brought into a small Compass. For as to the Anatomical part, it is certain, That every Instance of the Defect of Ancient Anatomy already mentioned, is a Proof how little the Texture of the Inward Parts of all these Creatures could possibly be known, and consequently, that no old Descriptions of these Animals which should go beyond the Parts immediately visible, could have been considerable. There is hardly one eminent Modern Discovery in Anatomy, which was not first found in Brutes, and afterwards examined in Humane Bodies. Many of them could never have been known without the Help of Live-Dissections; and the rest required abundance of Trials upon great Numbers of different sorts of Beasts, some appearing plainer in one sort of Animals, and some in another, before the Discoverers themselves could frame such a clear Idea of the Things which they were then in pursuit of, as that they could readily look for them in Humane Bodies, which could not be procured in so great Plenty, and of which they had not always the Convenience. All which things extremely tended to the Perfecting the Anatomy of all sorts of Brutes. About the other Part, which may comprehend an Account of their Way of Living, their Uses to Humane Life, their Sagacity, and the like, the Ancients took much Pains, and went very far: And there are a great many admirable things in *Aristotle's History of Animals*, concerning all these Matters. What Helps he had from Writers that lived before his own time, we know not; if he had but little, it must be owned that his Book is one of the greatest Instances of Industry and Sagacity that perhaps has ever been given. But since the Question is not so much, whether that is an excellent Book, as, whether it is perfect; it ought to be compared with Mr. *Willughby's Histories of Fishes and Birds*, and Mr. *Ray's Synopsis of Quadrupeds*, as the perfectest Modern Books upon these Matters; and then it will be easie to make a Judgment. I shall not make it my self, because no Man can mistake, that compares them, though never so negligently, together.

I

I name only *Aristotle*; because he is, to us at least, an Original Author: He had examined abundance of things himself; and though he took a great deal upon trust, yet that could not be avoided, since he had so little, that we know of, from more remote Antiquity, and it was too vast a Work for any one single Man to go through with by himself. *Aelian* and *Pliny* seem only to have Copied; and, with submission be it spoken, their Writings are *Rhapsodies* of Stories and Relations partly true, and partly fabulous, which themselves, very often, had not Skill enough to separate one from the other, rather than *Natural Histories*: From which Accusation, even *Aristotle* himself cannot wholly be excused. Though this must be said in Vindication of *Pliny*, That he neither Believed himself, nor proposed, as Credible, abundance of those strange things which he related in his *Natural History*. His Design was, to set down whatsoever he had found in all his Reading, which was very diffuse, upon those Heads which he treated of: And accordingly, where-ever he met with a shocking Story, he told it, indeed, (as *Gesner* and *Aldrovandus* did afterwards, though they were infinitely better Naturalists than he,) but it was almost always in such a manner, that a Reader must be exceedingly careless that is imposed upon

either

either to believe the thing himself, or to think that *Pliny* believed it, and set it down for Credible. (*o*) Which is a great deal more than can be said for *Aelian*, whose Authority is not near so good as his *Greek*, for the Elegancy of which he was extremely valued, and the more, because being by Birth a *Roman*, he had never (*p*) in his Life been out of *Italy*. But it is time to return.

(*o*) *Quaedam tamen haud omittenda duco, maxime que longius a mari degentium: in quibus prodigiosa aliqua & incredibilia multis visum iri haud dubito. Quis enim Aethiopas, antequam cerneret, credidit? aut quid non miraculo est, cum primùm in notitiam venit? ——— Nec tamen Ego in plerisq; eorum obstringam fidem meam; potiusq; ad Auctores relegabo, qui dubiis reddentur omnibus.* Plin. Nat. Hist. lib. vii. cap. 1. It is plain by this, that *Pliny* forewarns his Readers what they are to expect; and then if they are deceived, it is they deceive themselves, not he them.

(*p*) Vid. *Philostrat. de Vitis Sophist. in Aelian.*

If we would make this Comparison the easier, we should consult *Gesner* and *Aldrovandus*; or, if they are too voluminous, *Woton De Differentiis Animalium*, who has put under one View, in several Heads, almost every thing that is to be found in any ancient Authors concerning these Things. What he has collected of the Elephant, may be compared with Doctor *Moulin*'s Anatomy of the same Creature: The Ancients Observation concerning Vipers, may be read along with *Redi*'s and *Charas*'s. Their Anatomical Descriptions of many other Animals, may be examined with those excellent ones published by the

Mem-

Members of the *French Academy*, and Mr. *Ray* in his *Synopsis*: And then the Imperfections of the one, and the Excellencies of the other, will be clearly seen, and the Distance between each exactly stated; though perhaps this may seem too far about, since it is manifest at first sight, That no ancient Descriptions of any Creatures could be such as would be at present valuable, when their whole Anatomy was so imperfect. Some Mistakes however, might, methinks, have been prevented; the *Aegyptian Sages*, sure, might have taught them, that a Crocodile moves his Under-Jaw, and not his Upper; they might soon have found, that a Lion has Vertebres in his Neck, and with them, by consequence, can move it upon occasion, and has as large a Heart as other Creatures of his Size; that a (*q*) Porcupine doth not shoot his long Quills upon those that set upon him; and several other things, which would have prevented several Oversights that are not much for the Honour of *Ancient Diligence*. This would have saved

(*q*) Borellus de Motu Animalium, Part II. Prop 219. *Fabulosa narratio passim circumfertur de Hystrice, quae cutem tendendo, spinas illas praelongas quibus dorsum ejus tegitur, longiùs ejaculatur. De hoc Animali enarrabo ea, quae propriis oculis vidi. Hystrix non ejaculatur spinas suas praelongas, sed tantummodo eas arrectas retinendo tremulâ concussione agitat & vibrat. Hoc quidem efficitur à pelle musculosâ, & à musculis semilunaribus, quibus interna cutis stipata est, qui radices spinarum erigunt & concutiunt.* Vid. quoque Raii Synopsin Animal. Quadruped. pag. 209.

abun-

abundance of fabulous Relations that are to be met with in ancient Naturalists. Their heaping up monstrous Stories, without giving distinguishing Marks, many times, to testifie which they believed, and which not, is an evident Sign that they were not enough acquainted with these Creatures, to make a thorough Judgment what might be relied upon, and what ought to be rejected. For accurate Skill in these things helps a Man to judge as certainly of those Relations which himself never saw, as Political Skill does to judge of Accounts of Matters that belong to Civil Life; and a great deal better, since Nature goes in an evener Course than the Wills and Fancies of Men, which alone, and not Rules of Prudence, are the Foundations of some of the most considerable Actions that are done in the World.

CHAP. XXIV.

Of Ancient and Modern *Astronomy*, and *Optics*.

Having now gone through with the several Parts of *Natural History*, I am to enquire into the State of *Physico-Mathe-*

Mathematical and *Physical* Sciences: Such as *Astronomy, Optics, Music* and *Medics*. I put *Astronomy* first, because of the vast Extent, and real Nobleness of its Subject; and also, because it has suffered the least Eclipse of any part of Knowledge whatsoever in the barbarous Times: For when the *Greeks* neglected it, the *Arabs*, and from them the *Spaniards*, took it up. That this Enquiry might be the more exactly made, and that the Truth might be fully and clearly stated, Mr. *Edmond Halley*, who has, since the Publication of these Papers, been thought worthy to succeed the great Dr. *Wallis* in his Geometrical Chair at *Oxford*, and whose Labours towards the Advancement of this Science, have made him Famous in so many distant Parts of the World, did me the Favour to communicate this following Paper:

' As for the *Astronomy* of the Ancients,
' this is usually reckoned for one of those
' Sciences wherein consisted the Learning
' of the *Aegyptians*; and *Strabo* expresly
' declares, That there were in *Babylonia*
' several Universities, wherein Astronomy
' was chiefly professed; and *Pliny* tells us
' much the same thing: So that it might
' well be exspected, that where such a
' Science was so much studied, it ought
' to have been proportionably cultivated.
' Notwithstanding all which, it does ap-
                                    ' pear,

'pear, That there was nothing done by
'the *Chaldaeans* older than about CCCC
'Years before *Alexander's* Conquest, that
'could be serviceable either to *Hipparchus*
'or *Ptolemee*, in their Determination of
'the Celestial Motions: For had there
'been any Observations older than those
'we have, it cannot be doubted but the
'Victorious *Greeks* must have procured
'them, as well as those they did, they
'being still more valuable for their Anti-
'quity. All we have of them, is only
'Seven Eclipses of the Moon, preserved
'in *Ptolemee's Syntaxis*; and even those
'but very coursely set down, and the old-
'est not much above DCC Years before
'Christ; so that after all the Fame of
'these *Chaldaeans*, we may be sure that
'they had not gone far in this Science;
'and though *Callisthenes* be said, by *Por-*
'*phyry*, to have brought from *Babylon* to
'*Greece*, Observations above MDCCCC
'Years older than *Alexander*, yet the pro-
'per Authors making no Mention or Use
'of any such, renders it justly suspected
'for a Fable. What the *Aegyptians* did in
'this Matter is less evident, no one Ob-
'servation made by them being to be
'found in their Country-man *Ptolemee*,
'excepting what was done by the *Greeks* of
'*Alexandria*, under CCC Years before
'*Christ*. So that whatever was the Lear-
'ning

'ning of these two ancient Nations, as to
' the Motions of the Stars, it seems to
' have been chiefly Theorical; and I will
' not deny but some of them might very
' long since be apprized of the Sun's be-
' ing the Centre of our System, for such
' was the Doctrine of *Pythagoras* and *Phi-*
' *lolaus*, and some others who were said to
' have travelled into these Parts.

' From hence it may appear, That the
' *Greeks* were the first Practical Astrono-
' mers, who endeavoured in earnest to
' make themselves Masters of the Science,
' and to whom we owe all the old Obser-
' vations of the Planets, and of the Equi-
' noxes and Tropics: *Thales* was the first
' that could predict an Eclipse in *Greece*,
' not DC Years before *Christ*, and without
' doubt it was but a rude Account he had
' of the Motions; and 'twas *Hipparchus*
' who made the first Catalogue of the
' Fix'd-Stars, not above CL Years before
' *Christ*; without which Catalogue there
' could be scarce such a Science as *Astro-*
' *nomy*; and it is to the Subtilty and Dili-
' gence of that great Author that the World
' was beholding for all its Astronomy, for
' above MD Years. All that *Ptolemee* did
' in his *Syntaxis*, was no more but a bare
' Transcription of the Theories of *Hip-*
' *parchus*, with some little Emendation of
' the Periodical Motions, after about CCC
' Years

'Years Interval; and this Book of *Pto-*
'*lemee*'s was, without Dispute, the utmost
'Perfection of the Ancient Astronomy,
'nor was there any thing in any Nation
'before it comparable thereto; for which
'Reason, all the other Authors thereof
'were disregarded and lost, and among
'them, *Hipparchus* himself. Nor did Po-
'sterity dare to alter the Theories delive-
'red by *Ptolemee*, though successively *Al-*
'*bategnius* and the *Arabs*, and after them
'the *Spanish* Astronomers under *Alphonsus*,
'endeavoured to amend the Errors they
'observed in their Computations. But their
'Labours were fruitless, whilst from the
'Defects of their Principles, it was im-
'possible to reconcile the Moon's Motion
'within a Degree, nor the Planets, *Mars*
'and *Mercury*, to a much greater Space.

'Now in this Science to compare the
'Ancients with the Moderns, and so make
'a Parallel as just as may be, I oppose the
'Noble *Tycho Brahe*, or *Hevelius* to *Hip-*
'*parchus*, and *John Kepler* to *Claudius Pto-*
'*lemee*; and I suppose, no one acquainted
'with the Stars, will doubt, That the Ca-
'talogue of the Fix'd Stars made by *Tycho*
'*Brahe*, about C Years since, does, be-
'yond Competition, far excel that of
'*Hipparchus*, being commonly true to a
'Minute or two, when the other, many
'times, fails half a Degree, both in Lon-
'gitude

'gitude and Latitude; and this is the
'fairlier carried, for that it was as easie
'for *Hipparchus* to observe the Fix'd-Stars,
'as for *Tycho* or *Hevelius*, had he made
'Use of the same Industry and Instruments,
'the *Telescope*, wherewith we now ob-
'serve to the utmost possible Nicety, be-
'ing equally unknown to *Tycho* as to *Hip-
'parchus*, and not used by *Hevelius*. But
'what may justly be exspected from Mon-
'sieur *Cassini*, and Mr. *Flamsteed*, in this
'Matter, does yet further advance in Pre-
'ciseness, as not capable to err half a Mi-
'nute, though made with Instruments
'(*r*) of the Production of Gresham. As to (*r*) P. 57
'the other Comparison between *Kepler*
'and *Ptolemee*, I question not but all that
'can judge, will be fully convinced that
'the Hypothesis of Eccentrics, and Epi-
'cycles introduced by the Ancients only
'to represent the Motions, and that but
'coursly too, with the Opinion of *Ptole-
'mee* himself thereon, that the Natural
'Motions were otherwise performed;
'ought not to be valued against that ele-
'gant Theory of the Planetary Motions,
'first invented by the acute Diligence of
'*Kepler*, and now lately demonstrated by
'that excellent Geometer Mr. *Newton*, viz.
'*That all the Planets move in Elliptic Orbs
'about the Sun, at whose Center, being pla-
'ced in one Focus of the Ellipse, they de-
'scribe*

'scribe *Equal Area's in Equal Times.* This, as it is the necessary Result of the Laws of Motion and Gravity, is also found rigorously to answer to all that is observed in the Motions; so that the Moderns may, with as much Reason as in any other Science whatsoever, value themselves, on their having Improved, I had almost said Perfected, this of *Astronomy.*

Optical Instruments have been so serviceable in the Advancement of *Astronomy,* that the Sciences which demonstrate their wonderful Properties ought next to be considered. Here also I must own my Obligation to Mr. *Halley,* for this following Account of what the Ancients have done in them, and how much they have been outdone by Modern Mathematicians:

'I suppose there are few so thorough-paced Fautors of Antiquity, as to brag much of their Skill, either in *Optics* or *Dioptrics.* Their Want of *Optics* appears in their want of Authors treating thereon; and yet much better in their want of *Ordonnance* (as it is called) in their Paintings, and *Basse Reliev's,* as has been already said in its proper place. And as to *Dioptrics,* though some of the Ancients mention *Refraction,* as a natural Effect of Transparent *Media;* yet *Des Cartes* was the first who, in this Age, has discovered the Laws of *Refraction,* and brought *Di-*
optrics

'*optrics* to a Science. And the Invention
'of *Telescopes* and *Microscopes*, which must
'be wholly allowed to this Century, has
'received no small Improvements from the
'Study and Charge of Sir *Paul Neile*, and
'some other *Members of Gresham*. And these
'are such Instruments of real Knowledge,
'that though we will allow the Ancients
'to have done all that great *Genii*, with
'due Application, could arrive at; yet,
'for want of them, their Philosophical Ar-
'gumentation could not come up to the
'present Pitch; not being able to fathom
'the boundless Depths of the Heavens, nor
'to unravel the *Minutiae* of Nature, with-
'out the Assistance of the Glasses we are
'now possessed of.'

CHAP. XXV.

Of Ancient and Modern Music.

SIR *William Temple* having assured us, (s), that *it is agreed by the Learned, that the Science of Music, so admired by the Ancients, is wholly lost in the World: And that what we have now, is made up of certain Notes that fell into the Fancy of a poor Friar, in chanting his Mattins*: it may seem im-

(s) P. 45

proper

proper to speak of *Music* here, which ought rather to have been ranked amongst those Sciences wherein the Moderns have, upon a strict Enquiry, been found to have been out-done by the Ancients. I have chosen, however, to speak of it in this Place, for these following Reasons.

(1.) That whereas all Modern Mathematicians have paid a mighty Deference to the Ancients, and have not only used the Names of *Archimedes, Apollonius, Diophantus,* and the other Ancient Mathematicians with great Respect; but have also acknowledged, that what farther Advancements have since been made, are, in a manner, wholly owing to the first Rudiments, formerly taught: Modern Musicians have rarely made use of the Writings of *Aristoxenus, Ptolemee,* and the rest of the Ancient Masters in that Art; and, of those that have studied them, very few, unless their Editors, have confessed that they could understand them; and others have laid them aside, as useless for their Purpose; so that it is very probable, many excellent Composers have scarce ever heard of their Names.

(2.) *Music* has still, and always will have very lasting Charms. Wherefore, since the Moderns have used their utmost Diligence to improve whatsoever was improvable in the Writings of all sorts of

Ancient

Ancient Authors, upon other equally difficult, and very often not so delightful Subjects, one can hardly imagine but that the World would, long e're now, have heard something more demonstrably proved of the Comparative Perfection of Ancient *Music*, with large Harangues in the Commendation of the respective Inventors, if their Memory had been preserved, than barely an Account of the fabulous Stories of *Orpheus* or *Amphion*, which either have no Foundation at all, or as *Horace* of old understood them (*t*), are allegorically to be interpreted of their reducing a Wild and Salvage People into Order and Regularity. But this is not urged against Sir *William Temple*, who is not convinced of the Extent of Modern Industry, Sagacity and Curiosity; tho' to other Admirers of Ancient *Music*, who, upon Hearsay, believe it to be more Perfect than the Modern, and yet are, for other Reasons, sufficiently convinced of the unwearied Diligence, and answerable Success of the Modern Learning, in retrieving and improving other Parts of Ancient Knowledge, it will not appear inconsiderable.

(3.) *Music* is a *Physico-Mathematical Science*, built upon fixed Rules, and stated

(*t*) *Silvestres homines, sacer interpresque Deorum, Caedibus & victu foedo deterruit Orpheus: Dictus ob hoc lenire Tigres, rabidosque Leones. Dictus & Amphion, Thebanae conditor arcis, Saxa movere sono Testudinis, & prece blandâ, Ducere quo vellet.*
Art. Poet.

Proportions; which, one would think, might have been as well improved upon the old Foundations, as upon new ones, since the Grounds of *Music* have always been the same: And *Guido*'s Scale, as Dr. *Wallis* assures us, is the same for Substance with the *Diagramma Veterum*.

(4.) The Ancients had not, in the Opinion of several who are Judges of the Matter, so many Gradations of Half-Notes and Quarter-Notes between the Whole ones, as are now used; which must of necessity introduce an unspeakable Variety into Modern *Music*, more than could formerly be had: Because it is in Notes, as it is in Numbers; the more there are of them, the more variously they may be combined together.

(5.) Excessive Commendations can signifie nothing here; because every Man gives the highest Applauses to the Perfectest thing he ever saw or heard, of any kind: And if he is not capable of Inventing in any particular Art himself, he can form no clear Idea of it, beyond what himself was then affected with, when he first heard those discourse of it, who pretended to be Judges of every thing relating to it.

(6.) It is very probable, that Ancient *Music* had all that which still most affects common

common Hearers. The generality of Auditors are moved with an excellent Voice, are pleased when Time is exactly kept, and love to hear an Instrument played true to a fine Voice, when the one does not so far drown the other, but that they can readily understand what is sung, and can, without previous Skill, perceive that the one exactly answers the other throughout; and their Passions will be effectually moved with sprightly or lamentable Compositions: In all which Things the Ancients, probably, were very perfect. To such Men, many of our Modern Compositions, where several Parts are sung or played at the same time, would seem confused, intricate and unpleasant: Though in those Cases, the greater this seeming Confusion is, the more Pleasure does the Skilful Hearer take, in unravelling every several Part, and in observing how artfully those seemingly disagreeing Tones join, like true-cut Tallies, one within another, to make up that united Concord, which very often gives little Satisfaction to common Ears; though in such sort of Compositions it is, that the Excellency of Modern *Music* chiefly consists For, in making a Judgment of *Music*, it is. much the same thing as it is in making a Judgment of *Pictures*. A great Judge in *Painting*, does not gaze upon an exquisite Piece, so much to raise his Passions, as to inform his Judgment, as to approve, or to find fault; His Eye runs over every Part, to find out every Excellency; and his Pleasure lies in the Reflex Act of his Mind, when he knows that he can judiciously tell where every Beauty lies, or where the Defects are discernible: Which an ordinary Spectator would never find out. The chiefest thing which this Man minds, is the Story; and if that is lively represented, if the Figures do not laugh when they should weep, or weep when they should appear pleased, he is satisfied, if there are no obvious Faults committed any where else: And this, perhaps, equally well, if the Piece be drawn by *Raphael*, as by an ordinary Master, who is just able to make Things look like Life. So likewise in *Music*; He that hears a *numerous* Song, set to a very moving Tune, exquisitely sung to a sweet Instrument, will find his Passions raised, whilst his Understanding, possibly, may have little or no share in the Business. He scarce knows, perhaps, the Names of the Notes, and so can be affected only with an Harmony, of which he can render no Account. To this Man, what is intricate, appears confused; and therefore he can make no Judgment of the true Excellency of those Things, which seem *fiddling* to him only, for want of Skill in *Music*.

Whereas,

Whereas, on the contrary, the Skill or Ignorance of the Composer, serve rather to entertain the Understanding, than to gratifie the Passions of a skilful Master, whose Passions are then the most thoroughly raised, when his Understanding receives the greatest Satisfaction.

(7.) It will be difficult to form a just Idea of the Pleasure which the Ancient *Music* afforded, unless one reflects upon the confessedly unimitable Sweetness of the Ancient *Poetry*, the *Greek* especially; which, when sung by clear and sweet Voices, in such a manner, as that the Hearer never lost a Syllable, could scarce fail of producing those Emotions of Soul which the Poet intended to raise. And, indeed, the great End of *Music*, which is to please the Audience, was anciently, perhaps, better answered than now; though a Modern Master would then have been dis-satisfied, because such Consorts as the Ancient *Symphonies* properly were, in which several Instruments, and perhaps Voices, play'd and sung the same Part together, cannot discover the Extent and Perfection of the Art, which here only is to be considered, so much as the Compositions of our Modern *Opera*'s

From all this it may, perhaps, be not unreasonable to conclude, that though *(u)* *(u)* P. 45
thofe

those Charms of Music, *by which Men and Beasts, Fishes, Fowls and Serpents, were so frequently enchanted, and their very Natures changed,* be really and irrecoverably lost, if ever they were had; yet the Art of *Music,* that is to say, of Singing, and Playing upon Harmonious Instruments, is, in it self, much a perfecter thing, though perhaps not much pleasanter to an unskilful Audience, than it ever was amongst the Ancient *Greeks* and *Romans.*

CHAP. XXVI.

Of Ancient and Modern Physic and Surgery.

After these *Mathematical* Sciences, it is convenient to go to those which are more properly *Physical,* and in our Language alone peculiarly so called. What these want in Certainty, they make up in Usefulness: For, if Life and Health be the greatest good Things which we can enjoy here, a Conjectural Knowledge, that may but sometimes give us Relief when those are in danger, is much more valuable than a certain Knowledge of other Things, which can only employ the Understanding, or furnish us with such Conveniencies as may be spared; since we see that several Nations which never had them, lived happily, and did great Things in the World.

Before I begin my Comparison between *Ancient* and *Modern* Skill in *Physic*, it may be necessary to state the Difference between an *Empiric* and a *Rational Physician*; and to enquire how far a *Rational Physician* may reason right, as to what relates to the Curing of his Patient's Distemper, though his general Hypotheses be wrong, and his Theories, in themselves consider'd, insufficient. An *Empiric* is properly he who, without considering the Constitution of his Patient the Symptoms of his Disease, or those Circumstances of his Case which arise from Outward Accidents, administers such *Physic* as has formerly done good to some Body else that was tormented with an Illness which was called by the same Name with this that his Patient now labours under. A *Rational Physician* is he who critically enquires into the Constitution, and peculiar Accidents of Life, of the Person to whom he is to administer: who weighs all the known Virtues of the Medicines which may be thought proper to the Case in hand; who balances all the Symptoms, and, from past Observations, finds which have been

fatal

fatal, and which safe; which arise from Outward Accidents, and which from the Disease it self; and who thence collects which ought soonest to be removed, and which may be neglected, and thereupon prescribes accordingly.

Now it is evident, that such a Man's Prescriptions may be very valuable, because they are founded upon repeated Observations of the *Phænomena* of Diseases. And he may form Secondary Theories, which, like *Ptolemee's Eccentrics* and *Epicycles*, shall be good Guides to Practice; not by giving a certain Insight into the first Causes, and several Steps, by which the Disease first began, and was afterwards carried on; but by enabling the Physician to make lucky Conjectures at proper Courses, and fit Medicines, whereby to relieve or cure his Patient. And herein he may be equally successful, whether he resolves every thing into Hot or Cold, Moist or Dry; into Acids, or *Alkali*'s; into Salt, Sulphur, or *Mercury*; or into any thing else. He does not know, for Instance, that Spittle, Bile, and the Pancreatic Juice, are the main Instruments of Digestion; yet he sees that his Patient digests his Meat with great Difficulty; He is sure, that as long as that lasts, the sick Man cannot have a good Habit of Body: He finds that the Distemper

arises

arises sometimes, though not always, from a Visible Cause; end he has tried the goodness of such and such Medicines, in seemingly parallel Cases. He may be able therefore to give very excellent Advice, though he cannot, perhaps, dive into the Original and Causes of the Distemper so well as another Man; who having greater Anatomical Helps, and being accustomed to reason upon more certain Physiological Principles, has made a strict Enquiry into that particular Case: And so by consequence, though he cannot be said to know so much of the Nature of the Disease as that other Man; yet, perhaps, their Method of Practice, notwithstanding the great Disparity of each others Knowledge, shall be, in the main, the same.

Though all this seems certain, yet, in the Argument before us, it is not an easie thing to state the Question so equally, as to satisfie all contending Sides. He that looks into the Writings of the generality of the *Rational Physicians*, as they called themselves, by way of Eminence; that is to say, of those who, about an Hundred Years ago, set up *Hippocrates* and *Galen*, for the Parents and Perfecters of Medicinal Knowledge, will find, throughout all their Writings, great Contempt of every thing that is not plainly deducible from those Texts. On the other hand, If he dips into the

Books of the Chymical Philosophers, he will meet with equal Scorn of those Books and Methods, which they, in Derision, have called *Galenical*. And yet it is evident, that Practising Physicians of both Parties, have often wrought extraordinary Cures by their own Methods. So that there seems to have been equal Injustice on all hands, in excluding all Methods of Cure not built upon their own Principles. Here therefore, without being positive in a Dispute, about which the Parties concerned are not themselves agreed, I shall only offer these few Things: (1.) That if the Greatness of any one particular Genius were all that was to be look'd after, *Hippocrates* alone seems to have been the Man, whose Assertions in the Practical Part of Physic might be blindly received: For He, without the Help of any great Assistances, that we know of, did that, which, if it were still to do, would seem sufficient to employ the united Force of more than one Age. He was scrupulously Exact in Distinguishing Diseases, in Observing the proper Symptoms of each, and taking Notice of their Duration, thereby to make a Judgment how far they might be esteemed dangerous, and how far safe. Herein his particular Excellency seems to have lain; and this, in the Order of Knowledge, is the first thing that a *Rational Physician* ought to make himself Master of:

Which

Which is a sure Argument, that *Hippocrates* thoroughly understood what things were necessary for him to study with the greatest Care, in order to make his Writings always useful to Posterity. (2.) That, in the Opinion of the ablest Judges, the *Natural History of Diseases* was as perfectly known, and they were as accurately distinguished by the Ancients, as ever they have been since; and consequently, that the Knowledge of the *Appearances*, or *Diagnostics* (as they call them) of every Distemper common to us and them, is owing to, at least may be found in the Writings of the Ancients; for this they appeal to the Writings of *Aretaeus*, and *Caelius Aurelianus*, whose Descriptions of the Diseases they treat of, are in a manner perfect: The Fragments of *Herophilus*, and some other Ancient Physicians preserved in *Caelius Aurelianus*, shew this not to have been peculiar to him, but common with the other great Men of Antiquity. (3.) That, setting aside Chymical Remedies, and some few Drugs brought to us out of the *West-Indies*, the Body of the *Materia Medica* now in Use, is owing to the Ancients, who applied their Remedies with as great Skill and Judgment as any Modern Physicians whatsoever. But yet, (4.) Though we should allow the Ancient Methods of Practice to have been as perfect, nay, perfecter than those now in use,

which

which some great Men have eagerly contended for; yet it does not follow, that the whole Compass of their Profession was so well understood by the Ancients as it is now; because it is absolutely impossible to form just Theories of all Diseases, so as to lay down the perfectest Methods of Cure possible, which shall be adapted to all Persons, in all Circumstances, till Anatomy and Physiology are perfectly known; and by consequence, later Theories will always be more estimable, as they are raised upon newer Discoveries in Anatomy and Physiology: So that we may be sure no Ancient Theories can be so excellent, as some of those which have been devised by Modern Philosophers. (5.) That if the Addition of every new Medicine be an useful Accession to the Body of *Physic*, then a new Method of Preparing known Medicines; of making those Things profitable and noble Remedies, which before were dreaded as Poysons, or laid by as useless; and of trying such Experiments upon Bodies yet unexamined, as will soon and certainly discover some of their most principal Virtues, must be of unspeakable Advantage, and make the Knowledge of those who possess such a Method justly more valuable than that of those who want it. But this relates more particularly to *Chymistry*, of which enough has been said already. (6.) That if the

Practice

Practice of proper Judges be a reasonable Prejudice for or against any thing, then this Science has received vast Improvements of late Years: For now the generality of Physicians acquiesce in Modern Theories, or, which in the present Dispute is all one, advance new ones upon Anatomical and Physical Principles, pursuant to those Discoveries which have been lately made. In their Practice, they mix *Galenical* and *Chymical* Medicines together. They own, that *Galenical* Ways of preparing Drugs, anciently made use of in the Practice of *Physic*, are, in many Cases, not so valuable as *Chymical* ones. In short, though they pay a due Respect to the Writings of the Ancients, and in those things where they find by their own Experience that the Ancient Observations hold, follow their Directions; yet their constant Language, and as constant Practice, whensoever one opposes Ancient Authorities to them, is, *That the Ancients did very well for their Time; but that Experience, and farther Light, has taught them better Things.* This, I must needs own, has very great Weight with me, who am apt, *caeteris paribus*, to believe every Man in his own Way; *Physicians* especially, because their Science is entirely got by a long Series of repeated Experiments and Observations: So that it seems to be almost impossible, but that, in all such Cases, where

Men have the Assistance of former Light, and where the Subject upon which they employ their Pains wanted a great deal of that Perfection, which those that study it have an Idea of, as still wanting, and can only be attained by a longer Experience, successive Ages must make great Additions to the former Stock. (7.) That though the noble Discoveries of these latter Ages, might, possibly, be found in *Hippocrates*, *Aristotle* and *Galen*; yet, since no Interpreters could ever find them there, till they were actually discovered anew by Modern Physicians, who followed Nature only as their Guide, these late Discoverers have as just Right to the Glory due to such Discoveries, as the Ancients could possibly have: They both copied after the same Original; they both decyphered the same Characters, that before were unintelligible; not by reading Books, but by trying Experiments, and making Observations. And therefore, *Vander Linden*, *Almeloveen*, and the rest of the Bigots for the Ancients, deal very unjustly, when they cry out, upon the Sight of any New Discovery, This *Hippocrates* knew; This *Aristotle* taught. Could these Men have made these Discoveries by studying those Ancient Authors, without the Assistance of Dr. *Harvey*, *Asellius*, *Pecquet*, *Malpighius*, or the rest? This would hold, in case the *Circulation of the Blood*, the *Chyle-Vessels*,

Vessels, Lympheducts, and the other great Discoveries in Anatomy, had really been in the Ancients. That they are not, I believe I have proved already. To which I shall only add, That former Commentators wanted neither *Greek*, nor Skill; and had such Things been in their Writings, they would infallibly have found them there.

It is easie now to tell what Acquisitions have been made since *Galen*'s Days. When *Hippocrates* lived, Anatomy was a rude, imperfect Thing: It has since been growing, and the Theories of all Diseases have been proportionably more compleat. *Chymistry* has been introduced into *Physic*; thereby the *Materia Medica* has been enlarged by some as noble Medicines as any the Ancients were acquainted with; the Nauseousness of many Medicines has been removed; and they have been made less clogging, and more efficacious, since they may be taken in lesser Quantities, and in more pleasant Vehicles, to as good if not better purpose than before. *Botanics* have been unspeakably enlarged; and thereby also the Dispensatories have been stocked with some excellent Remedies, that the Old World knew nothing of. If these Particulars be rightly stated, as they seem to be, they will go very far to decide the Question: And so I shall leave it, without determining any thing positively about it. So much for that part of *Medicine* which in our Language is peculiarly call *Physic*.

Surgery comes next to be considered; which though at present it be looked upon as inferior to *Physic*, yet it was much the ancientest, and is still the certainest part of *Medicine*. For here the Eye directs the *Surgeon* how he shall proceed, and if he knows but the Virtue of his Medicines, and how to apply them, he can, generally speaking, tell whether his Patient be curable or not. Anciently this was only a Branch of the *Physician*'s Work; and the Old *Physicians* in the Heroical Times, *Aesculapius*, *Chiron*, *Machaon*, and the rest, were little more than *Surgeons*, that could apply a Plaister, and cure a Green Wound. Nay, after Learning had emboldened Men to Reason upon the Causes of Diseases, whose Original was not visible to the naked Eye, and to try whether Inward Remedies would not cure them, *Surgery* was constantly treated of by *Physicians*, as a Part of their Profession. *Celsus* alone will convince every Man of the Truth of this Proposition.

But how they treated of it, I durst not adventure to assert; tho' the Public will thank me for leaving it untouch'd, since that eminently Learned Surgeon, *Charles Bernard*, Esq; since the former Editions of this Book, deservedly advanced to be First Surgeon to

Her

Her Majesty's Person, has done me the favour to communicate this following Paper, which I shall subjoin in his own words:

'If we enquire into the Improvements
'which have been made by the Moderns
'in *Surgery*, we shall be forced to confess,
'that we have so little reason to value our
'selves beyond the Ancients, or to be
'tempted to contemn them, as the fashion
'is among those who know little, and have
'read nothing, that we cannot give stron-
'ger or more convincing Proofs of our
'own Ignorance, as well as our Pride. I
'do not pretend that the Moderns have not
'at all contributed towards the Improve-
'ment of *Surgery*; that were both absurd
'and injurious, and would argue as much
'Folly as that which I am reproach-
'ing: but that which I am contesting for,
'is, That it consists rather in refining and
'dressing up the Inventions of the Ancients,
'and setting them in a better light, than
'in adding many important ones of our
'own. Whether it be, that the Art of
'Healing External Hurts, being principal-
'ly the Subject of our Senses, was earlier
'studied, and therefore capable of being
'sooner brought to a greater degree of Per-
'fection, than the other Branch of Medi-
'cine; or, that the majority of the meer Pro-
'fessors having been, for some Ages, illite-
'rate and Empirical, it hath not been ad-
'vanc'd

'vanc'd and cultivated so as it might have
' been, had they been better qualified than
' they generally were, and do yet, for the
' greatest part continue to be: For a Testi-
' mony of which, that exceeding Paucity
' of Good Writers which occur in *Surgery*,
' when compared with those in most of the
' other learned Arts and Sciences, is, in
' my Opinion sufficient; and yet were
' they fewer, 'twould in the Judgment of
' these *Scioli*, be no great detriment to the
' Art. For the Folly of which Assertion,
' the best Excuse that can be made, seems
' to be, that because some Methods of pro-
' ceeding both in *Physic* and *Surgery*, which
' are incommunicable, to which every Man
' must be directed by his own Judgment,
' and Natural Sagacity, not being to be
' found in those Authors whom these opini-
' onated Practitioners have had the luck to
' consult, they are led immediately to de-
' spise all Reading, as useless and uninstru-
' ctive; especially that of the Ancients,
' who do not generally, I confess, write to
' Novitiates and Fools, or to those who
' will be always such.

' But whoever hath been conversant in
' their Writings, and hath the Opportuni-
' ty and Capacity of Comparing and Judg-
' ing from his own Experience, will readi-
' ly confess, that one thing which does not
' a little recommend the Reading of them
' be-

'beyond moſt of the Moderns, is, that
'they are more accurate in deſcribing the
'*Pathognomonics*, and more juſt and nice in
'diſtinguiſhing the Species of Tumors and
'Ulcers, than our more refined Moderns are.

'If this Age hath par'd away any rude
'and ſuperfluous Methods of Practice, as
'it muſt be confeſſed they have, it cannot
'be demonſtrated that they were all deriv'd
'from the Ancients, but were in a great
'meaſure introduc'd by ignorant and bar-
'barous Profeſſors of a much later date.

'There is no queſtion but that the prin-
'cipal Improvements which have theſe lat-
'ter Ages been made in *Surgery*, are owing
'chiefly to the Diſcoveries which have
'been made in Anatomy, by which we
'are better enabled to ſolve many of thoſe
'*Phaenomena* which were before inexplica-
'ble, or explained amiſs; the moſt impor-
'tant part, in the mean while (I mean,
'the Art of Healing, to which all the others
'ought to be ſubſervient) remaining very
'little better than the Ancients left it.

'As an unconteſtable Proof of what I ſay,
'I appeal to all thoſe Bodies of *Surgery*
'which have been hitherto publiſhed by
'the moſt Learned and Celebrated of the
'Moderns, being all manifeſtly Tranſcripts
'from one another, and the beſt of them
'from the Ancients. But this may indeed
'be ſaid in Defenſe of the Moderns in this

'par-

'particular, That even Transcribing is not
' their Invention, though it be their Pra-
' ctice; for *Aetius* and *Aegineta* have bor-
' row'd not a little of what they have, from
' *Galen*; and *Marcellus Empiricus* more gro-
' sly from *Scribonius Largus*, without so
' much as remembring his Name among
' the rest of those Authors to whom he
' was less beholden.

'Among all the Systematical Writers, I
' think there are very few who refuse the
' Preference to *Hieron-Fabricius ab Aqua-
' pendente*, as a Person of unquestioned
' Learning and Judgment; and yet is not
' he ashamed, to let his Readers know,
' that *Celsus* among the *Latins* (who, he
' tells us, is *Mirabilis in Omnibus*, and ad-
' vises, in *Horace*'s words,

' *Nocturnâ versare manu, versare diurnâ,*)
' *Paulus Aegineta* among the *Greeks*, and *Albu-
' casis* among the *Arabians* (whom I am willing
' to place among the Moderns, being in the
' number of those whom our Modern Judges
' reject, either because they never read him,
' or because he had the misfortune to live
' DC Years since) are the Triumvirate to
' whom he principally stands indebted, for
' the Assistance he received from them, in
' composing his excellent Book.

'But how many Operations are there
' now in use, which were unknown to the
' Ancients? I fear, that upon a due Enqui-
'ry,

'ry, there would be more useful ones found
'to be omitted or discontinued, than to
'have been invented by us. But to descend
'a little to Particulars, that we may, with-
'out Prejudice or Partiality, be enabled to
'determine whether the Ancients are in-
'deed so contemtible, and their Writings
'useless, as some would represent them.
'*Cutting for the Stone* (to begin with that)
'was unquestionably theirs, and the man-
'ner accurately described by *Celsus* and o-
'thers; and yet, that no Person or Age
'may be defrauded of the Glory they de-
'serve, where we can do them right, we
'must confess, that that way of perform-
'ing it which in most Cases is preferrible,
'and in some only practicable, which by
'Authors is styl'd *Magnus apparatus*, the
'High Operation, or Cutting upon the Staff,
'was invented by one *Johannes de Romanis* of
'*Cremona*, who flourisht at *Rome*, about
'the Year MDXX. The Manner of the
'Operation, and the Instruments necessary,
'were first described and publish'd by his
'Scholar *Marianus Sanctus Barolitanus*, at
'*Venice*, in MDXXXV. The Use of the
'*Modiolus*, in Opening the Skull, was like-
'wise theirs; our Country-man *Woodall*
'only mending the Instrument, by making
'that taper, which was before cylindrical,
'and for that reason not altogether so se-
'cure: The *Alae*, or Wings, being the
'In-

'Invention of that Great Man *Aquapendens*,
' to whom we stand obliged for many other
' useful Instruments. The *Paracentesis*, in
' all its kinds, is theirs: *Barbette*, indeed,
' invented an Instrument which is some-
' times more commodiously made use of
' than the Ancient Methods are. *Laryngo-*
' *tomy*, or the Opening of the Wind-Pipe
' in a Quinsey, was practis'd by them; an
' Operation secure and necessary, however
' at this day so disus'd, that it is almost
' become obselete, either through the Ti-
' midity of the Patient, or Relations, or
' the Backwardness or Ignorance of the
' Physician or Surgeon; and though *Are-*
' *taeus*, *P. Aegineta*, and *Caelius Aurelianus*,
' seem, from the Authority of *Antyllus*, to
' discourse doubtfully of it, yet the greatest
' part of the Ancients, both *Greeks* and *A-*
' *rabians*, advise it; and *Galen* in particular,
' from Reason and Experience, as well as
' from the Authority of *Asclepiades*, justly
' recommends it as the last Refuge in a
' Quinsey. *Cutting for the Hernia Intesti-*
' *nalis*, with the true Distinctions and Cures
' of all the other Species, are accurately de-
' scribed by them. They taught us the
' Cure of the *Pterygion* and *Cataract*; they
' describ'd and distinguish'd all the Diseases
' of the Eyes, (which were not then, as
' now, to the reproach of the Age they
' are, almost solely in the Hands of Old
' Wo-

'Women and Mountebanks) as justly as
' any of our Modern Oculists, who, indeed,
' do little more than transcribe from them.
' *Opening an Artery*, and the *Jugular-Vein*,
' (pretended to be revived here in *England*)
' was no more first attempted by the Mo-
' derns, than making *Ligature* in an *Aneu-*
' *rism*, which though an Operation of no
' mighty difficulty, was certainly not un-
' derstood, very lately, by *Fred. Ruysch*, a
' considerable *Dutch* Anatomist, and Pro-
' fessor of that and Surgery at *Amsteldam*, [as
' may be seen in his *Observationes Anatomico-*
' *Chirurgicae*, Obs. 2. printed in *Quarto*, at
' *Amstel.* MDCXCI.] The *Extirpation of*
' *the Tonsils*, or *Uvula*, is not our Inventi-
' on; though, indeed, the removal of the
' former by *Potential Cauteries*, which we
' sometimes use, when the Patient will not
' admit Excision, or Fire, seems neither to
' have been practis'd nor known to the An-
' cients. The manner of treating the *Fistu-*
' *la Lacrymalis*, (a nice and difficult Cure,
' very often,) which we continue at this
' day, is no other than what was taught by
' them, only the Use of the *Cannula* for the
' Cautery seems owing to *Fabr. ab Aqua-*
' *pendente*. As for the *Actual Cautery*, no
' inconsiderable, however terrible a Branch
' of Surgery it may seem, though *Costaeus*,
' *Fienus* and *Severinus* have written so amply
' concerning it, yet from one single Apho-
' rism

'rifm 'tis demonstrable, that *Hippocrates*
'knew its true Use as well as any that
'have since succeeded him; not to menti-
'on how frequent it is in the Writings of
'all the rest of the Ancients, and us'd in
'many Cases, (I do not doubt but with
'admirable success) wherein it is wholly
'neglected, or not understood by us. The
'Cure of the *Varices*, by Incision, scarce
'talk'd of in our Days, seems to have been
'familiarly practis'd among the Ancients,
'as is manifest from *Celsus*, and *Paulus Ae-*
'*gineta*; though so painful an Operation,
'that, as *Tully* 2. *Tuscul.* and *Plutarch* tell
'us, *Marius* was the first who in one Leg
'underwent it, standing, and without be-
'ing bound, though he could not be pre-
'vail'd upon to purchase with so much
'Tortue a Cure in the other: And though
'*Pliny* tells us, that he was *unus Hominum*,
'the single Instance; yet *Tully* assures us,
'that by his Example, there were others
'that sustain'd it with equal Resolution
'and Fortitude. And whoever is conver-
'sant with those obstinate Varicous Ulcers
'which we frequently meet with, will con-
'fess, that for the effecting a Cure, 'tis ab-
'solutely necessary, however painful and
'superfluous an Operation some may esteem
'it. The Ancients mention the *Vari* and
'*Valgi*, and prescribe us a Method of
'Cure; but the manner of their Reducti-
'on

'on by the Instruments now in use they
'knew not, which were the Invention of
'*Fabricius ab Aquapendente*; as was also that
'for *Extraction* of the *Polypus*, which ne-
'vertheless the Ancients cur'd as frequent-
'ly, though not so commodiously as
'our selves. But the *Polypus* of the *Ear*
'(a Disease indeed which occurs not so of-
'ten as the preceeding) seems so little
'known to the Moderns, that the very
'Mention of any such Disease is rarely to
'be met with in any of their Writings, yet
'the Cure of it is not omitted by the An-
'cients. They were perfectly acquainted
'and furnished with convenient Instruments
'for the Reduction of all the Species of
'*Fractures* and *Luxations*, and the Methods
'of treating them afterwards; together
'with all the kinds of *Sutures* at this day
'in use among us, and some too that are
'now lost, at least so uncertain, that some
'very learned Men have thought they em-
'ployed not their time amiss, in endea-
'vouring to determine what they were,
'and to recover their Use. And though
'some have contended, that *Issues* were un-
'known to them, the contrary is evident,
'from *Celsus* and *Caelius Aurelianus*, though
'we must acknowledge, that the placing
'and continuing them as now we do, ap-
'pears not to have been in use among them.
'Nor is the *Seton* so extremely Modern,

'but

'but that *Lanfrancus*, who lived CCCC
'Years since, directs its Use, and describes
'the manner of Making, (yet mentions it
'not as an Invention of his time,) though,
'indeed, till *Hildanus* his days, it seems to
'have been always made with the Actual
'Cautery.

'There is no doubt but the Ὑστεροτομοτο-
'κία, or *Cutting the Infant out of the Mo-
'ther*, to preserve both, commonly call'd
'*Partus Caesareus*, (not often, if at all pra-
'ctis'd among us, though reviv'd by some
'of our Neighbours with a success which
'ought to provoke the Emulation of our
'Professors here) is owing purely to the Fe-
'licity of the Moderns of the last Century.
'For, not to enter into the Controversie,
'whether *Pliny*, *Nonius* or *Isidore* were in
'the right, in asserting, that the First of
'the *Caesars* was denominated from his man-
'ner of Birth; or *Probus* and *Festus*, in af-
'firming, that they were the *Caesones*;
'whereas the *Caesars* were only so called,
'from their Hair: Most certain it is, that
'neither Side pretend the Operation to have
'been done *Matre superstite*: Nor is there
'any Evidence, that cutting the *Foe-
'tus* out of the Womb, and preserving the
'Mother, was ever propos'd or thought of
'by the Ancients, whether *Greek*, *Latin* or
'*Arabian*; both the Story, and the Reason of
'the Name, being to be found only in the
' Hi-

'Historians and Grammarians. Who it was
' that first propos'd or practis'd it, I confess,
' I am not able to determine: For *Fr. Ros-*
' *setus*, who first wrote solemnly and ex-
' presly, or indeed at all, concerning it,
' produces several Examples of other Men's
' Experience and Success, before ever he
' attempted it himself.

' As for those Operations which the *Greeks*
' call'd Κολοβώματα, or *Curtorum Chirurgia*,
' they amounted to no more than cutting
' the Hair-Lip, or the like, for that they
' knew and practis'd; and therefore it be-
' comes us to do right to the Age whose it
' was, for the Discovery of that which
' *Gaspar Talzacotius* properly so calls, and
' which himself brought to Perfection; and
' (whatever Scruples some who have not
' examin'd the History, may entertain con-
' cerning either the Truth or Possibility of
' the Fact) practis'd with wonderful Dex-
' terity and Success, as may be prov'd from
' Authorities not to be contested. So that
' it is a most surprising thing to consider,
' that few or none should have since at-
' tempted to imitate so worthy and excel-
' lent a Pattern, especially in an Age wherein
' so many deplorable and scandalous Objects
' do every day seem either to beg or com-
' mand our Assistance. But I do not assert
' him to have been the first Inventor, be-
' cause it is what I find mentioned, though
' im-

'imperfectly, by *Alex. Benedictus*, before
'*Taliacotius* was born; and afterwards, by
'*Vesalius*, in his *Chirurgia Magna*, if at least
'that mean Piece be his, as we have it
'publish'd by *Borgarutius*, which *Fabr. Hil-*
'*danus* justly questions. There is likewise
'an Epistle quoted by *Steph. Gourmelenus*,
'in his *Ars Chirurgica*, written from one
'*Calentius* to his Friend *Orpianus*, (who it
'seems, had the misfortune to want a Nose,)
'giving him an Account, that there was
'one *Brauca*, a *Sicilian, qui didicit nares*
'*inserere*, which *Calentius* himself had seen
'perform'd, and therefore invites him to
'come, with this Encouragement, That he
'might be sure to return with a Nose of
'what size he pleas'd. Who this *Orpianus*
'was, is not material to enquire; nor can
'I, I confess, say much of this *Brauca*, (or
'*Branca*, as *Taliacotius* calls him, who seems
'to know no more of Him or his History,
'than what he transcrib'd from *Gourmelenus*;
'and *Gourmelenus* himself, no more than is
'express d in this Epistle of *Calentius*, which
'affords but little light into the History;)
'though it is very probable that he was
'the same Person whom *Ambr. Parey* men-
'tions to have practis'd this way of Inocu-
'lating Noses some Years before his time
'in *Italy*, and gives and Instance of a Ca-
'det of the Family *à S. Thoano*, who being
'weary and asham'd of a Silver Nose, ap-
'ply-

Ancient and Modern Learning.

'plying himself to this *Italian*, return'd with
'one of Flesh, to the Wonder and Satisfa-
'ction of all that knew him. As for this
'*Elisius Calentius*, from whom we have the
'first mention, that I can find, of any such
'Operation, he was Contemporary and
'Familiar with *Sannazarius*, and *Jov. Pon-*
'*tanus*, who mentions him; as does also
'*Lilius Gyraldus*, in his History of the Mo-
'dern Poets, and tells us, agreeably enough,
'that he was Poor, Amorous, and a Poet;
'that he was born at *Amphracta*, in *Apulia*,
'but liv'd generally at *Naples*: His Works
'were printed about MDIII; and after-
'wards, his *Epistles*, among other select
'ones, were publish'd by *Gilb. Cognatus*,
'and printed by *Oporinus*, in MDLVIII.
'But I must not omit, among the rest,
'(what indeed is so notorious, that no Man,
'I suppose will deny it,) That all the sorts
'of *Amputations*, as Limbs, and Breasts, &c.
'were as familiarly practis'd among the
'Ancients, as any can pretend they are a-
'mong us, if we had only the Authority
'of a Poet for it, *Immedicabile vulnus*
'*ense rescindendum est.*

'The Art of *Bandage*, or *Rowling*, no
'mean or unnecessary, though neglected
'piece of *Surgery*, and upon which the
'*French* do so much value themselves, they
'knew so well, and had in such perfection,
'that we have not pretended to add much

Z ' to

'to that excellent and useful Treatife which
'Galen hath exprefly written upon that Sub-
'ject. And though the Variety of Inftru-
'ments now in ufe may feem, in fome mea-
'fure, to be juftly challeng'd by the Mo-
'derns, every Man adding as his own Fan-
'cy fuggefted, and the Neceffity required;
'yet by what are tranfmitted to us by the
'Ancients, 'tis notorious, that they were
'neither ignorant nor deftitute of thofe
'which were moft neceffary; and that they
'had variety of others too, may, by what
'we fee defcrib'd by *Oribafius* and others,
'and are at this day made ufe of, more ea-
'fily be imagin'd than prov'd, but feems
'highly probable.

'As for Topical Medicines, moft certain
'it is that we are oblig'd to them, for in-
'ftructing us in the Nature and Proper-
'ties of almoft all thofe of which we do
'at this day form our Applications; fome
'few excepted, the Productions of Modern
'Chymiftry, in this or the preceding Cen-
'tury.

'And as for general Methods of Cure,
'many of them have been fo excellently
'well handled by the Ancients, (to in-
'ftance only in Wounds of the Head) that
'feveral of the Moderns who have written
'moft judicioufly upon them, have been
'of Opinion, that they could not ferve
'and oblige Pofterity better, than by Com-
'ment-

'menting upon that admirable Book of *Hip-*
'*pocrates* upon the same Subject.

'That which without Injury to the An-
'cients, or Vanity in our Selves, may be
'justly said, is, That the publishing Ob-
'servations after that Method which some
'of the Moderns have done, is that wherein
'we must be allowed infinitely to have ex-
'ceeded them; and is vastly of more Ad-
'vantage to the Reader, than the perusal of
'tedious Systems are capable of being, two
'or three of which generally comprehend-
'ing whatever is to be found in all the
'rest: But particular Cases, when judici-
'ously and faithfully reported, (of which
'too few, I fear, even of the Moderns,
'are guilty,) *Et prodesse solent & delectare*,
'are diverting and instructive at once, the
'Reader more effectually adding other
'Men's Experience to his own.

'But to insist upon every particular, and
'to pretend to demonstrate what hath been
'invented, discontinued, or lost in every
'Age, if it be to be done, requires a Per-
'son of greater Leasure, and infinitely
'more capable than my self. What I have
'said, is sufficient to shew, that it becomes
'us to speak of the Ancients with Respect
'and Civility at least, if it were only for
'this, That it was our Instruction, and the
'Benefit of Mankind in general, which in-
'duc'd them to take that Care, and to be

Z 2 'at

'at so much Expense of Time and Labour
'to communicate their Knowledge to the
'World: Not that we are implicitely to be
'determin'd by their Authority, or to sup-
'pose that they have not left room for suc-
'ceeding Ages to Invent, and to Improve
'all those Parts of *Surgery* wherein they
'appear either to have been mistaken or
'deficient. For my own part, I must
'confess, I do entirely concurr with *Tho-*
'*mas Bartholine,* [*Epist. Med.* Cent. 3.] who
'very well understood the Advantages
'which the Moderns had, and was himself
'as solicitous for the Improvement of Know-
'ledge, as inquisitive into Nature, and as
'happy in his Discoveries, as any of those
'who imagine it a part of their Wit and
'Breeding, to ridicule and contemn the
'Ancients; *Pessimè studiis suis consulant* (says
'he) *qui ita recentiorum scriptis se immer-*
'*gunt, ut veteres vel negligant vel contem-*
'*nant, quum plerarumque rerum lux ex illis*
'*pendeat:* And in another place; *Ita sem-*
'*per recentiorum sententiis & opinionibus cal-*
'*culum adjeci, ut sua antiquitati reverentia*
'*servaretur, cui artis nostrae fundamenta de-*
'*bemus.*

CHAP.

CHAP. XXVII.

Of Ancient and Modern Natural Philosophy.

Having gone through with the most considerable Branches of *Natural* and *Mathematical Knowledge*, I am now to enquire into the Comparative Excellency of Ancient and Modern *Books of Philosophy*, thereby to see in which of them Nature, and its Operations, are explained best. Here I shall first enquire into the several *Methods of Philosophizing*; and afterwards, into the Intrinsic Worth of the Doctrines themselves. *Moderns* here are taken in a very strict sence. I shall mention none who have made any *Entries upon this noble Stage of Nature* (w) above LXXX Years ago, since the time of those first Flights of the Restorers of Learning, that are so exceedingly applauded by Sir *William Temple*. For *Natural Philosophy* was the last part of Knowledge which was cultivated with any particular Care, upon the Revival of Learning; though *Natural History*, which is a principal Ground-work, had been long be-

(w) P. 44.

fore

fore encreasing, and a considerable Heap of Materials had been collected, in order to the Work.

As for *Modern Methods of Philosophizing*, when compared with the *Ancient*, I shall only observe these following Particulars. (1.) No Arguments are received as cogent, no Principles are allowed as current, amongst the celebrated Philosophers of the present Age, but what are in themselves intelligible; that so a Man may frame an Idea of them, of one sort or other. Matter and Motion, with their several Qualities, are only considered in Modern Solutions of Physical Problems. *Substantial Forms, Occult Qualities,* (x), *Intentional Species, Idiosyncrasies, Sympathies, and Antipathies of Things*, are exploded; not because they are Terms used by Ancient Philosophers, but because they are only empty Sounds, Words whereof no Man can form a certain and determinate Idea. (2.) Forming of Sects and Parties in Philosophy, that shall take their Denominations from, and think themselves obliged to stand by the Opinions of any particular Philosophers, is, in a manner, wholly laid aside. *Des Cartes* is not more believed upon his own Word, than *Aristotle*: Matter of Fact is the only thing appealed to; and Systems are little farther regarded, than as they are proper to instruct young Beginners, who

(x) P. 46.

must

must have a general Notion of the whole Work, before they can sufficiently comprehend any particular Part of it; and who must be taught to reason by the Solutions of other Men, before they can be able to give Rational Solutions of their own: In which Case, a false Hypothesis, ingeniously contrived, may now and then do the Service of a true one. (3.) *Mathematics* are joined along with *Physiology*, not only as Helps to Men's Understandings, and Quickeners of their Parts, but as absolutely necessary to the comprehending of the Oeconomy of Nature, in all her Works. (4.) The *New Philosophers*, as they are commonly called, avoid making general Conclusions, till they have collected a great Number of Experiments or Observations upon the Thing in hand; and, as new Light comes in, the old Hypotheses fall without any Noise or Stir. So that the Inferences that are now a-days made from any Enquiries into Natural Things, though perhaps they be set down in general Terms, yet are (as it were by Consent) received with this tacit Reserve, *As far as the Experiments or Observations already made, will warrant.*

How much the pursuing of these Four Things will enlarge *Natural Philosophy*, is easie to guess. I do not say, that none of these things were anciently minded; but only,

only, that they were not then so generally put in practice. The great Men of Antiquity often exprest themselves in unintelligible Cant: They chiefly aim'd at being Heads of particular Sects: Few of their Natural Philosophers were great Mathematicians: And they did in general establish Hypotheses without a sufficient Fund of Experiments and Observations whereupon to build them. The *Corpuscularian Philosophy* is in all probability the oldest, and its Principles are those intelligible ones I just now commended. But its Foundations being very large, and requiring much Time, Cost, and Patience, to build any great Matters upon, it soon fell, before it appears to have been thoroughly understood. For it seems evident, that *Epicurus* minded little but the raising of a Sect, which might talk as plausibly as those of *Aristotle*, or *Plato*, since he despised all manner of Learning, even Mathematics themselves, and gloried in his having spun all his Thoughts out of his own Brain; a good Argument of his Wit indeed, but a very ordinary one of that Skill in Nature which *Lucretius* extols in him, as often as he takes occasion to speak of him. The Ancient Physics look like a thing wholly of Ostentation and Pomp, otherwise I cannot understand why *Plato* should reprove *Eudoxus* and *Archytas*, for trying to make

their

their Skill in Geometry useful in Matters of Civil Life, by inventing of Instruments of public Advantage; or think that those sublime Truths were debased, when the unlearned part of Mankind were made the better for them. And therefore, as *Plutarch* complains, in his *Life of Marcellus*, Mechanical Arts were despised by Geometers till *Archimedes*'s Time: Now though this be particularly spoken there by *Plutarch*, of the Making of Instruments of Defense and Offense in War, yet it is equally applicable to all the Ancient Philosophy and Mathematics in general. The Old Philosophers seemed still to be afraid that the Common People should despise their Arts, if generally understood: This made them keep, for the most part, to those Studies which required few Hands and Mechanical Tools to compleat them: Which to any Man that has a right Notion of the Extent of a Natural Philosopher's Work, will appear absolutely necessary. Above all, the Ancients do not seem sufficiently to have understood the Connexion between Mathematical Proportions of Lines and Solids, in an abstracted Proposition, and in every Part of the Creation; at least, in their Reasonings about the Causes of Natural Things, they did not take much Pains to shew it. When *Galen* was to give an Account of Vision, in his

Books

Books (y) *de Usu Partium*, because he had Occasion to use some few Geometrical Terms, as *Cone*, *Axis*, *Triangle*, and the like; he makes a long Excuse, and tells a tedious Story of a Daemon that appear'd to him, and commanded him to write what he did; and all this, lest the Physicians of that Age should think he Conjur'd, and so take a Prejudice against all he said. This shews, that in *Galen*'s Time at least, there was little Correspondence between Mathematical and Physical Sciences, and that Mankind did not believe there was so intimate a Relation between them as it is now generally known there is. Many a Man that cannot demonstrate any one single Proposition in *Euclid*, takes it now for granted, that Geometry is of infinite Use to a Philosopher; and it is believed now upon Trust, because it is become an Axiom amongst the Learned in these Matters. And if it had been so received in *Galen*'s Time, or by those more Ancient Authors whom *Galen* and his Contemporaries followed, or pretended at least to follow, as their Patterns; such as *Hippocrates*, whom all Sides reverenced, *Herophilus*, *Erasistratus*, *Asclepiades*, and several more, there would have been no need of any Excuses for what he was doing; since his Readers being accustomed to such sort of Reasonings, would either readily have understood them,

(y) De U. P. l. x. c. 12, 13, 14.

them, or acquiesced in them as legitimate Ways of Proof. If Three or Four Mathematical Terms were so affrightning, how would those learned Discourses of *Steno* and *Croone*, concerning Muscular Motion, have moved them? How much would they have been amazed at such minute Calculations of the Motive-strength of all the Muscles in the several general sorts of Animals, as require great Skill in Geometry, even to understand them, which are made by *Borellus*, in his Discourses *of the Motion of Animals*? It is not enough, in this Case, to quote a Saying or two out of some great Man amongst the Ancients; or to tell us, that *Plato* said, long ago, *That God Geometrizes in all his Works*; as long as no Man can produce one Ancient Essay upon any Part of Physiology, where Mathematical Ratiocinations were introduced to salve those *Phaenomena* of Natural Things, upon which it was possible to talk plausibly without their Help. At least, it is certain, That they contented themselves with general Theories, without entring into minute Disquisitions into the several Varieties of Things, as is evident in the two Cases already alledged, *of Vision and Muscular Motion*.

Now as this Method of Philosophizing laid down above, is right, so it is easie to prove, that it has been carefully followed
by

by Modern Philosophers. My Lord *Bacon* was the first Great Man who took much pains to convince the World that they had hitherto been in a wrong Path, and that Nature her self, rather than her Secretaries, was to be addressed to by those who were desirous to know much of her Mind. Monsieur *Des Cartes*, who came soon after, did not perfectly tread in his Steps, since he was for doing too great a part of his Work in his Closet, concluding too soon, before he had made Experiments enough; but then to a vast Genius he joined exquisite Skill in Geometry, and working upon Intelligible Principles in an Intelligible Manner, though he very often failed of one part of his End, namely, a right Explication of the *Phaenomena* of Nature; yet by marrying Geometry and Physics together, he put the World in Hopes of a Masculine Off-spring in process of Time, though the first Productions should prove abortive. This was the state of Natural Philosophy, when those great Men who, after King *Charles* II[d]'s Restoration, joined in a Body, called by that Prince himself, the ROYAL SOCIETY, went on with the Design; they made it their Business to set their Members awork to collect a perfect History of Nature, in order to establish thereupon a Body of Physics. What has been done towards it by the Members of that Illustrious Body, will be evident to those who consider that *Boyle, Barrow, Newton, Huygens, Malpighius, Leeuwenhoek, Willughby, Willis*, and abundance more already named amongst the great Advancers of real Learning, have belonged to it: If it shall be thought too tedious an Undertaking, to examine all their Writings, Mr. *Boyle's Works*, Monsieur *Le Clerc's Physics*, any one good *System of the* Cartesian *Philosophy*, Monsieur *Rohault's* for Instance, or to comprehend all under one, a Book intituled, *Philosophia Vetus & Nova ad Usum Scholae accommodata*, may be consulted, and then there will be no difficulty to determine of which Side the Verdict ought to be given; in the last Book especially it is evident how very little the Ancients did in all Parts of Natural Philosophy, and what a great Compass it at present takes, since it makes the Comparison I all along appeal to.

Thus, it seems to me to be sufficiently plain, That the Ancients Knowledge in all Matters relating to *Mathematics* and *Physics*, was incomparably inferior to that of the Moderns. These are Subjects, many of them at least, which require great Intenseness of Thought, great Strength and Clearness of Imagination, even only to understand them; how much more then to invent them? The Ancient *Orators*, who spoke so great things in Praise of
Elo-

Eloquence, who made it so very hard a thing to be an Orator, had little or no Notion of the Difficulty of these Sciences; the *Romans* especially, who despised what they did not understand, and who did not without some Indignation learn of a People whom themselves had conquered. But if they could have conceived what a Force of Genius is required to invent such Propositions as are to be found in the Writings of their own Mathematicians, and of the Modern Geometers and Philosophers, they would soon have acknowledged that there was need of as great at least, if not greater Strength of Parts and Application to do very considerable things in these Sciences, as in their own admired Eloquence, which was never more artfully employed than in commending it self. The Panegyrics which they made upon Geometry, were rather Marks of their Pedantry, than of their Skill; *Plato* and *Pythagoras* admired them, and therefore they did so too, out of a blind Reverence to those great Names. Otherwise, amongst those numerous Commendations which are given to *Archimedes*, some would have been spent upon the many noble Theorems which he discovered, and not almost all upon the Engines wherewith he baffled *Marcellus* at the Siege of *Syracuse*. The Proposition, *That the Superficies of a Sphere is equal to the Area's of Four of*

its

its greatest Circles, which is one of the most wonderful Inventions that was ever found in Geometry, shews him to have been a much greater Man, than all that is said of him by the *Roman* or *Greek* Historians. Had Experimental Philosophy been anciently brought upon the Stage, had Geometry been solemnly and generally applied to the Mechanism of Nature, and not solely made use of to instruct Men in the Art of Reasoning, and even that too, not very frequently neither, the Moderns would not have had so great Reason to boast as now they have: For these are things which come under Ocular Demonstration, which do not depend upon the Fancies of Men for their Approbation, as Oratory and Poetry often do. So that one may not only in general say, that the Ancients are out-done by the Moderns in these Matters, but also assign most of the Particulars, and determine the Proportion wherein and how far they have been exceeded, and shew the several Steps whereby this sort of Learning has from Age to Age received Improvement. This ends Disputes and satisfies the Understanding at once.

CHAP.

CHAP. XXVIII.

Of the Philological Learning of the Moderns.

Hitherto, in the main, I please my self, that there cannot be much said against what I have asserted, though I have all along taken care not to speak too positively, where I found that it was not an easie thing to vindicate every Proposition without entring into a Controversie, which would bear plausible things on both Sides, and so might be run out into a multitude of Words, which in Matters of this kind are very tiresome. But there are other Parts of Learning still behind, where the bare offering to compare the Moderns to the Ancients, may seem a Paradox; where the subject Matter is entirely ancient, and is chiefly, if not altogether contained in Books that were written before the Ancient Learning suffered much Decay.

Under this Head *Philology* and *Divinity* may very properly be ranked. I place *Divinity* last, to avoid Repetition; because what I have to say concerning Modern *Philology*, will strengthen many things that may

may be urged in the Behalf of Modern *Divinity* as compared with the Ancient.

In speaking of the Extent and Excellency of the *Philological Learning* of the Moderns within these last CC Years, I would not be mis-understood. For the Question is not, whether any Modern Critic has understood *Plato* or *Aristotle*, *Homer* or *Pindar*, as well as they did themselves, or even so well as they were understood by the Age in which they wrote, for that were ridiculous; but whether Modern Industry may not have been able to discover a great many Mistakes in the Assertions of the Ancients about Matters not done in their own Times, but several Ages before they were born. For the Ancients did not live all in one Age; and though they appear all under one Denomination, and so seem to be in the same Line, like things seen at a vast Distance, to us who are very remote from the youngest of them; yet, upon a nearer View, they will be found exceedingly remote some from others; and so as liable to Mistakes, when they talk of Matters not transacted in their own Times, as we are when we reason of Matters of Fact, which were acted in the Reign of *William the Conqueror*. Wherefore, if one reflects upon the Alteration which Printing has introduced into the State of Learning, when every Book

A a once

once printed, becomes, in a manner, out of danger of being lost, or hurt by Copiers; and that Books may be compar'd, examin'd and canvass'd with much more ease than they could before; it will not seem ridiculous to say, That *Joseph Scaliger, Isaac Casaubon, Salmasius, Henricus Valesius, Selden, Usher, Bochart, Spanheim*, and other Philologers of their Stamp, may have had a very comprehensive View of Antiquity, such a one as Strangers to those Matters, can have no Idea of; nay, a much greater than, taken all together, any one of the Ancients themselves, ever had, or indeed, could have. *Demosthenes* and *Aristophanes* knew the State of their own Times better than *Casaubon* or *Salmasius*: But it is a question whether *Boëthius* or *Apollinaris Sidonius* knew the State of *Demosthenes*'s Time so well; yet these also are Ancients to us, and have left behind them Writings of a very estimable Value. Literary Commerce could not anciently be so frequent as now it is, tho' the *Roman* Empire made it more easie than otherwise it could have been.

In *Ecclesiastical Antiquity* this can be more fully proved than it can in *Civil*; because Monuments of that Kind are more numerous, and have been better preserved. How widely were the *Greek* Writers, many times mistaken, when they gave an Account of the Affairs of the *Latin* Churches. And how

how imperfect, many times, were the Accounts which the *Western* Churches had of Things of the greatest Moment, that had been determined in the *East*? Though the Council of *Nice* was Oecumenical, yet the *African* Churches knew so little of its Canons above L Years after it was held, that the Bishops of *Rome* imposed Canons made in another Council, held several Years after, in another Place, upon them, as Canons made in the Council of *Nice*: Yet they were all, at that time, under one common Government, and these things were acknowledged by all Sides to be of Eternal Concernment. The same Negligence, if not greater, is discernible in Matters which were studied, rather as Recreation and Diversion, than as necessary Business. How many of the Ancients busied themselves about Examining into the Antiquities of several Nations; especially after the *Old Testament* was translated into *Greek*? Yet, how few of them understood the Languages of those Countries of which they disputed? There were but Two of the Ancient Fathers, that we know of, that pretended to Learning, who understood *Hebrew* in any tolerable degree, *Origen*, and St. *Hierom*: And how well St. *Hierom* understood it, is now certainly known; not like the *Lightfoot*'s, the *Buxtorf*'s, the *Drusius*'s, and the *Cappell*'s of the present Age, one may be very well assured: The other *Oriental* Languages, even these Inquisitive Fathers knew little or nothing of. To how good Purpose they have been cultivated by the Moderns, the Writings of *Selden*, *Bochart*, *Pocock*, and several others, do abundantly declare. When *Pocock* and *Golius* went into the *East*, to bring away their Learning, *they* went to excellent purpose indeed. The *Bodleyan* and *Leyden* Libraries can witness what vast Heaps of *Eastern* MSS. have been brought, by such Men as these, into *Europe*. One would think I were drawing up a *Catalogue*, not writing of a *Discourse*, if I should enumerate the Books which have been printed about the *Oriental* Learning, within these last LXX Years: And how much they have enlightned all manner of Antiquity, is easie to tell.

How clearly has the *Old Chronology* and *Geography* been stated by Modern Critics and Philologers; and the Mistakes and Carelesness of many Writers detected, who were esteemed Authentic even in the Times wherein they lived? *Selden* and *Bochart*, to name no more at present, have plainly proved, that all the Ancient *Greek* Antiquaries were not near so well acquainted with the Originals of that *Mythology*, which then made up a good part of their Religion, as well as of their Learning, as they are known at present, since the Languages of those

those Countries, from whence most of those Rites and Stories took their Original, have been carefully examined, and critically studied. Is it not a very odd thing, that of so many as have written of the *Pyramids*, there should not be one exact Account of them, Ancient nor Modern, till Mr. *Greaves* described them? They were admired formerly, as much as now (z); reckoned amongst the Seven Wonders of the World; and mention'd from *Herodotus*'s Time, downwards, by all that gave any Account of *Aegypt*: Yet most Men copied after *Herodotus*; and many of the rest, who did not, spoke by guess. None of the exstant Ancient Authors was so Exact as Mr. *Sandy*'s, who wanted nothing but Mathematical Skill, to have left nothing for Mr. *Greaves*, who came after him, to do. This is an eminent Instance, whereby we may give a certain Judgment of the Historical Exactness of the Ancients, compared to that of the Moderns. It may be improved to considerable Purposes; at least, it is of great Use to justifie those Modern Writers, who have, with great freedom, accused some of the greatest of the Ancients, of Carelesness in their Accounts of Civil Occurrences, as well as of Natural Rarities; and who have dared to believe their own Reason, against the positive Evidence of an old Historian, in Matters wherein one would think that he had greater Op-

(z) *Barbara Pyramidum sileat miracula Memphis.* Martial.

portunities of knowing the certain Truth, than any Man that has lived for several Ages.

But here I exspect it should be objected, That this is not to be esteemed as a Part of Real Learning. To pore upon old MSS. to compare various Readings; to turn over *Glossaries*, and old *Scholia* upon Ancient Historians, Orators and Poets; to be minutely critical in all the little Fashions of the Ancient *Greeks* and *Romans*, the Memory whereof was, in a manner, lost within L or a C Years after they had been in use; may be good Arguments of a Man's Industry, and Willingness to drudge; but seem to signifie little to denominate him a great Genius, or one who was able to do considerable Things himself.

The Objection is specious enough, and the Indiscretions of many Modern Commentators have given but too much Colour for it; which has, in our Nation especially, been riveted in Men's Minds, more, perhaps, than in any other learned Nation in *Europe:* Though in Enquiries into the remotest Antiquities of the *Northern* Nations, no People have done near so much as some learned *Englishmen*. But this Objection lies chiefly against the Men, not the Knowledge, the Extent whereof it is only my Business to enquire into; and yet, ever there too, it is without Ground: For, who
ever

ever will be at the pains to reflect upon the vast Extent of the various Knowledge which such Men as those I named before have gathered together, which they were able to produce to such excellent Purposes in their Writings, must confess that their *Genius's* were little, if at all, inferior to their *Memories*; those among them, especially, who have busied themselves in restoring corrupted Places of Ancient Authors. There are Thousands of Corrections and Censures upon Authors to be found in the Annotations of Modern Critics, which required more Fineness of Thought, and Happiness of Invention, than, perhaps, Twenty such Volumes as those were, upon which these very Criticisms were made. For though, generally speaking, good Copies are absolutely necessary; though the Critic himself ought to have a perfect Command of the Language and particular Stile of his Author, should have a clear Idea of the Way and Humour of the Age in which he wrote; many of which Things require great Sagacity, as well as great Industry; yet there is a peculiar quickness in discerning what is proper to the Passage then to be corrected, in distinguishing all the particular Circumstances necessary to be observed, and those, perhaps, very numerous; which often raise a judicious Critic as much above the Author upon whom he tries his Skill,

Skill, as he that discerns another Man's Thoughts, is therein greater than he that thinks. And the Objection that is commonly made against Editors of old Books, that every Man cries up his own Author, beyond all that have ever written upon that Subject, or in that Way, will rarely hold of truly great Critics, when they pass their Judgments, and employ their Thoughts upon indifferent Books; since some have taken as much pains, in their Critical Annotations (*a*), to expose Authors who have had the good luck to be exceedingly commended by learned Men, as ever others did to praise them.

(*a*) *Vid* Petri Cunæi *Animadversiones in Nonni Dionysiaca.*

Soon after Learning was restored, when Copies of Books, by Printing, were pretty well multiplied, *Criticism* began; which first was exercised in setting out Correct Editions of Ancient Books; Men being forced to try to mend the Copies of Books, which they saw were so negligently written. It soon became the Fashionable Learning; and after *Erasmus*, *Budaeus*, *Beatus Rhenanus*, and *Turnebus* had dispersed that sort of Knowledge through *England*, *France*, *Germany*, and the *Low-Countries*, which before had been kept altogether amongst the *Italians*, it was, for about CXX Years, cultivated with very great Care: And if since it has been at a stand, it has not been

because

because the Parts of Men are sunk, but because the Subject is, in a good measure exhausted; or at least, so far drained, that it requires more Labour, and a greater Force of Genius, now to gather good Gleanings, than formerly to bring home a plentiful Harvest; and yet this Age has produced Men who, in the last, might have been reckon'd with the *Scaligers*, the *Lipsius's* the *Casaubons*. It is not very long since *Holstenius*, *Bochart*, and *Gerhard Vossius*, died; but if they will not be allowed to have been of our Age, yet *Isaac Vossius*, *Nicolas Heinsius*, *Frederic Gronovius*, *Ezekiel Spanheym*, and *Graevius*, may come in; the two last of whom are still alive, and the others died but a few Years since. *England*, perhaps, cannot shew a proportionable Stock of Critics of this Stamp. In *Henry* VIIIth's Time there was an admirable Set of Philologers in the Nation; though there is a great difference to be made between a good Critic, and a Man that writes *Latin* as easily and correctly as his Mother-Tongue. Sir *Thomas More*, Cardinal *Pole*, *Linacre*, *Collet*, *Cheek*, *Ascham*, and several more, often to be met with in *Erasmus's Epistles*, wrote *Latin* with a Purity that no *Italian* needed then to have been ashamed of. Let the Subject they treated of have been what it would, one may see by the Purity of their Stile, that they wrote in a Language which express'd press'd their Thoughts without Constraint. A great Familiarity with the Politest Authors of Antiquity, was what these Men valued themselves much upon; and it was then the Delight of the Learned Men of this Nation, as much as their Disputes in Religion would give them leave. Though this seemed to sink by degrees, yet that afterwards Critical Skill in Antiquity was valued and pursued by our greatest Scholars, will not be questioned by those who consider that Sir *Henry Savile*, Mr. *Camden*, Archbishop *Usher*, Mr. *Selden*, Sir *John Marsham*, Mr. *Gataker* (not to mention some now alive, whose Fame will one Day equal that of the *Salmasius*'s and the *Grotius*'s of other Nations) were the Glories of our Countrey, as well as of the Age they lived in.

In short, to conclude this Argument: Though Philological and Critical Learning has been generally accused of Pedantry, because it has sometimes been pursued by Men who seemed to value themselves upon Abundance of Quotations of *Greek* and *Latin*, and a vain Ostentation of diffused Reading, without any thing else in their Writings to recommend them; yet the Difficulty that there is, to do any thing considerable in it, joined with the great Advantages which thereby have accrued to the Commonwealth

wealth of Learning, have made this no mean Head whereon to commend the great *Sagacity*, as well as *Induſtry* of theſe later Ages.

CHAP. XXIX.

Of the Theological Learning of the Moderns.

TO *Philology*, I before added *Divinity*, and, as I hope to prove, not without Reaſon. As they relate to our Queſtion, they both agree in this, that the Subject of them both is truly Ancient; and that it is impoſſible to become truly excellent in either of them, without a familiar Converſation with thoſe Original Books, to which the great Maſters of both theſe Sciences do conſtantly appeal. Our *Bleſſed Saviour* did not reveal his Law by halves to his Apoſtles, nor is the *New Teſtament* an imperfect Rule of Faith: The *Old Teſtament* likewiſe has conſtantly been at hand; and the *Jews* have, ever ſince their Return from the *Babyloniſh* Captivity, been ſcrupulouſly ſollicitous to deliver the *Genuine Hebrew* and *Chaldee Text* of the *Old Teſtament* pure

pure and uncorrupted, to succeeding Ages. Yet, tho' these, together with the Writings of the *Greek* and *Latin* Fathers, be Instruments without which no Divine can work; and tho' it seems almost impossible that any Man should be able to perform all the Duties of his Profession, that are incumbent upon him as a Scholar, without a competent Exactness in all these Things; yet it is very possible that Modern Divines, who make use of these Instruments, may be better Work-men than those Ancient Fathers, who furnished them with the greatest part.

Now, that there may be no Disputes about Terms mis-understood, it will be necessary to explain what is here meant by *a Perfect Divine*; that is to say, such an one as may be a Standard whereon to found a Comparison. A *Perfect Divine* ought to understand the Text of the *Old* and *New Testament* so exactly, as to have a clear Notion of every Book in general, and of the Grammatical Meaning of every Text in particular; that so he may be able to reconcile all Difficulties, and answer all Objections that may arise: He ought to understand the State of the Church, as to its Doctrine and Discipline, in its several Ages: He ought to be thoroughly vers'd in all the General Notions of *Ethics*, taken in their utmost Extent, to enable him to

re-

resolve such Cases of Conscience as may occurr, with Judgment and Satisfaction: He ought to be a Master of all the Topics of Persuasion which can ever lie in his Way, that so his Exhortations may please and convince those whom he designs to persuade at the same time: Last of all He ought to be able to Answer all the Objections which may be, or have been raised against the Doctrine and Discipline of the Church, by its open or secret Enemies. These seem to be the necessary Qualifications of a *Perfect Divine*; it may, perhaps be question'd whether any Man did ever fully come up to this Description; neither is it necessary to the present Purpose that any should, since the Question will be as perfectly answered, by determining who have come the nearest to it, as by assigning any particular Person that ever quite reach'd up to it. For these Differences do not lie in a Mathematical Point, and I do not desire that any Disputable Things should ever be brought under Debate. One Qualification, indeed, and that the most valuable of all, I have omitted; but that relates not to the present Controversie, since we are not now enquiring who were the Holiest Men, but who were the Greatest Masters of their Profession, the Ancient Fathers, or the Modern Divines.

The first thing required, is, *an Exact Knowledge of the Text of the Old and New Testament*. In Understanding the *Old*, even the LXX Interpreters themselves have often failed, as has been abundantly proved by Modern Critics. The Copies they used were sometimes faulty; and since they did not mend those Faults, it is very probable they did not see them. It has been observed already, That scarce any of the Fathers understood *Hebrew* besides *Origen* and St. *Hierom*, who therefore were followed as Oracles by many of their Successors; even that alone will not suffice, because there are no other Books besides the *Old Testament* written in that Language: For which Reason, *Syriac*, *Chaldee*, *Samaritan* and *Arabic*, have been studied by Modern Critics; not to mention the Writings of the *Rabbins* and the *Talmudists*, to which the Ancients were utter Strangers. If we come to Particulars; Who of the Ancients ever unravelled the Chronology of the *Old Testament*, like Archbishop *Usher*, and Sir *John Marsham*? Though *Eusebius*'s *Chronicon* is a standing Evidence how much he, and *Julius Africanus* before him, endeavoured to clear that Argument, which was of so great Use to confound the vain Pretences to Antiquity of those other Nations that were so unwilling to yield to the *Jews* in this Particular. Who has ever gi-

ven

ven so rational and so intelligible an Account of the Design and Intent of the several Parts of the Ceremonial Law, as Dr. *Spenser*? Who has acquainted the World with the Geography of *Genesis*, or the Natural History of the Bible, like Monsieur *Bochart*? These are much harder things than the lengthning of a fine-spun Allegory, or than a few Moral Reflections, which constitute the greatest Part of the Ancient Comments. But the *New Testament*, it will be said, was written in a Time that was nearer at hand; and so was certainly better understood. Without doubt it was, by the First Fathers; for which Reason their Interpretations (c) and their Reasonings, if we could have recovered many of them would have been of infinite value: But when once the Synagogue and the Church broke off their Correspondence, when once the immediate Reasons of the first Establishment of many Parts of the Christian Discipline, and of great numbers of Allusions to *Jewish* Customs and Traditions which are to be found in the *New Testament*, could only be known by Study and Reading, all which the first Christians knew without Study, as we do the Manners and Fashions of our own Age and Country, then the ancient Interpretations of the *New Testament* began to fail; and though some of them, St. *Chrysostom*'s and *Theodoret*'s especially,

(c) See Mr *Dodwell*'s Two First Dissertations upon St. *Irenaeus*.

are

are in themselves, setting Antiquity aside, truly valuable; yet, for want of such a diffused Knowledge of Eastern Antiquities as was necessary, and which only could be had by a long Conversation with the Books that are written in those Languages, these admirable Commentators seem in several Places not to have found out the true Original of many things in the *New Testament* which have been discovered since.

To the next thing, which is Skill in *Ecclesiastical Antiquity*, I have spoken already. The *Third* and the *Fourth*, which relate to a Divine, as a *Casuist*, or as a *Preacher*, may be considered of together; wherein we of the present Age may, without Vanity, boast of having the best Books, and of them too the greatest Numbers, upon these Subjects, written in our own Language, and by our own Countrey-men, of any People in the World. The Excellency of a *Casuist*, is, to give such Resolutions of Doubts and Questions proposed to him, as may both suit with the particular Circumstances of the Person who desires Satisfaction; and also may be perfectly agreeable to the Law of God. A *Preacher* then seems to perform his Office best, when he can at once instruct and move his Auditors; can raise their Passions, and inform their Judgment; that so every Sermon upon a Doctrinal Head, may contain the Solution of

a Case

a Case of Conscience. For the first of these; It is certain, that many of the ablest of the Ancient Fathers were very excellent Casuists; as, indeed, every Man who has a right Judgment, an honest Mind, and a thorough Acquaintance with the Design of our *Blessed Saviour*, revealed in the Gospel, must of necessity be. And if, at this distance, many of their Decisions seem over severe, there is as great, at least, if not greater Reason to suspect, that the Complaints now-a-days raised against them, may arise from our Degeneracy, as from their unwarrantable Strictness. But for the *Ancient* Way of *Preaching*, there is much more to be said. The great Handle by which an Hearer is enabled to carry along with him a Preacher's Arguments, is, Method and Order. Herein the Ancient Homilists are exceedingly defective: Flights of Rhetoric, which are more or less judiciously applied, according to the Abilities of the several Preachers, make up the greatest part of their Discourses: And after *Origen*, most Men busied themselves in giving the People Allegorical Interpretations of Passages of Scriptures; which were infinite, according to the Fancies of those that used them. St. *Chrysostom*, indeed, reformed this Custom in the *Greek* Church: His Authority went a great way; and his Interpretations were almost always Literal, and, suitably

ably to his vaſt Genius, very Judicious. But he that conſiders *Preaching*, as an Art capable of Rules and Improvement, will find a mighty difference between a Juſt, Methodical Diſcourſe, built upon a proper Text of Scripture, wherein, after the Text is carefully explained, ſome one Duty or Doctrine of Religion, thence ariſing, is plainly proved by juſt and ſolid Arguments, from which ſuch Topics of Perſuaſion are drawn at laſt, as are the moſt likely to raiſe ſuch an Affection, and engage thoſe Paſſions in the Minds of all the Auditors as will pleaſe and move Good Men, and ſilence, at leaſt, if not perſuade the Bad; and between a Looſe, Paraphraſtical Explication of a large Portion of Scripture, ending, at laſt, in a general Ethical Harangue, which is the uſual Method of moſt of *St. Chryſoſtom*'s Homilies. Whereas by the former Method, ſtrictly followed, many of our *Engliſh* Sermons, (eſpecially of the Great Men of our own Church, ſince the Reſtauration,) are Solutions of the moſt difficult Queſtions in Divinity, and juſt Diſcourſes upon the ſeveral Duties of the Chriſtian Life; and this with ſo much Smoothneſs, ſo great Beauty of Language, and ſuch a juſt Application of the greateſt Ornaments of True and Maſculine Eloquence, to Things at firſt View, oftentimes, the moſt oppoſite, that the Hearer takes a Pleaſure to think,

think, that then he is most instructed, when he is best pleased. The Want of this Method in the Ancient Homilists, is the great Reason why they are so little read. It is not because they are hard to be understood, for an indifferent Skill in *Greek* and *Latin* is sufficient to go through with the greatest part of them: But Want of Method, great Multiplicity of Words, and frequent Repetitions, tire out most Readers: They know not how far they are got, but by the Number of the Leaves; and so having no Rest for their Minds to lean upon, when once they begin to be weary, they are soon disgusted. If therefore these Inconveniences are, in a great measure, avoided by Modern Preachers, their Sermons are, in their kind, more perfect, though the Matter which both of them work upon be the same. And if these Things be the Effects of great Study, and of an exact Judgment, at least in those who contributed the most to so great an Alteration; then this also may come in as a proper Evidence of the Encrease of Modern Learning; and with much more Reason than those Things which only tend to divert a Man, when he is unfit for serious Business. Who those are who have succeeded the *Hookers*, the *Chillingworths*, the *Sandersons*, and the *Hammonds* of the last Age, to such excellent purpose for the present, and those that shall come after,

after, I need not name; but shall rather conclude with that Saying in *Velleius Paterculus*, upon a not much unlike Occasion; *Vivorum ut admiratio magna, ita censura difficilis est.*

The last thing which I mention'd, as necessary for a Divine, is, *To be able to Answer such Objections as have been, or may be raised against the Christian Faith.* Of the Controversies which have arisen among Christians, and the Adversaries with whom they have been obliged to engage, there are in the present Account two Sorts; those which the Ancient Fathers were concerned with, and those that have appeared since.

Of the latter it may, possibly, seem hard to pass a Judgment, since one cannot well say how Men would have managed Disputes which never came in their way. The former may also be subdivided into those which have been renewed in our own Time; and those of which we have only the Memory in Ancient Books. So that one is rather to consider how Controversies were handled in general, and so inferr how these Modern ones, which have only engaged the Wits and Passions of later Ages, would have been managed, had there been an Occasion.

It is evident, that in their first Disputes with the *Gentiles*, the old Apologists did with great Accuracy expose both the Follies

lies of their Worship, and the Vanity of their Philosophy: They opened the Christian Religion with great Clearness; they shewed the Grounds of their Belief, and proved its Reasonableness upon such Principles as were both solid in themselves, and suitable to the Ways of Arguing, and the peculiar Notions of all their several Adversaries. Afterwards, when the Mysteries of the Christian Religion were so eagerly debated, in Ages wherein they feared no Foreign Force, the Men of Learning shewed as great Subtilty in their Arguments, and as great Dexterity in shifting off the Sophisms of their Opponents, as have ever been shewed in later Times. So that thus far the Moderns seem to have little Advantage: And, indeed, the Books that were written by the Ancients in Defense of the Christian Religion, were very admirable; But in the Controversies that were managed amongst themselves, there seem to be, many times, as visible Signs of too great a Subtilty, as of a judicious Understanding of the Point in hand: They used little Method in ranging their Arguments, and rarely stated the Question in plain and short Terms: This made them often multiply Words to a tedious length, which both tired the Readers, and darkned the Dispute. That all these Faults are too often found in the Polemical Discourses of the Moderns, is most certain: But Comparisons are always laid between the ablest Men of both Sides. The Modern Defenses of the Doctrines of the *Trinity*, and the *Incarnation*, may be compared with the old Defences of the same Doctrines against the *Arians*, and other Ancient Heretics. If Heretics may be compared with Heretics, there is no question but the *Socinians* are much abler Disputants than the *Arians* and *Eunomians* were of old: They have collected every thing that can look like an Argument: They have critically canvass'd every Text of Scripture which anciently was not so Grammatically understood as now it is, and have spared no Pains nor Art to wrest every thing that, with any shew of Reason, could be drawn to their Side: They have refined upon the Philosophical Notions of God, and of his Attributes; and have taken great Care not to confound their Readers, or themselves, with Want of Method, or a Multiplicity of Words. Such able Adversaries have not failed of as able Opponents. And when Men of Skill manage any Dispute, whatsoever it be, they will teach one another the Art of Reasoning, even though before-hand they should not well have understood it, if their Debates continue to any length. Whence also it has followed, that though these Great Men, who have defended our Faith against such subtile

tile Adverfaries, would have fhewn their Skill equally upon any other Subject which they might have undertaken; yet upon thefe Queftions, the Truth would otherwife never have been fo perfectly known.

And here it ought to be obferved, That the Art of making Controverfies eafie and intelligible, even though the Arguments fhould be all the fame that had formerly been urged, fhews much greater Skill, and a more thorough Underftanding of thofe Matters, than had been difcovered before: For, he that makes another underftand a thing in few Words, has a more clear and comprehenfive Knowledge of that thing, than another Man who ufes a great many. Such a Man's Excurfions, if he has a mind at any time to go out of the way, or to enlarge, for the eafe of thofe who love to have things expreffed in an Homiletical manner, will never tire; becaufe, having his Point ftill in view, he will take care that his Readers or Auditors fhall always know where he is. Hence it is, that there are many Sermons in our Language, upon the moft abftrufe Queftions in the Chriftian Religion, wherein *Englifh* Readers, who have never read Fathers nor School-men, whofe Heads have never been fill'd with Terms of Art, and Diftinctions, many times, without a difference, may both in few and clear

clear Propositions, know what they are to believe, and at the same time know how to defend it. Hereby, in all our Controversies with *Papists*, *Socinians*, and *Dissenters*, many admirable Discourses have been written, wherein one sees the Question rightly stated, presently brought to an Head, and accurately proved by such Arguments as its particular Nature may require. It cannot be denied, but a good deal of this Methodical Exactness was at first owing to the School-men; but they are Moderns here: And if their Writings have some Excellencies, which the elegant Composures of more learned Ages want; this also affords us a convincing Argument, that Mankind will, in something or other, be always improving; and that Men of working Heads, what Subject soever they handle, though they live in Times when they have none but barbarous Patterns to copy after, will do many things which politer People did not know, or else overlook'd.

Upon this Occasion, I cannot but take notice, that the Moderns have drawn up clearer and shorter Institutions of all manner of Arts and Sciences, than any which the Ancients have left us. I have already instanced in the Method whereto all the Parts of Natural History have been reduced. It is evident, That Method in all those

Things,

Things, must be the Effect of a Comprehensive Knowledge of the Bodies so ranged, and of a Nice Comparison of every several Body and Animal one with another, since otherwise their mutual Differences and Agreements cannot possibly be adjusted; the same has been done in *Medics* and *Surgery*, in *Anatomy*, in *Chymistry*, in all Parts of *Physics* and *Mathematics*: How confused, many times, and always lax, are *Galen*'s Anatomical Discourses, in comparison of *Bartholin*'s, *Diemerbroek*'s, and *Gibson*'s? Monsieur *Perrault* has observed already, (c) that *Aristotle* expressed himself so obscurely in his *Physical Discourses*, that his Meaning is almost as variously represented, as there have been Commentators who have written upon him; whereas no Man ever doubted of the precise Meaning of the Writings of *Des Cartes* and *Rohault*, tho' all Men are not of their Opinion. In *Mathematics* the thing is yet more visible: How long and tedious are *Euclid*'s *Demonstrations*, either in *Greek*, or as they are Commented upon by *Clavius*, in Comparison of *Tacquet*'s or *Barrow*'s? *Tacquet* has made *Astronomy* intelligible, with a very little Help, which before was not to be attain'd without a Master, and abundance of Patience; the same has *Varenius* done in the *Mathematical Part of Geography*; *Tacquet*, in *Practical Geometry, Optics,* and *Catoptrics*. The *Doctrine* of the *Conic Sections,*

(c) *Paralléle des Anciens & des Modernes*, Dialog III pag. 251, —— 257.

ctions, in *Apollonius Pergaeus*, is so intricate, the Demonstrations are so long, and so perplexed, that they have usually deterred all but First-Rate Geometers: This, Pensioner *De Witt* has made so easie, in his *Elements of Curve Lines*, (*d*), that it is readily mastered by any Man who has read the First Six Books of *Euclid*. Such Abridgments save a great deal of Labour, and make Knowledge pleasant to those who, in the last Age, were so exceedingly frightned with the Thoughts of the Difficulty of these Studies, that Sir *Henry Savile* made as formal a Business of his *Praelections upon the Definitions, Axioms, and Eight First Propositions of the First Book of Euclid*, which may be thoroughly comprehended, by a Man of ordinary Parts, in Two Hours time, by the help of *Tacquet's Elements*, as a Man would now of Lectures upon the hardest Propositions, in Mr. *Newton's Mathematical Principles of Natural Philosophy*. To these judicious Abridgments, the wonderful Encrease of this part of Knowledge, for these last LXX Years, is in a great measure to be attributed; and though Methodizers and Compilers of Systems have commonly the hard Fate to be undervalued by those who have been Inventors themselves; yet, in Mathematical Sciences, the case is something different; for things cannot be abbreviated there,

(*d*) Annexed to the last Editions of *Des Cartes's Geometry*.

there, without a very exact Knowledge of the Subjects then to be abridged, and brought into one view. In *Moral*, or *Historical Discourses*, an Epitomizer immediately sees what is either in it self superfluous, or not to his particular Purpose; and so when he has cut it off, what remains, is in some sort entire, and may be understood without the rest, so that there is no harm done: But here that will by no means suffice; for the most verbose Mathematicians have rarely ever said any thing for Saying sake, theirs being Subjects in which Figures of Rhetoric could have no sort of place; but they made every Conclusion depend upon such a Chain of Premises already proved, that if one Link were broken, the whole Chain fell in pieces; and therefore, he that would reduce those Demonstrations into a narrower Compass, must take the whole Proposition anew in pieces, must turn it several ways, must consider all the relations which that Line, or that Solid, has to other Lines or Solids, must carefully have considered how many several Ways it can be generated, before he can be able to demonstrate it by a shorter Method, and by other Arguments, than those by which it was proved before: In short, he must, in a manner, be able to invent the Proposition of himself, before he can put it into this

this new Dress; for which Reason, *Tacquet*, *Barrow*, and *De Witt*, have been reckoned amongst the principal Geometers of the Age, as well as for their other Inventions in Geometry. *Tschirnhaus*'s *Medicina Mentis* will give a clear Idea of many things relating to this Matter.

And now, having gone through the several Parts of the Parallel which I proposed at first to make, I shall close all with Sir *William Temple*'s Words, a little altered:

(e) P 30. (*e*) 'Though *Thales*, *Pythagoras*, *Democritus*, *Hippocrates*, *Plato*, *Aristotle* and
' *Epicurus*, may be reckoned amongst the
' First mighty Conquerors of Ignorance,
' in our World; and though they made
' great Progresses in the several Empires of
' Science, yet not so great in very many
' Parts, as their Successors have since been
' able to reach. These have pretended to
' much more, than barely to learn what
' the others taught, or to remember what
' they invented; and being able to com-
' pass that it self, have set up for Authors
' upon their own Stocks, and not content-
' ing themselves only with Commenting
' upon those Texts, have both copied af-
' ter former Originals already set them,
' and have added Originals of their own
' in many things of a much greater Va-
' lue.

CHAP.

CHAP. XXX.

Reflections upon the Reasons of the Decay of Modern Learning, assign'd by Sir William Temple.

Having therefore, as I hope, sufficiently proved, that there has not been such a Fall in Modern Learning, as Sir *William Temple* supposes, (though in many Particulars it may have fallen short of, and in others not out-done the Ancient;) nay, even that, if we take it in the gross, the Extent of Knowledge is, at this Time, vastly greater than it was in former Ages; It may seem, perhaps, a needless thing to examine those Reasons which he alledges, of the Decrease of that, which in the main has suffered no Decay. Something, however, I shall say to them; because if they do not prove what Sir *William Temple* designs, yet they will prove at least, what a perfect thing Learning might have been, if it had not met with such Impediments.

The first Blow which he says (*f*) that Learning received, was by the Disputes which arose about Religion in *Europe*, (*f*) P 64, 65.

soon

soon after the Revival of Learning in these Parts of the World. There is no doubt, but the Thoughts of many very able Men were taken up with those Controversies; who, if they had turn'd them with the same Application to Natural or Civil Knowledge, would therein have done extraordinary things. Yet, considering all things, it may be justly question'd, whether Learning may not, by these very Disputes, have received either immediately, or occasionally, a great Improvement, or at least, suffered not any considerable Diminution. For, (1.) It is certain, That whatsoever relates to *Divinity* as a Science, has hereby been better scann'd, and more accurately understood and explained, than otherwise it would ever have been; and, I suppose, this will be readily owned to be one of the most excellent Parts of Knowledge. (2.) It is a question whether a great many of the chiefest Promoters of any Part of this Theological Knowledge, would, or could have done so great things, upon any other Subject. Opposition, in general, whets Men's Parts extremely; and that inward Satisfaction which a good Man takes, in thinking that he is employed upon Arguments of greatest Concern to the Souls of Men, inspires him with an Ardour that adds Wings to his native Alacrity, and makes him, in all such Cases, even out-

out-doe himself. (3.) When different Parties are once formed, and great Numbers of Youths are constantly trained up to succeed the older Champions of their respective Sides; as these shall drop off, all those after-Comers will not apply their Minds to Studies immediately relating to their own Professions, but here and there one, as his Genius shall lead him, will try to excell in different Ways, for the Glory of his own Party; especially if he sees any of his Adversaries eminently Famous before him, in those things. Thus *Petavius* set himself to contradict *Joseph Scaliger*'s Books *de Emendatione Temporum*, and *Scioppius* fell upon his other Critical Writings. Whilst *Isaac Casaubon* concerned himself only with Publishing and Commenting upon *Strabo*, *Athenaeus*, *Polybius*, and *Theophrastus*, he was complemented by all Sides; but when once he wrote against the Annals of Cardinal *Baronius*, he met with numerous Adversaries; and there was scarce a Critic of the Church of *Rome*, for some time afterwards, that did not peck at something or other in his other Writings. This Emulation eminently appeared in the Order of the Jesuits, a principal Design of whose Institution seems to have been to engross all Learning, as well as all Politics, to themselves; and therefore we see so many extraordinary Men amongst them

for

for all sorts of things, thereby to give the World Occasion to think, that there must certainly be something more than ordinary in the Constitution of a Body, which every Day produced such excellent Persons. So that if one considers how far this Emulation went, which even yet is not wholly extinct, it is hard to say, whether Disputes in Religion have not rather helped to encrease the Stock of Learning, than otherwise; at least, one may venture to say, that they have not diminish'd it.

It is most certain, that the different Political Interests in *Europe*, have done it a mighty Kindness. During the Establishment of the *Roman* Empire, one Common Interest guided that vast Body, and these Western Kingdoms amongst the rest. *Rome* was the Center of the Learning of the West, as well as of their Hopes, and thither the Provinces of this Part of the World had always Resort: Whereas now every Kingdom standing upon its own Bottom, they are all mutually jealous of each others Glory, and in nothing more than in Matters of Learning in those Countries where they have Opportunities to pursue it. About an CL, or CC Years since, it was esteemed a very honourable Thing to write a true *Ciceronian* Style: This the *Italians* pretended to keep to themselves, and they would scarce allow that any Man beyond
the

the *Alpes*, unless, perhaps, *Longolius* and Cardinal *Pole*, wrote pure *Roman* Latin: This made other Nations strive to equal them; and one rarely meets with a Book written at that time upon a Subject that would bear the Elegancies of Style, in bad Latin. When *Critical Learning* was in fashion, every Nation had some few Great Men at the same time, or very near it, to set against those of another: *Italy* boasted of *Carolus Sigonius*, *Fulvius Ursinus*, and *Petrus Victorius*; *France* had *Joseph Scaliger*, *Isaac Casaubon*, *Cujacius*, *Pithaeus*, *Brissonius*, and several more; *Switzerland* produced *Gesner*, for that and almost every thing else; *Germany* had *Leopardus*, *Gruter*, *Putschius*, and others; the *Low Countries* had *Justus Lipsius*; *England* had Sir *Henry Savile*; every Country had some Great Men to keep up its Glory in those things which then were in greatest request. In this last Age, *Mathematical* and *Physical Sciences* seem to have been the Darling Studies of the Learned Men of *Europe*; there also the same Emulation has been equally visible. When *Great Britain* could shew such Men as my Lord *Bacon*, my Lord *Napier* (the Inventor of Logarithms,) Mr. *Harriot*, Mr. *Oughtred*, and M. *Horrox*; *Holland* had *Stevinus*, who first found out Decimal Arithmetic, and *Snellius*; *France* could reckon up *Des Cartes*, *Mer-*

Fermat, and *Gassendi*; *Italy* had *Galileo*, *Torricellius*, and *Cavallerius*; *Germany*, *Kepler*; and *Denmark*, not long before, *Tycho Brahe*. When afterwards the Philosophers of *England* grew numerous, and united their Strength, *France* also took the Hint, and its King set up a *Royal Society*, to Rival ours. The Duke of *Tuscany* had set up already, at *Florence*, the *Academy del Cimento*, whose Members employed themselves in pursuing the same Methods. In *Germany*, an *Academy* of the same nature has been raised. Even *Ireland* has had its *Philosophical Society*. From all which, such Swarms of Great Men, in every Part of Natural and Mathematical Knowledge, have within these few Years appeared, that it may, perhaps, without Vanity, be believed, that if this Humour lasts much longer, and Learned Men do not divert their Thoughts to Speculations of another kind, the next Age will not find much Work of this kind to do: For this sort of Learning has spread wherever Letters have had any Encouragement in *Europe*, so successfully, that even the Northern Kingdoms have had their *Bartholin's*, their *Borrichius's*, their *Rudbek's*, their *Wormius's*, and their *Hevelius's*, who have put in for that Prize which the Inhabitants of warmer Climates seemed already in possession of. This has occasion'd the Writing of abundance

dance of Books, to vindicate the Glory of every great Invention to some eminent Man of that Country that the Authors of those Books belonged to. Which Disputes, though many times very pedantically managed, and with an Heat mis-becoming Learned Men, yet has had this good Effect, that while some were zealous to secure the Glory of the Invention of Things already discovered, to their own Countries; others were equally sollicitous to add a more undisputed Honour to them, by new Inventions, which they were sure no Man could possibly challenge.

Another Reason of the Decay of Learning, according to Sir *William Temple* (g), is, the want of Protection from Great Men, and an unsatiable Thirst after Gain, now grown the Humour of the Age. That Princes do not now delight to talk of Matters of Learning in their public Conversations, as they did about an CL Years ago, is but too evident: When Learning first came up, Men fansied that every thing could be done by it, and they were charm'd with the Eloquence of its Professors, who did not fail to set forth all its Advantages in the most engaging Dress. It was so very modish, that the Fair Sex seemed to believe that *Greek* and *Latin* added to their Charms; and *Plato* and *Aristotle* untranslated, were frequent Ornaments of their

(g) p 67, — 71.

C c 2 Closets.

Closets. One would think by the Effects, that it was a proper Way of Educating them, since there are no Accounts in History of so many truly great Women in any one Age, as are to be found between the Years MD and MDC. This Humour in both Sexes abated by degrees; and the Great Men being either disgusted with the Labour that was requisite to become thoroughly Learned, or with the frequent Repetitions of the same things, Business and Diversions took up their Thoughts, as they had done formerly. But yet, in the main, the Learned Men of this Age have not so much reason to think themselves ill used, as it is commonly thought. What by Fellowships of Colleges, and Ecclesiastical Preferments, here in *England*; and by the same sort of Preferments, added to the Allowances in several Monastical Orders, in Popish Countries, there are very fair Settlements for Men of Studious and Sedentary Lives; and innumerable Instances can be given, in these two last Ages, of the excellent Uses which great Numbers of Men have made of them: So that every such Preferment bestowed upon any learned Man, upon the score of his Merit, by Princes, or Great Men, in whose Gift they were, is an Instance of their Beneficence to Men of Letters: And whether a Man is considered by a Pension out of a

Prince's

Prince's Exchequer, or by the Collation of a Preferment in that Prince's Gift, it is, to a Man who enjoys it, the self-same thing. Neither have Examples been wanting in the present Age, of Sovereign Princes who have made it as much their Business to encourage Learned Men, as, perhaps, in any of the former, that are so much commended for that very Reason. *Christina* Queen of *Sweden*, who, in other respects, was by no means the Glory of her Sex, did, whilst she liv'd at *Stockholm*, send for the learnedest Men of *Europe* to come to her, that she might converse with them about those things wherein they were most excellent. *Des Cartes, Salmasius, Bochart, Nicolas Heinsius, Isaac Vossius*, were of that number: And her Profuseness, which knew no bounds, was scarce in any thing more visible, than in her Marks of Respect to Men of Letters. Afterwards, when she setled at *Rome*, her Palace was always an Academy of the *Virtuosi* of that City. The present *French* King, whilst Monsieur *Colbert* liv'd, took a singular Pride in sending Presents to the most celebrated Scholars of *Europe*; without regarding whether they were his own Subjects, or of his own Religion, or no. This he did purely *for his Glory*, the Principle which Sir *William Temple* (*h*) so exceedingly applauds. His own Protestant Subjects, before he in-

(*h*) P 68.

volved

volved them in one Common Ruine, tasted of his Liberality of that kind, upon Occasion: And whatsoever his other Actions are, or have been, yet his extraordinary Care to breed up his Son to Learning, his erecting of Academies for Arts and Sciences at *Paris*, and his frequent Bounties to Men of Letters, justly require that, upon this account, he should be mention'd with Honour. Cardinal *de Richelieu*, Cardinal *Mazarin*, Monsieur *Fouquet*, and Monsieur *Colbert*, though no Sovereign Princes, yet had Purses greater than many of them. Cardinal *de Richelieu* was himself a Scholar; and all of them were eminently Favourers of Learned Men. I have mention'd my own Country last, that I might once more observe, that it was a Prince of our own, who founded the ROYAL SO-CIETY, (i) *whose Studies, Writings and Productions, though they have not out-shined or eclipsed the* Lycaeum *of* Plato, *the Academy of* Aristotle, *the Stoa of* Zeno, *or the* Garden *of* Epicurus; *because they were neither written at the same Time, nor, for the most part, upon the same Subjects; yet will always help to keep alive the Memory of that Prince who incorporated them into a Body, that so they might the easier do that by their Joint-Labours, which singly would have been, in a manner, impossible to be effected,*

(i) P. 57.

The

The last of Sir *William Temple*'s Reasons of the great Decay of Modern Learning, (*k*) is *Pedantry*. The urging of which, is an evident Argument, that his Discourse is levelled against Learning, not as it stands now, but as it was L or LX Years ago. For the New Philosophy has introduced so great a Correspondence between Men of Learning and Men of Business, which has also been encreased by other Accidents amongst the Masters of other learned Professions, that that *Pedantry* which formerly was almost universal, is now in a great measure dis-used; especially amongst the Young Men, who are taught, in the Universities, to laugh at that frequent Citation of Scraps of *Latin*, in common Discourse, or upon Arguments that do not require it; and that nauseous Ostentation of Reading and Scholarship, in public Companies, which formerly was so much in fashion. Affecting to write politely in Modern Languages, especially the *French* and ours, has also not a little helpt to lessen it; because it has enabled abundance of Men who want Academical Education, to talk plausibly, and some exactly, upon abundance of learned Subjects. This also has made Writers habitually careful to avoid those Impertinencies which they know would be taken notice of, and ridiculed; and it is probable, that a careful perusal

(*k*) P. 7

of the fine new *French* Books, which of late Years have been greedily fought after by the politer fort of Gentlemen and Scholars, may, in this Particular, have done a great deal of good. By this means, and by the help alſo of ſome other concurrent Cauſes, thoſe who were not learned themſelves, being able to maintain Diſputes with thoſe that were, forced them to talk more warily, and brought them by little and little to be out of countenance at that vain thruſting of their Learning into every thing, which before had been but too viſible.

CONCLUSION.

THIS ſeems to me to be the preſent State of Learning, as it may be compared with what it was in former Ages. Whether Knowledge will improve in the next Age, proportionably as it has done in this, is a Queſtion not eaſily decided. It depends upon a great many Circumſtances; which, ſingly, will be ineffectual; and, which no Man can now be be assured, will ever meet. There seems Reason, indeed, to fear that it may decay, both because Ancient Learning is too much studied in Modern Books, and taken upon trust by Modern Writers, who are not enough acquainted with Antiquity, to correct their own Mistakes; and because Natural and Mathematical Knowledge, wherein chiefly the Moderns are to be studied as Originals, begin to be neglected by the generality of those who would set up for Scholars. For the Humour of the Age, as to those things, is visibly altered from what it was XX or XXX Years ago: So that though the *ROYAL SOCIETY* has weathered the rude Attacks of such sort of Adversaries as *Stubbe*, who endeavoured to have it thought, That Studying of Natural Philosophy and Mathematics, was a ready Method to introduce Scepticism at least, if not Atheism, into the World: Yet the sly Insinuations of the *Men of Wit*, That no great Things have ever, or are ever like to be performed by the *Men of Gresham*, and, That every Man whom they call a *Virtuoso*, must needs be a *Sir Nicolas Gimcrack*: together with the *public Ridiculing* of all those who spend their Time and Fortunes in seeking after what some call Useless Natural Rarities; who dissect all Animals, little as well as great; who think no part

of

of God's Workmanship below their strictest Examination, and nicest Search: have so far taken off the Edge of those who have opulent Fortunes, and a Love to Learning, that Physiological Studies begin to be contracted amongst Physicians and Mechanics. For nothing wounds more effectually as a Jest; and when Men once become ridiculous, their Labours will be slighted, and they will find few Imitators. How far this may deaden the Industry of the Philosophers of the next Age, is not easie to tell; for almost all the Parts of Mathematical and Natural Knowledge require a good deal of Time and Pains, of Industry and Attention, before a Man can thoroughly relish them: And those who do not, rarely know their Worth, and consequently do very seldom pass a right Judgment upon them. However, be the Studies of the Men of the next Age what they will, the Writings of the Learned Men of the present Time will be preserved; and as they have raised a nobler Monument to the Memory of *Archimedes* and *Diophantus*, of *Hippocrates* and *Aristotle*, of *Herophilus* and *Galen*, by building upon their Discovery's, and Improving of their Inventions, than had been raised for a Thousand Years before; so some future Age, though, perhaps, not the next, and in a Country now possibly little thought of, may do that which our Great Men

Men would be glad to see done; that is to say, may raise real Knowledge, upon the Foundations laid in this our Age, to the utmost possible Perfection to which it can be brought by Mortal Men in this imperfect state, and thereby effectually immortalize the Memories of those who laid those Foundations, and collected those Materials which were so serviceable to them in compleating the noble Work.

But this is what every Man would gladly hope might be reserved for his own Posterity, and his own Country. How it may be reserved is obvious: It must be by joining Ancient and Modern Learning together, and by studying each as Originals, in those things wherein they do severally most excell; by that means few Mistakes will be committed, the World will soon see what remains unfinish'd, and Men will furnish themselves with fitting Methods to make it perfect: And by doing Justice to every Side, they will have Reason to exspect, that those that come after them will do the same Justice to them, whenever they shall think fit to submit their Productions to public Censure.

F I N I S.

A DISSERTATION UPON THE EPISTLES OF THEMISTOCLES, SOCRATES, EURIPIDES, and Others; AND THE FABLES of AESOP.

BY
RICHARD BENTLEY, D.D.
Master of *Trinity College* in *Cambridge*, Chaplain in Ordinary and Library-keeper to Her MAJESTY.

LONDON:
Printed for *Tim.* Goodwin, at the *Queen's Head*, against St. *Dunstan*'s Church in *Fleetstreet*. MDCCV.

ADVERTISEMENT.

THE Reader *possibly may wonder that the* Dissertation *of* Dr. Bentley *is not reprinted entire, as it was annexed to the* Second Edition *of these* Reflections *which came out in* 1697. *The Reason why that Part of his* Dissertation *which concerned* Phalaris's *Epistles, is left out is this. It is well known that* Mr. Boile *(now* E. *of* Orrery*) wrote against it, and that* Dr. Bentley *thereupon reprinted all that Part of his* Dissertation *entire, and added great Additions to it in his Defense, which was printed in* 1699. *So that if what related to the Epistles of* Phalaris *in this Dissertation had been reprinted, it would have swelled this Book unnecessarily, since it may be had in another Place, to greater Advantage. Whereas what concerned the Epistles of* Themistocles, Socrates, Euripides, *and the Fables of* Aesop, *being printed no where else, is here reprinted just as it was in the former Edition.*

A DISSERTATION UPON The EPISTLES of THEMISTOCLES, SOCRATES, EURIPIDES, and Others; and the FABLES of AESOP.

To Mr. Wotton.

SIR,

THE *Epistles* of *Themistocles* were printed first at *Rome*, in MDCXXVI, out of a Manuscript in the *Vatican*. The Editor, a *Greek* Bishop, believed them genuine; but there were some that suspected a Forgery, as (a) *Leo Allatius* informs us: who himself leaves the matter in doubt; but withal observes in their favour, that no body

(a) *De Script. Socrat. p. 78.*

dy had ever said a Word in print, to prove them to be spurious. (b) *Suidas* is an Evidence in their behalf, for speaking of their reputed Author, he says, *he has writ Letters full of Spirit,* ἔγραψεν ἐπιστολὰς φρονήματος γεμούσας. He, I think, is the only old Writer that makes any mention of them. Which alone, as before in *Phalaris's* case, is a shrewd prejudice against their Credit and Reputation. (c) *Thucydides* and *Charon Lampsacenus* say that *Themistocles*, when he fled into *Asia*, made his Address to *Artaxerxes*, who was newly come to the Throne; wherein they are followed by (d) *Cornelius Nepos* and *Plutarch*; against the common Tradition of *Ephorus*, *Heraclides*, and most others, that make *Xerxes* the Father to be then alive. Some (e) Writers relate, that he had five Cities given him by the *Persian*; others, but three. Now, if the Letters had been known to any of those Authors, both these Disputes had been soon at an end, or rather never had been raised. For he himself expressly says, (f) it was *Xerxes* he went to, and that he gave him but three Cities. Now, where could these Epistles lie, unknown and invisible from *Themistocles*'s Time to *Suidas*? We must needs say, that the Letters had a worse Exostracism than their Author: since he was banisht but for five Years, but they for a Thousand.

(b) V. Θεμιστ.

(c) Lib. 1. p. 90.

(d) Vita Themistoc.

(e) Plutarch, Dioder Athenaeus, &c.

(f) Ep xx.

II. 'Tis

II. 'Tis obfervable, That every one of the Letters bear date after his Banifhment; and contain a compleat Narrative of all his Story afterwards, without the leaft gap or interruption. Now 'tis hard to fay, whether is the more ftrange of the two; That not one fingle Letter of his, before that time, fhould be preferved; or not one, afterwards, loft, though written from fo diftant places, *Argos, Corcyra, Epirus, Ephefus, Magnefia*, from whence there was no very fure conveyance to *Athens*. What a crofs Viciffitude of Fortune! while the Author is in Profperity, all his Letters are unlucky; and not one of them is miffing, after he himfelf mifcarried. But the Sophift can eafily account for this, though *Themiftocles* cannot; for here are no Letters before his Exile; becaufe the latter part of his Life was the whole Tour and Compafs that the Sophift defigned to write of: and not a Letter afterwards perifhed; becaufe being forged in a Sophift's Clofet, they run no hazard at all of being loft in the carriage.

III. *Themiftocles* was an Eloquent Man; but here are fome touches in his Letters of fuch an elevated ftrain, that if he did not go to School to *Gorgias Leontinus* the Sophift of that time, I can hardly believe he writ them. The Hiftorians tell us moderately, That after he was driven from home, he was made much on at *Argos*: but He himself is all melting, when he talks on that Subject. (g) He was met, he says, on the Road by two *Argivans* of his acquaintance; who, when he told them the News of his Banishment, rail'd bitterly at the *Athenians*: but when they heard he was going to *Delphi*, rather than to their Town; in a kind Quarrel they tell him, That (h) *the Athenians had justly punished him*; since he so much wronged the City of *Argos*, to think of any Sanctuary but that. Well, he goes with them to *Argos*; and there the whole City (i) *teazes him by meer force* to take the Government upon him; taking it as the greatest *injury*, that he offer'd to decline it. These, you'll say, are choice Flowers both of Courtesy and of Rhetoric: but there's another clearly beyond them; where he tells us, (k) That he is so resolved of going to the *Persian* Court, though it was a desperate risque; *that neither the Advice of his Friends, nor his Father* Neocles's *Ghost, nor his Uncle* Themistocles's, *nor Augury, nor Omen, nor* Apollo's *Oracle it self, should be able to dissuade him.* Here's a bold resolute Blade for you! here's your Stoical κάκεργα! 'Tis almost impossible for a Sophist not to betray himself. Nothing will relish and go down with them, that is ordinary and natural. Then they applaud themselves most, when they have said a forced,

(g) Ep. i

(h) Ἐπαινεῖν Ἀθηναίους, ὡς δικαίως τινύντων ἡμῶν.

(i) Ἀναγκάζεσθαι ὡς ἀδικησόμενον ἢν μὴ ἄρχω ων.

(k) Ep. xiv

forced, extravagant thing. If one speaks of any Civility; the Complement must be strain'd beyond all Decorum. If he makes a Resolution; he must needs swagger and swear, and be as wilful as a Mad Man.

IV. The Subject of many of the Letters is Common Place; mere Chat, and telling a Tale, without any Business; an Errand not worth sending to the next Town, much less to be brought from remote Countries some hundreds of Leagues. The xv and xviii Letters are written to Enemies; his Friends, I suppose, failing in their Correspondence: and contain nothing but a little Scolding; which was scarce worth the long carriage from *Ephesus* to *Athens*.

V. In the xx Epistle we have this Story: When *Themistocles* was at *Corcyra*, he design'd for *Sicily*, to *Gelo* the *Syracusian* Tyrant. But just as he was going a Shipboard, the News came that *Gelo* was dead, and his Brother *Hiero* succeeded him. Now, if we make it appear, that *Hiero* was come to the Crown some Years before *Themistocles*'s Banishment, and this Voyage to *Corcyra*; what becomes of the Credit of our Epistles? 'Tis true, the Chronology of this part of History is not so (*l*) setled and agreed, as to amount to a Demonstration against the Letters; but however, when joined with the Arguments preceeding, at least it will come

(*l*) Οὐδὲ αὐτοῖς χρονικοῖς ἀτρέμα συντεταγμένοις
Plut Them p. 227

406 Dissertation upon Themistocles Epistles

(m) Περὶ Βασιλείας apud Plut Them p 225

come up to a high Probability. (m) Theophrastus, in his Treatise *of Monarchy*, relates, That when *Hiero* had sent Race-horses, and a most sumptuous Tent, to the *Olympian* Games; *Themistocles* advised the *Greeks* to plunder the *Tyrant*'s Tent, τȣ̃ τυράννȣ, and not to let his Horses run. 'Tis evident then, if *Theophrastus* speak properly, that *Hiero* was Monarch of *Syracuse*, when *Themistocles* was at *Olympia*; but its most certain he never came thither after his Exile.

(n) Var H.f. 18, 5

But, to deal fairly, it must be confessed, that *Aelian*, in telling this Story, varies from *Theophrastus*; for he says, (n) *Hiero* himself came to the Games. But that he would go thither in Person, after he got the Government, is wholly improbable. So that, if *Aelian* be believed, this Business must have been done, before *Hiero* came to the Throne. For even in *Gelo*'s life-time, who left him the Monarchy, he kept Horses for the Race; and won at the *Pythian* Games,

(o) Pind Schol Pyth 1, & 3

(o) *Pythiad* the XXVI, which answers to Olymp. LXXIV. 3. But besides that *Theophrastus* is of much greater Authority, the other refutes himself in the very next Words. For he says, *Themistocles* hindred *Hiero* upon this Pretence; *That he that had not shared in the common Dangers, ought not to share in the Common Joys*. Where it's certain, by the Common Dangers he means *Xerxes*

Expedition; when (*p*) *Gelo* either refused or delayed to give the *Greeks* his assistance. This Affront then was put upon *Hiero*, after that Expedition. But the very next (*q*) Olympiad after, *Hiero* was in the Monarchy. It cannot be true then, that his first accession to the Throne, was, according to the Letters, while *Themistocles* stay'd at *Corcyra*.

(*p*) Herod. vii. c 163. Diod. xi p. 21
(*q*) Diod. xi. p. 29.

Besides these Inferences and Deductions, we have the express Verdict and Declaration of most of the (*r*) Chronologers, who place the beginning of *Hiero*'s Reign Olymp. LXXV. 3. and *Themistocles*'s Banishment seven years after, Olymp. LXXVII, 2. The *Arundelian* Marble, indeed, differs from all these, in the Periods of *Gelo* and *Hiero*: which would quite confound all this Argumentation from Notes of Time. But either that Chronologer is quite out, or we can safely believe nothing in History. For he makes *Gelo* first invade the Government, two years after *Xerxes*'s Expedition. But (*s*) *Herodotus* spends half a dozen Pages in the Account of an Embassy to *Gelo* from *Sparta* and *Athens*, to desire his assistance against the *Persian*. And 'tis agreed among all, (*t*) That *Gelo*'s Victory over the *Carthaginians* in *Sicily* was got the very same day with the Battle at *Salamis*.

(*r*) Schol. Pind Pyth. 1. Diod. xi. p. 29, 41. Eusen in Chron.

(*s*) Lib vii

(*t*) Herodot. ibid & Diod. l xi.

VI. The whole Volume of *Themistocles*'s Letters consists of XXI only; and Three of these

these are taken up in the Story of *Pausanias*. The Second is writ to *Pausanias* himself, before that *Spartan's* Conspiracy with the *Persian* was discovered. There he exhorts him to Moderation in his Prosperity; lest some very great turn of Fortune should speedily befall him. Can you desire now a surer indication of a Sophist? Without doubt, he that penn'd this Epistle, knew beforehand what happen'd to *Pausanias*: who was soon after recall'd home by the Magistrates, and put to death for Treason. The XIX is to *Pausanias* again; but after his Conspiracy was detected. Here he tells the Particulars of that Plot as exactly, as if he had been one of the *Ephori*, that over-heard it. Nay, he foretells him, that the *Lacedaemonians* would take away his Life. Now besides that *Themistocles* would scorn to insult so, and rail to no purpose, as this Letter does; he would surely have had more wit, than knowingly to write to the Dead. For at the same time he heard those Particulars of *Pausanias's* Treason, he must needs hear of his Execution; since those Things were not known till after his Death, and the rifling of his Papers. The VI Epistle is a long Narrative of the whole Business of *Pausanias*: for that was a Subject worthy of Eloquence, and therefore was to receive ornament from the Pen of the Sophist. But it was scarce worthy of *Themistocles*, to send

such

such a long News-Letter to *Athens*; where, in all likelihood, the Story was common, before he heard of it himself.

But how shall we reconcile this Affair of *Pausanias* according to the Letters, with what *Diodorus* has left us upon the same Subject? The Letters, we see, make *Themistocles* to be banisht, (*u*) before *Pausanias* was suspected; and make the one reside at *Argos*, (*x*) while the other was convicted and put to death. But *Diodorus*, who has brought all his History into the method of *Annals*, places the Death of *Pausanias* (*y*) Olymp. LXXV, 4; and the Exile of *Themistocles*, (*z*) six years after, Olymp. LXXVII, 2. Now, I would fain know of our Sophist, how he came to dispose and suit his matters so negligently; to bring *Pausanias* upon the Stage again, when he had been six years in his Grave? I imagine he will referr me to (*a*) *Thucydides*, who makes an immediate transition from one Story to the other; 'That the *Spar-*' *tans* accused *Themistocles*, who was then ' banisht from home, of conspiring with ' *Pausanias*.' This, indeed, might draw the Sophist and some others into a Mistake. But it may be taken two ways: either that it was done presently, upon the Death of *Pausanias*; or a few years after, when *Themistocles*'s Exile gave the *Spartans*, that ...ed and fear'd him, an opportunity to

(*u*) Ep. ii.

(*x*) Ep. xix. vi

(*y*) Lib. xi. p. 36.

(*z*) Lib. xi. p. 41

(*a*) Lib i. p 88

ruine

ruine him. (b) *Plutarch* follows the first way; for he makes *Themistocles*, after his Banishment, to have private dealings with *Pausanias*: in which opinion he favours the Author of these Letters. But the second will rather appear to be the sense of *Thucydides*: if we consider, that he places the matter of *Pausanias* (c) just after the flight of *Xerxes*; but when *Themistocles* went into *Asia*, he makes (d) *Artaxerxes* to be in the Throne: which was a considerable while after. Besides that *Diodorus*, whose design was to referr all Occurrences to Years, and not to follow the thread of Story beyond the annual Period, is of more credit in a point of Chronology; than *Plutarch* or any other, that write Lives by the Lump.

(b) In *Themist* p. 224
(c) P. 63
(d) P. 90

OF SOCRATES'S EPISTLES.

THE *Epistles* of *Socrates*, and his Scholars, *Xenophon*, *Aristippus*, &c. were publish'd out of the *Vatican* Library by the Learned *Leo Allatius*; and printed at *Paris*, MDCXXXVII. He was so fully persuaded himself, and so concerned to have others think, that they are the legitimate

mate Off-spring of those Authors they are laid to; that he has guarded and protected them, in a Dialogue of LVII Pages in *quarto*, against all the Objections that He or his Friends could raise. And no body since, that ever I heard of, has brought the matter into controversie. But I am enclined to believe, that by that time I have done with them, it will be no more a Controversie, but that they are spurious. I shall make use of nothing that *Allatius* has brought, except one Objection only; and that I shall both manage in a new way, and defend it against all his Exceptions.

I. The First Letter is *Socrates*'s to some King, 'tis supposed to *Archelaus* King of *Macedonia*; in which he refuses to go to him, though invited in the most kind and obliging manner. That he really denied his company to *Archelaus* and others, we are assured from very good hands: which was the ground for our Falsary to forge this Epistle. But I believe, none of those that mention it, make so tall a Complement to *Socrates*, as he does here to himself. For he says, (e) *The King offer'd him part of his Kingdom; and, that he should not come thither to be commanded, but to command both his Subjects and Himself.* Can you desire a better token of a Sophist, than this? 'Tis a fine offer, indeed, to a poor old Man, that had nothing but his

(e) Τῆς βασιλείας ἔφης μέρος δοῦναι & Ἄρξονία κ) τῶν ἄλ-λων κ) σε αυτε.

Staff

Staff and one Coat to his back. But a Sophist abhorrs mediocrity; he must always say the greatest thing; and make a Tide and a Flood, though it be but in a Bason of Water.

II. Well; our Philosopher goes on, and gives a reason of his refusal; That his Daemon forbid him to go: and then he falls into the long Story of what happen'd to him in the Battle at *Delium*; which was a Tale of twenty years standing at the date of this Letter. But the Sophist had read it in *Plato*; and he would not miss the opportunity of an eloquent Narration. I will not here insist upon the testimony of (*f*) *Athenaeus*; That the whole business is a mere fiction of *Plato*'s: let that be left in the middle. But we may safely inferr thus much from it; That even *Athenaeus* himself, whose curiosity nothing escaped, never met with these Epistles. Which alone creates a just suspicion, that they were forged since his days; especially when the universal silence of all Antiquity gives a general consent to it.

(*f*) Lib. v. p 215

There's a passage, indeed, in (*g*) *Libanius*, which, in *Allatius*'s Judgment, seems plainly to declare, that he had seen this very Epistle. For after he had mention'd *Socrates*'s refusal to go to *Scopas*, and *Eurylochus*, and *Archelaus*; he adds: Αὐτῶν ἢ ἐδεήθην τῆς Ἐπιστολῶν, ὂν ἐκείναις τ᾽ ἄνθρωπον καὶ λ-

(*g*) *Analogia Socrat.*

κάλλιστα ἂν ἴδῃς. Now should we concede, what *Allatius* would have; this is all that can be inferred from thence in their favour; That they are older than *Libanius*; which I am willing to believe: and, That He believed them true; which I matter not at all. For so we have seen *Stobaeus*, *Suidas* and others, cry up *Phalaris* for a genuine Book; and yet I fansie none of my Readers are now of their opinion. But with *Allatius*'s good leave, I would draw the words of *Libanius* to a quite contrary purpose. After he had said, that many Princes had sollicited *Socrates*, by Letter, to come and live in their Courts; and he answer'd them all with a denial: *But* (says he) *I want the Letters themselves; in which you might perfectly see the Spirit of the Man.* This, to me, is an Indication, that the Letters he means were not extant. For if he had them in his hand, according to *Allatius*, how could he *want* them? And 'tis plain, he speaks here of several Letters, being Replies to several Messages; but in this Collection here's but a single one. *I wish* (says he) *the Letters were to be had; in those you might read his Character.* If this be the sense of those words, as probably it is; *Libanius* is so far from being Patron to our Epistles, that he is a positive Witness against them.

III. The

III. The VII Letter is writ by *Socrates* to one of those that had fled to *Thebes* from the violence of the XXX Tyrants: in which he gives him an account of the State of *Athens* since their departure; *That himself was now hated by the Tyrants, because he would have no hand in the condemnation of* Leon *the* Salaminian: and then he tells the Story at large. Now, here's a manifest discovery that the Letters are suppositious. For the business of *Leon* was quite over, before those Fugitives left the Town. For *Leon* was murder'd (*h*) before *Theramenes* was: and *Theramenes* was murder'd, before *Thrasybulus* and his Party fled to *Thebes*. And that *Socrates* means them in this Letter, 'tis evident from hence; That he speaks here of their Conspiracy, to resort privately towards *Athens* and set upon the Tyrants: which afterwards came to pass.

(*h*) *Xenoph Hist* lib. II p 467, 470 *Diod* l XIV.

IV. The VIII, IX, XII, and XIII, are Letters of Jest and Raillery between *Antisthenes* and *Aristippus* and *Simon* the Shoomaker. 'Tis an affront to the memory of those Men, to believe they would fool and trifle in that manner; especially send such impertinent stuff as far as from *Sicily* to *Athens*, which could not decently be spoken even in merriment at a Table.

V. In the XIII Epistle among the acquaintance of *Simon* he names *Phædrus*, the same that gives the Title to our Dialogue

logue of *Plato*: and the XXV is writ by *Phaedrus* himself to *Plato*: and both these are dated after *Socrates*'s death. I will appeal now to *Athenaeus*, if these two Letters can be genuine. He, among other Errors in Chronology for which he chastises *Plato*, brings this in for one; (*i*) *That he introduces* Phaedrus *discoursing with Socrates; who must certainly be dead before the days of that Philosopher.* How comes he then to survive him, in these Epistles; and discourse so passionately of his Death? 'Tis true; for want of ancient History, we cannot back this Authority with any other Testimony. But I am sure, all those that have a just esteem for *Athenaeus*, can have no slight one of this Argument against the credit of the Letters.

(*i*) Lib xi. pag 505. Ἀδύνατον ᾗ ᾧ Φαῖδρον κατὰ Σωκράτην ᾖ.

VI. The XIV Epistle gives *Xenophon* a long Narrative of *Socrates*'s Tryal and Death; being writ presently after by one of his Scholars that was present at both. Among other particulars, he tells him, (*k*) *That the Oration or Charge against* Socrates *was drawn up by* Polycrates *the Sophist.* But I doubt this will turn to a Charge against another Sophist, for counterfeiting Letters. For, I think, I can plainly prove, That at the date of this Letter there was no such report ever mention'd, that *Polycrates* had any hand it; and, that this false Tradition, which afterwards obtained in the World,

(*k*) Ἦν ᾗ λόγος Πολυκράτης τὸ λόγον γράφε.

and

and gave occasion to our Writer to say it in his Letter, did not begin till some years after *Socrates*'s Condemnation.

Diogenes Laertius brings *Hermippus*'s testimony, That *Polycrates* made the (*l*) Charge. Συνέγραψε δ᾽ τ̄ λόγον Πολυκράτης ὁ σοφιστής, ὥς φησιν Ἕρμιππ۞. But, in opposition to this, he presently subjoins; "That "*Favorinus*, in the First Book of his *Commentaries*, says, That *Polycrates*'s Oration against *Socrates* is not *true* and *real*: "because he mentions in it the Walls, built "by *Conon* six years after *Socrates*'s death." To which *Laertius* subscribes his own assent, Καὶ ἔςιν ὅτως ἔχον, *And so it is*. I may freely say, that this passage of *Favorinus* has not been yet rightly understood. It is generally interpreted, as if he denied the Oration that is attributed to *Polycrates* to be really his. But this is very far from being his Opinion. For then he would be flatly confuted by *Isocrates*, a Witness unanswerable; who, in a Discourse which he addresses to this very *Polycrates*, tells him; (*m*) *I perceive you value your self most upon two Orations*, The Apology of Busiris, *and* Accusation of Socrates. But *Favorinus*'s meaning was; That *Polycrates* did not make that Oration for a true Charge to be spoke at the Tryal of *Socrates*; but writ it several years after, for no other Trial than that of his own Wit. The words in the

Greek

(*l*) *Vita Socrat.*

(*m*) Ἐπὶ τῇ Βυσίειδος ἀπολογία, ᾗ τῇ Σωκράτες κατηγορία Isoc. Busir.

Greek can admit of no other sense; Μὴ εἶ ἀληθῆ τ̄ λόγον τ̄ Πολυκράτες κ[ατὰ] Σωκράτες· ἐν αὐτῷ γὰρ μνημονεύει τῶς ὑπὸ Κόνωνος τειχῶ, &c. Observe, that he says μνημονεύει, *Polycrates mentions*: if he had denied him to be the Author, he would have said in the Passive, *There is mention'd.* Besides he expresly calls it τ̄ λόγον τ̄ Πολυκράτες, only denies it to be ἀληθῆ. But if he had denied it to be His, he would have said, Μὴ εἶ Πολυκράτες τ̄ λόγον τ̄ κ[ατὰ] Σωκράτες: as *Laertius* speaks in other places; (*n*) Λακεδαιμονίων Πολιτείαν, ἥν φησιν ἐκ εἶ Ξενοφῶντος ὁ Μάγνης Δημήτριος. (*o*) Διαλόγες, ἃς Πεισίςρατος ὁ Ἐφέσιος ἔλεγε μὴ εἶ Αἰσχίνε. This, I think, is sufficiently clear. Now we are to know, it was the custom of the old Sophists to make an Ostentation of their Art, upon some difficult Subjects and Paradoxes, such as other People could speak nothing to: as the commendation of a Fever or the Gout. *Polycrates* therefore, to shew his Rhetoric in this way, writ an Apology of *Busiris*, that kill'd and eat his Guests; (*p*) and of *Clytemnestra*, that murder'd her Husband: and to give a proof of his skill, as well in accusing Vertue, as in excusing Vice, he writ an Indictment against *Socrates*; not ἀληθῆ, *the true one*, as *Favorinus* truly says, but only a Scholastic Exercise; such as *Plato*, *Xenophon*, *Libanius* and others writ in his Defense.

(*n*) In *Xenoph.*
(*o*) In *Aeschine.*
(*p*) *Quintil* lib 11 cap 18

So that we are no more forced to believe, that his Oration was the true Charge that was spoken at *Socrates*'s Tryal; than, that he really pleaded for *Clytemnestra*, when *Orestes* was going to kill her. Nay, it appears to me, from *Isocrates* himself, that it was but a Scholastic Exercise, and after *Socrates*'s death. For he blames *Polycrates*, for reckoning *Alcibiades* among *Socrates*'s Disciples: since, besides that no body else ever counted him his Scholar; had he really been so, he had been a commendation to his Master; and not a disparagement, which was the aim of the Sophist, (q) *So that* (says he) *if the dead could have knowledge of your Writings,* Socrates *would thank you*. Is not this a clear Indication, that *Socrates* was *dead*, before the Oration was made? and that this was not the true Charge? For then he would have heard it at his Tryal: and there had been no occasion to say, *if the dead could have knowledge of it*. In the close of all, he advises him to leave off shewing his Parts upon such *villainous Themes*, πονηράς ὑποθέσεις; lest he do public mischief by putting false colours upon things. Here again we are plainly told, that his Action against *Socrates*, like those for *Busiris* and *Clytemnestra*, was but a Declamation, a Theme and Exercise in the School

(q) Εἰ γίνοιτο ἔξουσία τοῖς τετελευτηκόσι βουλεύσασθαι περὶ τῶν εἰρημένων, ὁ μὲν χάριν ἂν εἰδείη σοι. *Isoc. Busir.*

School, and not a real Indictment in the *Areopagus* at *Athens*. To all which let me add, That neither *Plato* nor *Xenophon*, nor any body contemporary with *Socrates*, ever once mention *Polycrates* for the Author of the Charge: which, had the thing been true, they would certainly have thrown in his teeth, considering the perpetual quarrel between Sophists and Philosophers. And 'tis well known; that the *Athenians*, in a penitential mood, either banisht or put to death all those that had any hand in *Socrates*'s Accusation. If *Polycrates* then were so eminently guilty, as to draw up the Impeachment; how could he escape untoucht, when all the rest suffer'd?

But when the *Accusation of Socrates*, though only a Sophistical Exercise, came abroad in the World; it was natural enough, in some process of time, that those that heard of it only, or but perfunctorily read it, should believe it to be the real *Charge*. We have seen already, that *Hermippus* was in that mistake, who lived an hundred years after; and with him *Quintilian*, *Themistius*, and others innumerable. *Favorinus*, it seems, alone had the sagacity, by a notice from Chronology, to find it of a more recent date than *Socrates*'s Tryal. And even that very Passage of *Favorinus* has lain hitherto in the dark: so that my Reader may forgive me this prolixity and niceness; since he learns by it a piece of News. As for *Hermippus*, left the Authority of so celebrated an Author should deterr one from so plain a truth; I will shew another slip of his, and a worse than this, in the Story of *Socrates*. When *Gryllus* the Son of *Xenophon* was slain in the same Battle that *Epaminondas* was; most of the Wits of that Age writ Elegies and Encomiums on him, in Complement and Consolation to his Father. Among the rest, (*r*) *Hermippus* says, *Socrates* was one. Which is a blunder of no less than XXXVII Years, the interval between *Socrates*'s death, and the Battle of *Mantinea*.

Socrates was put to death Olymp. XCV, 1. when *Laches* was Magistrate. This is universally (*s*) acknowledged; and to go about to prove it, were to add Light to the Sun. And six years after this, Olymp. XCVI, 3. (*t*) in *Eubulides*'s Magistracy, *Conon* repair'd the Walls. Which gave the hint to *Favorinus*, and after him to *Diogenes*, to discover the common mistake about *Polycrates*'s Oration. But *Leo Allatius*, to avoid the force of their Argument, undertakes an impossible thing; to prolong *Socrates*'s life above twenty years beyond *Laches*: so that He might see *Conon*'s Walls, and *Polycrates*'s Declamation

(*r*) *Laert. in Zenoph*

(*s*) See *Diodorus, Favorinus, Diog Laertius Aristides, Marmor Arund Euseb Argumentum Isocr Busir* &c

(*t*) *Diodor* XIV p 303 *Favorin. Diog Laert.*

mation be the true Charge at his Tryal. Which he would make out by comparing together some Scraps of different Authors, and some Synchronisms of other Men's Lives with *Socrates*'s. As if those things which are only mistakes and unwary slips of the Writers, could have any force or credit against so many express Authorities. By the same way that he proceeds, I will shew the quite contrary; that *Socrates* died twenty years before *Laches*'s Government. For we have it from good Hands, (*u*) That *Euripides*, in a Play of his call'd *Palamedes*, using these Words, Ἐκάνετ', ἐκάνετε τὰν πάνσοφον, &c. design'd to lash the *Athenians* for *Socrates*'s Murder: and the whole Theatre perceiving it, burst into Tears. *Socrates* therefore died before *Euripides*. But 'tis well known, that the latter died six years before *Laches* was Archon. Nay, *Socrates* must needs be dead, before *Palamedes* was acted. But that was acted Olymp. XCI, 1. (*x*), which is sixteen years before *Laches*. Have I not proved now exactly the quite contrary to *Allatius*? But still, I hope, I have more Judgment, than to credit such an oblique Argument against so many direct Testimonies. If *Allatius* had looked round about him, he would not have committed so great a Blunder; while he defends his Epistles at one Post, to expose them to worse Assaults. If *Socrates* died

(*u*) *Diog. Laert. in Socrat Argum. Isoc Busir.*

(*x*) *Ælian. Var Hist* ii,1 *Schol. Aristoph* Ὄρνιθ p. 401

died in *Laches*'s Magistracy, one Epistle must be spurious, that mentions *Polycrates*. This Breach *Allatius* would secure; and therefore he will needs make him live several years longer. But then, say I, if we concede this to *Allatius*; not one Epistle only, but the whole Bundle of them are spurious. For most of them plainly suppose, that *Socrates* died under *Laches*. Even this very Epistle complains (y) that *Xenophon* was abroad when *Socrates* suffer'd; and that the Expedition of *Cyrus* hindred him from being present then at *Athens*: and a second Letter, to name no more, dated after *Socrates*'s Death, makes *Xenophon* to have newly escaped the dangers of his long March through Enemies Countries. Now, all the world knows, (z) that *Cyrus*'s Expedition, and *Xenophon*'s March was in *Laches*'s time, and the year before him. So that upon the whole; there is no escape, no evasion from this Argument; but our Epistles must be convicted of a manifest Cheat.

(y) Ep xiv

xviii

(z) Marm. Arund Laert Diodor. &c.

VII. In the XVII Letter, one of *Socrates*'s Scholars, supposed to be present at *Athens*, when the things he speaks of were acted, says, the *Athenians* (a) put to death both *Anytus* and *Melitus*, the Prosecutors of *Socrates*: which being contrary to known matter of fact, proves the Epistle to be a Forgery. *Melitus*, indeed, was killed;
but

(a) Ἄνυτον τε ἡ Μέλιτον ἀπέκτειναν.

but *Anytus* was only banisht; and (*b*) several Writers speak of him afterwards at *Heraclea* in *Pontus*.

VIII. The XVIII is a Letter of *Xenophon*'s inviting some Friends to come to see him, at his Plantation near *Olympia*. He says, *Aristippus* and *Phaedo* had made him a Visit: and that he recited to them his (*c*) *Memoirs of Socrates*; which both of them (*d*) *approved* of. This alone is sufficient to blast the Reputation of our Famous Epistles. For, how is it likely that *Aristippus* would go so far to see *Xenophon*, who (*e*) was always his Enemy? Much less would he have given his approbation to a Book, that was a Satyr against himself. For the Book is yet in being; and in it he introduces *Socrates*, in a long Lecture, reprehending *Aristippus* (*f*) for his Intemperance and Lust. Even *Laertius* takes notice, That he brought in *Aristippus*'s Name upon that scandalous occasion, out of the enmity he bare him.

IX. We have already seen *Xenophon* writing *Socrates*'s Memoirs at *Scillus*, near *Olympia*. But in the XXII, to *Cebes* and *Simmias*, he is writing them at *Megara*; for there the Letter is dated. And in the XXI. to *Xanthippe*, he invites her to come to him to *Megara*. One would think, there was more Sophists than one had a Finger in this

(*b*) *Laert. in Socrat. & in Antisth. Themist. O, at 11 Augustin. de Civ Dei, VIII, 3.*

(*c*) Ἀπομνημονεύματα.
(*d*) ὅτι ἐρμόδια τινα ἐῇ.

(*e*) Ξενοφῶν ᾗ εἶχε πρὸς αὐτὸν δυσμενῶς *Laert. in Aristippo.*

(*f*) *Xenoph. Memo. ab lib II in princip.*

Volume of Letters: or if he was but one Author, Nature gave him a short Memory without the Blessing of a great Wit. 'Tis true, upon *Socrates*'s Execution, his Scholars left *Athens* for fear, (*g*) and retired to *Megara*, to the House of *Euclides:* which occasion'd our Sophist to bring *Xenophon* thither too. But he should have remembred, That while They were scared out of *Athens* for fear of their own Lives, He was safe at a great distance in the Retinue of *Agesilaus*; from whose company he went to *Scillus*, without ever residing at *Megara*. Nay, the Sophist is so indiscreet, as to bring in *Xenophon* in *forma pauperis*, to beg and receive relief from *Cebes* and *Simmias:* whereas every body knows, that he got great Riches in the War, (*h*) and lived in very great splendor and hospitality at *Scillus*.

X. In the XXIV Epistle, *Plato* says, he is quite weary of a City Life; and had therefore retired into the Country, διατεί-βων ἒ μακρὰν Ἐφεστιάδων, which *Allatius* translates, *non longe ab Ephestiadibus*. He ought to have said, *ab Hephaestiadis*. For the true word in the *Greek*, is Ἡφαιστιαδῶν. *Plato* had some Estate there, which he disposed of in his Will: τὸ ἐν Ἡφαιστιαδῶν χωρίον, as 'tis in (*i*) *Laertius*. *Hesychius*; Ἡφαιστιάδαι, Ἀθηναῖοι. *Stephanus Byz*. Ἡφαιστιάδαι, δῆμ⸳ Ἀθηναίων τᾶ τιπικᾶ. ἐξ Ἡφαιστιαδῶν, &c. In the *Roman* Manuscript of *Laertius*,

(*g*) *Laert. in Euclid.*

(*h*) *Laert. in Xenoph. Xenoph. Exp Cyri, l.v.p.350.*

(*i*) *Vita Platon.*

ertius, 'tis writ ἐνιφισιάδων: which manner of Spelling is found also in *Hesychius*, Ἰφισ-ιᾶς, ἥρως, ἀφ᾽ ὃ Ἰφισιάδαι. If the Reader does believe, that our Letter-monger, like *Hesychius*, spelt the word wrong; he will be satisfied of the Forgery: For surely, *Plato* himself knew the true name of his own Estate. But if he encline to absolve the Author, and lay the blame upon the Copyers; he may please to accept of this, only as an Emendation.

XI. The XXVII Epistle is *Aristippus*'s to his Daughter *Arete*: which, perhaps, is the very same that is mention'd by *Laertius*; who, among the Writings of this Philosopher, names Ἐπιστολὴν πρὸς Ἀρήτην τ̄ Θυγατέρα. *Allatius*, indeed, is ready to vouch it: but I am not so easie of belief. For here are (*k*) two other Letters of his in this Parcel, and both of them writ in the *Doric* Dialect, though directed to *Athens*: because, forsooth, he was a *Cyrenaean*, and the *Doric* his native Tongue. Pray, what was the matter then, that in this he uses the *Attic*; though he writ from *Sicily* a *Dorian* Country, to his own Daughter at *Cyrene*? One would suspect, as I observed before, that a couple of Sophists clubb'd to this Collection. 'Tis true, we know, from *Laertius*; that of xxv *Dialogues* publisht by *Aristippus*, some were in the *Doric* Idiom, and some in the *Attic*. But that, I suppose,

(*k*) IX. & XI.

pose, was done because of the variety of his Persons. In some Dialogues the Speakers were *Sicilians*, and those were writ in the *Doric*; and where the *Athenians* were introduced, the *Attic* was proper. But now, in this Letter to his Daughter, both Parties are *Dorians*; and so this Epistle should rather be *Doric*, than either of the other two.

XII. In the same Letter he mentions her Estate in *Bernice*, τὸ ἐν Βερνίκῃ κτῆμα. There is no question but he means Βερενίκη; perhaps that City not far from *Cyrene*. But there was nothing then in all *Afric* called by that name: for Βερενίκη is the *Macedonian* Idiom for Φερενίκη, *the Victorious*. In that Countrey, φ was generally changed into β: as (*l*) instead of κεφαλὴ they said κεβλὴ for Φίλιππος, Βίλιππος; for φαλακρὸς, Βαλακρὸς; and so in others. So that Βερενίκη was unknown in *Afric*, till the *Macedonians* came thither: and indeed, they had their names from the Wives of the *Ptolemees*, a whole Century of years after the date of this Letter.

(*l*) *Etym. Magn.* &c.

XIII. He goes on, and tells his Daughter, *That if he should die, he would have her go to* Athens, *and live with* Myrto *and* Xanthippe, *the two Wives of* Socrates. It was a common Tradition among the Writers of Philosophic History, that *Socrates* had these two Wives at once; and from thence our
Sophist

Sophist made them the Complement of a Place in this Epistle. *(m)* There are cited as Authors of this Story, *Callisthenes, Demetrius Phalereus, Satyrus,* and *Aristoxenus,* who all took it from *Aristotle* in his Book *Of Nobility,* περὶ Εὐγενείας. But Polygamy being against the Law of that Commonwealth, and the Story therefore improbable; *Hieronymus Rhodius* produces a temporary Statute made in *Socrates*'s Days, That by reason of the scarcity of People, a Man might marry two Wives at a time. But notwithstanding such a flush of Authorities, *(n) Panaetius* the Stoic, a very great Man, writ expresly against all those named above; and, in the Opinion of *Plutarch,* *(o) sufficiently* confuted the Tradition of the Two Wives. For my own part, I dare pin my Belief upon two such excellent Judgments, as *Plutarch*'s and *Panaetius*'s; and upon their Credit alone, pronounce this Letter to be an Imposture. What grounds they proceeded on, I cannot now tell; but I think there is apparent reason for rejecting the Story, even laying aside their Testimony. For none of *Socrates*'s Acquaintance, not *Plato,* not *Xenophon,* say one word of this *Myrto. Aristotle,* we see, was the first that mention'd her: but *(p)* *Plutarch* suspects that Book to be spurious. So that all this Tradition rose at first from a Falsary, that counterfeited *Aristotle*'s Name.

(m) Laert. in Socrat. Plutarch. Aristid. Athen. xiii. p. 556.

(n) Athenaeus Plutarch ib.

(o) ἱκανῶς.

(p) Ibid.

Name. Besides, they do not agree in telling their Tale; one says, that he had both Wives together: another, that *Myrto* was his first Wife, and the second came after her death: another, that *Xanthippe* was the first. Let either of them come first, and our Epistles are false; for here we have Both surviving him, and living together. (*q*) One says, this *Myrto* was *Aristides*'s Daughter; another his Grand-daughter; and another, his Grandson's Daughter. Whatsoever she was; if she outliv'd her Husband, according to the Letters, pray where was her Ladyship at the time of his suffering? (*r*) *Xanthippe*, like a loving Wife, attended him in the Prison; but the other ne'er came near him. 'Tis a mistake, sure, that has past upon the World, that *Xanthippe* was the Scold: it should seem, that *Myrto* had the better title to that honourable Name. But what shall we say to *Hieronymus*, who brings you the very Statute, that gave allowance of two Wives at once? *Panaetius*, you see, believed it not: and why may not a Statute be forged, as easily as these Epistles? If there was such an Act, there appears no great wisdom in it. It is certain, there is near an equality in the births of Males and Females. So that if some Men had two Wives for their share, others must go without: and what remedy would that be against the scarcity of

People?

(*q*) Ibid.

(*r*) Plato *Apolog.*

People? Besides that by such a Law the Rich only would be accommodated, who were able to maintain a couple: the poorer sort, who are always the most fruitful, would be in worse circumstances than before. And without doubt, a very strong interest would have been made against the passing of such a Bill; (*s*) as we know what the *Roman* Matrons did, when *Papirius Praetextatus* made a like Story to his Mother. 'Tis very odd too, that no body but *Hieronymus* should ever hear of this Statute; and He too a suspected Witness, because he brings it to serve a turn, and to help at a hard pinch. But certainly such a Political Occurrence, had it been true, could never have lain hid from the whole Tribe of Historians. It had very well deserved not only a mention, but a remark. But how could it possibly escape the fancy and spleen of all the Comoedians of that Age? how could they miss so pleasant an Argument of Jest and Ridicule? Those that are acquainted with the condition of those times, will look upon this as next to a Demonstration. But let us grant, if you will, half a dozen Wives to *Socrates*; yet nevertheless our Epistles will be still in the mire. For here our Sophist makes the two Women live amicably together: which is pretty hard to believe: for (as (*t*) those that make them Two, tell the Story of them

(*s*) *A. Gellius*, lib. 1. c. 23.

(*t*) *Aristoxenus apud Theodoret*, Serm xii. ad *Graecos*

them) while their Husband was alive, they were perpetually fighting. But, which is worse yet, there are other Letters in the bundle, that plainly suppose *Socrates* to (*u*) Ep iv. have had but one Wife. (*u*) He himself, writing to some body, tells him this Domestic News, *That* Xanthippe *and the Children are well:* but says not a word of my (*x*)Ep xxi Lady *Myrto*. (*x*) *Xenophon* sends a Letter top full of kindness and commendation to *Xanthippe* and the Little ones; but it was very uncivil in him, to take no notice of the other; since, according to the Story, she brought her Husband the more Children. Nay, if we allow this Letter of *Xenophon*'s to be genuine, he play'd a false and dirty trick, much against his Character. For at the date of this Epistle, if (*y*) Ep. we believe the very next (*y*) to it, he was xxii writing *Socrates*'s *Memoirs*. So that while he here in his Letter wheedles the poor Woman, and makes her little Presents, and commends her for her love to her Husband, and for many good qualities; in his Book (*z*)Xenoph. (*z*) he traduces her to that present Age, Conviv. and to all Posterity, for the most curst and p. 876. devilish Shrew, *that ever was or ever would be*. Nay, which makes it the baser, he was the only Man that said this of her; for neither *Plato* nor any of the old *Socra-* (*a*) Lib v *tics* writ a word about her Scolding. Which p. 219. made (*a*) *Athenaeus* suspect it was a Calumny:

lumny: especially since *Aristophanes* and his Brethren of the Stage, in all their Railery and Satyr upon *Socrates*, never once twitted him about his Wife. Well, let that be as it will: but what shall we say to *Xenophon*'s double dealing? For my part, rather than I'll harbour such a thought of that great Man, I'll quit a whole Cart-load of such Letters as these.

XIV. *Xenophon*, in the xv Letter, tells this Story of *Plato*, to whom he bore a grudge; That he should say, *None of his Writings were to be ascribed to himself, but to* Socrates *young and handsom*; Φησὶ μηδὲν ἔτι ποίημα αὐτῶ, Σωκράτης μένΤοι νέθ κỳ καλῶ ὄντος. Now, this Sentence is taken out of *Plato*'s Second Epistle to *Dionysius* the Younger: Οὐδ' ἔτι σύγγραμμα Πλάτωνος ἐδὲν, ἐδ' ἔςαμ τὰ ἢ νῦν λεγόμενα Σωκράτης ὅτι, καλῶ ỳ νέῳ γεγονότος. Here's a blunder with a witness, from the Sophist's Ignorance in Chronology. For his forged Letter of *Xenophon* bears date immediately after *Socrates*'s Death: but the true one of *Plato*, which *Xenophon* here alludes to, is recenter by a vast while. For *Dionysius* came but to the Crown Olymp. CIII, 1. which is XXXII years after the Tryal of *Socrates*.

I must observe one thing more, that by no means should be omitted. There were formerly more Epistles of *Xenophon* extant, than appear in this Collection.

A large Fragment is cited in (*b*) *Stobaeus*, out of his Letter to *Crito*; (*c*) two Fragments out of a Letter to *Sotira*; (*d*) and two more out of one to *Lamprocles*: none of which are found here in *Allatius*'s Parcel. *Theodoret* produces a Passage out of a Letter of his to *Aeschines*; wherein he jerks *Plato* (*e*) for his Ambition and Voluptuousness; to gratifie which, he went to *Sicily, to Dionysius's* Court. (*f*) *Eusebius* has this Passage and more out of the same Epistle: and the whole is extant in (*g*) *Stobaeus*. What shall we say? that the true Letters of *Xenophon* were extant in those days? or that those too were a Cheat, and belong'd to the same Volume whence these of *Allatius* were taken? And so, as I observ'd before, they will be older than *Libanius*'s time. I am afraid it will be thought ill manners to question the Judgment of *Eusebius* and *Theodoret*. But we know, (*h*) they have made other Mistakes of a like nature: and the very Letter which they cite, betrays it self to be a counterfeit. *Xenophon*, we see, reproaches *Plato*, in a Letter to *Aeschines*. If this were true, it was a most rude affront to the Person he writ to, whose Friendship he courts so much in the rest of his Letter. For *Aeschines* himself was guilty of the very same fault, and is wounded through *Plato*'s side. 'Tis well known, that He too,

(*b*) Serm. 81.
(*c*) Serm. 120, 123
(*d*) Serm. 5.
(*e*) Ἔρως τυραννίδος, κὶ ἀντὶ λιτῆς διαίτης Σικελιώτης παρεθὺς ἀμέτρε τραπέζα.
(*f*) Praep. Evang XIV. 12.
(*g*) Serm. 78.

(*h*) See Dissert upon Jo. Malal.

too, as well as *Plato* and *Aristippus* and others, made a Voyage to *Sicily*, and struck in with *Dionysius*; (*i*) and that purely for Money and the Table. (*k*) *Lucian* says, He was Parasite to the Tyrant; and (*l*) another tells us, he liked his Entertainment so well, that he did not stir from him, till he was deposed. I would ask any Man now, if he can still believe it a genuine Letter; let him have what veneration he can for the Learning of *Eusebius*.

(*i*) *Laert. & Suidas in Aesch. Plut de Adulat.*
(*k*) *In Parasito.*
(*l*) *Polycritus apud Laert.*

In the beginning of this Discourse, I have said, *That I heard of none, that, since the first publication of these Letters, called them into question.* But I was shewn to day (after mine was in the Press) in Bishop *Pearson*'s *Vindiciae Epp. Sancti Ignatii*, a (*m*) Digression made on purpose against *Socrates*'s *Epistles*. I must confess, with some shame, I had either never read that Chapter, or utterly forgot it. But I am glad now to find that incomparable Man both to think it worth going out of his way to discover this Imposture, and to confirm me in my Judgment by the accession of his great Authority. There is nothing there disagreeing with what I had said; but that his Lordship allows the Epistle to *Aeschines*, cited by *Eusebius*, to be genuine: which I had endeavoured to convict of a Forgery. I referr it to those that please to read both;

(*m*) *Part II. p. 12, 13.*

whether they think I have juſt reaſon to change my Opinion: eſpecially when I ſhall tell them, That not *Aeſchines* only, but even *Xenophon* himſelf made a Viſit to *Dionyſius.* I have (n) *Athenaeus* for my Authority, a Witneſs beyond all exception. Ξενοφῶν γοῦν ὁ Γρύλλου πρὸς Διονυσίῳ. &c. Xenophon (ſays he) *the Son of* Gryllus, *when at* Dyoniſius *the Sicilian's Table the Cup-bearer forced the Company to drink;* Pray, ſays he, Dionyſius (ſpeaking aloud to the Tyrant,) *if your Butler forces Wine upon us againſt our wills, why may not your Cook as well compell us to eat?* So that if we ſuppoſe the Letter genuine, the Abſurdity will double it ſelf; both Parties being guilty of the very ſame thing, that is charged upon *Plato.*

(n) Lib. x. p. 427

OF EURIPIDES'S EPISTLES.

'TIS a bold and dangerous venture, to attack *Euripides*'s *Letters*; ſince a very Learned *Greek* Profeſſor has ſo paſſionately eſpouſed them; that he declares it to be (o) *great Impudence and want of all Judgment* to queſtion the Truth of them.
I do

(o) Perfrictae frontis & judicii imminuti Eurip Edit Cantab. par II p 523

&c. *and* Aesop's Fables.

I do not care to meddle with Controversie upon such high Wagers as those: but if I may have leave to give my opinion, without staking such valuable things as Modesty and good Sense upon it, I am very ready to speak my Mind candidly and freely.

I. There are only five Epistles now extant, ascribed to *Euripides*: but without doubt there were formerly more of them; as we have seen just before, that we have not now the whole Sett of *Xenophon's* Letters. Neither can we suppose a Sophist of so barren an Invention, as to have his Fancy quite crampt and jaded with poor Five. We have here a peculiar happiness, which we wanted in the rest; to know whom we are obliged to for the great blessing of these Epistles. *Apollonides*, that writ a Treatise Περὶ κατεψευσμένης Ἱστορίας, 'About falsified 'History, says, one (p) *Sabirius Pollo* for-'ged them, the same Man that counterfeited the Letters of *Aratus*.' This we are told by the Writer of *Aratus's* Life, no unlearned Author: who does not contradict him about these of *Euripides*; but for *Aratus's*, he says, that, bating this *Apollonides*, every body else believed them to be genuine. I cannot pass any judgment of what I never saw; for *Aratus's* Letters are not now to be had: but if they were no better than these of our Tragedian, I should, in

(p) Σαβί- ε.Θ. Πόλ- λων.

F f 2 spite

spite of the Common Vogue, be of *Apollonides*'s Mind; and I wish that Book of his were now extant. One may know by the manner of the Name, that this *Sabirius Pollo* was a *Roman*: but I do not find such a Family as the *Sabirii*, nor such a Sirname as *Pollo*. What if we read *Sabinius*, or *Sabidius Pollio*?

Non amo te, Sabidi; nec possum dicere quare.

If that *Sabidius* in *Martial* was the Forger of our Epistles; though the Poet could give none, yet I can give a very good Reason why I do not love him.

But the Learned Advocate for the Letters makes several Exceptions against the Testimony of *Apollonides*. As first, *That we may fairly inferr from it, that a great many others believed them to be true.* Alas! How many more, both Ancients and Moderns, believed *Phalaris*'s to be true? If that Argument would have done the Work, I might have spared this Dissertation. *But prove, that these Letters now extant are the same that were forged by* Sabirius. Commend to me an Argument, that, like a Hail, there's no Fence against it. Why, had we been told too, that he made *Phalaris's Epistles*: yet how could we *prove*, unless some Passages were cited out of them, that they were the same that we have now? But

But though I cannot demonstrate that these are *Sabirius*'s; yet I'll demonstrate them by and by to be an Imposture; and I hope then it will be no injustice to lay them at his door. *But 'tis an Evidence, that the true* Epistles *of* Euripides *were once extant; because some body thought it not improper to father false ones upon him.* Now, I should think the very contrary; that the Cuckow does not lay her Egg, where the Nest is already full. At least, I am resolved I'll never go a book-hunting after the genuine Epistles of *Phalaris*; though some body has cheated the World with a parcel of false ones.

II. It might easily have happen'd, though we suppose the Letters spurious, that in so small a number as five, there could be nothing found to convict them by. But so well as the Writer managed his Business; that every one of them has matter enough to their own Detection. The last and principal of them is dated from *Macedonia*, in answer to some Reproaches, that were cast upon him at *Athens* for his going to *Archelaus*. *As for what you write from* Athens; says he, *pray know, that I value no more,* ὧν νῦν Ἀγάθων ἢ Μέσατος λέγει, *what* Agatho *or* Mesatus *now say; than I formerly did, what* Aristophanes *babbled*. Here we have the Poet *Agatho*, (for without doubt he means the Poet, since he has joined him with *A-ristophanes*)

ristophanes) residing at *Athens*, and blaming *Euripides* for living with *Archelaus*. Now, could any thing be more unfortunate for our *Sabirius Pollo*, than the naming of this Man? For even this *Agatho* himself was then with *Archelaus* in (*q*) *Euripides*'s Company: besides that they were always good Friends and Acquaintance, not there only, but before at *Athens*.

But perhaps some may suspect, it was another *Agatho* a (*r*) Comic Poet, that was meant in the Letter, and not the famous *Agatho* the Tragedian. This I find to be the Opinion of the Learned Person above named. But I will make bold to expunge this Comic *Agatho* out of the Catalogue of Mankind. For he sprung but up, like a Mushroom, out of a rotten Passage in *Suidas*; who, after he has spoken of *Agatho* the Tragic Poet, has these Words; κωμῳδοποιὸς Σωκράτης διδασκάλῳ· ἐκωμῳδεῖτο δ᾽ εἰς θηλύτητα: which his Interpreters (*Wolfius* and *Portus*) thus translate, *Fuit & alius Agatho Comoediarum Scriptor*. But there's nothing like *Fuit & alius* in the Original; but the same *Agatho* is here meant, that was mentioned before. This they might have known from the following words, ἐκωμῳδεῖτο δ᾽ εἰς θηλύτητα, he was libelled for his *Effeminateness*. For whom can that belong to, but to *Agatho* the Tragoedian;

(*q*) *Aelian.* II, 21 & XIII, 4 *Plut in Apoph Schol Aristoph. Βάτραχ.*
(*r*) *Vita Eurip p 9 Ed. Cant.*

dian; whom (s) *Lucian* ranks with *Cinyras* and *Sardanapalus?* Do but read *Aristophanes*'s *Thesmophoriazusae*; and you'll see him ridiculed upon that score for some Pages together. The Scholiast upon Βάτραχοι of the same Poet; Ἀγάθων (says he) ἕτος τραγικὸς ποιητὴς ὅτι μαλακίᾳ διεβάλλετο. Here you see, it is expresly said, (t) Agatho *the Tragoedian was traduced as Effeminate*, It follows presently in the same Scholiast; Οὗτος ἢ ὁ Ἀγάθων κωμῳδοποιὸς τῦ Σωκράτυς διδασκάλυ; where we have the very words of *Suidas* applied to the Tragoedian: ἕτος, *this same* Agatho *was a Comoedian*, Socrates *being his Master*: not *another*, as the Translators of *Suidas* interpolate the Text. But is it true then, that our spruce *Agatho* writ Comedies too? Nothing like it; though the Learned (u) *Gregorius Gyraldus* affirms it from this very Passage. 'Tis a mere oscitation of our Scholiast, and of *Suidas* that gaped after him: the occasion and ground of the Story being nothing but this. *Plato*'s *Convivium* was in the House of this *Agatho*: in the (x) conclusion of which, *Socrates* is introduced proving to *Agatho* and *Aristophanes*; *That it belonged to the same Man, and required the same Parts, to write both Comedy and Tragedy; and that he that was a skilful Tragoedian, was also a Comoedian.*

(s) Πάναβρόν τινα Σαρδανάπαλον, ἢ Κινύραν, ἢ αὐτὸν Ἀγάθωνα τ̄ τραγῳδίας ἐπίερσον ποιητὺν. *Rhet Præc.*

(t) P.133.

(u) *Dialog. de Poet.*

(x) P.336. Τὸν τέχνῃ τραγῳδοποιὸν ὄντα κ̄ κωμῳδοποιὸν εἶ).

Hence

Hence have our wise Grammarians dress'd up a fine Story, That *Agatho* was a Comoedian, and of *Socrates*'s teaching. And now, I hope, I have evidently proved the thing that I proposed; to the utter disgrace of our admired Epistles.

III. *Euripides*, we have seen, did not value one farthing, *what either* Agatho *or* (y) Mesatus *said of him*. I would gladly be better acquainted with this same *Mesatus*; for I never once met with him but here in this Letter. He must be a Brother of the Stage too, by the Company he is placed in: But what was the matter? Was he so hiss'd and exploded, that he durst never shew his Head since? I have a fancy, he was of the same Family with (z) *Phalaris*'s two Fairy Tragoedians, *Aristolochus* and *Lysinus*: and that these Letters too are a kin to those of the Tyrant. But, perhaps, you'll say, this *Mesatus* is but a Fault in the Copies. It may be so: and I could help you to another Tragoedian of those Times, not altogether unlike him; one *Melitus*, the same that afterwards accused *Socrates*; who was likely enough to hate *Euripides*, that was the Philosopher's Friend. Or I could invent some other Medicine for the Place: but let those look to that, that believe the Epistles true, or think them worth the curing.

(y) ἢ Μέσατος.

(z) Epist. lxiii, & xcvii.

The very Learned Defender of the Epistles, one of a singular Industry and a most diffuse Reading, has proposed some Objections against the Letters, communicated to him by a private Hand. That private Person, at the Request of the Editor, imparted his opinion to him in a very short Letter: to which he had no Answer returned; till he found it, with some surprize, brought upon the Stage in (*a*) print; and his Reasons routed and triumph'd. But let us see if we can rally them again: perhaps they may keep their ground in a second Engagement.

(*a*) *Eurip.* Edit Cant. p. 27, & 523.

IV. Our Friend *Sabirius Pollo*, to make the whole Work throughout worthy of himself, has directed this same Letter to *Cephisophon*, who was *Euripides*'s Actor for his Plays. For he had often heard of *Cephisophon*; and so he would not let him pass without a share in his Epistles. But he should have minded Time and History a little better, if he hoped to put himself upon Us for the Author he mimic's. 'Tis true, *Cephisophon* and our Poet were once mighty dear acquaintance: but there fell out a foul accident, that broke off the Friendship. For *Euripides* caught him Acting for him, not upon the Stage, but in private with his Wife. Which business taking wind abroad, and making a perpetual Jest, was one of the main Reasons why he left *Athens* and went

went to *Macedonia*. And is it likely, after all this, that our Poet should write a Letter to him, as soon as he got thither? that he should use him as his most intimate Friend, nearer to him than his own Children? I know, there are some so fond of our Epistles, that *they value all this as nothing*. *Cephisophon* is so much in their Books; that whatsoever is said against him, must be Calumny and Detraction. Give me an Advocate, that will stick close and hang upon a Cause. By being their Editor, he is retain'd for the Letters; and therefore he must not desert his Client. But why shall no Testimony be allowed, that touches *Cephisophon*? Are not (*b*) *Aristophanes* and his Commentator, and *Suidas* and (*c*) *Thomas Magister* all lawful and good Evidence? And is there one single Witness against them in his behalf? Not a Writer is now extant, that mentions his Name, but what tells the Story of him: and if we must not believe them, we shall want new Evidence to prove, there ever was such a Man.

V. In a Disquisition of this nature, an inconsistency in Time and Place is an Argument that reaches every body. All will cry out, that *Phalaris*, &c. are spurious, when they see such Breaches upon Chronology. But I must profess, I should as fully have believed them so; though the Writers

(*b*) P 167, 184
(*c*) In *Vita Eurip*

ters had escaped all Mistakes of that kind. For as they were commonly Men of small Endowments, that affected to make these Forgeries; a great Man disdaining so base and ignoble a Work: so they did their business accordingly; and expressed rather themselves, than those they acted. For they knew not how to observe Decorum, in a Quality so different from their own: like the silly Player, that would represent *Hercules*; tall indeed, but slender, without bulk and substance. Let us see the Conduct of this Author: In the first Letter, *Archelaus* sends *Euripides* some Money; and our Poet, as if his Profession were like a Monastic Vow of Poverty, *utterly refuses it*. And why, forsooth, does he refuse it? Why, *it was too great a Summ for his Condition*. Yes, to be sure; when a Sophist makes a Present, the greatest Summ costs no more than the least. *But it was difficult to be kept, and the Fingers of Thieves would itch at it*. Alas for him; with the Expence of one Bag, out of many, he might have provided a strong Box, and new Doors and Locks to his House. But why could he not accept a Little of it? Even (*d*) *Socrates* himself and *Xenocrates* took a Modicum out of Presents, and return'd the rest again. And is a Poet more self-denying, than the most mortified of the Philosophers? But the best of all, is, *That* Clito *the King's chief*

(*d*) *Laertius, in Socrat & Xenoc.*

chief Minister, threatned to be angry with him, if he refused it. What, could *Clito* expect before-hand, that the Present would be refused? The most sagacious States-Man, sure, that ever Monarch was blest with. *Alexander* could not fore-see such a thing; but was mightily surprized, when *Xenocrates* would not receive some Money that he sent him: (e) "What, says he, has "*Xenocrates* no Friends to give it to, if " he need it not himself?" As for our Poet, he had Friends, I assure you; but all of his own Kidney, *Men of Contentment, that would not finger a Penny of it,* τὸ ἀυταρκὲς ἡμῖν τε κỳ τοῖς φίλοις παρόν. What would one give to purchase a Sett of such Acquaintance? And yet, I know not how, in the Fifth Letter, their Appetites were come to 'em; For in that, *Euripides* himself, from *Archelaus*'s Court, shared some Presents among them; and we hear not one word, but that all was well taken.

VI. The rest of this Letter is employed in begging Pardon (f) *for the two Sons of a Pellaean old Fellow,* who had done something to deserve Imprisonment. And the Third and Fourth are Common Places of Thanks for granting this Request. Now, besides that the whole Business has the Air and Visage of Sophistry; for this same is a mighty Topic too in *Phalaris*'s Epistles: 'tis a plain Violation of good Sense, to Petition

(e) *Plut. Apoph.*

(f) Πελλαῖ⊕ γέρων

tition for a Man without telling his Name: as if *Pella* the Royal City had no Old Man in it but one. How can such an Address be real? But to this they give a double Answer; *That a Sophist, if this was one, could not be at a loss for a Name: he might easily have put one here; as hereafter he names* Amphias, Lapretes *and others.* But the Point is not, what he *might* have done, but what he *has* done. He *might* have named some other Poet at *Athens*, and not *Agatho* that was then in *Macedonia*. All those Mistakes and Blunders of *Phalaris* and the rest *might* easily have been avoided, had the Writers had more History and Discretion. (g) *But he had writ a Letter before this about the same business; and there we must suppose he had mention'd his name.* This indeed would be something, if it would carry water. But though the Sophist has told you so; do not rashly believe him. For it is plain, that pretended Letter must have been sent to *Archelaus*, before this vast Present came from him. Why then did not the same Messenger that brought the Money, bring the Grant too of his Petition? Would the King, that did him this mighty Honour and Kindness, deny him at the same time that small and just Request? For the Crime of those Prisoners was surely no hainous business. Had it been a design to Assassinate the King, he would

(g) Πρότερον ἐπεστείλαμέν σοι.

would never have interceded for them. The Charge against them was a Venial Fault: or were it the blackest Accusation, their Innocence at least would clear them: for our Poet himself tells us, (*h*) *They had done no body any wrong.*

(*h*) Οὐδὲν ἀδικεῖν ἐ- φίκασιν

VII. The Second Epistle is to *Sophocles*, whom he makes to be Shipwrack'd at the Island *Chios*; the Vessel and Goods being lost, but all the Men saved. That *Sophocles* was at *Chios*, we are informed by (*i*) *Ion Chius* the Tragoedian; who relates a long Conversation of his there. If our Author here means the same Voyage, as probably he does; he is Convicted of a Cheat. For (*k*) then *Sophocles* was Commander of a Fleet with *Pericles* in the *Samian* War; and went to *Chios*, and thence to *Lesbos*, for Auxiliary Forces. But our Mock-*Euripides* never thinks of his publick Employment; but advises him to return home at his leisure; as if it had been a Voyage for Diversion. *Yes,* says his Advocate; *but why might he not be at* Chios *another time, though no body speak of it, about private Affairs?* Yes; why not, indeed? For *Sophocles* was so (*l*) courteous and good-natur'd a Man, that, to do our Letter-Monger a kindness, he would have gone to every Island in the *Archipelago*. But 'tis hard though, that a good Ship must be lost, and our Poet swim for't, to oblige the little Sophist. For I fear

(*i*) *Athen.* XIII, 603

(*k*) Ibid. & *Thucyd.* 1, 75.

(*l*) *Ion Chius,* ib. *Aristoph. Ranis*

the

the Vessel was Cast away, purely to bring in *(m) the great loss of Sophocles's Plays.* Alas! alas! Could he not go over the water, but he must needs take his Plays with him? And must *Euripides*, of all Men, lament the loss of them; whose own Plays must, probably, have truckled to them at the next Feast of *Bacchus?* Must *Euripides*, his Rival, his Antagonist, tell him, *(n) That his Orders about Family Affairs were Executed:* as if He had been employed by him, as Steward of his Houshold?

(m) Ἡ περὶ τὰ δράματα συμφορά.

(n) Τὰ οἴκοι ἴσθι χθὲς νῦν ὄντα.

VIII. The Fifth Letter is a long Apology for his going to *Macedonia.* " Can they " think, says he, that I came hither for " love of Money? I should have come " then, when I was younger; and not now, " to lay *(o)* my Bones in a Barbarous Coun- " try, and make *Archelaus* richer by my " Death." I observed it, as no small Mark of a Sophist, That our Author foretels, he was to die in *Macedonia*; where, we know, he was worried to Death by a Pack of Dogs. *But what wonder*, say they, *if an Old Man of Seventy predict his own Death?* I do not question, but our Poet might presage himself to be Mortal. But 'twas an odd guess to hit upon the time and place, when and where he was to Die. For, what ground was there to be so positive? The Letter, we see, carries Date just after his Arrival at Court. He had, as yet, had very short

(o) Ἵνα ἐν βαρβάρῳ γῇ ἀποθάνωμεν.

Trial,

Trial, whether all things would continue to his liking. And we have no reason to suppose, that he came thither for good and all; never to see *Athens* again. Might he not, by some Accident, or supplanted by some Rival, lose the King's Favour? Or, was he sure His Life would last as long as his own? 'Twas a violent Death, and not mere Age and Craziness, that took our Poet away at last: and he knew *Sophocles* to be then alive and hearty and making of Plays still; that was Fourteen Years older than himself. In these Circumstances to be so positive about his Dying there, was a Prophecy as bold as any of the *Pythian* Oracle. *But,* say they, *he gives a hint too, that* Archelaus *might be deposed: which a Sophist would not say, because it never came to pass.* That was true and came to pass every day, that he *might* be deposed: and he does not suggest, that it actually would be so; for he expresly says, (*p*) *God would always stand by the King, and support him.* But indeed, as they interpret the Passage there; it looks as if he had foreboded real Mischief; Οὐδὲ ἀνιάσῃ, ὅτι οἴχεται ὁ καιρὸς εἰς ἀνθρώπων ἐυεργεσίαν, ἀνεθεὶς φροῦδος ἤδη. Which last words they Translate, *ubi jam destitutus fueris & abdicatus,* "when you are Deserted and Deposed." But with all due Submission, I will assume the freedom of changing the Version. For ἀνεθεὶς and φροῦδος belong

(*p*) Παρέσαι μὲν ἀεί ὁ θεὸς, κ̀, ϛήσει κα- τ̀ όπιν.

long to the word καιρὸς, and not to *Archelaus*: and the distinction is to be put thus; ὅτι οἴχε(ται) ὁ καιρὸς, εἰς ἀνθρώπων ἐυεργεσίαν ἀνεθεὶς, φροῦδος ἤδη; *Tempus ad exercendam benignitatem concessum*; "You will not grieve, that "the time is gone past recalling, which was "granted you by God to do good to Man- "kind in." Thus, I suppose, is now clear enough; and *Archelaus* is in no danger of being deposed by this Sentence. But let us examine our Author's next words; (*q*) *To make* Archelaus *richer by my Death*. A very good Thought indeed, and worthy of *Euripides*. But pray what could the King get by his Death? Would the Poet be compell'd to make him his Heir; as some were forced by the *Roman* Emperors? Or, would the King seize upon his Estate, and defraud the true Inheritor? If the Poet had such Suspicions as these, he would never have gone to him. But though he had left all to him at his Death; what would the King have been richer for him? For surely *Euripides*, having setled Affairs at home, carried no great Stock with him to *Macedonia*; unless he thought *Archelaus* would make him pay for his Board. He might well expect to be maintain'd by the King's Liberality; (*r*) as he found it in the Event. The King therefore, were he his Heir, would only have received again, what himself had given before. Nay, even

(*q*) Ἵνα πλείονα Ἀρχελάῳ καταλίποις μὲν χρήματα.

(*r*) Ep. v.

G g

a great part of that had been loſt beyond recovery. For our Poet, by the very firſt Meſſenger, had packt more away to *Athens,* that *Archelaus* had given him, than all that he carried with him could amount to; perhaps, than all he was worth before.

IX. But he has more ſtill to ſay to thoſe, that blamed him for leaving *Athens.* " If " Riches (ſays he) could draw me to " *Macedonia*; why did I refuſe (*s*) *theſe* " *very ſame Riches*; when I was (*t*) *young,* " or *middle-aged*; and while my Mother " was alive; for whoſe ſake alone, if at " all, I ſhould have deſired to be rich?" He alludes here to the Firſt Letter, (and perhaps to others now loſt,) where he refuſes an ample Summ of Money ſent him by *Archelaus.* Alas, poor Sophiſt! 'twas ill luck he took none of the Money, to Fee his Advocates luſtily: for this is like to be a hard bruſh. For how could the Poet, while young, or middle-aged, refuſe Preſents from *Archelaus*? ſince, according (*u*) to moſt Chronologers, he was about Seventy; and, by the moſt favourable account, above Sixty; when *Archelaus* came to the Crown.

X. But what a dutiful Child had Mother *Clito* the Herb-woman? *For her ſake alone, her Son* Euripides *could wiſh to be Rich;* to buy her Oil to her Sallads. But what had the Old Gentleman the Father done, that

(*s*) Τὸν αὐτὸν τῦτον πλῦτον.
(*t*) Νέοι τε ὁμέσοι τἱω ἡλικίαν.

(*u*) *Diod. Sicul. & alii apud Athen* l.v. p. 217.

that he wishes nothing for His sake? And how had his (*x*) three Sons offended him, that They have no share in his good wishes? 'Tis a fine piece of Conduct that our Sophist has shewn. He had read something of our Poet's Mother; for she was famous in old Comedy for her Lettuce and Cabbage: but having heard nothing of his Sons; he represents him through all his Letters, as if he had no Children. As here, the only motive to desire Wealth, is his care of the *Old Woman:* and when she is supposed to be dead, all his concern is only for his *Friends.* In the First Letter, (*y*) He and his Friends are such contented Men, that they refuse the Royal Gift. Not a word of the three young Sparks; who, 'tis hard to think, were so self-denying. In the Fifth, he keeps none of the King's Presents by him, but sends all away to *Athens,* to be shared among his (*z*) Friends and Companions. How, again, would the young Gentlemen look, to be forgot thus by their own Father? If it be suspected, in favour of the Letters, that the Sons might be all dead before; I can soon put a stop to that, from a good Evidence, *Aristophanes;* who, in a Play made (*a*) the very Year of our Poet's Death, mentions the Sons as then alive.

(*x*) *Suidas, Tho. Magister.*

(*y*) Ἡμῶν τε κὴ τοῖς φίλοις.

(*z*) Τοῖς ἑταίροις κὴ ἐπιτηδείοις.

(*a*) Βάτραχοι p. 184 Edit *Basil.*

XI. The *Romans* may brag as much as they please of *Mecoenas* and others: but of all Patrons of Learning, *Archelaus* of *Macedonia* shall have my Commendations. Within two or three days after *Euripides*'s Arrival, he makes him a Present of (b) *Forty Talents.* Which was a greater Summ of Money than our Poet could ever have raised before; though all that he had should have been sold four times over. The Great *Themistocles* (c) was not worth Three Talents, before he meddled with Public Affairs: and (d) Two Talents was thought a good Portion for a Substantial Man's Daughter. *Alexander the Great,* when he was Lord of the World, sent *Xenocrates* the Philosopher a Present of Thirty Talents, or, as others say, Fifty; which (e) *Cicero* calls a vast Summ, especially for those times. But *Alexander*'s natural Munificence was stimulated and exalted to that extraordinary Act of Bounty, out of a Peak (f) he had to *Aristotle.* How generous then, nay, how profuse was *Archelaus*; that out of his little and scanty Revenue could give as much, as his great Successor in the midst of the *Persian* Treasures? But all this is spoil'd again; when we consider, 'tis a Sophist's Present: who is liberal, indeed, of his Paper Notes, but never makes solid Payment.

(b) Ep v.

(c) Plut Themist.

(d) Terent Heaut.

(e) Cicero T sc v Pecunia temporibus illis, Athens praesertim maxima.

(f) Laert in Arist.

And,

And now, I suppose, it will be thought no great matter, whether *Sabirius Pollo*, as *Apollonides* affirms, or any other unknown Sophist, have the Honour of the Epistles. I will take my leave of Him and Them; after I have done the same kindness to *Apollonides*, that I did to *Sabirius*. For as I read the name of the one, Σαβίδιος Πολλίων, instead of Σαβίριος Πόλλων: so, for Ἀπολλωνίδης ὁ Κηφεύς, I dare make bold to substitute Ἀπολλωνίδης ὁ Νικαεύς. The former was never heard of but here. This latter is mention'd by *Laertius*, *Harpocration* and others. He writ several Books, and Dedicated one of them (g) to *Tiberius*. The time therefore agrees exactly with this Emendation; for living in that Emperor's days, he might well cite a *Roman* Author *Sabidius Pollio*. But to take away all manner of scruple; this very Book *About Falsified History*, is ascribed to *Apollonides Nicenus* by (h) *Ammonius*; Ἀπολλωνίδης, says he, ὁ Νικαεὺς ἐν τῷ τρίτῳ περὶ κατεψευσμένων; just as the Writer of *Aratus*'s Life says; Ἀπολλωνίδης ὁ Κηφεὺς ἐν τῷ ὀγδόῳ περὶ κατεψευσμένης Ἱστορίας.

(g) *Laert. in Timone.*

(h) v Κατοίκησις. *De Differ Vocab.*

OF AESOP's FABLES.

I Could easily go on, and discover to you many more Impostures of this kind, The Epistles of *Anacharsis, Heraclitus, Democritus, Hippocrates, Diogenes, Crates,* and others. But perhaps I may be *exhorted* hereafter to put this Dissertation into *Latin,* with large Additions: till which time I will adjourn the further Discourse upon those several Authors; and proceed now to the last thing proposed, *The Fables of Aesop.*

And here I am glad to find a good part of the Work done ready to my hand. For Monsieur *Bachet S. de Meziriac,* has writ *The Life of Aesop,* in *French:* which Book, though I could never meet with it, I can guess from the great Learning of the Author, known to me by his other Works, to have in a manner exhausted the Subject. *Vavasor* too, *De Ludicra Dictione,* ascribes the present *Fables* to *Maximus Planudes,* and not to *Aesop* himself. See also a great deal upon this Head in the late *Historical Dictionary* of Mr. *Baile.* All which make me look upon Sir *W. T*'s mighty Commendation of the *Aesopean Fables* now extant, which is occasion of this Treatise, to be an unhappy Paradox; neither worthy of the great Author, nor agreeable to the rest of his excellent Book. For if I do not much deceive my self, I shall soon make it appear, That of all the Compositions of the *Aesopic Fables,* these that we have now left us, are both the Last and the Worst. Though I do not intend a set Discourse; but only a few loose things, that I fansie may have escaped the Observation of Others.

I. 'Tis very uncertain, if *Aesop* himself left any *Fables* behind him in Writing: the Old Man in (*i*) *Aristophanes* learned his Fables in Conversation, and not out of a Book. (*i*) *In Vespis,* p. 357.

Αἰσωπικὸν γελοῖον ἢ Συβαριτικὸν
Ὧν ἔμαθες ἐν τῷ συμποσίῳ ——

There's another (*k*) Passage in the same Poet, Οὐδ' Αἴσωπον πεπάτηκας; which (*l*) *Suidas,* and from him *Erasmus, Scaliger,* &c. affirm to be used proverbially; *You have not read so much as* Aesop, (spoken of Ideots and Illiterates.) From whence one might conclude, that *Aesop* wrote his own Fables, which were in every Bodies hands. But it plainly appears from the Poet himself, that it is not a Proverbial Saying: For when One had said, *He never heard before, that Birds were older than the Earth:* the Other tells him, *He is unlearned, and unacquainted with* Aesop; who said, (*k*) *In Avibus,* p. 387. (*l*) Πατῆσαι.

said, "That the *Lark* was the first of Things; and she, when her Father died (after he had laid five days unburied, because the Earth was not yet in being) at last buried him in her own Head. Now, what is there here like a Proverb? But pray take notice, that this Fable is not extant in our present Collection; a good Testimony, that Ours are not of the *Phrygian*'s own Composing.

I will mention another place of our Poet; that I may, on this occasion, correct a gross Error of the Scholiast. 'Tis extant *in Vespis*, p. 330.

Οἱ δ᾽ λεγεσι μύθες ἡμῖν, οἱ δ᾽ Αἰσώπε τι γελοῖον.

Where he interprets Αἰσώπε γελοῖον; of one *Aesop* a *ridiculous Actor of Tragedy*. But our Scholiast himself is more ridiculous: if it was He that writ this; and not some Trifler, that foisted it in among the other's Annotations. For there was no *Aesop* a *Greek* Actor in the Days of *Aristophanes*: he mistakes him for the Famous *Aesop* in *Cicero*'s Time, an Actor of Tragedy on the *Roman* Stage; and far from being ridiculous;

Quæ gravis Aesopus, quæ doctus Roscius egit.

But the *Aesop* meant by our Poet is the *Phrygian* himself, whose Fables were called *Jests*, Γελοῖα: so in the other Passage, already cited,

ted, Αἰσωπικὸν γελοῖον. *Hesychius*, Αἰσώπε γελοῖα· ὅπως ἔλεγον τὲς Αἰσώπε μύθες. (m) *Dion Chrysostom*, speaking of our *Aesop*, Ἡύχοντο αὐτὸν, says he, ἡδόμβροι ἐπὶ τῷ γελοίῳ ᾗ τοῖς μύθοις. *Avienus*, in his Preface; *Aesopus responso Delphici Apollinis monitus, RIDICULA orsus est.*

(m) *Orat. lxxii p. 631*

II. The first, that we know of, who essayed to put the *Aesopic Fables* into Verse, was (n) *Socrates* the Philosopher. *Laertius* seems to hint, that he did but one Fable; and that with no great success; the beginning of it was this:

(n) *Plato in Phaedone. Plutarch. de Aud. Poet Laert in Socrat.*

Αἴσωπός ποτ' ἔλεξε Κορίνθιον ἄςυ νέμεσι,
Μὴ κρίνειν ἀρετὴν λαοδίκῳ σοφίη.

'Tis observable again, that *Socrates* does not say, he made use of a *Book* of Fables: but, I wrote, says he, ὦν ἠπιςάμω, *those that I knew, and that I could first call to mind.* And this Fable too does not appear in our present Collection; if we may gather so much, from his naming the *Corinthians*.

III. After *Socrates*'s time, (o) *Demetrius Phalereus* made Λόγων Αἰσωπείων Συναγωγάς, *Collections of Aesopean Fables*: which, perhaps, were the first in their kind, committed to writing; I mean, in form of a Book. These seem to have been in Prose: and some, perhaps, may imagine, that they are the same that are now extant. I wish they were; for then they would have been well writ,

(o) *Laert. in Demet.*

with

with some Genius and Spirit. But I shall demonstrate ours to be of a Modern Date; and the Composition it self speaks too loud, and that it is not *Demetrius's*.

IV. After him, there was some body, whose name is now lost, that made a new Edition of the *Fables* in Elegiac Verse; I find no mention of them, but in *Suidas*; who cites them often under the name of Μῦθοι, or Μυθικοί. I will set down a few Fragments of them; both to shew that they belong to the *Aesopic Fables*, which has not yet been observed, that I know of; and to enable you to judge whether, if we could change our Modern Collection for these, we should not get by the bargain.

(p) *Suidas in* Δύη.

(p) Τὅνεκα τἠν ἰδίην ὅτις ὄπωπε δύην.

This belongs to the Fable about the Two Baggs that every Man carries; one before, where he puts other Men's Faults; another behind him, where he puts his own. This is mention'd by *Catullus, Horace, Phaedrus, Galen, Themistius, Stobaeus,* &c. and it is a Blot upon our Modern Sett, that there it is wanting.

(q) Id *in* Αἰπεινῇ.
(r) vulgo τεμνομένῃ.

(q) Αἰπειναῖς ἐλάταις ἔρισεν βάτος· ἡ μὲν ἔσπε Καὶ ναῦς κ̀ νηὸς (r) τεμνομένη τελέειν.

And,

Αἰπεινὴν ἐλάτην ἐρὶς ὤρσεν αἴσυλα φάσθῃ.

And,

And, [θυμῷ

(s) Οὐδὲ οἱ ἐδλ' αἴθων ἄδε πάρδαλις, ἕνεκα (s) Id. in
Ἐμπλείη——— Ἀδεν.

And, [ἀκηδής.

(t) Πικρὴ μὲν τε λύκοισιν, ἀτὰρ χειμέριοιν (t) Id.
Ἀκηδής.

Some of them, it seems, were all Hexameters:

———(u) Ὅθι στυφελῶν ἐπὶ πετρᾶν (u) Id.
Ὀςρεφθέντά τε νῶτα κ̣ αἰπύλα γυῖα κεάθη. Στυφ &
Schol. Ari-
stoph. p.
229.

'Tis an easie matter to find what Fables these Pieces relate to; and I think they are all extant in the present Collection.

V. This, you see by this Specimen, was no contemptible Author: And after him came one *Babrius*, that (x) gave a new Turn (x) *Suidas* of the Fables into Choliambics. No body, *in Βάβριος.* that I know of, mentions him; but *Suidas*, *Avienus*, and *Jo. Tzetzes*. There's one *Gabrias*, indeed, yet extant, that has comprized each Fable in four sorry Iambics. But our *Babrius* is a Writer of another Size and Quality; and were his Book now extant, it might justly be opposed, if not preferred, to the *Latin* of *Phaedrus*. There's a whole Fable of his yet preserved at the end of *Gabrias*, of the *Swallow and the Nightingale*. *Suidas* brings many Citations out of him; all which shew him an excellent Poet: as this of the *Sick Lion*,

(y)

——— (y) οἷά τις νόσῳ
Κάμνων ἐβέβλητ', ἐκ ἀληθὲς ἀσθμαίνων:

(y) *Suidas in Ἀσθμ.*

And that of the *Bore*,

Φρίξας ἢ χαίτην (z) ἔκθορε φωλάδος κοίλης:

(z) *Suidas in Ἔκθορε*

And a great many others.

VI. I need not mention the *Latin* Writers of the *Aesopean Fables*; *Phaedrus*, (a) *Julius Titianus*, and *Avienus*; the two first in Iambic, the last in Elegiac: but I shall proceed to examine those *Greek* ones now extant, that assume the name of *Aesop* himself. There are two Parcels of the present *Fables*; the one, which are the more ancient, CXXXVI, in number, were first publisht out of the *Heidelberg* Library, by *Neveletus*, A.D. MDCX. The Editor himself well observed; That they were falsly ascribed to *Aesop*, because they (b) mention Holy Monks. To which I will add another Remark; That there is a Sentence out of *Job*, (c) Γυμνοὶ γὰρ ἤλθομεν οἱ πάντες, γυμνοὶ ἓν ἀπελευσόμεθα; *Naked we all came, and naked shall we return.* But because these two Passages are in the *Epimythion*, and belong not to the Fable it self; they may justly be supposed to be Additions only, and Interpolations of the true Book. I shall therefore give some better Reasons, to prove they are a recent Work. That they cannot be *Aesop*'s own, the CLXXXI Fable

(a) *Ausonius*, Ep. XVI.

(b) Φιλερήμοις κ/τ/ θεὸν Μοναχοῖς, Fab. 152.
(c) See Fab 288.
Job 1 21.

Fable is a demonstrative proof. For that is a Story of *Demades* the Rhetor, who lived above CC years after our *Phrygian*'s time. The CXCIII is, about *Momus*'s Carping at the Works of the Gods. There he finds this Fault in the Bull *That his Eyes were not placed in his Horns, so as he might see where he pusht*. But (d) *Lucian* (speaking of the same Fable) has it thus; *That his Horns were not placed right before his Eyes*. And (e) *Aristotle* has it a third way; *That his Horns were not placed about his Shoulders, where he might make the strongest push; but in the tenderest part, his Head*. Again, *Momus* blames this in the Man; *that his* Φρένες *did not hang on the out-side of him, so as his Thoughts might be seen*: but in (f) *Lucian*, the fault is; *That he had not a Window in his Breast*. I think it probable from hence, that *Aesop* did not write a Book of his Fables: for then there would not have been such a difference in the telling. Or, at least, if these that are now extant were *Aesop*'s; I should guess from this Specimen, that *Lucian* had the better on't, and beat him at his own play.

(d) *In Nigrino.*
(e) *De Part. Anim.* l. iii. p. 54
(f) *In Hermotimo.*

VII. But that they are recenter than even *Babrius*, who is himself one of the latest Age of good Writers, I discovered by this means. I observed in 'em several Passages, that were not of a piece with the rest; but had a turn and composition plainly Poetical: as in the CCLXIII.

CCLXIII Fable, which begins thus; Ὄνος πατήσας σκόλοπα χωλὸς ἑστήκει. This, I saw, was a Choliambic Verse; and I presently suspected, that the Writer had taken it out of *Babrius*. And I was soon confirmed in my Judgment by this (g) Fragment of his, that belongs to the same Fable:

(g) *Suidas in* Κνηκίας

Ὁ δ' ἐκλυθεὶς πόνων τε καὶ νίας πάσης,
Τὸν κνηκίαν χάσκοντα λακτίσας φεύγει.

For in the Fable in Prose there are these words; Ὁ ὄνος ἢ ΛΥΘΕΙΣ ΤΟΥ ΠΟΝΟΥ, ἐπὶ τ̕ λύκον ΧΑΣΚΟΝΤΑ ΛΑΚΤΙΣΑΣ ΦΕΥΓΕΙ. Whence it evidently appears, that the Author of that Parcel, which was published by *Neveletus*, did nothing else but epitomize *Babrius*, and put him into Prose. But I will give you some further Proofs of it. The CCLXI begins thus; Ὄνῳ τις ἐπιθεὶς ξόανον ἦγε. Which, at the first reading, one perceives to be part of a Scazon: And thus it is in a (h) Fragment of *Babrius*:

(h) *Suidas in* Κωμῇ

Ὄνῳ τις ἐπιθεὶς ξόανον εἶχε κωμήτης.

In the CLVI, about the *Fox* with the *Firebrand*; Ταύτην ἢ δαίμων εἰς τὰς ἀρούρας τοῦ βαλόντος ὡδήγει. Who does not discover here a Scazon of *Babrius*?

Εἰς

Εἰς τὰς ἀρέρας τε͂ βαλόντος ὡδήγει.

The CCXLIII is a manifest turning out of Choliambics into Prose; for the whole is made up either of Pieces or entire Verses:

―――ἡλίε πλέον λάμπει.

And,
Ἀνέμων δ' συρρεύσαντες, οὐδεὶς ἐσβέσθη.

And,
Ἐκ δευτέρε δ' ἅπλων τις ―――

And,
―――φαῖνε λύχνε κὴ σίγα,
Τῶν ἀςέρων τὸ φέγγος ὅπωτ' ἐκλείπει.

In the CCXCIII, there are these Remnants of *Babrius*:

Πόση γδ ὁλκῆ τ' ἔμον αἷμα προδήσῃ.

And,
Ἔςαι μάγειρος, ὅς με συντόμως δύσει.

And,
――― κὴ πάλιν κερεῖ με, κὴ σώσει.

The CLXV begins thus; Ἀνὴρ μεσοπόλιος δύο ἐρωμθίας εἶχεν· ὧν ἡ μψὺ μία νεᾶνις, ἡ δ' ἄλλη

ἄλλη πρεσβῦτις: which I suppose to have been in *Babrius* thus:

Ἀνὴρ μεσοπολιὸς δὔ ἐρωμένας εἶχεν,
Ὧν ἡ μία νεᾶνις, ἡ δὲ πρεσβῦτις.

Or, Ὧν ἡ μὲν ἦν ν:

In all these Passages here are most visible footsteps by which we may trace our Imitator: but generally he has so disguised the Fables, that no body can find they ever belong'd to *Babrius*. In the CCXLV, about the Priests of *Cybele*, there's nothing but a short dry Story, and no Reliques of a Verse. But there's a noble Fragment of *Babrius* belonging to the same Fable, which I will here set down, both to correct it, (for he that hath given it us, (1) has printed it false, and to shew you how much we have lost:

(1) Natal Com l IX c 5

Τά᾽ ιοις ἀγύρταις εἰς τὸ κοινὸν ἐπεράθη
Ὄντος τις ἐκ εὖ μοιρος, ἀλλὰ δυσδαίμων
Οἷς φέρη πτωχοῖσι κὴ πανέργοισι
Πείνης ἄκος δίψης τε, κὴ κακῶν τέχνην.
Οὗτοι ᾗ κύκλῳ πᾶσαν ἐξ ἔθος κώμην
Περιίοντες ἐλέγοντο· τίς γὰρ ἀγροίκων
Οὐκ οἶδεν Ἄτλιν λόυκὸν, ὡς ἐπηρώθη;
Τίς ἐκ ἀπαρχαῖς ὀσπρίων τε κὴ σίτων
Αἰνῷ φέρων δίδωσι τυμπάνῳ Ῥείης:

VIII. Thus I have proved one Half of the *Fables* now extant, that carry the name of *Aesop*, to be above a Thousand Years more

recent

recent than He. And the other Half, that were public before *Neveletus*, will be found to be yet more modern, and the latest of all. That they are not from *Aesop*'s own Hand, we may know from the LXX, *Of the Serpent and the Crab-fish*: which is taken from a *Scolion* or Catch, much older than *Aesop*, that is extant in (*k*) *Athenaeus*, and must be corrected thus: (*k*) Lib. xv. c. 15.

Ὁ καρκίνος ὧδε ἔφα, χαλᾷ τ̓ ὄφιν λαβών·
Εὐθὺν χρὴ ἕταρον ἔμμην, κὴ μὴ σκολιὰ φρονεῖν.

And there is great reason to believe, that they were drawn up by *Planudes*, one of the Later *Greeks*, that translated into his Native Tongue *Ovid's Metamorphoses*, *Cato's Distich's*, *Caesar's Commentaries*, and *Macrobius*. For there is no Manuscript any where above CCC Years old, that has the *Fables* according to that Copy. Besides that there are several Passages, that betray a Modern Writer; as in the LXXVII, Βέταλις, a *Bird*; and XXXIX, Βένδρον, a *Beast*; both unknown to all Ancient Authors: and in the CXXIX βοᾶν ἐν τῇ καρδίᾳ, *Crying in his Heart*, a manifest Hebraism, in imitation of *Ecclef.* xi. 1. εἶπον ἐν τῇ καρδίᾳ μου. The LXXV, about the *Aethiopian*, is taken almost word for word out of the VI of *Apthonius* the Rhetorician; who made an Essay upon some *Aesopic Fables*, that is yet extant.

tant. The IV, as appears from the last Sentence of it, is a Paraphrase on the CCLXXXIV of *Neveletus*'s Parcel; which Parcel, as I have proved above, are a Traduction of *Babrius*: and particularly in this very Fable there are Footsteps of his Verses;

——— κατῆλθεν εἰς βαθὺν κρημνόν.

And,

——— μετενδει, κ βοηδὸν ἐζήτει.

This Collection therefore is more recent than that Other; and coming first abroad with *Aesop's Life*, writ by *Planudes*, 'tis justly believed to be owing to the same Writer.

IX. That Idiot of a Monk has given us a Book, which he calls *The Life of Aesop*, that, perhaps, cannot be match'd in any Language, for Ignorance and Nonsense. He had pick'd up two or three true Stories, That *Aesop* was Slave to one *Xanthus*, (*l*) carried a Burthen of Bread, conversed with *Croesus*, and was put to death at *Delphi*: but the Circumstances of these, and all his other Tales, are pure Invention. He makes *Xanthus*, an ordinary *Lydian* or *Samian*, to be a (*m*) *Philosopher*: which word was not heard of in those days, but invented afterwards by *Pythagoras*. He makes him attended too, like *Plato* and *Aristotle*, by a Com-

(*l*) Eustath. in X Odyss. p. 785.

(*m*) Ξάνθος ὁ Φιλόσοφος

Company of Scholars, whom he calls Σχολαστικοί: tho' the word was not yet used in that sense, even in *Aristotle*'s time. 'Twas the (n) King of *Aethiopia*'s Problem to *Amasis* King of *Aegypt*, *To drink up the Sea:* but *Planudes* makes it a Wager of *Xanthus* with one of his Scholars. To say nothing of his Chronological Errors, Mistakes of a Hundred or Two Hundred Years: Who can read with any patience, that silly Discourse between *Xanthus* and his Man *Aesop*; not a bit better than our *Penny-Merriments*, printed at *London-Bridge*?

(n) Plutarch in Conviv.

X. But of all his Injuries to *Aesop*, that which can least be forgiven him, is, the making such a Monster of him for Ugliness: an Abuse, that has found credit so universally; that all the Modern Painters, since the time of *Planudes*, have drawn him in the worst Shapes and Features, that Fancy could invent. 'Twas an (o) old Tradition among the *Greeks*, That *Aesop* revived again, and lived a second Life. Should he revive once more, and see the Picture before the Book that carries his Name; could he think it drawn for Himself? or for the Monkey, or some strange Beast introduced in the *Fables*? But what Revelation had this Monk about *Aesop*'s Deformity? For he must learn it by Dream and Vision, and not by ordinary Methods of Knowledge. He Liv'd (p) about Two thousand Years after him: and in all that tract

(o) Suidas in Αἴσ & Ἀραβιῶναι Schol Aristoph. p 357, & 387.

(p) A D Mcccclxx

of time, there's not one single Author that has given the least hint, that *Aesop* was ugly. What credit then can be given to an ignorant Monk, that broaches a new Story after so many Ages? In *Plutarch*'s *Convivium* our *Aesop* is one of the Guests with *Solon* and the other Sages of *Greece*: there is abundance of Jest and Raillery there among them: and particularly upon *Aesop*: but no body drolls upon his ugly Face; which could hardly have escaped, had he had such a bad one. Perhaps you'll say, it had been rude and indecent, to touch upon a natural Imperfection. Not at all, if it had been done softly and jocosely. In *Plato*'s *Feast*, they are very merry upon *Socrates*'s Face, that resembled old *Silenus*: and in this, they twit *Aesop* for having been a Slave: which was no more his Fault, than Deformity would have been. *Philostratus* has given us, in Two Books, a Description of a Gallery of Pictures; (q) one of which is *Aesop* with a Chorus of Animals about him. There he is represented *smiling and looking towards the ground, in a posture of Thought*; but not a word of his Deformity; which, were it true, must needs have been touch'd on, in an account of a Picture. The *Athenians* set up a noble Statue to his Honour and Memory:

(q) P 735.

(r) *Aesopo*

(r) *Aesopo ingentem Statuam posuere Attici,*
Servumque collocarunt aeterna in basi;
Patere honoris scirent ut cuncti viam,
Nec generi tribui, sed virtuti gloriam.

(r) Phaedrus l. xi. ult.

But had he been such a Monster, as *Planudes* has made of him, a Statue had been no better than a Monument of his Ugliness: it had been kinder to his Memory, to have let that alone. But the famous *Lysippus* was the Statuary that made it. And must so great a Hand be employed to dress up a Lump of Deformity? *Agathias* the Poet has left us an (s) Epigram upon that Statue:

(s) Anthol. lib iv. Lis Φιλοσ.

Εὖγε ποιῶν, Λύσιππε γέρων, Σικυώνιε πλάστα,
Δείκελον Αἰσώπε ςήσαο τῶ Σαμίε, &c.

How could He too have omitted to speak of it, had his Ugliness been so notorious? The *Greeks* have several Proverbs about Persons deformed; Θερσίτειον βλέμμα, Εἰδεχθὴς Κορυδεύς, &c. Our *Aesop*, if so very ugly, had been in the first Rank of them; especially when his Statue had stood there, to put every body in mind of it. He was a great Favourite of *Croesus* King of *Lydia*; who employ'd him, as his Embassador to *Corinth* and *Delphi*. But would such a Monster, as *Planudes* has set out, be a fit Companion for a Prince? or a proper Embassador; to be hooted at by all the Boys, where-ever he came? *Plutarch* represents him as a polite and elegant Courtier; rebuking *Solon* for his gruff and clownish behaviour with *Croesus*; telling him, he must converse with Princes, (t) ἢ ὡς ἥδιστα, ἢ ὡς ἥκιστα, *either agreeably, or not at all.* Now, could either such a Station, or such a Discourse befit *Aesop*; if he was truly that Scare-crow, as he is now commonly Painted? But I wish I could do that Justice to the Memory of our *Phrygian*, to oblige the Painters to change their Pencil. For 'tis certain, he was no Deformed Person; and 'tis probable, he was very Handsom. For whether he was a *Phrygian*, or, as others say, a *Thracian*; he must have been sold into *Samos* by a Trader in *Slaves*. And 'tis well known, that that sort of People commonly bought up the most Beautiful they could light on; because they would yield the most Profit. And there is mention of two Slaves, Fellow-Servants together, *Aesop* and *Rhodopis* a Woman; and if we may guess him by his Companion and (u) *Contubernalis*, we must needs believe him a Comely Person. For (x) that *Rhodopis* was the greatest Beauty of all her Age: and even a Proverb arose in Memory of it;

Ἅπαιθ᾽ ἔμρια, ἢ Ῥοδῶπις ἡ καλή.

(t) Plut *in Solone*

(u) Plaut *XXXVI, 12*

(x) Herodotus Suidas. Strabo.

FINIS.

A DEFENSE OF THE REFLECTIONS UPON

Ancient and *Modern Learning*,

In Answer to the

OBJECTIONS OF

Sir *W. Temple*, and Others.

With OBSERVATIONS upon *The Tale of a Tub*.

LONDON:
Printed for *Tim. Goodwin*, at the *Queen's Head*, against St. *Dunstan's* Church in *Fleetstreet*. MDCCV.

A DEFENSE OF THE REFLECTIONS UPON *Ancient* and *Modern Learning*,

In Answer to the OBJECTIONS of Sir *W. Temple*, and Others.

To Anthony Hammond, *Esq;*

Honoured SIR,

WHEN I first began at your Desire to draw up my Thoughts concerning the comparative Extent and Excellency of the Learning of the Ancients and the Moderns, I did not imagine that what I intended to say upon that Subject, could have met with that Opposition which I found

I found it did. One would think that a Vindication of the Designs and Performances of the Age one lives in, should be grateful to every Man; especially to those who think they can do any Thing considerable, since upon this Foot all Parties should in all probability be pleased. Let Mens Studies lie which way they will, towards Divinity, Mathematic's, Philosophy, Philology, or Natural History, such a Design can only tend towards putting the World upon setting a due Value upon the Labors of these Men, especially if they be really excellent or useful. And he whose whole Aim is to lessen and disparage the Performances of Learned Men, ought, methink, so far to be looked upon as a Common Adversary. It is plain both by Sir *W. Temple's Essay*, and by his *Defense of that Essay*, that it was his Drift to represent Mankind, in these latter Ages, as languid and *effoete*, when compared with what it was 3 or 4000 Years ago. The Inventions and Discoveries of the present Age, especially by the *Men of Gresham*, have been treated with Contempt, and the value which has been put upon them, by truly Competent Judges, has been attributed by him to Pride and Ignorance. His Censure was manifestly rash, because in several Things he plainly shew'd that he understood nothing of the Matter. And his Quality and Wit did by

no

no means enable him to pass such a Judgment. I never thought my self tolerably qualified to make the due Comparison, I only pointed at some of the most considerable Things, thereby designing to assist those who were more unacquainted with the Question to make a general Judgment. I endeavoured likewise to write as decently towards Sir *W. Temple* as I could, since he was wholly a Stranger to me, and had very agreeably entertained the World with several ingenious Treatises. The Society which I principally had in my Eye to defend, whom he more than once contemptuously calls, *the Men of Gresham*, were many of them every way as considerable for Birth and Quality, for Parts and Wit as Sir *W. Temple* himself, and their Labors were what in Truth deserved the just Applauses of the Lovers of Learning and Religion; they having been, as they still are, so eminently serviceable to both. So that setting Sir. *W. T.* himself aside, from whom I did not expect any Commendation, I thought the rest of the Learned Men of this Age would not be ill pleased with my Design, how much soever they might be dissatisfied with the Performance.

I was surprized therefore to see Mr. *Keill* in his *Examination of Dr. Burnet's Theory*, fall so severely upon me in these words; " I wonder therefore why Mr. *Wotton* in
" his

"his Reflections upon Ancient and Modern
"Learning, should say, *That* Des Cartes
"*joined to his great Genius an exquisite Skill
"in Geometry; so that he wrought upon in-
"telligible Principles in an intelligible man-
"ner, tho' he very often failed of one Part
"of his End; namely, a right Explication
"of the Phaenomena of Nature; yet, by
"marrying Geometry and Physics together,
"he put the World in hopes of a Masculine
"Off-spring.* This, I think, is a clearer
"Demonstration than any in Des Cartes's
"Principles of Philosophy, that Mr. *Wot-
"ton* either understands no Geometry, or
"else *that he never read* Des Cartes's *Prin-
"ciples*; for from the beginning to the
"end of them, there is not one Demon-
"stration drawn from Geometry, or in-
"deed any Demonstration at all; except
"Mr. *Wotton* will say, that every Thing
"that is Illustrated by a Figure is a De-
"monstration, and then indeed he may
"produce enough of such Demonstrati-
"ons in his Philosophical *Works*. So far
"was *Des Cartes* from marrying Physics
"with Geometry, that it was his great
"Fault that he made 𝖓𝖔 𝖚𝖘𝖊 𝖆𝖙 𝖆𝖑𝖑 𝖔𝖋
"𝕲𝖊𝖔𝖒𝖊𝖙𝖗𝖞 𝖎𝖓 𝕻𝖍𝖎𝖑𝖔𝖘𝖔𝖕𝖍𝖞." (b) For
had I made a Mistake, and had *Des Cartes*
never joined Mathematics and Philosophy
together, yet still, since Mr. *Keill* sets up
for Skill in those Parts of Learning particularly,

(b) *Exa-
minat of
Dr Bur-
net's Theo-
ry,* P. 14,
15.

cularly, whose Increases in this Age I chiefly contend for, I thought I might reasonably have look'd for fairer Quarter; and I could not forbear crying out, *Et Tu Brute,* when he fell upon me. But then one would certainly take it for granted, that this Great Mathematician should Accuse me of what he can prove me Guilty, and not Charge me with what he full well knows is **not** Deducible from my Words. He says *Des Cartes made no use at all of Geometry in Philosophy:* Let the Excellent Mr. *Halley,* now the worthy Professor of Geometry in *Oxford,* be Judge. In the *Paper concerning Optics,* which he did me the Honor to Communicate to me, he has these words; " As to *Dioptrics,* tho' some " of the Ancients mention *Refraction,* as " a Natural Effect of *Transparent Media;* " yet *Des Cartes* was the **first**, who in " this Age has **Discovered the Laws of** " **Refraction, and brought Dioptrics** " **to a Science.**" (c) The Question is not whether *Des Cartes* demonstrates every Thing in his *Principles,* but whether he found out any thing in Natural Philosophy, by the help of Geometry. This Mr. *Halley* averrs he did in his *Dioptrics,* and I never said he did it in his *Principles:* So that when Mr. *Keill* falls upon me on the Account of *Des Cartes's Principles,* he shews himself to be but an indifferent Logician, by

(c) *Vide Supra* Reflex. p. 306.

by putting into his Conclusion what he did not find in his Premises: For I am sure he will not deny *Dioptrics* to be a very Noble Part of Philosophy.

Having said thus much in Vindication of my self, I think I am bound to say something too in Vindication of my most Learned Friend Dr. *Bentley*, who has suffered for being Engaged in a Controversy, into which I at first drew him. Mr. *Keill* in the first Place accuses him for Asserting, that *tho' the Axis of the Earth were Perpendicular to the Plane of the Ecliptic, yet take the* whole Year about, *we* should have the same Measure of *Heat* as *we* have now: WE, *i. e. The Inhabitants of the Temperate Zone.* Whereas it is certain, that if the *Sun* had moved continually in the Aequator, these Temperate Regions of the Earth would not, take the whole Year about, have had so much Heat as they have now. Now this is all a Cavil upon the word WE: Dr. *Bentley* means the Inhabitants of the whole Globe; not *Englishmen*, *Frenchmen*, or *Germans*, in opposition to the Inhabitants of *Guinea*, *Persia*, or the *East-Indies:* He is there speaking of the whole Race of Mankind, and in their Names setting forth the Praises of our Great Creator, who in every Thing has considered what was best for us; and by a long Induction of Particulars, shewing that Meliority in abundance of
In-

Inſtances. And if the WE be taken of Mankind in general, diſperſed over the greateſt part of the Terreſtrial Globe, Dr. *Bentley*'s Propoſition is ſtrictly true; and therefore to prevent all future Cavils or Miſinterpretations, he has put *the Earth* inſtead of *We* in the Edition of his Sermons which he put out in 1699, (*d*).

(*d*) In the firſt Edition of 1693, it is thus; " Tho' the Axis then had been Perpen-" dicular, yet take the whole Year about, and WE ſhould have " had the ſame Meaſure of Heat, that WE have now." *Bentley*'s *Conf of Atheiſm from Origin and Frame of World*, Part. III Pag 23. In the Edition of 1699, it is alter'd thus; " Tho' the Axis then " had been Perpendicular, yet take the whole Year about, and " THE EARTH would have had the ſame Meaſure of Heat " that IT has now, *Ibid.* Pag. 259

The next Thing for which he accuſes Dr. *Bentley*, is his Aſſerting, *That 'tis Matter of Fact and Experience, that the Moon always ſhews the ſame Face to us, not once wheeling about her own Center*, (*e*). " Whereas, (ſays Mr. *Keill*,) 'tis evident to any " one who thinks, that the Moon ſhews " the ſame Face to us, for this very Rea-" ſon, becauſe ſhe does turn once in the " Time of her Period, about her own " Center." (*f*) This is ſo heavy a Crime in Dr. *Bentley*, that Mr. *Keill* cannot forbear Crying out with great Concern, " That it were to be wiſhed, that Great " Critics would confine their Labors to " their Lexicons, and not venture to Gueſs " in thoſe Parts of Learning which are
" capable

(*e*) *Examinat of Dr.* Burnet's *Theory*, Pag 70.

(*f*) Ibid

(g) Ibid. "capable of Demonstration." (g) I am sure *it were to be wished,* that Men that endeavour to deserve well of Religion and Learning, might be treated with Candor and Decency by other Men, who themselves are Men of Merit. Mr. *Keill*'s Physical Lectures shew him to be both willing to do, and capable of doing good Service to Learning, in that Noble University where he lives: And for that Reason, I shall overlook his Usage of Dr. *Bentley* and of my self. As he grows older he will grow wiser, and not run a-muck at Men that never provoked him, nor go out of his way to vilifie and lessen their Reputations.

In the Case before us, he knows that Sir *Isaac Newton* was the first Man that made that Inference from the Moon's shewing the same Face to us, that Mr. *Keill* has done; namely, that therefore she turns about her Axis, and that the Time of one Rotation is equal to the Period of her Motion round the Earth. Nay, Mr. *Mercator*, who gave the first hint of this *proper diurnal Rotation of the Moon,* in his Astronomy which he Publisht in 1676, declares in so many words, that he had it from Sir *Isaac Newton,* who afterwards Published it himself, (and that too just as a Hint in a Line or two) in his own Famous Book which came out in 1687. You will be surprized, Sir,

if

if I should tell you that I have heard it very credibly related, that this Notion of a *Diurnal Rotation of the Moon about its own Axis*, was so new and strange to Dr. *Wallis*, that he never could rightly apprehend nor embrace it; and long after Mr. *Newton*'s Book came out, he speaks of it as if he could not digest it. (*h*) Dr. *Bentley* therefore spake the Language of all the Astronomers before Sir *Isaac Newton*: So that it was *not so evident to any one that Thought, that the Moon shews the same Face to us for that very Reason, because she does turn once in the Time of her Period about her own Center*; since, it seems, many Men that *Thought* in their Generations, never found it out. Dr. *Bentley* has shewn that he will not persist in an Error; for in the Edition of that Sermon in 1699, he has left out the words, *not once wheeling about her Center*. It is no want of Judgment, not to know all Sir *Isaac Newton*'s Discoveries; especially when they come in by the bye, and are so thick crouded as they are in his Incomparable Book. But it is something which deserves a severer Name than I give to it, to Insult a Learned Man for not knowing an Astronomical Discovery which

(*h*) *Jam vero, quod & Telluri competat hujusmodi circa suum Axem Conversio (qui & Lunam circumferre apta sit) ex ipsius Motu Diurno Constat Nec minus certum videtur, hujusmodi Motum Lunae non competere, cum semper eadem Lunae facies nos respiciat. Quod fieri non posset si Luna Terram circumferret; ni si forsan diceretur, eadem plane Temporis Periodo Terram circumferre, qua circa suum Axem ipsa vertitur, contra quam in reliquis fit* Wallisius de Aestu Maris, Pag 743. Edit Oxon, 1693

Dr. *Wallis* could never give a full assent to. And before I leave Mr. *Keill*, I shall take the Freedom to tell him, that Dr. *Bentley* may, Mr. *Keill* himself being Judge, be *allowed to leave his* Lexicons, *and venture to Reason in those parts of Learning which are capable of Demonstration*; since there is scarce one single Instance that Dr. *Bentley* had urged before of the *Wisdom of God in forming of the World, and of Human Bodies*, in his *Six last Discourses*, which Mr. *Keill*'s Countreyman, Dr. *Cheyne*, has not urged in the same way, and drawn the same Conclusions from them, that Dr. *Bentley* had done so long before. (*h*) Dr. *Cheyne*'s Authority will pass with Mr. *Keill*, because his Book was approved by Dr. *Freind* of *Christchurch*, and by two excellent Mathematicians, my very worthy Friends, Dr. *Arbuthnott*, and Mr. *Craig*: This is what I thought necessary to say to Mr. *Keill*, who sees that I have not gone one Step out of my way to reckon with him.

(*h*) See Dr *Cheyne's Philosophical Principles of Natural Religion*: London. 1705

Some time after this Admonition from Mr. *Keill*, I receiv'd several from the Noble *Examiner of Dr. Bentley's Dissertation upon the Epistles* which go abroad under the Name of *Phalaris*. One of them is concerning a Grammatical Observation of mine about *Delphi* and *Delphos*, which that Noble Author has with *greater plainness of Speech*, than any of mine towards Sir *W. Temple*

Temple, chastized me for; asserting that *Delphos* was more analogous to the Genius of our Tongue than *Delphi*. What Dr. *Bentley* has said in my Defence, is unanswerable; to which I shall only add, That Mr. *Moile*, a Gentleman of great Learning and Politeness in his Translation of *Xenophon*'s Περὶ, or *of the Improvement of the Revenue of the State of* Athens, which came out after the first Edition of the *Reflexions*, always says *Delphi*, and not *Delphos*. So does my excellent Friend Mr. *Jenkin*, in his *Reasonableness of Christianity*; and which is incomparably more to my present purpose, so did the very Learned Dr. *Gale*, late Dean of *York*, in one of his Sermons (*k*) which was printed after the *Noble Examiner's* Book came out: To which Book there is reason to believe Dr. *Gale* was by no means a Stranger. (*l*) As far as an Argument can be *ad hominem*, Dr. *Gale*'s Authority is here decisive. To you and me, Sir, Mr. *Stanley*'s Authority is so, who, as Dr. *Bentley* has observed already, constantly says, *Delphi* in his *Lives of the Philosophers*, as did

(*k*) Serm. III. p. 19.

(*l*) I am glad of this Opportunity of mentioning the Worthy Dean of *York*, and of paying my Public Acknowledgments to him for the particular Kindness and Favours I receiv'd from him, while I was under his Care. The Foundation of all the little Knowlege I have in these Matters, was laid by him, which I gratefully own: for I think my self obliged to let the World know whom I have been beholden to. Boile *Examen of Dr. Bentley's Dissertation upon the Epistles of* Phalaris; *pag.* 59, 60.

our dear Friend, your Kinsman, Mr. *Tho. Stanley* his Son, in his *Translation of* Aelian's *Various History.* The Truth is, in Words of daily use, which we have from the Common People, the Construction and Analogy, as we have received it from them, must be followed. They gave us those Words, and we must take them as they have given them; but in Words which Learned Men first introduced, which they chiefly have occasion to use, it is inexcusable to pretend Custom is to be follow'd, when the Analogy of a Language is manifestly violated. If therefore a Learned Man has ever used such a Word wrong, he has nothing to do but to mend the Fault, when once he is made acquainted with it.

This therefore is the true Reason why I did not strike out this *Remark*, when I *purged the Reflexions* from the other *unbecoming Passages*, as the *Noble Examiner* calls them. (*m*) Had I struck it out, I had owned my self mistaken in the Observation, which I can by no means do.

(*m*) This Digression might have been spared, but that Mr. *Wotton*, when he was purging his Book of some unbecoming Passages, in a second Edition of it, thought fit still to retain this Grammatical Reflection there: Perhaps in a Third Edition he'll take care that this too shall bear the rest Company. *Id. ibid. page* 97.

Another Admonition I have also received from the same Noble Author, in the Foundation

dation of which I must say, I think he is mistaken. When he is giving Dr. *Bentley* some Plain Advice about coining of new Words, and tells him, That that *is the Work of great Masters, and a Privilege allowed only to Writers of the first Rate, who know the compass of a Language, and see through all its several Beauties and Blemishes*; He adds, *Sir* W. Temple *may say sufficiency, and the World will speak after him.* (n) 'Tis plain, by these Words, that this Noble Author thought I had tacitly reproved Sir *W. Temple* for making a new Word, or using an old one, at least, in a wrong Sense. Now I had never blamed Sir *W. Temple* for coining that Word, and had I done so, I had been my self in fault; since I knew, that Mr. *Hobbes* had used it, in a not much unlike Sense, long before, in his *Leviathan* (o). And after all, how *great a Master* soever Sir *W. Temple* may be thought to be, there are a great many Words and *Phrases* which he uses, that in all probability will not be commonly received among us in haste: *Rapport* for *Proportion*; *Defense of Commerse* for *Prohibition of Trade*; *Surintendance* for *Superintendence*; and very many such sort of Expressions, especially in his *Memoirs* and *Letters*, are purely *French*, and not yet naturalized among us.

(n) *Id. ibid* pag. 286.

(o) Part I. cap. 11. pag. 49. Edit. 1651. His words are these, *Vain-glorious Men, such as without being conscious to themselves of great* Sufficiency, *delight in* And

supposing themselves Gallant Men, are enclined only to Ostentation And again in the Margen, *Ambition from Opinion of* Sufficiency. It is

These

plain from hence, that Mr *Hobbes* takes *Sufficiency* for an Opinion of ones own Ability's *right or wrong*. For Mr. *Hobbes* never looked upon *Ambition* to be a *Vice*. Sir *W. Temple* always takes it in an evil Sense, for *Vanity* and *Presumption*, which are Senses which the *French Academy* in their *Dictionary* put upon *Suffisance*, from whence Mr. *Hobbes* seems to have taken it.

These are the chief Exceptions which have been occasionally made to what I have said. Had not Sir *W. Temple* left a *Defense of his Essay* behind him, I should have said nothing to them; but since Dr. *Swift* has thought fit to publish that Sketch of an Answer, I looked upon my self as obliged to say something in Defense of what I had formerly written upon this Argument.

Dr. *Swift* in his Preface to the *Third Vol.* of Sir *W. Temple's Miscellanea*, says, *That for the Paper relating to the Controversie about Ancient and Modern Learning, he cannot well inform the Reader upon what Occasion it was writ, having been at that time in another Kingdom.* This is an odd Passage; because both his own Brother, who lived at that Time near Sir *W. Temple*, and was a great Admirer of that Gentleman, who was his Patron, could have certainly informed him of the true Reason why it was written, which also we may reasonably suppose he did; and also because he might by reading of it, plainly see that it was designed for an Answer to some Book or other; which therefore every Prudent Editor should for his Author's sake have consulted; and after that

that have taken Measures whether to publish it or no; and if Orders had been particularly left, that such a Discourse should be published right or wrong, then some way or other to have let the World know it. For otherwise an Editor may either hurt the Reputation of him whose Posthumous Discourses he undertakes to publish, or his own. This, however, I think may certainly be inferred, that Dr. *Swift* had no mind to defend that Paper, and thought it best by such a Declaration, to insinuate, that he was willing to have it shift for it self. So that I think I may build upon his Judgment, that this Paper of Sir *W. Temple's* is by no means an Answer to the *Reflexions*. So much for the *Editor's Preface:* I come now to the Discourse it self.

This *Paper* begins with *Three Reasons* why Sir *W. Temple* took a New *Survey of his Essay concerning Ancient and Modern Learning.* I. *The Common Interest of Learning in general, and particularly in our Universities; and to prevent the Discouragement of Scholars in all Degrees, from reading the Ancient Authors, who must be acknowledged to have been the Foundation of all Modern Learning, whatever the Superstructures may have been.* This does not at all relate to me. It is the very first Reason which I gave in the Preface of the Reflexions, why they were at first written. There is no Question but if the Youth in our Universities should once leave off the Study of the Ancients, Learning would quickly sink: Infinite Mistakes would be perpetually committed, and those great and noble Parts of Knowledge in which they indisputably excelled, would remain uncultivated. II. *A just Indignation at the Insolence of the Modern Advocates, in defaming those Heroes among the Ancients, whose Memory has been sacred and admired for so many Ages, as* Homer, Virgil, Pythagoras, Democritus, *&c.* It was a like *Indignation at the same Insolence* that induced him to write his First Essay. A good deal of this likewise does not belong to me. *Homer* and *Virgil* were, as they ought, always treated honourably; concerning my Usage of *Pythagoras* and *Democritus* I shall speak hereafter. III. *To vindicate the Credit of our Nation, as others have done that of the* French, *from the Imputation of this Injustice and Presumption that the Modern Advocates have used in this Case.* (p) If what I have said be right, I have been guilty of no Injustice; and how small soever my Quality is, it is no Presumption to attaque Propositions in Print, let who will lay them down. We have seen Superiors treated by their immediate Inferiors, to whom by the Laws of God and Man they ow'd a Reverence, with *great plainness of Speech*; and yet these Inferiors did not take themselves to be in fault,

but

(p) Temple's *Miscellanea*, 3d Part, pag 204, 205.

but affirmed that it was their Duty to admonish their Superiors freely from the Press, when they could come at them no other way. However justifiable this Practice may be in Matters relating to Religion and Government, let others dispute; it is certainly justifiable in Matters of Learning: No Man there has a right to use another ill; he may expose his Errors, but then it ought to be with a regard to his Person. And in the Case before us, with a very true Esteem for the *Minister of State*, and *the Bel Esprit*, I only disputed against the Author of the *Miscellanea*, and even there when I saw some Personal Reflexions had unawares crept into the First Edition, I voluntarily, and not admonished from the Press, struck them out in my Second. This Dr. *Swift* should have weighed before he had publish'd this Paper; he would then have seen it was a regard to Sir *W. Temple*, that made me strike out what I had said about *the Sergian Monk*, about Sir W. Temple's *omitting* Moses *and* Jesus Christ, when he mentioned the Famous Legislators of Antiquity, in his Essay *upon Heroic Virtue*, and the *Hint about Prince* Maurice's *Parrot*. And though Sir *W. Temple* had in the Interval between the *First* and *Second* Editions of the *Reflexions*, published his Introduction to the *History* of *England*, yet I said nothing of the strange Mistakes therein committed. I did not
mention

mention his *Aethelbert* King of the *South-Saxons*, to whom *Augustine* the Monk was sent by Pope *Boniface* to convert our Forefathers to Christianity; tho' every body knows that *Aethelbert* was only King of *Kent*, and that it was *Gregory* the Great who sent *Augustine* into *England*. These Things Dr. *Swift* should have informed himself about, and not in a Controversie purely literary, sent Papers into the World concerning Matters wherein Sir *W. Temple* seems not to have been a Competent Judge. And therefore those that stand up for the Honor of the present Age, have reason to complain that they are call'd *Young Barbarous Goths and Vandals*, (q) when they, backed by Antiquity, speak impartially of some of the Ancients. Why should it be call'd Injustice and Presumption, (r) and where is the Wit in saying that Men know the *Seven Sages*, *and the Seven Wise Men of Gotham alike*; (s) when out of *Diogenes*, *Censorinus*, and *Pliny*, and other Celebrated Writers of Antiquity, they endeavour to set the Peformances of the Ancient Philosophers in their true Light? My Arguments stand as they did in the *Reflexions*, and they are not weakened by the Negative Assertions of Sir *W. Temple*, who whenever he is prest, talks of *Conquests of Barbarous Nations*, *great Plagues, and great Inundations,*; (t) by which he thinks he has *demonstrated* in his

First

(q) Ibid pag 204

(r) P. 205.

(s) P. 222.

(t) P. 234.

First Essay, *how all the Traces and Memorials of Learning and Story may be lost in a Nation.* What is this to the purpose? If the *Traces and Memorials of Learning and Story* are lost, Sir *W. Temple* talks in the dark about what was formerly. His Schemes are then, for ought he knows, imaginary; and his Negations do not disprove one positive Argument which was brought to determine the Comparative Excellency and Extent of the Knowlege of our Forefathers and our selves. I allow from the Testimonies of Antiquity, that *Pythagoras* was a wise Law-giver, that he found out the XLVIIth Proposition of the First Book of *Euclid*, and I give Reasons why we may justly suppose him to have been well versed in Arithmetical Speculations. One would think this had been enough; of this we have certain Proofs; when Sir *W. Temple's* Friends can shew from proper Evidences that the Knowledge of *Pythagoras* in Physic's and Mathematic's was *in its self greater* than that of the Moderns, I shall acquiesce; in the mean time I must believe that *Archimedes* and *Apollonius*, and *Conon*, and *Diophantus* were incomparably better Mathematicians than he. Upon the same Grounds I must believe Sir *Isaac Newton*, and Dr. *Gregory* to know vastly more of the System of the Heavens, and of the Operations of Heavenly Bodies one upon another, of the Periodical

riodical Times in which the Planets of our System move, with their Distances from the Sun, of the Laws of Attraction by which those Times are fixed, of the Quantity of Matter of these mighty Bodies, and of many other amazing Theorems of this sort, than *Hipparchus* or *Ptolemee*. It is imposing upon Mens Understandings (which sometimes indeed arises from being imposed upon first ones self) to cry up *Thales* as a First Rate Mathematician, when one of the chiefest Things that is recorded of him in this way, is, that he first calculated Eclipses among the *Greeks*. Astronomy then must have been in its Infancy; yet what he did was wonderful at that Time, and deserves great praise. The *Chaldaeans* we know did not believe the Moon to have been an Opake Body; (*u*) and Mr. *Halley*, who is a competent Judge, says, There was nothing done by the *Chaldaeans* in Astronomy older than about 400 Years before the Conquest of *Alexander*, *i. e.* within that Period, which, after *Herodotus*, who is the oldest *Greek* Historian, I set for the Rise of the *Assyrian* Monarchy, and about 100 Years before the

(*u*) "Berosus qui a Chaldaeorum Civitate sive Natione progressus in Asia etiam Disciplinam patefecit, ita est profcssus, Pilam esse ex dimidiâ parte candentem, reliqua habere caeruleo colore. Cum autem cursum Itineris sui pergens subiret orbem Solis, tunc eam Radiis, & Impetu Caloris corripi, convertiq; candentem, propter ejus proprietatem Luminis ad Lumen" Vitruvius Lib. IX. cap. 4. This whole Passage is quite misunderstood by the *French* Translator Mr. *Claude Perault*.

Time

Time when *Thales* lived in the *Lesser Asia*. But as far as Sir *W. Temple* is concerned in this Controversy, I must declare that I except against him as an Incompetent Judge, since he excepts against the *Doctrine of the Circulation of the Blood*, as not true, because *Sense can very hardly allow it; which*, says he, *in this Dispute must be satisfied as well as Reason, before Mankind will concurr* (w). One would think, when he was abroad, he had conversed with none but *Spaniards*, who, 'tis said, do scarce even at this Day believe it.

(w) Essay of Ancient and Modern Learning, *pag.* 44, 45.

But he that will answer Sir *W. Temple*, must go along with him in his Way; and therefore when he has no Arguments, he recurrs to Surmizes. Something must be said to his *Plagues* and *Floods*, and *Conquests by Barbarous Nations*, which have brought Learning to the pass in which we now see it. Very well, let us set it upon this Foot. The oldest and the biggest Flood that ever was, was that in the Time of *Noah*: We know now from Philosophical Principles, that either that Flood was wholly miraculous, or depended upon Causes foreign to this of our Earth; yet as general as it was, there were Men enough preserved to inform us that the Use of Iron and Copper, of Musical Instruments, and of Agriculture was known before. So that even in that Case which we are sure happen'd but once, *the Traces*

Traces and *Memorials* of the Heads of the Knowledge of the Ante-Diluvian World are preserved. Where ever was there a Plague which destroyed a whole People? If one City suffered, another escaped; and Inventions of General Use have never been lost, unless they have been superseded by others of the same Nature, which have done the Business better. Here again, Sir, I can only referr you to the *Preface* of the *Reflexions*, wherein this Question is at large Discussed.

In short, it is from what we *do know* of the *Chaldaean* and *Aegyptian* Knowledge, that we Argue to what we *do not*. Some Opinions, or Glimpses that Men once held such Opinions, are Demonstrations many times as well of their Ignorance, in those Sciences, as of their Knowledge. A long Induction of Particulars of this Nature, may be seen in the XVIIth XVIIIth and XIXth Chapters of the *Reflexions*, to which, Sir, I will beg leave to referr you. I use few or no Negative Arguments, in the whole Book, but argue from *positive Knowledge* to *positive Ignorance*. Mr. *Halley* distrusts the Tradition of *Callisthenes*'s bringing Astronomical Observations out of *Chaldaea* into *Greece*, above M^r CCC ears older than *Alexander*, Lec he proper Authors say nothing o have no Observations of t er than

than CCCC Years before that Prince's time: So that you see, Sir, there is a positive Argument upon which he builds, tho' it may look like a Negative one, (*x*). *(x)* Vide Supra Reflexions, Pag. 302.

This Negative way of Reasoning, which Sir *W. Temple* is so fond of, is so much the more suspicious, because he never uses it when he thinks he can help it. Where he has Room to Declaim, he does it plentifully. He thinks, when I speak of Eloquence, I talk very absurdly, and so he runs out thus; *Upon the Subject of Eloquence, they will have it, that* Padre Paola's *Council of* Trent, *and* Comines's *Memoirs, are equal to* Herodotus *and* Livy, *and so would* Strada *be too, if he were but Impartial,* (*y*). *This*, says he, *is very wonderful, if it be not a Jest.* It is one; but then the *Jest lies* in Asserting, that I set up *Comines* and F. *Paul* as Patterns of Eloquence, when I say the contrary: For after I had declared (and not unwillingly (*z*) I do assure you) that I thought the Prize of Eloquence belonged of Right to the Ancients, I then took notice of such Performances wherein *Oratory can only claim a share* (*a*), *and where Rhetorical Ornaments are only Secondary Beauties; without which, that Discourse wherein they are found may be justly valuable, and that in a very high degree.* (*b*) Can I then be said to affirm, that upon the Subject of Eloquence, *(y)* Defense of Essay, Pag. 250.

(z) Ibid Pag. 230.

(a) Vide Supra Reflex P. 41.

(b) Ibid. Pag. 37.

F. *Paul*

F. *Paul* and *Comines* are equal to *Herodotus* and *Livy*? No; F. *Paul* and *Comines* were pitched upon, becaufe Eloquence was the Talent of neither of them. *Fra. Fulgentio* the great Friend of F. *Paul*'s, who wrote his Life, fays, *He never profeft the Art of Speaking, nor had ever Studied it, but only fo far as was neceffary to exprefs his Thoughts*, (c): And this was fo well known at that time, that for that Reafon *John Baptifta Leoni*, who had formerly been Secretary to Cardinal *Commendone*, was order'd to draw up an Account of the Controverfy between the *Venetians* and Pope *Paul* the V. from the Minutes which F. *Paul* gave him in Writing. *Polybius* therefore was mentioned among the Ancients, as an Inftance that a Hiftory may be Incomparable, that has not Rhetorical Ornaments to fet it off. There lay the Strefs of the Argument: The Queftion was only concerning Greatnefs of Genius, proper to Execute Noble Performances; and therefore when Sir *W. Temple* had asked *whether D'Avila's and Strada's Hiftories be beyond thofe of* Herodotus *and* Livy (d), I named two Modern Hiftorians, F. *Paul* and *Philip Comines*, whom there I was only to confider as Hiftorians, and not at all as Orators. And the Queftion between us was not, *whether the Modern Hiftories abfolutely taken, Exceeded the Ancients*; but whether fome Moderns

(c) *Il Padre non hà mai fatto Profeffione di Lingua, nella quale non haveva mai fatto Studio, fe non per fervirfi all' Explicatione de' fuoi fenfi.* Vite del Padre Paolo, Pag 134

(d) *Effay*, Pag. 57

derns have not, (considering the Subjects they wrote upon) *Composed as Instructing Histories as any of the Ancients;* and whether the Subjects which some of these Modern Writers chose, did not require as great Men to manage them, and consequently whether the Dignity of those Subjects was not preserved in those Performances?

Now if it be a *Jest* in Sir *W. Temple*, to make me say what I did not, it is more so for him to deny Father *Paul's* to have been a *History*. F. *Paul's History of the Council of* Trent *is indeed no History of any great Action; but only an Account of a long and artificial Negotiation between the Court and Prelates of* Rome, *and those of other Christian Princes. So that I do not see how it can properly be stiled an History; the Subjects whereof are great Actions and Revolutions:* And by all the *Ancient Critics upon History,* the first part of the Excellence of an Historian, is the Choice of a Noble and Great Subject that may be worth his Pains (e). This is imposing upon his Readers: The Council of *Trent* not a *Noble and Great Subject!* When a Mighty Empire, far exceeding in Extent of Territory, and perhaps in Number of Subjects, any of the Four Ancient ones, was to Stand or Fall by what that Assembly did; When *Germany* and *France* struck at the Root of the Papacy; When not the Protestant Powers alone, which had

(e) *Defense of Essay,* Pag. 251.

made the Defection, but all the Obedient Kingdoms, *Spain* and *Portugal* alone excepted, were just shaking off the Papal Yoak; When a General Council, which was the chiefest Battery which the Protestants desired to have Play'd against the Supremacy of the Bishop of *Rome*, was employed against it for XL Years together; When after it had been put by for above Three Quarters of that Time, that at last the whole Force of it should be turned upon those that raised it, and so thereby the Power of the Popes of *Rome* to be secured, and settled upon a safer Bottom than it ever had before: These Things shew such a Depth of Contrivance, and such a Train of Refined Politics, that no Genius less than F. *Paul's* could have done Justice to his Argument, and acquainted us with the Springs of every Debate, and the Reasons of every Resolution. But there was no Fighting indeed, no Burning of Towns, and laying Wast whole Countreys, no knocking out of Mens Brains, in order to do them good, in F. *Paul's* History; all which I suppose are necessary to make up such a *Great and a Noble Subject, as may be worth the Pains of an Historian.*

For *Philip de Comines*, (says Sir *W. Temple*) *None ever called it a History; nor he himself other than Memoirs, nor does either the Subject deserve it, or the Author, who is valued*

valued only for his great Truth of Relation, and Simplicity of Stile, (f). Then *Caesar's Accounts of the* Gallic *and Civil-Wars,* are no Histories, because he calls them only *Comentaries.* I never knew a modest Title was a Prejudice to a Work before. Mr. *Locke* called his *Discourse upon Humane Understanding,* only an *Essay;* and yet the World has always esteemed it a very just Treatise upon that Subject. Some *Essays* indeed, have now and then appeared, which have not Merited a higher Title; so that it is not always a wrong way of Arguing from a *Title* to a Book. But the Subject of the *Memoirs of Philip de Comines* deserves no higher a Title. Be it so; *Thucydides* wrote the History of the *Peloponnesian* War, and thought so well of it, that he called it Κτῆμα ἐς ἀεί: *A neverfailing Possession.* And yet that was chiefly a Dispute between the Republics of *Athens* and *Lacedaemon,* which was Contested upon not much more Ground than the Kingdom of *France :* Whereas in the *Memoirs of Philip de Comines,* we have *France* and *England, Italy,* and the *Low-Countries,* (the Governors at least of all these Nations) concerned; every one of which Powers were severally as great, some much greater than *Athens* and *Sparta* were in *Thucydides's* Time. But *Comines* is not commended by

(f) Ibid. Pag. 251.

(g) Vide Supra Reflex P 39, 40.

me as an Orator, (g); (I say little more of him, than Sir *W. Temple* himself) no more is Cardinal *D' Ossat*; and yet his Letters are so Excellent in their kind, that we have nothing in Antiquity of that sort to oppose to them. I forgot to mention them before, which I am sorry for, because Sir *W. Temple* was a truly competent Judge of their Worth, they being an Account of one of the nicest Embassys to the most Politic Court in the World, that ever was sent from one Prince to another; that Cardinal and Cardinal *Perron* being employed by *Henry* IV. of *France*, to Negotiate his Reconciliation with the Pope, after he had declared himself a *Roman-Catholic*.

Having named *Thucidides* upon this Occasion, I can't without doing Injustice to my Argument, forbear mentioning my Lord *Clarendon's History of the late Rebellion*, which has lately seen the Light. That will be Κτῆμα ἐς ἀεί indeed, as the Publishers justly call it in the Title-Page. The Subject is every way as Great, the Events as Surprizing, and the Conclusion as Miraculous, as Sir *W. Temple* himself could have desired. Here is Fighting enough, (too much in Truth) for those that love it, and Negotiations abundance, for those that had rather read them. Great Examples of true Virtue; I would have said *Heroic*, (but

(h) Sir

(h) Sir *W. Temple* allows no *Virtue* to be (*except that is Unfortunate*) wonderful Fortitude shewn by Great Men under the greatest Sufferings; Mankind described under so many different Characters of Good and Evil Men, that one would hardly think it possible the Mind of Man should be capable of so much Variety, are every where to be met with in that Work; and all this with so much strength of Stile, and such a rich Copia of Words, that when the Prejudices of the present Age shall be worn off, and the Faction then raised be quite extinguished, I doubt not but *Dispassionate* Posterity (give me leave, Sir, to use a word which my Lord *Clarendon* seems to have been so fond of) will oppose it for Matter and Elocution, to the most Celebrated Performances of all Antiquity. But to return to Sir *W. Temple.*

[margin:] must be assisted by Fortune to preserve it to Maturity, because the Noblest Spirit or Genius in the World, if it falls, tho' never so bravely in its first Enterprizes, cannot deserve enough of Mankind to pretend to so great a Reward as the Esteem of Heroic Virtue. And yet perhaps many a Person has Died in the first Battle or Adventure he atchieved, and lies buried in Silence and Oblivion; who, had he outlived as many Dangers as *Alexander* did, might have shined as bright in Honor and Fame. *Essay upon Heroic Virtue,* Pag. 146, 147.

He spends next a good deal of Time in Declaiming against me for bringing *Chymistry, Philology,* and *Divinity,* into the Number of *Sciences.* (i) The First of these I was so far from reckoning among the Sciences, that I expresly call it only an Instrument by which Sciences have been Advanced

(i) *Defense of Essay,* P 252, &c.

vanced (*k*), and the Stock of Knowledge Enlarged; which no Man will deny to have been done by its Means: And what he says about *Philology, Criticism* and *Divinity*, is not at all to his purpose. The Question which I labour to Discuss, is, *Who knew most, the Ancients or Moderns?* (*l*) and I there particularly separate this Question from that which Sir *W. Temple* had put, *Who were the greatest Men, the Ancients, or the Men of these latter Ages?* This naturally led me into an Enquiry about the whole Compass of Knowledge of any sort; And as ludicrously as Sir *W. Temple* is pleased to describe it, I had an Example before me, of a Learned Man, who upon the same Subject had long ago done the very same Thing. In the Year MDCXX, *Alessandro Tassoni*, a Learned *Modenese*, Published his *Pensieri Diversi*; which are *Miscellaneous Discourses* upon all manner of Subjects, after the manner of *Pasquiers Recherches*, or rather of *A. Gellius*'s *Noctes Atticae*; a Work exceedingly admired in *Italy*, and there several times Reprinted. One whole Book of the Ten, into which his Work is divided, is upon this very Subject, and the Introductory Chapter has this Title, *Whether in Sciences and Arts, the Ancients have shew'd a greater Genius than the Moderns* (*m*)?

(*k*) *Reflex.* Pag. 172, 173

(*l*) Ibid. Pag. 7.

(*m*) *Se nelle Dottrine, e nell' Arti gli Antichi prevalessero d' Ingegno a i Moderni.* Tassoni Pens. Divers. Lib x Cap 1

And

And after he has divided his Heads of Enquiry into Three Parts, *Contemplation, Action*, and *Manufacture*, he Discourses upon these following Particulars, Grammar, Logic, Divinity, Natural Philosophy, Medicine, Moral Philosophy, Monarchs, Commonwealths, Lawyers, War, Horsemanship, Historians, Poets, Orators, Agriculture, Building, Houſholdſtuff, Statuary, Painting, Apparel, Mathematical Sciences of all ſorts, Curioſities and Subtilties. Here was a Noble Pattern ſet by a Man of great Repute in the Commonwealth of Letters; and a Pattern which I need by no means be aſhamed to follow. And as to what I ſay concerning *Philology* and *Divinity*, I only beg the Curious Reader to compare the XXVIII.th and XXIX.th Chapters of the Reflexions with what Sir *W. Temple* has ſaid upon that Argument, and then I ſhall willingly ſtand to his Award.

Upon the occaſion of *Taſſoni's Thoughts*, I ſhall obſerve that what I ſay concerning the Care with which the *Italians* have Cultivated their Language, ſo that even diſtinct Treatiſes have been written concerning the Uſe of particular Letters, which Dr. *King* has thought fit to Ridicule in his *Dialogues of the Dead*, is taken out of this Writer, who did not think ſuch Things below his Notice, when he was writing upon this very Subject. Such Writers as *Taſſoni*, a

Man may very laudably Copy after, when he does not Steal from them; and a Man is got but a very little way, that is concerned as often as such a merry Gentleman as Dr. *King* shall think fit to make himself Sport.

You see now, Sir, that mine was no new nor strange Undertaking; that in an Enquiry of this Nature formerly, every thing that could be imagined to be an Increase of Knowledge was brought in; and that the Nature of my Undertaking (which barrs all Disputes about Superiority of Genius in one Age above another) led me to favour no one side more than another; and last of all, that Divines, Philologers and Chymists had as much right to be remembred as Architects and Painters, as Poets and Historians. This therefore is a proper Place to take notice that the Stock of Knowledge still encreases; and since the Second Edition of the Reflexions came out, we have seen several Learned Performances, and some Executed by Men of our own Nation: I shall name but two, Sir *Isaac Newton's Optics*, and Dr. *Hicks's Thesaurus of the Northern Languages*.

Sir *Isaac Newton's Optics* is so entirely an Addition to the Stock of Knowledge, that till he first gave some Hints (of what he has now fully explained in that Book,) in the Philosophical Transactions about 30 Years

Years ago, it never enter'd into Mens Minds to conceive where the Truth lay in those Matters. The Subjects too, were of the greatest Importance in all Philosophy, even Light and Heat, and their Operations upon this Earth. Men never before imagined that all Light consists of Rays differently, but regularly *Refrangible* and *Reflexible*, and that those Rays are differently, and in the same Order *Reflexible*, which are differently *Refrangible*; that all Rays have their own Colours, which are constantly and regularly varied according to the different Refrangibility or Reflexibility of every such Ray; that no Position, no Refraction, no Reflexion alters the Nature of any single Ray; but that that Ray for Instance which appears Red, or Violet, or Orange, upon a single Refraction, will appear so upon a double one, if other Rays of different Colours are not blended with it; that Colour consequently is Essential and proper to every Ray of Light, and depends not upon the Position, or Surface, or Texture of the Bodies from which it is reflected, or thro' which it is refracted; that all which visible Bodies do, is by the Disposition of their Parts, to reflect Rays of one Colour more Copiously than Rays of another; that every several Ray of Light has an Innate Disposition to Excite such a determinate Sensation in us which we call by the Name of

such

such a Colour; and that the Original Colours are only these, Violet, Indigo, Blew, Green, Yellow, Orange and Red; that all the Colours of the Universe which are made by Light, are either these Homogeneal ones, or Compounded out of a Mixture of these; that Whiteness is caused by a due Mixture of all Primary Colours of Homogeneal Light, and Blackness by an entire Suffocation or Non-Reflexion of any Luminous Rays; and that if the Solar Rays were all alike Refrangible, there would be but one Colour of all Visible Bodies, since all Colours unchangeably depend upon the different Refrangibility of every Individual Ray of Light. These, with innumerable other Discoveries of the Nature of Light and Heat, and their several Actions upon all other Bodies, were before very obscurely known; and the Mechanism of the Great Architect in the Management of that which is the main Preserver and Cherisher of all the Life and Motion in this our Planet, are in a manner solely owing to the single Discoveries of that admirable Man.

The Second Work which I shall mention here, is of a very different Nature, and that is Dr. *Hicks's Thesaurus of the Northern Tongues.* By this Excellent Writer's means, we have an Accurate and large Grammar of that Language which our Ancestors

cestors the *Anglo-Saxons* spake at first: We have an Historical Account of the several Changes which the *Danes* first, and then the *Normans* and the *French* introduced into it: We have a full Description of their Poetry under all those Periods, and of the several Dialects of the *English* Language, from about the Year DCCC to *Henry* II's Time: We are able now to draw up an Accurate History of the Alterations of our Language since we were a People, to this Time; to ascertain the true Original of almost every Word, and thereby to fix its Signification for the time to come, and so hinder the future Fickleness of our truly Noble Language, if once such a Dictionary were made of it, as the Members of the *French* Academy have made of theirs. The *French* and the *Germans*, the *Italians* and *Spaniards* have like Obligations to this Industrious Author for what he has done upon the old *Gothic* and *Francic* Languages, which were the Tongues of their *Gothic* and *Teutonic* Ancestors DCCC or M Years ago. Hereby they will see how little their Learnedest Men have understood of the Originals of their own Languages, (any farther than as they are derived from *Latin*) comparatively to what may be now learnt; and how often, and how childishly *Menage* and *Ferrari*, and all their *Etymologists* have been mistaken in their Accounts of the most

Com-

Common Words for want of these Assistances: Assistances which the *English* Antiquary must not neglect, how perfect soever he may reckon his own *Anglo-Saxon* Monuments, if he will thoroughly comprehend his Native Tongue. Would a Man imagine that *Iseland*, and *Norwey*, and *Denmark*, and *Sweden* are Countries from whence the Southern Nations should need to fetch the Knowledge of their own Originals? Dr. *Hicks* will inform us that multitudes of Words of the most daily use, which we have not from the *Anglo-Saxons* are still preserved in the *Norwegian* Tongue, which is still spoken in its Primitive Perfection in *Iseland*; of the Learned Men of which Island we have abundance of valuable Productions, many of which have been published by Northern Antiquaries in this Age.

What use the Poetry of the old *Runic Scalders*, the Fabulous Mythology's of the *Iselandic Edda*'s, and the Histories or *Saga*'s, as they call them, of the other Learned Men who lived in the utmost *North*, during the most Barbarous Ages of Learning, might be applied to, was in a manner unknown, till the great *Olaus Wormius* first broke the Ice. And though since (to name no others) *Resenius* and *Bartholin* among the *Danes*; *Verelius*, *Peringskiold* and *Rudbeckius* among the *Swedes*, have made many Surprizing Discoveries in the Learning of these *Northern*

Nations which broke the *Roman* Empire, and founded thefe Noble mixt Governments, of which we ftill (and long may we do fo!) reap the Benefit: Yet what this *Englishman* has done towards explaining and illuftrating the *Northern* Languages, will make the Work incomparably eafier, and we may reafonably expect in the next Age to fee the Learning of our *Northern* Anceftors better known to us, than it ever was to them in any fingle Age in which any of them lived. This is a part of Learning Sir *W. Temple* would not have defpifed, if he had been alive when this Book appeared; who in his *Effay upon Heroic Virtue*, makes laudable ufe of fome of the Ancient *Runic* Monuments, which *Wormius* or *Bartholin*, or both, helpt him to. The truth is, thofe Nations which in their Time did fuch wonderful Things; which broke that Power that for fo many Ages had kept fo great a part of the World in fubjection; which eftablifht fuch Juft and Reafonable Governments in its place; which were fo eminent for true Courage and Contempt of Death (*n*) even when Idolaters, and for true, zealous, unaffected Piety when once converted to the Chriftian Faith, ought to have all we know of them carefully preferved: And the Helps which Dr. *Hicks* has given us to preferve them, and the mighty and various Ufes which he has fhewn may be made of them when underftood, are Benefits

(*n*) See *Thomas Bartholin* the *Younger*'s Admirable Book, *De Caufis Contemtæ a Dantis adhuc Gentilibus Mortis.*

nefits for which he ought to be remembred, especially by a *young Barbarous Goth or Vandal*, the Off-spring of some one of these Northern People, with particular Honour. These Words of Sir *W. Temple*'s, which are part of the Character that he has thought fit to bestow upon me, admonish me whither I must return, tho' what I have said is no Digression from my first Design.

What I say of the *Assyrian* Monarchy in the *Reflexions* comes next to be considered. Sir *W. Temple* thinks he has a large Scope to fall upon me there, and he is not wanting to say all he can upon it. The Account of the First Race of Kings from *Ninus* to *Sardanapalus*, I do I think with Reason disallow, because *Herodotus* is silent, whose Business it was to have given an Account of them. Besides, had there been such a mighty Monarchy in *Assyria* or *Babylonia* before the Time of *Pul*, the *Jewish* Historians must have mention'd it. To prove this, I use a positive Argument, which Sir *W. Temple* represents as if it had been only a Negative one. " These Moderns (says he) will
" not allow the plainest Accounts given us
" by the best *Greek* and *Latin* Authors of
" the Duration of those Empires, though
" not contrary to the Periods allow'd us
" by the Scriptures. But the Reasons they
" give for not believing them, seem too
" weak and frivolous to be taken notice of:
" As

" As first, That we have no Account of
" the *Assyrian* Kings in Scripture till *Tig-*
" *lath-Pileser* and others, (*o*) whereas the
" Scriptures take no notice of the Story of
" either the *Aegyptian, Assyrian, Tyrian* or
" *Sidonian* Governments, but as they had
" at some certain times a Relation to the
" Affairs of the *Jews*, or their Common-
" wealth." Here all that I said concerning
Amraphel and *Chushan-Rishathaim* (*p*) is un-
touched, though therein lay the strength of
my Argument. I produce, you see, Sir,
a positive Argument first, that there was no
great *Assyrian* Monarchy before the Time
of *Pul*, which is, that *Amraphel* King of
Shinar is described by *Moses*, and *Chu-*
shan Risha-thaim in the Book of *Judges*,
but as *Heads of Clans*, or at least as *Petty*
Reguli. To this Argument he should have
replied, before he had found fault with what
I said about *Pul* and *Tiglath-Pileser*. Now
the several Accounts which the *Jewish* Historians give of these several Monarchs,
shew the Ancientest to have been but small
ones, and those nearer the Captivity to
have been very powerful Princes. And
though the *Jewish* Writers do indeed take
no farther *notice of the Aegyptian, Assyrian,*
Tyrian or Sidonian Governments, than as they
had to do with their own Commonwealth, yet
it is impossible to write the Civil History of
any one Nation, and not to say so much of

(*o*) *Defense of Essay*, pag. 235, 236.

(*p*) *Vide supra Reflex* p 130.

its

its Neighbouring States as may give us to understand something positive concerning their Greatness or Smalness. Take *England* for Instance: No Man can go over its History since the Invasion of *William* the Conqueror, but he will find, if he carries on his Enquiries to the Death of King *Charles* II, that *Scotland* was a distinct entire Monarchy till the Death of Queen *Elizabeth*; that *Ireland* was divided into several Petty Sovereignties in *Henry* II's Time, that *France* consisted of several distinct Dominions, the chief of which was governed by the King of *France*, to whom the rest were feudatary; that all these Subordinate Dominions did not fall into the possession of the Kings of *France* till our *Henry* VII's Time, when *Charles* VIII of *France* married the Heiress of the Duke of *Britany*: that *Germany*, and *Spain*, and *Italy*, and the *Low-Countries* had distinct Sovereignties respectively within themselves for several Ages; that in *Edw.* IV's time the House of *Burgundy* had got all the *Low-Countries* into its own possession: that in *Henry* VII's Time the Heir of *Burgundy* married the Heiress of *Spain*, which was then as good as united under one Head, and so laid the Foundation of the greatest Western Monarchy which had been seen since the *Roman* Times: that after this Monarchy became terrible, it invaded *England*, which made

such

such an Opposition to it by the Wife Conduct of Queen *Elizabeth*, as went very far to pull down its Greatness; and that upon its Ruines a Monarchy mightier in Intrinsic Strength, though less in Extent of Territory, arose in *France*, which affrighted all the States and Kingdoms that lay round about it. All this, and abundance more relating to our Neigbouring Countries, a Man cannot avoid knowing by the bare reading of the *English* History from the Year MLXVI, to the Year MDCXCIV. And yet such a History will concern it self with the Affairs of Foreign Countries no farther than as they have had an immediate relation to our own Affairs. So now in *Abraham*'s Time we find *Phoenicia, Syria* and *Assyria* in the hands of Petty Princes, whilst *Aegypt* was a great and a powerful Monarchy, capable in *Moses*'s Time to hinder an Army of 600,000 Men, besides Women and Children, from going out of the Country against the Governors Wills. We find likewise that it continued to be a distinct Kingdom till the Time of *Nebuchadnezzar*. In *Syria* we find a considerable Kingdom, with *Damascus* its Capital City, during the Reigns of the Kings of *Israel*, which, and all the lesser Monarchies round about, fell a Prey to the *Assyrian* and *Babylonian* Kings after they became powerful. Thus *Herodotus*, and the Canon of *Ptolemee*, and the Astronomical

Observations of the *Chaldaeans* and the *Jewish* Writers agree. Consider, Sir, how near *Mesopotamia* and *Judaea* ly to one another. Such Monarchs as the old *Assyrians* of the Family of *Ninus*, would soon have made the *Jews* and *Syrians* tributary, or have attempted it at least, and then we must have heard of it. The History of Q. *Elizabeth* is full of the Attempts of *Phil.* II. upon *England*. Great Monarchies in the nature of Things will always be striking at their smaller Neighbours, who of course will fall into Alliances to keep the Balance of Power even, as well and as long as they can; or else they will be cajoled and bribed, and so made Tools by which they will contribute to devour the rest. Sir *W. Temple* knew this better than I do, his Business led him to it, and when he was a Public Minister Abroad, as far as we may judge by his Political Writings, he seems to have had very true and just Notions of Matters of this kind. Whatsoever therefore he here gravely urges against his *Young Barbarous Adversary*, it is impossible he could ever believe that there was a mighty Monarchy in *Assyria* so near to *Judaea* upon the same Continent, so long as from the Time of *Ninus* to the Time of *Sardanapalus*, of which we should have had no Footsteps older than the History of *Ctesias*, whom *Aristotle*

tle in his own Time branded for a Lyar (*q*).

(*q*) Ἐν τῇ Ἰνδικῇ, ὥς φησι Κτησίας, ἐκ ὦν ἀξιόπιςΘ, ὅτε ἥμερΘ, ἔτ' ἄγριΘ σῦς. *Aristot. De Hist Animal Lib.* VIII *cap* 28. This thing alone is sufficient to determine concerning *Ctesias*'s Authority. He says, There are no Hogs Wild or Tame in the *East-Indies*; now on the contrary, we know there are both. Hunting of the Wild-Boar is a great Diversion in that Country at this Day. *Aristotle* we see was better informed, and therefore declares that *Ctesias* was not ἀξιόπιςΘ, *worthy of Credit*.

But Arguments drawn from the Agreement of Sacred and Prophane History, have no weight with Sir *W. Temple*. "As it has "never succeeded with so many Learned "Men, that have spent their whole Time "and Pains to *agree* (*r*) the Sacred with "the Prophane Chronology (not to except "Sir *John Marsham*'s great Industry) so I "never exspect to see it done to any pur- "pose." (*s*) Where then must the Fault lie? Not in the *Jewish* History, which is consistently and regularly delivered down to us from the Creation, to the Destruction of the first Temple. It must be then in those *Pagan* Historians who have given Accounts of the Originals of the most Famous *Gentile* Nations: But the oldest of these is *Herodotus*, and his Accounts of the *Median*, *Assyrian* and *Persian* Monarchies agree well enough with the Sacred Historians. It brings them down indeed many Ages lower than the *Jewish* Accounts; and this morti- fied

(*r*) Sir *W. Temple* here puts *Agree* for *Reconcile*, and so uses it transitively, for *to make agree*. Perhaps the being a Great Master will bear him out; lesser Men must beware of such Things.
(*s*) Defense of *Essay*, pag. 236.

fied the Vanity of these Nations. This probably set *Ctesias* a work, who is followed by almost all the Ancients who treat of these Matters. That the Sacred and Prophane Historians therefore do not agree, is not the fault of the Truth, but of those who have corrupted it. But indeed if the *Assyrian* Race from *Ninus* to *Sardanapalus*, for which we are beholden to *Ctesias*, is removed, a great deal of Sir *W. Temple*'s *Hypothesis* falls to the Ground, and that made him so zealous for the *Ctesian* Race of the *Assyrian* Monarchs.

After all, if the Controversie between Sir *W. Temple* and me were to be decided by the *Greek* Writers, and of those there were a due choice, the Incompetent Authorities being set aside, when more competent ones can be substituted in their Rooms, the Dispute would soon be at an end. The *Greek* Writers are the Men I appeal to, and by their Accounts of the Knowledge of the Ancients, I desire the Extent of Modern Knowledge may be measured. But then it is fit those Authorities should be clear and proper: it is fit that a Man treating of his own Art or Science, should be credited beyond a Writer who seems not to speak of his own Knowledge concerning that Matter: it is fit that the Authors who are the nearest to the Times or Facts in question should first be heard, and

and that nothing be admitted that is not reconcileable to the *Jewish* Text. Let the Old Testament be admitted barely as a History without any regard in the present Dispute to its Inspiration, but such a History as has had a whole Nation for very many Ages together to attest its Truth, whilst there is no consistent *Anti-History* of any other People to oppose it. Thus the Scriptures will *not* be of *Private Interpretation*, but will help us to correct the *Private Interpretations* of other Writers. And herein are Sir *John Marsham's Disquisitions* upon his *Canon Chronicus* particularly to be prized, that he has reduced the wild incoherent Antiquities of the *Aegyptians* to a fixt *Aera*, and has set aside all those remote *Assyrian* Accounts which only confounded Mens Belief of the History of the Old Testament.

I have now given a full Answer, as I think, Sir, to all the Argumentative part of Sir *W. Temple's Thoughts* upon the *Reflexions*. If we do not allow that he misunderstood the Question as I had plainly stated it (*t*), we must believe that he wilfully mistook it; and the rather, because when he was to examine the several Particulars in which I apprehended that the Preference was to be given to the Moderns, he drops the Question. It is done decently indeed, and there is a *Hiatus in Manuscripto*, as the

(*t*) *Vide supra Reflex pag 7.*

Publisher of the Tale of a Tub expresses it (u), that so we may suppose the Comparison was intended to be made, and only by accident left imperfect. For after Sir *William Temple* had said, "Since the Modern Advocates yield, though very unwillingly, the Pre-eminence of the Ancients in Poetry, Oratory, Painting, Statuary and Architecture; I shall proceed to examine the Account they give of those Sciences, wherein they affirm the Moderns to excel the Ancients; whereof they make the chief to be the Invention of Instruments; Chymistry; Anatomy; Natural History of Minerals, Plants, and Animals; Astronomy and Optics; Music; Physick; Natural Philosophy; Philology and Theology; of all which I shall take a short survey." There is a Gap, and Dr. *Swift* fills it up thus, *Here it is supposed, the Knowledge of the Ancients and Moderns last mentioned, was to have been compared: But whether the Author designed to have gone through such a Work himself, or intended these Papers only for Hints to some body else that desired them, is not known. After which, the rest was to follow written in his own Hand as before.* (w) This Method of answering of Books, and of publishing such Answers, is very dissatisfactory. Just where the Pinch of the Question lay, there the Copy fails, and where there was more

(u) P. 42.

(w) Defense of Essay, p. 230. 231.

Room for flourishing, there Sir *W. Temple* was as copious as one would wish. To use his own Words, *This is very wonderful, if it be not a Jest*; and I take it for granted, Dr. *Swift* had express Orders to print these *Fragments* of an Answer.

This way of printing Bits of Books that in their Nature are intended for Continued Discourses, and are not loose Apophthegms, Occasional Thoughts, or incoherent Sentences, is what I have seen few Instances of; none more remarkable than this, and one more which may be supposed to imitate this, *The Tale of a Tub*, of which a Brother of Dr. *Swift*'s is publicly reported to have been the Editor at least, if not the Author. In which though Dr. *Bentley* and my self are coursely treated, yet I believe I may safely answer for us both, that we should not have taken any manner of notice of it, if upon this Occasion I had not been obliged to say something in answer to what has been seriously said against us.

For, believe me, Sir, what concerns us, is much the innocentest part of the Book, tending chiefly to make Men laugh for half an Hour, after which it leaves no farther Effects behind it. When Men are jested upon for what is in it self praiseworthy, the World will do them Justice: And on the other hand, if they deserve it, they ought to sit down quietly under it. Our Cause therefore we shall leave to the Public very willingly, there being no occasion to be concerned at any Man's Raillery about it. But the rest of the Book which does not relate to us, is of so irreligious a nature, is so crude a Banter upon all that is esteemed as Sacred among all Sects and Religions among Men, that, having so fair an Opportunity, I thought it might be useful to many People who pretend they see no harm in it, to lay open the Mischief of the Ludicrous Allegory, and to shew what that drives at which has been so greedily bought up and read. In one Word, God and Religion, Truth and Moral Honesty, Learning and Industry are made a May-Game, and the most serious Things in the World are described as so many several Scenes in a *Tale of a Tub*.

That this is the true Design of that Book, will appear by these Particulars. The *Tale* in substance is this; " A Man " had three Sons, all at a Birth, by one " Wife; to whom when he died, because " he had purchased no Estate, nor was " born to any, he only provided to each " of them a New Coat, which were to last " them fresh and sound as long as they " lived, and would lengthen and widen of " themselves, so as to be always fit."

(x) By

(*x*) By the Sequel of the *Tale* it appears, (*x*) p. 54.
that by these three Sons, *Peter*, *Martin*,
and *Jack*; *Popery*, the *Church of England*,
and our *Protestant Dissenters* are designed.
What can now be more infamous than such
a *Tale*? The Father is *Jesus Christ*, who at
his Death left his WILL or TESTA-
MENT to his Disciples, with a Promise
of Happiness to them, and the Churches
which they and their Successors should
found for ever. So the Tale-teller's Father
to his three Sons, "You will find in my
"WILL full Instructions in every Parti-
"cular concerning the wearing and ma-
"naging of your Coats; wherein you must
"be very exact, to avoid the Penalties I
"have appointed for every Transgression
"or Neglect, upon which your *Future*
"*Fortunes* will *entirely* depend." (*y*) By (*y*) Ibid. p. 54, 55.
his Coats which he gave his Sons, the Gar-
ments of the *Israelites* are exposed, which
by the Miraculous Power of God waxed
not old, nor were worn out for Forty Years
together in the Wilderness. (*z*) The num- (*z*) Deut VIII. 4.
ber of these Sons born thus at one Birth,
looks asquint at the TRINITY, and one
of the Books in our Author's Catalogue in
the Off-page over-against the Title, is a
Panegyric upon the Number THREE,
which Word is the only one that is put
in Capitals in that whole Page (*a*). (*a*) In the Citations
out of the *Tale of a Tub*, the first Impression is constantly quoted.

In the pursuit of his Allegory, we are entertain'd with the Lewdness of the Three Sparks. Their Mistresses are the *Dutchess d'Argent*, Madamoizelle *de Grands Titres*, (b) P. and the Countess *d'Orgueil* (b) i. e. *Covetousness*, *Ambition* and *Pride*, which were the Three great Vices that the Ancient Fathers inveighed against as the first Corrupters of Christianity. Their Coats having such an extraordinary Virtue of never wearing out, give him large Scope for his Mirth, which he employs in burlesquing *Religion*, *Moral Honesty* and *Conscience*, which are the strongest Ties by which Men can be tied to one another. *Is not Religion a Cloak, Honesty a Pair of Shoes worn out in the Dirt, Self-love a Surtout, Vanity a Shirt, and Con-*
(c) P. 60. *science a Pair of Breeches?* (c) Which last Allusion gives him an opportunity that he never misses of talking obscenely.

His Whim of Clothes is one of his chiefest Favourites. " Man, says he, is an Animal
" compounded of two *Dresses*, the *Natural*
" and the *Coelestial-Suit*, which were the
(d) P. 61 " Body and the Soul." (d) And " That
" the Soul was by daily Creation and Cir-
" cumfusion they proved by Scripture, be-
" cause *In them we live, and move, and have*
" *our Being.*" *In them* (i. e. *in the Clothes of the Body :*) Words applicable only to the Great God of Heaven and Earth, of whom they were first spoken by St. *Paul*
(e).

(e). Thus he introduces his Tale; then that he might shelter himself the better from any Censure here in *England*, he falls most unmercifully upon *Peter* and *Jack*, *i.e.* upon *Popery* and *Fanaticism*, and gives *Martin*, who represents the *Church of England*, extream good Quarter. I confess, Sir, I abhor making Sport with any way of worshipping God, and he that diverts himself too much at the Expense of the *Roman Catholics* and the *Protestant Dissenters*, may lose his own Religion e're he is aware of it, at least the Power of it in his Heart. But to go on.

(e) Acts XVII, 28.

The first Part of the *Tale* is the *History of Peter*. Thereby *Popery* is exposed. Every body knows the *Papists* have made great Additions to Christianity. That indeed is the great Exception which the Church of *England* makes against them. Accordingly *Peter* begins his Pranks with *adding a Shoulderknot to his Coat,* " whereas his
" Father's Will was very precise, and it was
" the main Precept in it with the greatest
" Penalties annexed, not to add to, or di-
" minish from their Coats one Thread,
" without a positive Command in the
" W.I.L.L." (f) His Description of the Cloth of which the Coat was made, has a farther Meaning than the Words may seem to import. " The Coats their Father
" had left them were of very good Cloth,
" and

(f) P 63.

"and besides so neatly sown, you would swear they were all of a Piece, but at the same time very plain, with little or no Ornament." *(f)* This is the Distinguishing Character of the Christian Religion. *Christiana Religio absoluta & simplex*, was *Ammianus Marcellinus*'s Description of it, who was himself a Heathen. *(g)* When the *Papists* cannot find any thing which they want in Scripture, they go to *Oral Tradition*: Thus *Peter* is introduced dissatisfied with the tedious Way of looking for all the Letters of any Word which he had occasion for in the *Will*, when neither the constituent Syllables, nor much less the whole Word were there *in Terminis*, and he expresses himself thus; "Brothers, if you remember, we heard a Fellow say when we were Boys, that he heard my Father's Man say, that he heard my Father say, that he would advise his Sons to get *Gold-Lace* on their Coats, as soon as ever they could procure Money to buy it." *(h)* Which way of coming at any thing that was not expresly in his Father's WILL, stood him afterwards in great stead.

The next Subject of our *Tale-teller*'s Wit is the *Glosses* and *Interpretations of Scripture*, very many absurd ones of which kind are allow'd in the most Authentic Books of the Church of *Rome*: The Sparks wanted Silver

(f) Ibid.

(g) Lib. XXI. *in fine.*

(h) P. 67

ver Fringe to put upon their Coats. Why, says *Peter*, (seemingly perhaps to laugh at Dr. *Bentley* and his Criticisms); "I have "found in a certain Author, which shall be "nameless, that the same Word which in "the Will is called *Fringe*, does also sig-"nifie a *Broomstick*, and doubtless ought to "have the same Interpretation in this Para-"graph." (*i*) This affording great Diversion to one of the Brothers; "You speak, "says *Peter*, very irreverently of a *Myste-*"*ry*, which doubtless was very useful and "significant, but ought not to be overcuri-"ously pry'd into, or nicely reason'd up-"on." (*k*) The Author, one would think, copies from Mr. *Toland*, who always raises a Laugh at the Word *Mystery*, the Word and Thing whereof he is known to believe to be no more than a *Tale of a Tub*.

(*i*) P. 70.

(*k*) Ibid

Images in the Church of *Rome* give our *Tale-teller* but too fair a Handle. "The "Brothers remembred but too well how "their Father abhorred the Fashion of Em-"broidering their Clothes with *Indian* Fi-"gures of Men, Women and Children; "that he made several Paragraphs on pur-"pose, importing his utter Detestation of "it, and bestowing his Everlasting Curse "to his Sons, whenever they should wear "it." (*l*) The Allegory here is direct. The *Papists* formerly forbad the People the use of Scripture in a Vulgar Tongue; *Pe-*

(*l*) P. 71.

ter

ter therefore *locks up his Father's Will in a strong Box brought out of* Greece *or* Italy: Those Countries are named, because the *New Testament* is written in *Greek*; and the *Vulgar Latin*, which is the Authentic Edition of the Bible in the Church of *Rome*, is in the Language of Old *Italy*. (*m*) The Popes in their *Decretals* and *Bulls* have given their Sanction to very many gainful Doctrines which are now receiv'd in the Church of *Rome*, that are not mentioned in Scripture, and are unknown to the Primitive Church. *Peter* accordingly pronounces *ex Cathedra*, that *Points tagged with Silver were absolutely Jure Paterno*, and so they wore them in great numbers. (*n*) The Bishops of *Rome* enjoy'd their Privileges in *Rome* at first by the Favour of Emperors, whom at last they shut out of their own Capital City, and then forged a Donation from *Constantine the Great*, the better to justifie what they did. In imitation of this, *Peter*, " having run something behindhand
" with the World, obtained leave of a cer-
" tain Lord to receive him into his House,
" and to teach his Children. A while after
" the Lord died, and he by long Practise
" upon his Father's Will, found the way of
" contriving a Deed of Conveyance of that
" House to himself and his Heirs: Upon
" which he took possession, turned the
" Young Squires out, and receiv'd his Bro-
" thers

(*m*) P 72.

(*n*) Ibid.

" thers in their stead." (*o*) *Pennance* and *Absolution* are plaid upon under the Notion of a Sovereign Remedy for the Worms, especially in the Spleen, which by observing of *Peter*'s Prescriptions, would void insensibly by Perspiration ascending through the Brain. (*p*) By his *Whispering Office* for the Relief of Eves-droppers, Physicians, Bawds and Privy-Couneellors, he ridicules *Auricular Confession*, and the Priest who takes it is described by the Ass's Head. (*q*) Holy-Water he calls an Universal Pickle, *to preserve Houses, Gardens, Towns, Men, Women, Children and Cattle*, wherein he could preserve them as sound as Insects in Amber; (*r*) and because Holy-Water differs only in Consecration from Common Water, therefore our Tale-teller tells us that his Pickle by the Powder of *Pimperlimpimp* receives new Virtues, though it differs not in Sight nor Smell from the Common Pickle which preserves Beef, and Butter, nor Herrings. (*s*) The *Papal Bulls* are ridiculed by Name, so there we are at no loss for our *Tale-teller*'s Meaning. (*t*) *Absolution in Articulo Mortis*, and the *Taxa Camerae Apostolicae* are jested upon in Emperor *Peter*'s Letter. (*u*) The *Pope's Universal Monarchy*, and his *Triple Crown*, and *Key*'s and *Fishers Ring* have their turns of being laughed at; (*w*) nor does his Arrogant way of requiring Men to kiss his Slipper,

(*o*) P. 73.

(*p*) P. 94

(*q*) P. 95.

(*r*) P. 96, 97.

(*s*) P 97

(*t*) P 97—100.

(*u*) P 101.

(*w*) P 103

per, escape Reflexion (*x*). The *Celibacy of the Romish Clergy* is struck at in *Peter*'s turning his own and Brothers Wives out of Doors. (*y*) But nothing makes him so merry as *Transubstantiation* (*z*): *Peter* turns his Bread into Mutton, and according to the Popish Doctrine of Concomitance, his Wine too, which in his way he calls *pauming his damned Crusts upon the Brothers for Mutton* (*a*). The ridiculous multiplying of the *Virgin Mary's Milk* among the Papists, he banters under the Allegory of a *Cow* which gave as much Milk at a Meal, as would fill Three thousand Churches: (*b*) and the *Wood of the Cross* on which our Saviour suffered, is prophanely likened to an " Old Sign-post that belonged to his " Father, with Nails and Timber enough " upon it to build Sixteen large Men of " War ": (*c*) And when one talked to *Peter* of *Chinese* Waggons which were made so light as to sail over Mountains, he swears and curses four times in Eleven Lines, that the *Chapell* of *Loretto* had travelled Two Thousand *German* Leagues, though built with Lime and Stone, over Sea and Land (*d*).

(*x*) Ibid.
(*y*) P. 104.
(*z*) P. 104-108.
(*a*) P. 130.
(*b*) P. 108.
(*c*) P. 109.
(*d*) Ibid.

But I expect, Sir, that you should tell me, that the *Tale-teller* falls here only upon the Ridiculous Inventions of Popery; that the Church of *Rome* intended by these things to gull silly Superstitious People; and to rook them of their Money; that the World had been but too long in Slavery; that our Ancestors gloriously redeemed us from that Yoak; that the Church of *Rome* therefore ought to be exposed, and that he deserves well of Mankind that does expose it.

All this, Sir, I own to be true: but then I would not so shoot at an Enemy, as to hurt my self at the same time. The Foundation of the Doctrines of the Church of *England* is right, and came from God: Upon this the Popes, and Councils called and confirmed by them, have built, as St. *Paul* speaks, *Hay and Stubble*, perishable and slight Materials, which when they are once consum'd, that the Foundation may appear; then we shall see what is faulty, and what is not. But our *Tale-teller* strikes at the very Root. *'Tis all* with him *a Farce, and all a Ladle*, as a very facetious Poet says upon another occasion. The *Father*, and the *WILL*, and *his Son Martin*, are part of the *Tale*, as well as *Peter* and *Jack*, and are all usher'd in with the Common Old Wives Introduction, *Once upon a Time* (e). And the *main Body of the Will* we are told consisted in *certain admirable Rules about the wearing of* their Coats (f). So that let *Peter* be mad one way, and *Jack* another, and let *Martin* be sober, and spend his Time with Patience and Phlegm in picking the

(e) P. 54

(f) P. 124

Embroidery off his Coat never so carefully, "firmly resolving to alter whatever was already amiss, and reduce all their future Measures to the strictest Obedience prescribed therein" (g); Yet still this is all part of a *Tale of a Tub*, it does but enhance the *Teller*'s Guilt, and shews at the bottom his contemptible Opinion of every Thing which is called Christianity.

For pray, Sir, take notice that it is not saying he personates none but Papists or Fanatics, that will excuse him; for in other Places, where he speaks in his own Person, and imitates none but himself, he discovers an equal mixture of Lewdness and Irreligion. Would any Christian compare a *Mountebank*'s-*Stage*, a *Pulpit*, and a *Ladder* together? A *Mountebank* is a profess'd Cheat, who turns it off when he is press'd, with the Common Jest, *Men must live*; and with this Man the Preacher of the Word of God is compared, and the Pulpit in which he preaches, is called *an Edifice* (or Castle) *in the Air* : (h) This is not said by *Peter*, or *Jack*, but by the Author himself, who after he has gravely told us, that he has had Poxes ill cured by trusting to Bawds and Surgeons, reflects with "unspeakable Comfort, upon his having past a long Life with a *Conscience void of Offence towards God and towards Man*" (i).

(g) Ibid.

(h) P. 34.

(i) P. 51.

In

In his own Person, the Author speaks in one of his Digressions of "Books being not bound to Everlasting Chains of Darkness in a Library; but that when the Fulness of Time should come, they should happily undergo the Tryal of Purgatory, in order to ascend the Sky." (k) In another Digression our Author describes one of his Madmen in *Bedlam*, who was distemper'd by the Loose Behaviour of his Wife, to be like *Moses: Ecce Cornuta erat ejus Facies*; (l) which is the rendring of the *Vulgar Latin* of that which in the *English* Bible is called *the shining of his Face* when he came down from the Mount. (m) Our Author himself asserts, that the "Fumes issuing from a Jakes, will furnish as comely and useful a Vapor, as Incense from an Altar." (n). And 'tis our Author in his own Capacity, who among many other Ludicrous Similes upon those that get their Learning out of *Indices*, which are commonly at the End of a Book, says, "Thus Human Life is best understood by the *Wise-man*'s Rule of *regarding the End*." (o) 'Tis in the *Fragment*, which has nothing to do with the *Tale*, that Sir *Humphrey Edwin* is made to apply the Words of the *Psalmist*, *Thy Word is a Lanthorn to my Feet, and a Light to my Paths*, to a Whimsical Dark Lanthorn of our Authors own contrivance; wherein he poorly alludes to *Hudibras*'s

(k) P.144.

(l) P.179.

(m) Exod. XXXIV. 29, 30, 35.

(n) P.160.

(o) P.139.

Dark-Lanthorn of the Spirit, which none see by but those that bear it. (*p*) His whole VIIIth Section concerning the *Aeolists*, in which he banters Inspiration, is such a Mixture of Impiety and Immodesty, that I should have as little regard to you, Sir, as this Author has had to the Public, if I should barely repeat after him what is there. And it is somewhat surprizing that the Citation out of *Irenaeus*, in the Title-Page, which seems to be all *Gibberish*, should be a Form of Initiation used anciently by the *Marcosian* Heretics (*q*). So great a delight has this Unhappy Writer, to play with what some part or other of Mankind have always esteemed as Sacred!

(*p*) P. 307.

(*q*) The Words of this *Form of Redemption*, as these Heretics called it, are *Basima eaca basa ea naa irraurista, diarbada caeotaba fobor camelanthi*. So it is in the Old Editions of *Irenaeus*, from one of which it is here transcribed. *Irenaeus* thus interprets them, *Hoc quod est super omnem virtutem Patris invoco, quod vocatur Lumen & Spiritus & Vita, quoniam in corpore regnasti* i.e. *I call upon this, which is above all the Power of the Father, which is called Light, and Spirit, and Life, because thou hast reigned in the Body*. The Greek Words which were faulty at first, made the *Latin* ones yet more so; it is probable that *Irenaeus* might not understand them right at first. They are *Syriac*, and in the very Learned Mr *Grabe*'s Edition of *Irenaeus*, they are very ingeniously restored out of *Jacobus Rhenferdius*'s *Dissertation, upon the Redemption of the Marcosians and Heracleonites*.

And therefore when he falls upon *Jack*, he deals as freely with him, and wounds Christianity through his Sides as much as he had done before through *Peter's*. The *Protestant Dissenters use Scripture-Phrases* in their Serious Discourses and Composures more than the Church of *England-men*. Accordingly *Jack* is introduced, making "his Common Talk and Converſation to run wholly in the Phraſe of his WILL, and circumſcribing the utmoſt of his Eloquence within that compaſs, not daring to let ſlip a Syllable without Authority from thence." (*r*) And becauſe he could not of a ſudden recollect *an AuthenticPhraſe*, for the Neceſſities of Nature, he would uſe no other: (*s*) Can any thing be prophaner than this? Things compared, always ſhew the Eſteem or Scorn of the Comparer. To ridicule Praedeſtination, *Jack* walks blindfold through the Streets; the Body of our Diſſenters having till of late been *Calviniſts* in the Queſtions concerning the *Five Points*. "It was ordained, ſaid he, ſome few days *before* the Creation (*i.e.* immediately by God himſelf) that my Noſe and this very Poſt ſhould have a Rencounter; and therefore Providence thought fit to ſend us both into the World in the ſame Age, and to make us Country-men and Fellow Citizens." (*t*) This is a direct Prophanation of the Majeſty of God. "*Jack* would run Dog-mad at the Noiſe of Muſic, eſpecially a Pair of Bagpipes." (*u*) This is to expoſe our Diſſenters Averſion to Inſtrumental Muſic in Churches. The Agreement of our Diſſenters and the Papiſts, in that which Biſhop *Stillingfleet* called

(*r*) P.197.

(*s*) P.198.

(*t*) P 199.

(*u*) P.203.

led the *Fanaticism of the Church of Rome*, is ludicrously described for several Pages together, by *Jack's* likeness to *Peter*, and their being often mistaken for each other, and their frequent meeting when they least intended it: (w) In this, singly taken, there might possibly be little harm, if one did not see from what Principle the whole proceeded.

(w) P. 206, 207, 208.

This 'tis which makes the difference between the sharp and virulent Books written in this Age against any Sect of Christians, and those which were written about the beginning of the Reformation between the several contending Parties then in *Europe*. For tho' the Rage and Spight with which Men treated one another was as keen and as picquant then as it is now, yet the Inclination of Mankind was not then irreligious, and so their Writings had little other effect but to encrease Mens Hatred against any one particular Sect, whilst Christianity, as such, was not hereby at all undermined. But now the Common Enemy appears barefaced, and strikes in with some one or other Sect of Christians, to wound the whole by that means. And this is the Case of this Book, which is one of the Prophanest Banters upon the Religion of *Jesus Christ*, as such, that ever yet appeared. In the *Tale*, in the *Digressions*, in the *Fragment*, the same Spirit runs through, but rather most in the
Fragment,

Fragment, in which all extraordinary Inspirations are the Subjects of his Scorn and Mockery, whilst the Protestant Dissenters are, to outward appearance, the most directly levelled at. The Bookseller indeed in his Advertisement prefixed to the *Fragment*, pretends to be *wholly ignorant of the Author, and he says, he cannot conjecture whether it be the same with that of the two foregoing Pieces, the Original having been sent him at a different Time, and in a different Hand.* It may be so; but the Stile, and Turn, and Spirit of this *Fragment*, and of the *Tale* being the same, no body, I believe, has doubted of their being written by the same Author: If the Authors are different, so much the worse, because it shews there are more Men in the World acted by the same Spirit. But be the Author one or more, the Mask is more plainly taken off in the *Fragment*. The Writer uses the Allegory of an *Ass's bearing his Rider up to Heaven*: (*x*) And presently after he owns his Ass to be allegorical, and says, " That " if we please, instead of the Term *Ass*, we " may make use of *Gifted* or *Enlightned* " *Preacher*, and the Word *Rider* we may " exchange for that of *Fanatic Auditory*, or ' any other Denomination of the like Im- " port : " (*y*) And now *having setled this Weighty Point*, (as he contemptuously calls it) he enquires *by what Methods this Teacher arrives*

(*x*) P. 287.

(*y*) P. 2 §

arrives at his *Gifts*, or *Spirit*, or *Light* (z). Enthusiasm with him is an Universal Deception which has run through all Sciences in all Kingdoms, and every thing has some *Fanatic Branch annexed to it*; (a) among which he reckons the *Summum Bonum*, or *an Enquiry after Happiness*. The *Descent of the H. Ghost* after our Blessed Saviour's Ascension in the Shape of Cloven Tongues, at the First *Pentecost*, in the Second of the *Acts*, is one of the Subjects of his Mirth: And because in our Dissenting Congregations, the Auditory used formerly with great Indecency to keep on their Hats in Sermon Time, therefore, says he, "They will needs have "it as a Point clearly gained, that the Clo- "ven Tongues never sat upon the Apostles "Heads, while their Hats were on:" (b) using that Ridiculous Argument to prove that the Dissenting Ministers are not divinely inspired. And he does not mince the Matter when he says, "That he is resolved imme- "diately to weed this Error out of Man- "kind, by making it clear, that this My- "stery of venting Spiritual Gifts is nothing "but a Trade acquired by as much Instru- "ction, and master'd by equal Practice and "Application as others are." (c) Can any "thing be more blasphemous than his *Game* "at *Leap-Frog between the Flesh and Spirit* (d) This affects the Doctrine of St. *Paul*, (e) and not the Private Interpretations of

this

(z) Ibid

(a) P. 189.

(b) P 295, 296

(c) P 303.

(d) P 310.
(e) Rom. VII

this or that Particular Sect; and this too is described in the Language of the Stews, which with now and then a Scripture-Expression, compose this Writer's Stile. Thus when the *Snuffling* of Men who have lost their Noses by Lewd Courses, is said to have given rise to that Tone which our Dissenters did too much affect formerly, He subjoins, " That when our Earthly Tabernacles are disordered and desolate, shaken and out of Repair, the *Spirit* delights to dwell within them, as Houses are said to be haunted, when they are forsaken and gone to decay.(*f*)" And in his Account of Fanaticism, he tells us, *That the Thorn in the Flesh, serves* for a Spur to the Spirit. (*g*) Is not this to ridicule St. *Paul*'s own Description of his own Temptation; in which the Apostle manifestly alludes to a Passage in the Prophet *Ezekiel* (*h*)?

(*f*) P. 313.
(*g*) P. 319.
(*h*) 2 Cor. XII 7. *and* Ezek XXVIII. 24.

What would Men say in any Country in the World but this, to see their Religion so vilely treated from the Press? I remember to have seen a *French* Translation of the Learned Dr. *Prideaux* (the present Worthy Dean of *Norwich*'s) *Life of Mahomet*, printed in *France*, I think at *Paris*, in the *Advertisement* before which, the Translator tells the Public, That he did not translate the *Letter to the Deists*, thereto annexed in *English*, because, says he, our Government suffers no such People, and there is no need of

Anti-

Antidotes where there is no Poison. Be this true or false in *France*, it matters not to our present Purpose; but it shews that no Man dares publickly play with Religion in that Country. How much do the *Mahometans* reverence the *Alcoran*? Dares any Man among them openly despise their Prophet, or ridicule the Words of his Law? How strictly do the *Banians*, and the other Sects of the *Gentile East-Indians* worship their Pagods, and respect their Temples? This Sir, you well know, is not Superstition nor Bigottry. It is of the Essence of Religion, that the utmost Regard should be paid to the *Name* and *Words of God*, both which upon the slightest, and the most ridiculous Occasions, are play'd upon by Common Oaths, and Idle Allusions to Scripture Expressions in this whole Book. I do not carry my Charge too far.

For admitting that this Writer intended to make himself and his Readers Sport, by exercising his Wit and Mirth upon a Couple of Pedants, as he esteems Dr. *Bentley* and my self; yet since the *Tale* may thus be explain'd, and since to your knowledge and mine, Sir, it has been thus interpreted by Unconcerned Readers, the Mischief which it does is equally great to Mankind. Besides, even that Excuse will not serve in the *Fragment*, which is levelled at no particular Man that I can find whatsoever. Dr. *King*, late

late of *Christ-Church* was so sensible of this, that when by reason of the Personalities (as the *French* call them) in the Book, it was laid at his Door, he took care immediately to print such *Remarks* upon it, as effectually cleared him from the Imputation of having writ it: He therein did like a Christian; and he that is one, would be very uneasie under the Character of being none. And this is what Mr. *Swift* is yet under greater Obligations to do, because of his Profession. The World besides will think it odd, that a Man should in a Dedication play upon that Great Man, to whom he is more obliged than to any other Man now living; for it was at Sir *William Temple*'s Request, that my Lord *Sommers*, then Lord-Keeper of the Great-Seal of *England*, gave Mr. *Swift* a very good Benefice in one of the most Delicious Parts of one of the Pleasantest Counties of *England*. It is publicly reported that he wrote this Book: It is a Story, which you know, Sir, I neither made, nor spread; for it has been long as public as it can well be. The Injury done to *Religion*, that any of its Ministers should lie under the Imputation of writing such a *Burlesque* upon it, will be irreparable, if the Person so charged does not do *it* and *himself* Justice. I say *Himself*, for *in my own Conscience* I acquit him from composing it. The Author, I believe, is dead, and it is probable that it

was

was writ in the Year 1697, when it is said to have been written.

Before I leave this Author, be he who he will, I shall observe, Sir, that his *Wit* is *not his own*, in many places. The *Actors* in his *Farce*, *Peter*, *Martin*, and *Jack*, are by Name borrowed from a Letter written by the late Witty D. of *Buckingham*, concerning Mr. *Clifford's Human Reason*: (*ı*) And *Peter's* Banter upon *Transubstantiation*, is taken from the same D. of *Buckingham's Conference with an Irish Priest*, (*k*) only here. *Bread* is *changed into Mutton* and *Wine*, that the Banter might be the more crude; there a *Cork* is *turned into a Horse*. But the *Wondrings* on the one side, and the *Asseverations* on the other, are otherwise exactly alike. And I have been assured that the *Battel in St. James's Library* is *Mutatis Mutandis* taken out of a *French* Book, entituled, *Combat des Livres*, if I misremember not.

(*ı*) P. 67.

(*k*) P. 37.

And now, Sir, I heartily ask your Pardon for troubling you with so long a Letter. You know the true Reasons and Inducements of my Writing the *Reflexions* at first; I cannot think it needed any Apology then, and so I do not write this Letter as an Apology now. I wrote then of the Writings of one Gentleman at the Command of another, who is an exact Judge of Decency and Good Manners. I would say a great deal more, but that I write *to*, as well as

of

of your felf. But I should have been inexcusable, if, when you saw and gave your felf the Trouble of reading the *Reflections* before they went to the Press, I should not have composed them so, as that you should not have needed to disown them afterwards. Your Friendship, in truth, has been for many Years so generous towards me, and so disinterested, that I have often found you could as willingly have made Excuses for my Failings, as have commended my good Management. But as the Office of an Excuser is what for ones Friend's sake, as well as ones own, a Man is not too frequently to put his Friend upon, so the principal Design of my Writing this long Narrative, was to satisfie you, Sir, who are so very much concerned, that all the Objections hitherto made against the *Reflexions*, will easily admit of a direct and full Answer. I have nothing more to say, but that it is necessary for your sake, that I should inform the Public, that the Faults in this Letter are all my own, and that I will not desire you to stand by me upon the account of any Mistakes of which I may have been guilty. I am,

SIR,

May 21. 1705

Your most Obliged and Faithful Servant,

W. Wotton.

FINIS.

MVSEVM BRITANNICVM

BOOKS Printed for *Tim. Goodwin.*

NEW Book of Declarations, Pleadings, Verdicts, Judgments and Judicial Writs, with the Entries thereupon; Compiled by Mr. *Henry Clift*, late of *Furnivalls-Inn*, and digested for Benefit of the Professors of the Law, by Sir *Charles Ingleby*, Knt. Serjeant at Law. Fol

Fables of *Æsop* and other Eminent Mythologists, with Morals and Reflections; by Sir *Roger Lestrange*. Fol

Leges Marchiarum, or, *Border-Laws*. Containing several Original Articles and Treaties, Made and Agreed upon by the Commissioners of the Respective Kings of *England* and *Scotland*, for the better Preservation of Peace and Commerce upon the *Marches* of both Kingdoms: From the Reign of *Henry* III to the Union of the Two Crowns, in King *James* I. With a Preface and an Appendix of Charters and Records, relating to the said Treaties: By *William* Lord Bishop of *Carlisle* 8vo.

The Gentleman's Dictionary In Three Parts; viz. 1. The *Art of Riding the Great Horse*, containing the Terms and Phrases us'd in the *Manage*, and the Diseases and Accidents of Horses 2. The *Military Art*; explaining the Terms and Phrases us'd in Field or Garison; the Terms relating to *Artillery*; the Works and Motions of *Attack* and *Defence*; and the Post and Duty of all the Officers of the Army: Illustrated with Historical Instances, taken from the Actions of our Armies. 3. The Art of *Navigation*; explaining the Terms of Naval Affairs, as Building, Rigging, Working, and Fighting of Ships; the Post and Duty of Sea-Officers, *&c* with Historical Examples taken from the Actions of our Fleet Each Part done Alphabetically, from the Sixteenth Edition of the Original *French*, Published by the Sieur *Guillet*, and Dedicated to the *Dauphin*. With large Additions, Alterations and Improvements, adapted to the Customs and Actions of the *English*, and above forty Curious Cuts that were not in the Original. 8vo

A Paraphrase and Comment upon the Epistles and Gospels on all Sundays and Holy-Days throughout the Year, Vol 1st. and 2d by *George Stanhope*, D D. Dean of *Canterbury*, and Chaplain in Ordinary to Her Majesty. 8vo.

BOOKS Printed for Tim. Goodwin.

Of Wisdom; three Books, written originally in *French* by Sieur *de Charron*; with an Account of the Author; done into *English* by Dr. *Stanhope*. 8vo.

The History of *Rome*, from the Death of *Antoninus Pius*, to the Death of *Severus Alexander*; by *W. Wotton*. B.D. 8vo.

—— Letter to *Eusebia*; occasion'd by Mr *Toland's* Letter to *Serena* 8vo.

Titi Livii Historia, Juxta Edit. Gronov. diligenter recens. Duob. Vol. 8vo.

Mr. *Echard's Roman* History, in 2 Vol. 8vo.

—— *Roman* History, 3d Vol. being a Continuation of Mr *Echard's* 1st. and 2d. 8vo

A Political Essay, or a Summary Review of the Kings and Government of *England* since the *Norman* Conquest; by W—. P—. Esq; 8vo.

The Constitution of the Laws of *England* considered, by *W. P.* Esq;. 8vo.

Lex Parliamentaria. Or a Treatise of the Law and Custom of the Parliaments of *England*; by G-. P-. Esq;.

Angliæ Notitia; or the Present State of *England*; by Dr *Chamberlayn*. 8vo.

An Account of *Denmark*, as it was in the Year 1692. 8vo.

An Account of *Sueden*, together with an Extract of the History of that Kingdom 8vo.

Travels into divers Parts of *Europe* and *Asia*, undertaken by the *French* King's Order, to discover a New Way by Land into *China*, containing many Curious Remarks, together with a Description of *Great Tartary*; by Father *Avril*, of the Order of the Jesuits Done out of *French* 12o

A New Voyage to *Italy*, with Curious Observations on several other Countries, as *Germany*, *Switzerland*, *Savoy*, *Geneva*, *Flanders* and *Holland*; together with useful Instructions for those who travel thither, by *Maximilian Misson*; done out of *French*; in two Vol. 8vo

Dumont's New Voyage to the *Levant*; containing an Account of the most Remarkable Curiosities in *Germany*, *France*, *Italy*, *Maltha* and *Turky*, with Historical Observations relating to the Present and Ancient State of those Countries. 8vo.

A Relation of a Voyage made in the Years 1695, 1696, 1697 on the Coasts of *Africa*, Streights of *Magellan*, *Brazile*, *Cayenna* and the *Antilles*, by a Squadron of *French* Men

of

BOOKS Printed for Tim. Goodwin.

of War, under the M. *de Gennes*; by the Sieur *Froger*; done into *English*. 8vo.

New Voyages to *North-America*, containing an Account of the several Nations of that vast Continent, their Customs, Commerce and way of Navigation, the several Attempts of the *English* and *French* to dispossess one another, with the Reasons of the Miscarriage of the former, and the various Adventures between the *French* and the *Iroquese* Confederates of *England*, from 1683 to 1694, &c. written in *French* by the Baron *Lahontan*, Lord Lieutenant of the *French Colony* at *Placentia* in *Newfoundland*. 8vo.

History of the Revolution in *Portugal*, in the Year 1640, or an Account of their Revolt from *Spain*, and setling the Crown on the Head of *Don John* of *Braganza*, Father to *Don Pedro* the present King, and *Catherine* Queen Dowager of *England*; written in *French* by the Abbot *Vertot*; done into *English*. 12o.

Memoirs of the most Material Transactions in *England* for the Last Hundred Years, preceeding the Revolution in 1688, by *James Welwood*, M.D. 8vo.

Memoirs of *Denzill* Lord *Holles*, Baron of *Ifeild* in *Sussex*, from 1641 to 1648. 8vo.

Miscellanea, 3d Part, containing 1st an Essay on Popular Discontents; 2d. An Essay upon Health and Long Life: 3d. A Defence of the Essay upon Ancient and Modern Learning; with some other Pieces; by the late Sir *W Temple*. 8vo.

———Letters to the King, the Prince of *Orange*, the Chief Ministers of State, and other persons; by Sir *W Temple*, being the 3d and last Volume; published by *Jonathan Swift*, D.D. 8vo.

Bellamira, or the Mistress: A Comedy by Sir *Charles Sedley*.

Practical Essay on Fevers; containing Remarks on the Hot and Cool Methods of their Cure, wherein the first is rejected, and the last recommended: To which is annext a Dissertation on the *Bath* Waters; by *W Oliver*, M.D. Fellow of the Royal Society. 12o.

A Compendium of Universal History, from the Beginning of the World, to the Reign of the Emperor *Charles* the Great, 8vo.

Reflections upon what the World commonly call Good-Luck and Ill-Luck, with regard to Lotteries, and of the Good Use which may be made of them. These Two last written in *French* by Monsieur *Le Clerk*, and done into *English*. 12o.

Lightning Source UK Ltd.
Milton Keynes UK
UKOW07f1952210817
307701UK00006B/557/P